MW00633196

The Virgin Mary assumed a position of central importance in Byzantium. This book examines her portrayal in liturgical texts during approximately the first six centuries of Byzantine history. Focusing on three main literary genres that celebrated this holy figure, it highlights the ways in which writers adapted their messages for different audiences. Mary is portrayed variously as defender of the imperial city, Constantinople, virginal Mother of God and ascetic disciple of Christ. Preachers, hymnographers and hagiographers used rhetoric to enhance Mary's powerful status in Eastern Christian society, depicting her as virgin and mother, warrior and ascetic, human and all-holy figure. Their paradoxical statements were based on the fundamental mystery that Mary embodied: she was the mother of Christ, the Word of God, who provided him with the human nature that he assumed in his incarnation. Dr Cunningham's authoritative study makes a major contribution to the history of Christianity. This title is also available as Open Access on Cambridge Core.

MARY B. CUNNINGHAM is Honorary Associate Professor of Historical Theology at the University of Nottingham. She has published books and articles in the fields of Byzantine hagiography, homiletics, and theology. In addition to translating Byzantine homilies on the Virgin Mary (2008), she has co-edited books on this subject with Leslie Brubaker (2011) and Thomas Arentzen (Cambridge, 2019). She also sits on the editorial boards of various series, including Translated Texts for Byzantinists and the Society for the Promotion of Byzantine Studies' book series.

THE VIRGIN MARY IN BYZANTIUM, c. 400–1000 CE

Hymns, Homilies and Hagiography

MARY B. CUNNINGHAM

CAMBRIDGE
UNIVERSITY PRESS

CAMBRIDGE
UNIVERSITY PRESS

University Printing House, Cambridge CB2 8BS, United Kingdom

One Liberty Plaza, 20th Floor, New York, NY 10006, USA

477 Williamstown Road, Port Melbourne, VIC 3207, Australia

314–321, 3rd Floor, Plot 3, Splendor Forum, Jasola District Centre, New Delhi – 110025, India

103 Penang Road, #05–06/07, Visioncrest Commercial, Singapore 238467

Cambridge University Press & Assessment is part of the University of Cambridge.

It furthers the University's mission by disseminating knowledge in the pursuit of education, learning, and research at the highest international levels of excellence.

www.cambridge.org
Information on this title: www.cambridge.org/9781009327251
DOI: 10.1017/9781009327244

© Mary B. Cunningham 2022

Reissued as Open Access, 2022

First published 2022

A catalogue record for this publication is available from the British Library.

Library of Congress Cataloging-in-Publication Data
NAMES: Cunningham, Mary (Lecturer in historical theology and Othodox Christian studies), author.
TITLE: The Virgin Mary in Byzantium, c.400–1000 : hymns, homilies and hagiography / Mary B. Cunningham.
DESCRIPTION: Cambridge ; New York, NY : Cambridge University Press, 2021. | Includes bibliographical references and index.
IDENTIFIERS: LCCN 2021028269 (print) | LCCN 2021028270 (ebook) | ISBN 9781108845694 (hardback) | ISBN 9781108964869 (paperback) | ISBN 9781108990530 (ebook)
SUBJECTS: LCSH: Mary, Blessed Virgin, Saint – Devotion to – Byzantine Empire. | Orthodox Eastern Church – Liturgy. | Mary, Blessed Virgin, Saint, in the liturgy – Orthodox Eastern Church. | Sermons, Greek – Byzantine Empire – History and criticism. | Hymns, Greek – Byzantine Empire – History and criticism. | Byzantine Empire – Religious life and customs.
CLASSIFICATION: LCC BT645.3 .C86 2021 (print) | LCC BT645.3 (ebook) | DDC 232.91–dc23
LC record available at https://lccn.loc.gov/2021028269
LC ebook record available at https://lccn.loc.gov/2021028270

ISBN 978-1-009-32725-1 Paperback

Contents

Acknowledgements

This book has been in preparation for a long time and it is wonderful at last to have completed it. I am delighted to acknowledge here the help, both financial and intellectual, that contributed to this project. I would like first to thank the British government funding body, the Arts and Humanities Research Council (AHRC), for supporting a three-year project at the University of Birmingham between 2003 and 2006 on the Virgin Mary in Byzantium. The project was led by Professor Leslie Brubaker, of the Centre for Byzantine, Ottoman and Modern Greek Studies within the Institute of Archaeology and Antiquity, and it provided a three-year research post for me at the University of Birmingham. I thus owe thanks to that institution, which furnished me with both financial assistance and bibliographical resources during that initial phase of the project. The Department of Theology and Religious Studies at the University of Nottingham, which offered me a Lectureship from 2006 onward, supported my research activities for the next ten years and I remain indebted to that institution for its belief in my scholarly and teaching abilities. Following this, I was offered a one-year Fellowship at Dumbarton Oaks Research Library and Collection in the academic year 2015–16. I worked specifically on this project throughout that year, which helped immeasurably in pushing it towards completion. In addition to giving me access to its unparalleled library and museum resources, Dumbarton Oaks provided a friendly community in which I learned much from the other Fellows and Junior Fellows. I would like to express my deepest thanks to all three of these institutions in which I enjoyed such dynamic and productive intellectual exchanges with fellow teachers and scholars.

As for the many individuals who helped me to complete this project, I would like to acknowledge first my original director and collaborator, Leslie Brubaker. She took the initiative in submitting a proposal to the AHRC in 2002, overseeing its successful completion and advising me not only during the three years of official funding but also thereafter. It is unfortunate that our respective work schedules did not in the end allow us to write this book together; however, Leslie graciously agreed that it would make better sense for each of us to write separate works. We hope that the two volumes, which will cover the textual and the material evidence for the cult of the Virgin Mary during the early and middle Byzantine periods, will complement each other since they both reflect the aims of our joint project. In addition to providing stimulus at the beginning of the project, Leslie read and commented on various chapters that I wrote in the years that followed. I would also like to thank Thomas Arentzen, Fr Maximos Constas, Stig Frøyshov, Susan Ashbrook Harvey, Dirk Krausmüller and Andrea Olsen Lam, who have read either the whole or separate parts of the book and offered valuable criticisms. I take full responsibility for any errors that remain. In addition to those scholars, Pauline Allen, Theodora Antonopoulou, Barbara Crostini, Beatrice Daskas, Francesca Dell'Acqua, Uffe Holmsgaard Eriksen, Jeffrey Michael Featherstone, Georgia Frank, Antonia Giannouli, Brad Hostetler, Ally Kateusz, Karen Kilby, Derek Krueger, Fr Andrew Louth, Wendy Mayer, Andrew Mellas, Fr Damaskinos Olkinuora, Leena Mari Peltomaa, Maroula Perisanidi, Nancy Ševčenko, Stephen Shoemaker, Christos Simelidis, Kosta Simić, Alice-Mary Talbot, Gabrielle Thomas, Niki Tsironis, Annemarie Weyl Carr, Monica White and Mary Whitby have provided me with ideas and advice over the years. Michael Whitby suggested several important corrections, for which I am grateful. There are many other colleagues, whose names are too numerous to list, who have also assisted me. Professor Dame Averil Cameron helped me to overcome my doubts and complete the manuscript in the course of the last year – for that, along with the inspiration that she has provided by means of her own contributions to the subject, I remain hugely grateful. Two anonymous readers offered useful advice and approved my manuscript for publication. Terry J. Wright compiled the index for me, thus relieving me of a technical challenge that I found difficult to face. Michael Sharp has been immensely helpful during the preparation of this work and I would like to take this opportunity to thank him along with the rest of the production team at Cambridge University Press. Thanks are also due to Kay McKechnie, the copy-editor, who saved me from many errors as we prepared the manuscript for publication.

Finally, I would like to express my gratitude and love for various close friends and family members who have encouraged me throughout my career – and sometimes especially with respect to this project. My children, Emily and James, generously believed in a career that frequently distracted my attention from themselves. Emily, since becoming a successful scholar herself, has been an indefatigable and helpful mentor with regard both to the bigger questions and to detailed matters of presentation. My sisters, Sarah and Conti, provide me with moral support and love, as our parents did throughout their lives. Finally, I would like to acknowledge the enduring encouragement of my husband, Richard Corran, who has always stood behind whatever enterprise I undertake. I hope that this offering is worthy of the 'infinitely capacious' and compassionate Mother of God who is its subject.

This title is part of the Cambridge University Press *Flip it Open* Open Access Books program and has been "flipped" from a traditional book to an Open Access book through the program.

Flip it Open sells books through regular channels, treating them at the outset in the same way as any other book; they are part of our library collections for Cambridge Core, and sell as hardbacks and ebooks. The one crucial difference is that we make an upfront commitment that when each of these books meets a set revenue threshold we make them available to everyone Open Access via Cambridge Core.

This paperback edition has been released as part of our Open Access commitment and we would like to use this as an opportunity to thank the libraries and other buyers who have helped us flip this and the other titles in the program to Open Access.

To see the full list of libraries that we know have contributed to *Flip it Open*, as well as the other titles in the program please visit www.cambridge.org/fio-acknowledgements

A Note on Capitalisation, Spelling and Recent Publications

I apologise that this book displays the usual inconsistencies that afflict most publications in Byzantine Studies, owing to the difficulty of reconciling clarity with changing trends in presentation. I have decided to follow traditional spellings or versions of names that are well known to modern readers, such as John Chrysostom or John of Damascus. However, I have adopted the hellenised version of less common names, such as Nikephoros or Proklos. In general, the latter follow the rules for spelling that are set out in the *Oxford Dictionary of Byzantium* (*ODB*). I capitalise the names of Marian feasts (such as the 'Annunciation' and the 'Dormition'), but not the events or legends that inspired them. My object, above all, is to present a book that is understandable and attractive to modern readers. Fashions will no doubt change, but I hope that my choices in presentation will endure at least as long as the content remains useful. A more serious, but also unavoidable, problem has been my inability to incorporate some recently published texts, such as the new edition of the *Book of Ceremonies* by Constantine VII Porphyrogennetos (ed. G. Dagron, B. Flusin and D. Feissel, Paris, 2020, in 5 vols.). Owing to the slow process of preparing a work for publication, it is impossible to keep up with all of the latest developments in the field. Nevertheless, it will remain for future scholars to advance and refine some of the ideas that I present in this book.

Introduction

> For she alone always knows how to defeat nature,
> first by giving birth, and second, by battle.
> For just as she then needed to give birth without a seed,
> so does she now give birth to salvation without weapons
> in order that she may be found to be a virgin through both acts,
> as immutable in battle as she was when giving birth.[1]

This short passage describes two main characteristics of the Byzantine Virgin Mary: she is the young woman who gave birth to Christ, the Son and Word of God, and also the fearless warrior who defended Constantinople from its enemies from about the early seventh century onward. The author, George of Pisidia, who celebrated the defeat of the Persian and Avar siege that took place in 626 CE, viewed both of these events as miraculous. Mary's virginity, which remained intact throughout the conception and birth of Christ, bore witness to his divine nature while her humanity assured the reality of the incarnation. It was also her virginity, according to George, which provided her with the strength to defeat potential invaders of the imperial city. This powerful and paradoxical figure was thus a dominant figure in the doctrine and devotion of the Eastern Roman empire, with her cult flourishing in Constantinople especially from about the sixth century onward.

As noted in several recent publications,[2] there has been an explosion of interest in the Virgin Mary during the last few decades.[3] Articles, monographs and proceedings of conferences have approached Eastern Christian manifestations of her cult in various ways, focusing on texts, feasts, relics and material objects that were produced in Mary's honour throughout the

---

[1] George of Pisidia, *Bellum Avaricum*, ed. Pertusi 1959, 176.4–9 (my own translation). For further discussion of this passage, see Whitby 2020, 406–7.
[2] For example, Cameron 2004, 1–2; Cameron 2011, 1–3; Mullett 2011, 279–81; Harvey 2019, 344–5.
[3] Two important collections of essays that approach the Virgin Mary from a broader interdisciplinary perspective are Boss 2007 and Maunder 2019.

Byzantine centuries.[4] The early Christian and Byzantine period (between approximately the second and seventh centuries) remains the most closely studied, since late antique and patristic scholars view Mary as important for theological, liturgical and historical reasons.[5] Controversy continues, however, over questions such as the period when Marian devotion began,[6] the extent to which emperors or empresses were involved in promoting the cult,[7] and whether or not it became a focus of theological controversy.[8] Several recent studies, such as Thomas Arentzen's book on Romanos the Melodist's treatment of the Virgin, explore her transition in the course of the sixth century from theological symbol to multifaceted woman.[9] The middle and late periods of Byzantine history remain less studied, although several conferences and their proceedings offer new approaches.[10] Bissera Pentcheva's book on Mary's role as defender of Constantinople, along with her commemoration through relics, icons and processions, from the beginning of the seventh century until about 1204, provides analysis of these aspects of the cult.[11] There is no comparable study of the Virgin's ongoing veneration in the late Byzantine period (c. 1204–1453); however, various articles address manifestations of Marian devotion, including the pictorial representation of the Virgin's life in the fourteenth-century mosaics of the Chora monastery in Constantinople and her celebration in later hymns and homilies.[12] The whole field is opening up, but much work on the surviving textual, liturgical and material evidence remains to be done.

[4] See, for example (in order of publication), Vassilaki 2000; Swanson 2004; Vassilaki 2005; Pentcheva 2006; Brubaker and Cunningham 2011; Allen, Külzer and Peltomaa 2015; Arentzen and Cunningham 2019.

[5] Good introductions to this period include Shoemaker 2002; Maunder 2008; Shoemaker 2016a.

[6] Those arguing for a very early date include Shoemaker 2016a and Kateusz 2019. Scholars who see the Council of Ephesus (431 CE) as a major watershed for the Byzantine Marian cult include Cameron 2004, 8–9; Price 2004; Price 2007.

[7] For scholarly controversy concerning whether the future empress Pulcheria played an essential role in the events leading up to the deposition of the patriarch Nestorios in 431, see Holum 1982; Limberis 1994; Cooper 1998; Price 2004; James 2005.

[8] For example, during the period of Iconoclasm (c. 730–87 and 815–43). For recent views on this subject, see Parry 1996, 191–201; Kalavrezou 2000; Tsironis 2000; Brubaker and Haldon 2011, esp. 32–3, 199–212.

[9] Arentzen 2017. The PhD thesis that formed the basis of this monograph can be found in Arentzen 2014.

[10] Brubaker and Cunningham 2011; Arentzen and Cunningham 2019.   [11] Pentcheva 2006.

[12] Lafontaine-Dosogne 1964 (1992); Lafontaine-Dosogne 1975; for texts, see for example the important verses called 'enkomia' that were inserted into the so-called *epitaphios threnos* of Holy Saturday *Orthros* in about the fourteenth century and which express the lament of the Mother of God at the cross, see Eustratiades 1937–8; Touliatos-Banker 1984; Detorakis 1987–9; Ševčenko 2011, 249, nn. 9–10.

This book does not pretend to cover every aspect of the cult of the Virgin Mary during the early and middle Byzantine periods.[13] However, it does engage with the idea that Mary was a multifaceted figure – or to use Averil Cameron's memorable words, a model of extraordinary 'capaciousness' that was 'all things to people at different times and places'.[14] To some extent, the message was determined by purpose, intended audience or viewer, and physical setting or context. Liturgical texts, such as homilies and hymns, emphasised the Christological importance of the Virgin although they also began to weave intercessory invocation and prayer into this theological context from about the late fifth century onward.[15] Historical texts, which were concerned mainly with political or military events, meanwhile described the Virgin's role in defending the imperial city from its external foes.[16] Mary appears as a powerful figure in both contexts, assuming a more symbolic than realistic aspect – although hymnographers such as Romanos sometimes portrayed her human and maternal qualities.[17] I have chosen to focus on three important categories of Marian literature in Byzantium: homilies or sermons, hymns and hagiography (including not only *Lives* of the Virgin or of saints, but also miracle stories and apocalyptic narratives). Other, less religious or liturgical sources, such as histories, chronicles, poems and epigrams, must await a separate study. The sheer amount of surviving material, much of which remains to be critically edited and translated into modern languages, forbids universal coverage in the present work. I also regret that material or art historical evidence can only be mentioned briefly, or in passing, here – however, a forthcoming monograph will soon offer new approaches to this large field.[18]

The scope of this book, in terms of chronology and geographical boundaries, reflects my choice of literary material. Although the years 400 and 1000 CE represent rough boundaries for the study, it will be necessary occasionally to stray earlier or later by a few centuries in order to

---

[13] Throughout this book, I define the 'early' period of Byzantine as lasting roughly from 330 to 843; the 'middle' as *c.* 843–1204; and the 'late' as 1204–1453. For discussion of various alternatives to this system, see *ODB*, vol. 1, 345–62.

[14] Cameron 2004, 20.   [15] See Chapters 1 and 2.

[16] See Pentcheva 2006, 61–103, for texts and bibliography on the Persian and Avar siege of 626, for example. Some homiletic texts, such as Theodore Synkellos' homily on the same siege, also portray the Virgin Mary in such terms; see Theodore Synkellos, *De obsidione.*

[17] For the kontakia of Romanos the Melodist, see Maas and Trypanis 1963 (1997); Grosdidier de Matons 1964–81; Maisano 2002; Koder 2005; Eng. trans. Lash 1995; Barkhuizen 2012.

[18] Leslie Brubaker is currently working on a separate volume that will follow this one; it will cover the material evidence, including churches, icons and other artefacts that commemorated the Virgin Mary in Byzantium. See also Acknowledgements, viii–ix, and Conclusion, 218.

include a few, but significant, sources that influenced the Greek religious texts that we will be examining. I decided, for example, to include Syriac religious poetry, including the second-century *Odes of Solomon* and the hymns and sung homilies of the fourth-century writer Ephrem the Syrian, owing to the fact that these works – along with the fifth- and sixth-century Syriac texts that followed them – provided such an important foundation for the sixth-century hymnographer Romanos the Melodist.[19] The works that survive in the Georgian hymnbook which is known as the *Ancient Iadgari* were originally written in Greek; these are thus precious survivals of hymns that were sung in Greek churches and monasteries of Jerusalem and Palestine between about the fourth and sixth centuries. My study focuses inevitably on Constantinople between the fifth and tenth centuries since this is where and when the majority of Greek Marian texts were produced. However, some regional preachers and hymnographers, a few of whom (like John of Damascus and Kosmas of Maïuma) lived under Muslim rule in Palestine, also contributed to the tradition. The choice of texts may in some ways be arbitrary, but it reflects the direction that this book has taken in its exploration of the development of Greek Marian religious texts during the early and middle Byzantine periods. I have chosen to stop at the end of the first Christian millennium because of the wealth of texts that survives before that date. This is not to say, however, that later material, including the homilies of the twelfth-century writer James of Kokkinobaphos, are not important too.[20] I hope that future studies, including the forthcoming edition of these works by Elizabeth Jeffreys, will fill this gap.[21]

The aim of the present book is therefore to examine Mary's multifaceted aspect in Byzantine homilies, hymnography and hagiography between about 400 and 1000 CE. If we approach these separate, although closely related, literary genres on the basis of their particular liturgical or didactic aims, we see interesting developments in all three. First, it is noticeable that the earliest hymns and homilies that were composed in honour of the

---

[19] On the question of Syriac influence on the kontakia of Romanos the Melodist, see Grosdidier de Matons 1977, 16–27; Papoutsakis 2007; Petersen 1985; Gador-Whyte 2013; Gador-Whyte 2017, 12–13; Arentzen 2017, 39.

[20] James of Kokkinobaphos, *Homilies*; for discussion, see Linardou 2004; Linardou 2007; Jeffreys 2019.

[21] Elizabeth Jeffreys is currently working on a critical edition of the *Homilies*; see Jeffreys 2019. I am grateful to Professor Jeffreys for sharing the forthcoming text and translation of the *Homilies* with me. The two illustrated manuscripts, Cod. Paris. Gr. 1208 and Cod. Vat. Gr. 1162, that contain the *Homilies* are now digitised and available online at: https://gallica.bnf.fr/ark:/12148/btv1b55013447b/f1 .image and https://digi.vatlib.it/view/MSS_Vat.gr.1162.

Virgin Mary praised above all her role in the Christological mystery. Such texts, most of which were intended for delivery in liturgical contexts, used not only discursive, but also poetic and typological, language in order to teach Christians that a human, but perpetually virginal, woman conceived and gave birth to Jesus Christ, the Word of God. The inclusion of intercessory invocation and prayer to Mary began slowly but was in place by the beginning or middle of the sixth century. In subsequent centuries, but especially after about the beginning of the eighth, preachers and hymnographers also displayed an interest in legendary narratives, first expressed in apocryphal texts such as the *Protevangelion of James* and (several centuries later) various accounts of Mary's death or dormition and assumption into heaven, which they embellished with dialogue, monologue and other dramatic rhetorical devices.[22] Such narrative freedom developed further in the surviving hagiographical texts, some of which departed significantly from the canonical Gospels in their accounts of Mary's life. The form, or genre, of individual texts does seem to have played a part in how Byzantine writers shaped their content.[23] I argue therefore that the Virgin's many aspects depend first on the literary genres that portray her, and second on the stage of cultic development in which they appear.

The richest and most developed phase begins after about the end of the ninth century when the whole range of Mary's qualities becomes visible. She remains above all a symbol of the incarnation in this period; however, this aspect may be overlaid with human and maternal characteristics, as she weeps at the foot of Christ's cross, and with monastic virtues, as she becomes a model of asceticism for Byzantine monks and nuns. An additional (and fascinating) quality of leadership also appears in a few hagiographical texts such as the probably late tenth-century *Life of the Virgin* that is falsely attributed to Maximos the Confessor, which describes Mary directing the activities of both female and male followers of Jesus.[24] To some extent, however, this wide expanse of Marian portraiture remains dependent on individual writers' choices of literary form, potential audiences and contexts of writing. I therefore argue throughout this book that

---

[22] *Protevangelion of James* (*CANT* 50), ed. Tischendorf 1876; de Strycker 1961; trans. Elliott 1993 (2004); various Greek dormition accounts are listed at *CANT* 100; cf. Jugie 1944; Mimouni 1994 (2011); Shoemaker 2002. The title, 'Protevangelion' was only given to this work in the sixteenth century according to a Latin translation prepared by Postel 1552 (1570).

[23] Cunningham 2011a; Cunningham 2016.

[24] Georgian *Life of the Virgin* 94–102, ed. and trans. Shoemaker 2012, 121–9. The scholarly controversy surrounding the dates and authorship of this text is treated in Chapter 5, 192–4.

the Virgin Mary presented herself to Byzantine readers or auditors in the symbolic forms that they expected: although she became an increasingly compassionate and human interlocutor for Christian devotees, she encompassed in her person a full spectrum of theological, devotional and even polemical reflection that had developed over more than a millennium.

Marian Doctrine and Devotion in the Eastern Roman Empire up to *c.* 1000 CE

It is worth providing a short overview of the history of the cult of the Virgin in the late antique and Byzantine worlds, especially in view of the controversial areas in this field that were mentioned above. Although Stephen Shoemaker presents a forceful case for Marian devotion in the centuries preceding the Council of Ephesus in 431,[25] the textual evidence remains patchy. Shoemaker sets this phenomenon within the wider context of the emerging cult of saints, arguing that the lack of evidence concerning relics, shrines or other testimony of Marian devotion before the middle of the fifth century may be 'simply a matter of serendipity'.[26] He cites a number of apocryphal and heterodox literary sources, beginning with the mid to late second-century narrative known as the *Protevangelion of James*, as evidence for Mary's importance as a holy figure in her own right.[27] Such texts include several gnostic texts including the *Gospel of Mary*,[28] as well as early accounts of the Virgin's dormition and assumption that survive only in Ethiopic, Old Georgian and Syriac.[29] All of these sources, suggests Shoemaker, have escaped the notice of scholars who tend to focus on more 'orthodox' or mainstream Christian ones.[30] The suggestion that Marian devotion developed first – and indeed flourished – in heterodox Christian communities during the first four centuries of the common era is intriguing; it is reinforced by the late fourth-century father Epiphanios of Salamis's polemic against an otherwise unattested sect called the Kollyridians, who appear to have commemorated the Virgin Mary annually with a service at which bread was offered to God in her name.[31]

---

[25] Shoemaker 2016a; cf. Kateusz 2019.   [26] Shoemaker 2016a, 17.

[27] *Protevangelion of James*, ed. Tishendorf 1876, de Strycker 1961, trans. Elliott 1993 (2004). On the likely late second- to early third-century date for the *Protevangelion of James*, see Cullmann 1991, 423–4; Elliott 1993 (2004), 49; Vuong 2013, 32–9.

[28] *Gospel of Mary*, ed. Wilson and MacRae 1979; Shoemaker 2016a, 75–87. Shoemaker's view that the 'Mary' of this Gospel should be identified with Jesus' mother rather than with Mary Magdalen is not widely accepted by apocryphal scholars; see Norelli 2009, 69–70.

[29] Shoemaker 2016a, 100–45.   [30] Shoemaker 2016a, 2.

[31] Epiphanios of Salamis, *Panarion* 79.1.7, ed. Holl 1933, vol. 3, 476; Shoemaker 2016a, 145.

Shoemaker does not neglect other, more mainstream, textual and material evidence in support of an early cult of the Virgin Mary. However, whereas the evangelists, apostolic fathers and early patristic writers mention her frequently, this is almost always in connection with her roles as 'Second Eve' and virginal mother of Jesus Christ. Second-century theologians, including especially Justin Martyr and Irenaeus of Lyons, saw Mary as the antitype of Eve: whereas the latter disobeyed God and thereby helped to bring about the Fall of humankind from divine favour, the former obeyed him and initiated a new creation and redemption.[32] The qualifications of the female person who would thus reverse the disastrous consequences of God's gift of free will, by using it in the way that he intended, needed further justification – especially in response to questions about Mary's background that were circulating among pagan and Jewish opponents of Christianity.[33] It is likely that the *Protevangelion of James* was compiled partly in response to this challenge; its primary purpose is to describe, with the help of a highly symbolic and theological narrative, the purity of the young woman who gave birth to Christ, the Son of God.[34] As Trinitarian and Christological doctrine developed further in the course of the third and fourth centuries, Christian teachers began to focus more on Mary's role as 'Theotokos' or 'birth-giver of God'. Gregory of Nyssa, for example, describes her mysterious role as follows in his homily on the Nativity of Christ:

> O, what a marvel! The Virgin mother becomes and remains a virgin. Do you see the novelty of nature? In the case of other women, there is no mother as long as she remains a virgin. When she has become a mother, she does not have virginity. But in this case, the two titles have come together in this fashion. For the same woman is at once both mother and virgin. And neither has virginity hindered the birth, nor has the birth undone virginity. For it was fitting that [Christ], having entered human life in order to make us all incorruptible, should himself originate from an incorruptible birth.[35]

---

[32] Justin Martyr, *Dialogue with Trypho* 100.4-5, ed. Marcovich 1997, 242–3; trans. Falls 2003, 152; Irenaeus of Lyons, *Against Heresies* 3.22.4, ed. Sagnard 1952, vol. 3, 378–83.

[33] The main pagan opponent, according to Origen, was the philosopher Celsus. According to Origen, Celsus questioned the circumstances surrounding Jesus' birth, suggesting that Mary was a poor Jewish woman who committed adultery with a Roman soldier named 'Panthera'; see Origen, *Contra Celsum* 1.28-32, ed. Borret 1967 (2005), 162–5, 268–71. On Jewish questioning of the Virgin birth, see Vuong 2013, 44–51; cf. Shoemaker 2016, 54, who doubts that the *Protevangelion of James* was composed mainly for apologetic reasons.

[34] Vuong 2013; Shoemaker 2016a, 54.

[35] Gregory of Nyssa, *Homily on the Nativity of Christ*, ed. Mann 1975, 273. 9–20 (my own translation).

Shoemaker is certainly correct in suggesting that devotion to the Virgin Mary existed in Christian circles well before the Council of Ephesus took place in 431. However, the nature of such veneration differed – at least in the mainstream Church – from that which was offered to martyrs and saints in that Mary's importance lay in her role as the mother of Jesus Christ. The lack of relics and shrines in her honour also sets her apart from other holy people in this period.[36] The Fathers reflected on the Virgin's purity, acceptance of God's will and miraculous conception of Jesus, discerning prophetic and typological witness to her unique place in the history of salvation throughout the Old Testament. Even if some heterodox groups such as the Kollyridians expressed devotion to the Virgin Mary in more tangible ways, it is likely that her Christological role remained their primary impetus. In other words, whereas early Christians celebrated Mary's role as mediator of salvation and instrument of the incarnation, they did not yet appeal to her in the way that they addressed martyred saints, as intercessors and miracle workers.

It might be useful at this point to define some terms concerning Mary's relationship with the rest of humankind, which will be used throughout this book. I have chosen to follow Brian Reynolds's useful distinction, for example, between the terms 'mediation' (*mesiteia*) and 'intercession' (*presbeia*).[37] Although these terms are often used synonymously, they indicate different activities on the part of the Virgin Mary. According to Reynolds, mediation refers to Mary's role in cooperating with God in order to distribute grace and redemption to humankind through the incarnation of Christ. Although this definition is expressed in Roman Catholic language, it applies equally to the Eastern Christian view that Mary, who was chosen by God from the beginning of creation to give birth to his Son, the Word and Messiah, played an essential role in his dispensation for salvation. 'Intercession' meanwhile refers to Mary's intervention on behalf of humanity, either collectively or individually, before God. Owing to her privileged position as Christ's mother, which allows 'free speech' (*parresia*) with him, the Virgin intercedes on behalf of sinners, seeking to alleviate or even abolish their just punishments. Whereas mediation thus occurs at the point of Mary's acceptance of the incarnation – and continues to play a part in the process of human salvation – intercession takes place at

---

[36] On the development of the cult of saints in early Christianity, see Brown 1981; Markus 1994; Booth, Dal Santo and Sarris 2011; Dal Santo 2012.

[37] Reynolds 2012, 152–3.

discrete moments in human history when Christians turn to the Mother of God for help or healing.

The theological significance of the Virgin, as birth-giver of God and mediator of salvation, became controversial in Constantinople at the beginning of the fifth century. It is in this period, at some point after about 400, that the first feast in honour of the Virgin was established: it was celebrated on 15 August in Jerusalem and Palestine, but during the Nativity cycle (probably on 26 December) in Constantinople.[38] Preachers including Hesychios of Jerusalem and Attikos of Constantinople began to deliver high-flown, but well-grounded, theological orations in honour of the Virgin, as we shall see in Chapter 2. Such panegyrical language, in which the epithet 'Theotokos' featured, reflected the Alexandrian theological tradition according to which Christ remained the divine Word of God even after assuming human flesh in the incarnation.[39] It is this theological message that provoked Nestorios, who was appointed bishop of Constantinople in 428, along with his presbyter Anastasios, to preach against the use of the epithet 'Theotokos' for the Virgin Mary. The historian Socrates relates the story as follows:

> Preaching in the church one day, Anastasius warned his hearers that 'No one must call Mary "Theotokos", for Mary was but a human being and it is impossible that God could be born from a human being.'[40]

The subsequent struggle between Nestorios and his opponents, including especially the patriarch of Alexandria, Cyril, is well covered in secondary literature.[41] The role that the empress Pulcheria (the sister of Theodosios II) played in this conflict, however, remains unclear. Kenneth Holum, Vassiliki Limberis and Kate Cooper together constructed a persuasive case for Pulcheria's bid to harness popular devotion to the Theotokos, which included her role as a model of asceticism, in order to strengthen her own imperial and civic claims as female ruler.[42] This hypothesis rests especially on a text known as the *Letter to Cosmas*, which was written in support of

---

[38] Scholars believe that the feast 'in memory of Mary' was celebrated in Constantinople in connection with the Nativity of Christ, either on a Sunday before Christmas or on the day after (26 December). The latter is attested in the tenth-century *Typikon of the Great Church*, ed. Mateos 1962, vol. 1, 158–61. See also Jugie 1923b; Jugie 1944, 172–212, esp. 175–7; Capelle 1943; Constas 2003, 135.

[39] Recent scholarship has provided nuance to the concept of separate 'Antiochene' and 'Alexandrian' Christologies; see Daley 2015; Daley 2018, 174–99; however, some aspects of this categorisation remain useful: see Grillmeier 1975, 167–439; Hofer 2019, 461.

[40] Socrates, *Ecclesiastical History* 7.32.1-2, ed. Hansen 1995, 380. 1–3, trans. Constas 2003, 52; cf. Evagrios, *Ecclesiastical History* 1.2, ed. Bidez and Parmentier 1898, 7–8.

[41] See, for example, Young 1983, 213–65; McGuckin 1994 (2004); Wessel 2004.

[42] Holum 1982; Limberis 1994; Cooper 1998.

Nestorios and after his exile to Egypt, perhaps between *c.* 435 and 450.[43] Richard Price has shown, however, that the date and polemical tone of this text, when compared with earlier sources, undermines Holum's case. It appears that Pucheria's enmity towards Nestorios and promotion of the Marian cult represent later elaborations in the historical record.[44] Further, whereas later Byzantine historians and chroniclers assigned the discovery of the Virgin's robe in Palestine, its translation to Constantinople and the building of the Blachernai shrine, along with that of the Chalkoprateia, to Pulcheria, historians now believe that these activities took place somewhat later, during the reign of Leo I and his consort Verina.[45]

Two aspects of the scholarly controversy concerning the empress Pulcheria remain significant for our purposes. First, the questions concerning gender, patronage and imperial piety remain applicable to the Marian cult – whether or not they should be examined in relation to this early fifth-century ruler. I shall return to these questions throughout the present book since they should be posed at every stage of the cult's development in Byzantium. Second, it is clear that the Christological controversy that involved the Theotokos in the first half of the fifth century was, at least in part, a reaction to growing devotion to the Virgin as a holy figure in her own right. The homilies and hymns that can be dated to this period do not yet appeal to Mary as protector or intercessor, as we shall see in Chapters 1 and 2; however, the shift that allowed doctrine to become infused with devotion even in theological and liturgical contexts was beginning to take place, perhaps justified by the Christological controversies of the early fifth century.

The Third Ecumenical Council thus provided an incipient cult of the Virgin Mary with the seal of ecclesiastical approval.[46] It can be no accident that churches and shrines in honour of the Theotokos quickly followed, in both Palestine and Constantinople. The church of the Kathisma, which has recently been excavated at a site halfway between Jerusalem and

---

[43] The text tells the story of Nestorios' expulsion of Pulcheria from the sanctuary of Hagia Sophia, where she was in the habit of receiving communion. When the patriarch told her that this space was reserved for priests, she responded, 'Why? Have I not given birth to God?' Nestorios then answered, 'You have given birth to Satan!', thereby incurring her permanent displeasure. See Nau 1919 (1974), 279; Price 2004, 32–3.

[44] Price 2004; James 2005; Price 2008.   [45] Mango 1998, 65–6.

[46] Note, however, Richard Price's recent suggestion that scholars have exaggerated the focus that Mary, as Theotokos, received at the Council of Ephesus in 431. This Council did not issue a doctrinal definition concerning the status of the Virgin Mary; the only documents that affirm her role as Theotokos are Cyril of Alexandria's *Second and Third Letters to Nestorius*, as well as his *Homily IV, On the Virgin Mary*, which was delivered at Ephesus soon after the condemnation of Nestorios. See Price 2019, 71–4.

Bethlehem,[47] marked the place where (according to the *Protevangelion of James*) the Virgin rested on her way to give birth to Christ.[48] Textual sources, including the fifth-century *Armenian Lectionary* and an account by a sixth-century pilgrim named Theodosios, testify to the site, as well as to the liturgical celebrations that took place there.[49] It is only in the mid sixth century, however, that two saints' *Lives* mention the church of the Kathisma, which they attribute to the generosity of a woman named Ikelia during the reign of the bishop Juvenal in the mid fifth century.[50] Here we note once again the role of a female patron in promoting the commemoration of the Virgin Mary in a material way.

Meanwhile, Leo I and his consort Verina founded the shrines (*Soroi*) at Blachernai and Chalkoprateia in Constantinople between 468 and 474, as we saw above.[51] These housed (or came to house) Mary's most famous relics, the robe (or mantle) and belt.[52] In the course of the sixth century, the emperors Justin I and Justinian I built numerous churches, some of which (including the Blachernai and Chalkoprateia) were renewed by their successor, Justin II.[53] Other churches or shrines that were constructed during this period include that of the 'Source' (*Pege*), which contained a spring at which healing miracles took place, and a chapel of the Theotokos in the imperial palace.[54] Justinian's official historian, Prokopios, describes these foundations in Constantinople along with others throughout the empire.[55]

Another important development in this period was the addition of new Marian feast-days to the Constantinopolitan ecclesiastical calendar. To the existing feast of the 'Memory of Mary', which had been celebrated since the

[47] Avner 1999; Shoemaker 2002, 79–98; Avner 2011.

[48] *Protevangelion of James* 17.3; ed. Tischendorf 1876 (1966), 33; trans. Elliott, 1993 (2004), 64. For discussion of this site and its significance for the Palestinian cult of the Virgin, see Shoemaker 2002, 78–98.

[49] *Armenian Lectionary*, ed. Renoux 1971, vol. 2, 354–7; Theodosios, *De situ terrae sanctae*, ed. Geyer 1965, 119. See also Wilkinson 1977, 5; Shoemaker 2002, 82–3.

[50] Theodore of Petra, *Vita s. Theodosii*, ed. Usener 1890, 13–14; Cyril of Skythopolis, *Vita s. Theodosii*, ed. Schwartz 1939, 236; Shoemaker 2002, 83–4.

[51] Mango 1998; Mango 1993–4; Mango 2000, 19.

[52] Ebersolt 1921, 44–60. For the earliest texts on the discovery and translation of the robe, see Wenger 1955, 111–39.

[53] Mango 2000, esp. 19–21. The epithet 'Theotokoupolis' was coined by the early seventh-century writer Theodore Synkellos in his oration known as the *Invention*; see Combefis 1648, vol. 2, 754B: Ἡ βασιλὶς αὕτη καὶ θεοφύλακτος πόλις, ἣν τῆς Θεοτόκου πόλιν ὁ λέγων ἢ γράφων ἐπαινεθήσεται . . .

[54] Ebersolt 1921, 17–30, 61–6; Mango 2000, 21; Magdalino 2004 (palace chapel of the Theotokos of the Pharos).

[55] Prokopios, *Buildings* I.iii.6 (the shrine of the *Pege*); I.iii.10 (that of the *Heraion*); I.iii.11–13 (a shrine to St Anna, Mary's mother, in the Deuteron); I.iii.1-5, I.vi.3 (Blachernai); I.viii.20 (a Marian shrine on the Bosphoros); II.x.24 (Antioch); III.iv.12 (Theodosiopolis); v.vi.1 (Jerusalem); v.vii.7 (Mt Garizin); v.viii.5-6 (Mt Sinai); v.ix.5 (Jericho); v.ix.8 (Mt of Olives); and many others.

early fifth century in connection with the feast of Christ's Nativity (25 December), as we saw above, were added those of the Annunciation (25 March) and possibly of the Virgin's own birth (8 September).[56] A homily by Abraham of Ephesus, dated to before 553, mentions the introduction of the feast of the Annunciation.[57] Further support for the existence of this festival appears in a letter that was purportedly written by Justinian himself in 560, in which the emperor argues that its date, along with that of Christ's Presentation in the Temple or *Hypapante* (2 February), should be determined by that of Christmas (25 December).[58] As for the feast of the Nativity of the Virgin, a kontakion by the sixth-century hymnographer Romanos the Melodist suggests that this was also being celebrated by about the middle of the sixth century.[59] The feast of Mary's Dormition or *Koimesis* ('falling asleep') (15 August) was added to the liturgical calendar at the end of the sixth century during the reign of Maurice (582–602).[60] Although our witness, Nikephoros Kallistos Xanthopoulos, was writing in the early fourteenth century, his testimony is supported by the numerous festal sermons on the subject of Mary's Dormition that survive from the early seventh century onward.[61] The feasts of Mary's Conception (9 December) and Entrance into the Temple (21 November) may only have been added to the calendar at around the beginning of the eighth century.[62] The first homilies and hymns that celebrate these festivals are dated to that period; they include works by the early eighth-century preachers John of Euboea and Germanos of Constantinople.[63]

---

[56] Cunningham 2008b, 19–23.

[57] Abraham of Ephesus, *Homily on the Annunciation*, ed. Jugie 1922 (2003), 443.2.14–20; see also van Esbroeck 1968-9; Antonopoulou 1997, 167, n. 37; Allen 2011, 72, 73, n. 27.

[58] Van Esbroeck 1968–9; *ODB*, vol. 1, 106.

[59] See Romanos the Melodist, *Kontakion on the Nativity of the Virgin*, ed. Maas and Trypanis 1963 (1997), 276 80. It is likely that Romanos died in *c.* 560; see Arentzen 2017, 5. Romanos also composed at least one kontakion for the feast of the Annunciation; see Maas and Trypanis 1963 (1997), 280–89. Although Maas and Trypanis assign a second kontakion to the theme of the Annunciation, Archimandrite Ephrem Lash titles it 'On the Mother of God' and suggests that it might have been sung on 26 December; see Maas and Trypanis 1963 (1997), 289–93; trans. Lash 1995, 16–22.

[60] Jugie 1944, 172–84; Mimouni 1995, 46–71; Shoemaker 2002, 121–5. All of these scholars trace the development of the Constantinopolitan celebration of the feast of the Dormition from Eastern Christian (especially Palestinian) celebration of her memory on 15 August.

[61] Nikephoros Kallistos Xanthopoulos, *Ecclesiastical History* 28, PG 147, 292B. Translations of many of these sermons can be found in Daley 1998.

[62] For discussion, see Cunningham 2008b, 24–6; Krausmüller 2011, 228–30; Panou 2018, 41–8.

[63] John of Euboea, *Homily on the Conception of the Virgin Mary*, PG 96, 1460–1500; Germanos I of Constantinople, *Homilies I–II on the Entrance*, PG 98, 292–320.

Liturgical texts, including homilies and hymns, in honour of the new Marian feasts proliferated from the sixth century onward. Pauline Allen argues that these displayed an increasingly 'high' and affective Mariology, citing festal orations by seventh-century preachers such as Sophronios of Jerusalem and Leontios of Neapolis.[64] Allen further shows that in addition to including intercessory invocation of the Virgin alongside the usual Christological doctrine, sermons for the feast of the Presentation in the Temple (*Hypapante*) began to 'sanatise' problematic aspects of this story, including the necessity (according to Jewish tradition) for Mary's purification forty days after the birth of Jesus (Lk 2:22) and her grief at the foot of the cross according to the elder Symeon's prophecy (Lk 2:35).[65] Whereas early Church teachers or bishops, including Origen and Cyril of Alexandria, argued that these signs revealed Mary's humanity, along with her need to be saved,[66] festal preachers from about the sixth century onward expressed no such ambiguity.[67] Their purpose, when preaching on the recently instituted Marian feast-days, was to celebrate the all-pure Virgin and Theotokos while also offering an opportunity for congregations to pray collectively for her protection and intercession.

The sixth century thus represents, as Averil Cameron and Cyril Mango have already argued, a turning point in the cult of the Byzantine Virgin Mary.[68] The beginnings of Marian devotion, which involved appeals for intercession and protection, may be detected in historical accounts of the fifth-century theological controversy; however, this trend manifests itself in liturgical texts only from about the sixth century onward. We shall see in Chapter 1 how the sixth-century hymnographer Romanos, probably influenced by Syriac liturgical poetry, contributed to the development of a fully human and maternal Virgin Mary.[69] Although his hymns may have been inspired as much by post-Chalcedonian theological considerations as by growing popular devotion to the Virgin, he succeeded in juxtaposing the powerful – and fully divine – figure of Christ and his human mother. But Mary also represented an effective intercessor for Romanos; she remained close to her Son even after his resurrection and ascension into heaven, thus providing the rest of humanity with access to the Righteous

---

[64] Allen 2011, 74–7, 82–4.

[65] Christian exegetes from an early date interpreted Symeon's prophecy as referring to Mary's future response to the crucifixion of her son; see Allen 2011, 84–5.

[66] Allen 2011, 79. Cf. Origen, *Homilies on Luke* XVII.6, ed. Crouzel, Fournier and Périchon 1962, 256–59; commentary on 11–64; Cyril of Alexandria, *Homily XII, On the Presentation*, PG 77, 1049C.

[67] See, for example, Leontios of Neapolis, *Homily on Symeon*, PG 93, 1580C; cited in Allen 2011, 83, n. 91.

[68] Cameron 1978; Cameron 1979b; Mango 2000, 21–3.   [69] Gador-Whyte 2013; Arentzen 2017.

Judge.[70] Romanos laid the foundations for later liturgical treatment of the Theotokos, both in homiletics and hymnography, although the themes that he introduced would develop further, especially after the period of Iconoclasm (*c.* 730–843).[71]

It is worth suggesting (although difficult to prove) that opposition to the developing Marian cult did exist in some quarters. It is possible that such a position was related to the late sixth-century controversy concerning the souls of saints after death and their efficacy as mediators of miracles and healing.[72] Whereas some theologians argued that souls can only function through the bodies with which they are associated, thus meaning that they are inactive after death, others believed that they remain awake and can bring about miracles and healing. Narratives concerning the Virgin's own death and afterlife began to circulate widely in the Greek-speaking world, following their first appearance in both Syriac and Greek versions in about the late fifth century.[73] This took the debate to another level, since Mary was believed to have been assumed bodily into heaven after three days in the tomb following which, in her resurrected form, she sat at the right hand of Christ in heaven but could also appear in visions to believers at her various shrines on earth. Clear textual evidence of anti-Marian voices in the Byzantine world is nevertheless difficult to find. A few clues, such as the silence of some liturgical writers in relation to the Virgin or Maximos the Confessor's need to defend himself from an accusation of slandering the Virgin in a text known as the *Dispute of Bizya* (656/7), may suggest that opponents of the cult (even if they did not include Maximos himself) were active in the Byzantine world.[74] It is possible, as Gilbert Dagron has suggested, that some ecclesiastics were dismayed by what they viewed as an excess of devotion to saints, relics, images and the Virgin at the turn of the seventh and eighth centuries; they viewed such activity as 'idolatrous' because it involved too much belief in 'presbeia' or intercession.[75]

The evidence increases during the iconoclast period, although historians have so far failed to prove conclusively that the opponents of images were also suspicious of Marian devotion. The answer to this question is likely to be nuanced; whereas iconoclasts (apart perhaps from Constantine V)

---

[70] Peltomaa 2015.
[71] On the continuing influence of Romanos the Melodist on later liturgical texts, see Cunningham 2008a.
[72] Dal Santo 2012; Krausmüller 1998–9; Krausmüller 2008.   [73] Mimouni 1995; Shoemaker 2002.
[74] Maximos the Confessor and Anastasios, *Dispute at Bizya*, ed. Allen and Neil 1999, 143. On the attribution of this text to Maximos and his disciple Anastasios, see ibid., 36–7.
[75] Dagron 1992, 65.

upheld Mary's holy status as 'Theotokos', they discouraged popular veneration of her relics and icons, as well as appeals to her intercessory power.[76] At the very beginning of the controversy, the patriarch Germanos I of Constantinople (715–30) denounced unnamed people who failed to venerate Mother of God, associating them rhetorically with Jews or other non-believers.[77] Several decades later, according to the ninth-century chronicler Theophanes, Constantine V rejected the concept that the Virgin Mary, or indeed any of the saints, could intercede in response to Christian supplication; this emperor also suppressed the possession or veneration of their relics.[78] The patriarch Nikephoros claimed that Constantine tampered with the content of hymns in praise of the Virgin, implying that this had to do with excising sections that sought her help or intercession.[79] All of this evidence, which remains scattered and heavily biased, suggests that this iconoclast emperor, possibly backed by members of the clergy who were sympathetic to his cause, opposed aspects of the Marian cult including veneration of her relics and belief in her power of intercession. Nevertheless, the production of Marian festal sermons and hymns flourished as never before in this period, which suggests that suppression of the cult, if it did indeed occur, was confined to the period of Constantine V's reign and that it revived after 787 and flourished during the period of second Iconoclasm (815–43).

Eighth- and ninth-century preachers and hymnographers, backed up by historians such as Theophanes the Confessor, employed Marian praise in support of the iconophile cause. Ioli Kalavrezou and Niki Tsironis have shown how emphasis on Mary's – and by extension Christ's – humanity helped to prove that images not only could, but indeed must, be

---

[76] The 'Horos' or Acts of the Iconoclast Council of Hiereia in 754 repeatedly stresses Mary's holiness as 'Theotokos'; see the *Acts of the Seventh Ecumenical Council of Nicaea (787)*, ed. Lamberz 2008-12, 682, 690; trans. Price 2018, 675, 676. On Constantine V's alleged position with regard to the Theotokos, including the idea that she should be regarded as 'an empty purse', see Gero 1977, 146.

[77] See Germanos of Constantinople, *Homily II on the Entrance*, PG 98, 312. A century or so later, the patriarch Photios of Constantinople berated listeners (or putative listeners) who did not accept the story of Anna's miraculous conception of the Virgin Mary at an advanced age; see Photios, *Homily IX, On the Birth of the Virgin* 4–6, ed. Laourdas 1959, 91.9–94. 3; trans. Mango 1958, 166–71. It is difficult to determine, however, whether the polemic that appears in these homilies is directed at actual ideological opponents or included merely for rhetorical effect.

[78] Theophanes Confessor, *Chronicle*, ed. De Boor 1887, 439, 442; trans. Mango and Scott 1997, 607, 610. Some scholars argue, however, that passages such as these exaggerate the extent to which iconoclasts suppressed the cult of relics; see Auzépy 2001, 19–20; Brubaker and Haldon 2011, 38–40.

[79] Nikephoros, *Antirrhetikos* II.4, PG 100, 341D: Ἔπειτα παραχαράσσει καὶ παραποιεῖται ὅσα ἐπὶ τῷ ὀνόματι αὐτῆς ἐπεκέκλητο, καὶ ἐν λιταῖς πρὸς τὸν τεχθέντα ἐξ αὐτῆς καὶ δεήσεσιν ἐν ᾄσμασιν ἀεὶ ἀνεφώνουν ὑπὲρ τῆς τοῦ κοινοῦ παντὸς σωτηρίας οἱ δεόμενοι. I am grateful to Dirk Krausmüller for informing me of this reference.

constructed and venerated in order to witness to the reality of the incarnation.[80] Mary's human and maternal qualities, which manifested themselves especially at the time of Christ's birth and crucifixion, might be expressed with the help of affective rhetorical devices such as *enargeia* (making absent things present), *ekphrasis* (description), *ethopoiia* (dramatic speech) and others.[81] All of these elements had already been employed, as we saw earlier, by Romanos the Melodist in the middle of the sixth century; however, eighth- and especially ninth-century preachers and hymnographers took them to a higher level in their depiction of the loving and grieving Virgin Mary. Their purpose, by focusing on his mother, was to prove the humanity of Christ; however, this also served to make Mary appear even more accessible to human supplication as she sat in glory beside her resurrected Son in heaven.

One other product of the Iconoclast period was the elaboration of Mary's legendary life story. The late eighth- and early ninth-century hagiographer Epiphanios the Monk (of Kallistratos) produced the first biography, or *Life*, of the Virgin that survives in Greek,[82] although earlier examples circulated in the Syriac-speaking world.[83] This text differs from liturgical homilies and hymns in its 'historical' approach to the holy subject. As we shall see in Chapter 5, Epiphanios was followed in the tenth century by at least three other hagiographers; although the latter provided an interesting mix of panegyrical and narrative elements in their *Lives* of the Virgin,[84] Epiphanios adhered mainly to the latter approach. His effort must reflect increasing interest in the historical figure of the Virgin Mary, although he inevitably depended on New Testament, apocryphal and patristic sources for his narrative. In any case, this text inaugurates several new strands in the developing Marian tradition: these include the aforementioned interest in 'historical' narrative; the revival of emphasis on Mary's ascetic, or monastic, qualities; and, perhaps most interestingly, a willingness to diverge from apocryphal and even canonical narratives about the Virgin. Not only Epiphanios but also the later hagiographers embellish Mary's story for their own didactic purposes; such freedom indicates an ability not only of writers – but presumably also of readers or audiences – to associate certain

[80] Kalavrezou 1990; Kalavrezou 2000; Tsironis 2000.   [81] Tsironis 2010; Tsironis 2011.

[82] Epiphanios of Kallistratos, *Life of the Virgin*, ed. Dressel 1843; see also Cunningham 2019.

[83] Naffah 2009.

[84] John Geometres, *Life of the Virgin*, ed. Constas and Simelidis forthcoming; Georgian *Life of the Virgin*, ed. van Esbroeck 1986, Shoemaker 2012; Symeon the Metaphrast, *Life of the Virgin*, ed. Latyshev 1912. For discussion of the four *Lives* (either collectively or individually), see Mimouni 1994 (2011); Shoemaker 2005; Shoemaker 2011c; Cunningham 2016; Constas 2019; Cunningham 2019; Simelidis 2020.

aspects of the Virgin (such as personal qualities or narrative details) with particular theological messages.

The period that followed the end of Iconoclasm, or 'Triumph of Orthodoxy', in 843 thus saw the full elaboration of Marian veneration in Byzantium. The Virgin Mary, who was usually now addressed as 'Mother of God' (*Meter Theou*), presided over the apses of middle Byzantine Churches, symbolising not only the incarnation of Christ but also her own role as purveyor of his body and blood in the Eucharist.[85] Artisans, including not only icon painters but also mosaicists, sculptors, weavers and illuminators of manuscripts, began to depict the Mother of God in different aspects that were provided with recognisable epithets, such as 'Hodegetria' ('Guide'), 'Eleousa' ('Tender One') and others.[86] The ninth-century preacher George of Nikomedia described the figure of the lamenting Virgin who experienced 'searing flames of fire that penetrated her womb' as she witnessed her Son suffering on the cross.[87] And, perhaps following such homiletic treatment, the compilers and authors of liturgical books for weekdays throughout the year developed the short hymns known as *stavrotheotokia*, which commemorated the grieving Mary in concise but affective ways.[88] In addition to embodying the full act of spiritual surrender to Christ, the Virgin was envisioned as vicariously enduring his pain on the cross. Whereas Byzantine liturgical writers preferred to avoid detailed descriptions of the suffering Son of God, they could develop this aspect of divine *kenosis* fully in the person of his mother.

Another aspect of middle Byzantine devotion to the Virgin Mary was her appropriation by monastic or lay religious writers. This process began with the composition of hymnography in her honour, not only for the Marian feast-days but also for Wednesdays and Fridays throughout the year, by mainly monastic melodists.[89] As mentioned above, the early ninth-century writer Epiphanios, who may have belonged to the Monastery of Kallistratos in Constantinople, displayed an interest in Mary's ascetic prowess throughout his *Life of the Virgin*.[90] Although the late tenth-century *Life* by John Geometres may have been composed for a pious lay confraternity at the church of the Theotokos *ta Kyrou*, it also

[85] Evangelatou 2019, 77 and passim.

[86] For discussion of the epithets that are associated with particular icons of the Mother of God, see Ouspensky and Lossky 1983, 76–103; Baltoyanni 2000.

[87] George of Nikomedia, *Homily on Good Friday*, PG 100, 1480B (quoted and translated in Constas 2014, 127).

[88] *Oktoechos;* see especially the hymnography for Wednesdays and Fridays.

[89] For discussion of this process, see Ševčenko 1998, esp. 112–14.

[90] Cunningham 2016, 152–6; Cunningham 2019, 319–22.

celebrated the Virgin's prayerful way of life.[91] The main periods in Mary's legendary life that were significant, according to these authors, were the years (between the ages of three and twelve – or according to Epiphanios, seven and fourteen) that she spent in the Jewish temple and those that followed the ascension of Christ into heaven. She is described as engaging in constant vigils and prayer in the settings of the 'holy of holies', or innermost sanctuary, in the temple and of the 'upper room' on Zion where she lived in the care of the evangelist John after Christ's ascension. Even more significantly, the late tenth-century *Lives* of the Virgin attribute teaching and leadership roles to Mary at various points in her story. The Georgian *Life of the Virgin*, for example, goes so far as to describe the Virgin directing both the ascetic training and missionary activity of the apostles.[92] We may ask whether such attribution of power to a female figure reflects the desire or experience of the author or, alternatively, whether it is applied uniquely to the Mother of God and not to other women.

Miracle stories, along with longer *Lives* of saints that contain embedded stories of miracles involving the Virgin, meanwhile provide us with a glimpse of lay people's responses to her miraculous presence and intercession.[93] The miracles that were recorded at the shrine of the *Pege* (Source) in Constantinople, for example, belong to a collection of stories that date between the fifth and tenth centuries.[94] Interestingly, they record visions of a woman who takes various forms, depending on the witnesses who encounter her. One story describes a woman 'of modest means' (γυναῖκά τινα μετρίαν), whereas another portrays her as 'a woman robed in purple, towering as high as the lintel [of the church doors] in the majesty of her stature'.[95] It is possible that the stories in this collection reflect the individual experiences of pilgrims to the shrine; the compiler has apparently made no attempt to harmonise such different accounts of Mary's presence, remaining close to the narratives as they were originally told. Several middle Byzantine apocalypses that describe the Virgin's tours of heaven and hell, according to purported visions of individual Christians, portray yet another image of the Mother of God.[96] Jane Baun has analysed the didactic purpose of the *Apocalypse of Anastasia* and the *Apocalypse of the*

---

[91] John Geometres, *Life of the Virgin*. On the confraternity at the church of the Theotokos *ta Kyrou*, see Magdalino 2018.

[92] Georgian *Life of the Virgin* 93–102; ed. and trans. van Esbroeck 1986, vol. 479/ 22, 81–90; ed. and trans. Shoemaker 2012, 120–9.

[93] See Chapter 5.

[94] *Miracles of the Pege*, ed. and trans. Talbot and Johnson 2012, Introduction, xv.

[95] *Miracles of the Pege* 7 and 13, ed. and trans. Talbot and Johnson 2012, 220–1 and 234–5.

[96] *Apocalypse of Anastasia*, ed. Homburg 1903; *Apocalypse of the Theotokos*, ed. Tischendorf 1866 (1966).

Theotokos, as they portray sinners suffering in Hades for their various misdeeds in life.[97] The lively nature of these texts, as well as their hopeful portrayal of the Virgin Mary in her role as chief intercessor in heaven, assured their popularity not only in the Byzantine, but also the later Orthodox world.[98] In short, and as we will see in Chapter 5, the hagiographical or 'popular' treatment of the Virgin Mary differs in many ways from the theological, and increasingly formulaic, approach that predominates in homilies and hymns of the same period.

This brief overview of the development of Marian doctrine and devotion during the early and middle periods of Byzantine history does not differ significantly from that which has already achieved consensus among most historians and theologians. Although I disagree with some scholars about the extent and nature of Marian devotion in the early Church, it is undeniable that recognition of her personal holiness existed well before the beginning of the fifth century.[99] Mary's promotion as patron and defender of Constantinople, along with acknowledgement of her intercessory power, took place especially in the course of the sixth century and reached a high point at the siege of the imperial city in 626. Shrines that contained the main secondary relics, the robe and the belt, although founded as early as the second half of the fifth century, gained impetus after this date. The defeat of Iconoclasm in the course of the eighth and ninth centuries helped to promote the cult further and it flourished especially in the centuries that followed, with the late ninth and tenth centuries seeing increased production of hymnography, homiletics and hagiography in honour of the Virgin. To return to the theme with which I began, Mary represented all things to most people: she became a multilayered symbol that worked in theological, devotional and social ways. Her gender was important, as we shall see later, but this did not inhibit Christians of all three genders (male, female and eunuch) from approaching her.[100] Mary symbolised creation, the Church and every human being; at the same time, according to Byzantine hymnography, she 'was higher than the cherubim and more honourable than the seraphim' – in other words, a member of the celestial court who stood in close proximity to God himself. In short, Mary was the meeting place of the divine and created worlds, according to a society

[97] Baun 2007.
[98] For example, F. Dostoyevsky refers to a Slavonic version of the Theotokos apocalypse, calling it a 'monastic poem', in the 'Grand Inquisitor' section of *The Brothers Karamazov*; see Dostoyevsky, *The Brothers Karamazov*, trans. McDuff 1993 (2003), 322–3; cf. Baun 2007, 259.
[99] See above, 6–8.
[100] For the idea that three genders existed in Byzantine culture, see Ringrose 2003.

that never forgot its place in relation to the whole Christian cosmos.[101] Byzantine writers of every literary genre presented the variegated aspects of the Mother of God in response to, and for the benefit of, the liturgical, literary and civic circumstances in which they found themselves.

Literary Genre and Contexts of Textual Reception

The question of literary genre – that is, whether we can classify different types of text on the basis of their form, style and content – continues to perplex Byzantinists. Scholars debate whether Byzantine writers recognised separate literary forms and if so, whether they adhered strictly to such categories. Reacting in part to the German 'Handbuch' approach to Byzantine literature, Alexander Kazhdan questioned the concept of 'genre' and suggested that texts should be read on their own merits – especially with attention to the work of individual authors.[102] Margaret Mullett, Panagiotis Agapitos and Martin Hinterberger defend the concept, however, arguing that 'genre' refers to recognised literary 'forms' that provide authors both with models for inspiration and opportunities for parody.[103] Some of these are well-known genres from classical antiquity, such as histories, letters or epigrams. Others, including saints' *Lives* or *vitae*, homilies, and hymns such as kontakia and kanons, are Christian inventions. Nevertheless, some problems remain. First, as Agapitos points out, 'what the Byzantines have to say about genre and the way in which they compose texts belonging to ancient genres (e.g. epistolography or historiography) shows a steady trend in juxtaposing convention and innovation or in experimenting with mixture and deviation'.[104] In other words, the authors of all kinds of literary texts played with traditional rules about genre, combining these in new ways in order to create something slightly different. Second, as Mullett remarks, the rhetorical 'type', which depended on performative contexts, audiences and other factors, could

---

[101] Meyendorff 1974, 129–50; Theokritoff 2008; Cunningham 2010; Louth 2013, 33–49.

[102] Kazhdan with Franklin 1984, viii; see also Kazhdan 1999, 1–5. Classic German handbooks include Krumbacher 1897; Beck 1959; and Hunger 1978.

[103] Mullett 1992; Agapitos 2003; Agapitos 2008; Hinterberger 2014. Martin Hinterberger defines the concept as follows: 'The question of literary genres involves, on the one hand, the categorisation and classification of texts by modern scholarship on the basis of precise criteria and characteristic features, and, on the other, the literary practice according to which the writer, one way or another, refers to an extant tradition and texts of reference (or model texts) which he/she follows, adapts, rejects, or parodies. However, it also concerns the literary audience and their reception of a text according to their expectations of a particular genre, as developed by former experiences.' See Hinterberger 2014, 25, with reference to Duff 2000.

[104] Agapitos 2008, 79.

apply to a variety of literary forms – and indeed could shift from one setting to another according to multiple readings of the same text.[105] Third and finally, it is evident that the boundaries between literary genres are sometimes blurred or porous; what, for example, is the difference between a festal oration and a high-style saint's life, both of which might be delivered in a liturgical setting? I shall deal with these three problems one by one, aiming in the process to justify the classification of texts that I adopt in the present book and to explain why it is important.

To begin with the definition of individual genres, it is worth noting that many of the literary forms that are useful for scholarship would not be recognised by Byzantine writers or their audiences. Nor do they correspond to ancient categories, as defined by philosophers or rhetoricians. Festal sermons, to take one example, are based on early Christian models such as the theological orations of Gregory Nazianzen.[106] Although we may also call them 'homilies', they differ from the more conversational, or colloquial, exegetical orations that were delivered in church on a daily or weekly basis by preachers including Origen, the Cappadocian Fathers including Gregory, and John Chrysostom.[107] All of these homiletic forms are Christian inventions; they were employed for didactic, panegyrical and polemical reasons. There are various subgenres within the wider category of 'homiletics', but most were employed in liturgical settings – a purpose which usually governed their inclusion or not in later collections such as *menologia, panegyrika* and *homiliaria*.[108] Hagiography is also a Christian invention, which served both commemorative and liturgical functions.[109] The *Acts* or passions of martyrs, *Lives* (*vitae*) of ascetic saints and collections of miracles all belong to this category. Whereas *Acts* of martyrs follow earlier pagan and Jewish models, the *Lives* of saints are based more on rhetorical forms such as the *basilikos logos* or the *enkomion*, both of which offer praise to important people, whether living or dead. New forms of poetry that were sung primarily in liturgical contexts also developed in

---

[105] Mullett 1992, 235–6.
[106] Gregory Nazianzen, *Festal Orations*, ed. Bernardi 1978, Moreschini 1990; trans. Harrison 2008. Useful studies include Ruether 1969; McGuckin 2001a; Daley 2006; Beeley 2008; Elm 2012; Thomas 2019.
[107] On the distinctions between homiletic genres (along with the difficulty of such definitions), see Cunningham 2008c, 875–8; Mayer 2008, 570–72.
[108] The categorisation (and naming) of such collections is undertaken in Ehrhard 1936–52. On the possible uses of these collections in Byzantine monastic and liturgical settings, see Cunningham 2011b.
[109] For orientation on the genre as a whole, see Efthymiadis 2014, 1–21 ('Introduction'); Hinterberger 2014.

the Christian Church.[110] Hymns such as the kontakion (sometimes described as a 'sung homily'), the kanon, sticheron, and – specifically in honour of the Virgin Mary – the theotokion and stavrotheotokion all follow particular melodies, metrical patterns and didactic methods.

It is worth asking next whether Byzantine preachers, hagiographers and hymnographers consciously recognised these separate literary forms, along with the rules or formulaic qualities that became associated with each. The answer is not clear, especially since none of these specifically Christian genres corresponded directly with forms that Byzantine writers would have been taught in the course of their rhetorical or philosophical training. Sometimes the titles that are provided for individual texts in manuscripts provide clues – especially with regard to hymn forms that filled specific slots in liturgical service books by about the early eighth century. Festal sermons and *Lives* of saints, however, could both be called 'logoi' ('speeches') in middle Byzantine liturgical collections; they might both be read out in the course of offices such as the morning service (*Orthros*), although both might also have acted as private devotional reading or have been read aloud (not always all at once) in non-liturgical settings.[111] In short, whereas hymnography became increasingly well defined, as regards separate forms that occupied specific slots in liturgical celebration, the prose compositions are less easy to classify. It seems possible that Byzantine writers of homilies, *enkomia*, *Lives* of saints and other literary forms were aware of earlier prototypes, but were also happy to play with these malleable categories. Some other aspect of their composition, apart from 'genre', must determine their structure, style and content.

This brings us to Mullett's suggestion that 'the "rhetorical" type provides the occasion, function, and status and transactional relationships between the implied speaker and the implied recipient' in any given speech or text.[112] The epideictic types, such as *basilikos logos* (speech in praise of an emperor), *ekphrasis*, or other set compositions that determine the content of a text depend above all on the timing, physical location and intended audience or reader. Mullett suggests that these criteria intersect with the form of literary delivery that has been chosen, thus producing a particular genre that is suited to the occasion.[113] This analysis provides a way forward in our attempt to classify the various types of text that are identified in the chapters of this book. It is possible that the multifaceted Virgin Mary

---

[110] Introductions to Byzantine hymnography and music can be found in Wellesz 1961; Szövérffy 1978-9; Savas 1983; Lingas 2008.
[111] Mayer 2008; Cunningham 2011b; Antonopoulou 2013.   [112] Mullett 1992, 235.
[113] Mullett 1992, 235-7.

responds not to identifiable literary genres (although I have chosen to categorise texts in this way as a matter of convenience), but rather to the separate contexts and audiences for which individual texts are intended. Liturgical writers and hagiographers (who could sometimes be the same people, as in the case of John Geometres) portrayed the Mother of God in accordance to the particular settings in which they found themselves.[114] The tenth-century *Lives* of the Virgin were thus composed for audiences or readers who expected longer, more narrative treatment of the holy subject, whereas festal homilies occupied specific slots in the liturgical offices which both dictated their structure and limited their scope. Collections of miracle stories such as those that emanated from the Constantinopolitan shrine of the Source, which may be classified as 'hagiography', also fulfilled particular expectations: it is likely that these were read out *in situ* on particular festive occasions, such as the patronal feast of the monastery.[115]

My third point, namely, that the boundaries between these literary genres were porous, supports the hypothesis that Marian content reflected the particular contexts of oratorical or sung delivery. Byzantine preachers, hagiographers and hymnographers moved between literary form and rhetorical type with deliberate fluidity. John Geometres' *Life of the Virgin*, for example, combines hagiographical narrative (in that it covers Mary's legendary biography from conception through death and assumption), panegyrical praise and hymnic acclamation. The text is grounded in the liturgical calendar, in that it recognises the major feast-days of the Virgin and organises its narrative around these events in her life. Some festal homilies, beginning in about the seventh century, combine narrative with Christological teaching and praise. This genre, which adorned a liturgical calendar that contained a full set of Dominical and Marian feasts by about the end of the eighth century, adopted a wide variety of rhetorical tropes and devices in its aim to celebrate, teach and delight Byzantine congregations.

Hymnography differs from prose compositions in that more structured, metrical forms are assigned to specific liturgical slots in the offices and Divine Liturgy. Christian Hannick argues that such poetry occupies

---

[114] On the possible settings at which the tenth-century *Lives* were delivered, see Mimouni 1994 (2011), 75; Georgian *Life of the Virgin*, ed. and trans. Shoemaker 2012, 3, 161–64 (referring to the reading aloud of this text in Georgian monasteries); Constas 2019, 325–6 (on the liturgical settings for readings of John Geometres' *Life of the Virgin*); Simelidis 2020 (on the possible literary background, namely, a confraternity at the church of the Theotokos *ta Kyrou* in Constantinople, of the same text).

[115] *Miracles of the Pege*, ed. and trans. Talbot and Johnson 2012, Introduction, xiv–xviii.

a more ambiguous position than homiletics both because it is often
anonymous (or difficult to assign securely to known hymnographers)
and because it is unclear whether it is intended to serve a didactic or
a panegyrical purpose.[116] Nevertheless, studies such as those of Derek
Krueger have helped to open up our understanding of the multiple
purposes of hymnography.[117] Literary study of these texts, which analyses
the role of the author, or narrator, of individual texts, as well as the ways in
which congregations responded to them, suggest that hymns functioned in
similar ways to festal sermons. Christological teaching, dramatic treatment
of biblical or apocryphal stories, praise and invocation of the Virgin's
intercessory power played varying parts in both genres. The main difference lies in the strict and limited structure of hymnographic forms, as
opposed to the expandable form of festal or occasional sermons.

In spite of the flexibility and porousness of all of these Christian literary
genres, which allowed writers to draw inspiration from each when com-
posing a text for a particular setting, some fundamental differences in their
treatment of Mary, the Mother of God, remain. It is for this reason that
I organise the present book according to three main genres, homiletics,
hymnography and hagiography, and attempt to discern why she appears in
different aspects according to each. Whereas changes in her depiction also
develop in a diachronic way, as we shall see in the following chapters, some
basic differences seem to depend on the choice of literary form. I will argue
that these variations depend on the particular settings, or contexts, and
audiences for which the separate texts were intended. Whereas hymnography and festal sermons, for example, were expected to provide theological teaching and praise, hagiography (including *Lives* and miracle
collections) and occasional homilies offered more narrative treatment of
the holy subject.

One other aspect of the question should be mentioned here, especially in
view of recent discussions of the very nature of Byzantine texts and their
reception. I concur with the view that most Byzantine literature was
delivered orally, owing to the fact that only a small proportion of the
population was literate.[118] This applies especially to the liturgical or paraliturgical – but always religious – texts that are covered in this study.
Homilies and hymns were mostly performed in the context of church
services.[119] Although it is unclear how well Byzantine congregations

---

[116] Hannick 2005, 70.   [117] Krueger 2004; Krueger 2014.
[118] Saenger 1982; Shawcross 2018, esp. 23–5; Jeffreys and Jeffreys 2018.
[119] On the delivery of homilies during the Divine Liturgy or in offices, see Cunningham 1990;
Antonopoulou 1997, 95–115.

understood these texts, they were spoken, read, or sung either annually or else on a daily or weekly basis. The situation is more complicated than this, however, as we shall see in the course of Chapters 4 and 5: homilies, although perhaps delivered extempore at the time of composition, often experienced an 'afterlife' as readings both in liturgical and non-liturgical contexts.[120] It is likely especially from the twelfth century onward that homilies were performed, along with 'recited metrical prefaces', in lay literary settings such as the church of the Theotokos *ta Kyrou* in Constantinople.[121] They might also have been used as private devotional readings in some monasteries or lay settings. Hymns, although usually contained in service books and sung on a daily, weekly or annual basis, could occasionally be used as teaching tools or devotional readings.[122] This was not the fate of most Marian hymns, but it shows how much Byzantine readers appreciated the theological content of these works. The most important point about all of these works, however, which applies to many other Byzantine literary genres, is their oral and performative nature. This is a topic that offers rich potential for future study – and which should alter our approach to all forms of Marian literary expression.

Gender: The Subject and Her Supplicants

The Virgin Mary and Mother of God has always attracted scholarly interest on the grounds of her female gender. Feminist approaches have ranged from celebration of Mary's power and influence to disapproval of her role within patriarchal societies, as a symbol of obedience and submission; most studies recognise, however, the paradoxical ways in which these roles have been applied to Mary.[123] Gender Studies offers more nuanced methods, suggesting that literary texts and material evidence should be read with an understanding of the cultural backgrounds in which they were produced.[124] Many literary texts cannot be read at face value; they offer sophisticated and multi-layered messages that conceal deeper meanings. Since this problem pertains as much – if not more – to Marian texts of the early and middle Byzantine period as to any other form of literature, it is worth devoting some space to the subject of gender.

---

[120] Cunningham 2011b.   [121] Antonopoulou 2010; Simelidis 2020, 133.   [122] Skrekas 2018.

[123] Most scholarly studies offer nuanced approaches to Mary's gender; see, for example, Warner 1976; Ruether 1977; Hamington 1995; Gaventa 1999; Beattie 2002; Rubin 2009.

[124] Neville 2019, 36–43; James 1997, xi–xxiv; see also the collected essays on gender in James 1997; Brubaker and Smith 2004; Neil and Garland 2013; Constantinou and Meyer 2019; Betancourt 2020.

There are two aspects of the field that we need to consider: first, it is necessary to look at the various ways in which this holy woman is portrayed in Byzantine religious texts. Mary's female nature, especially in terms of her virginity and motherhood, is central to her role in this literary tradition. Second, we must consider whether the Virgin appealed especially to women and if so, why. We should also ask whether such popularity developed or changed in the course of our chosen period. The latter approach, which has to do with the reception of Mary's cult in Byzantium, has so far received more attention from scholars than has the former. However, both are important, so I shall deal with them one by one in the discussion that follows.

Bearing in mind Leonora Neville's useful identification of traits that the Byzantines (or, as she would prefer to call them, 'medieval Romans') considered 'feminine', aspects of the Virgin's character assume importance: she is virginal, obedient to God, maternal, compassionate, and protective both of her Son, Christ, and of her devotees. However, as the early seventh-century poet George of Pisidia reminded us at the beginning of this Introduction, Mary was also pictured as an invincible warrior, defending the imperial city of Constantinople in the siege of 626.[125] If we accept Neville's view that Byzantine ideas about gender were more to do with ethical behaviour than with biological identity, then it becomes evident that the Virgin Mary – perhaps more than most other biblical or literary personages – is an ambiguous or paradoxical figure.[126] She represents the extremes of both femininity and masculinity in her person: in short, this larger-than-life figure embodies aspects of both genders. In the discussion that follows, I shall focus first on examples that reveal Mary's 'feminine' qualities, which include above all her virginal motherhood, and second on virtues that betray more 'masculine' attributes. Above all, we should bear in mind a second strand in Neville's argumentation, namely, that texts convey complex messages and should not be read literally. In their transmission of a gendered message regarding the Virgin Mary, Byzantine religious writers are less interested in discovering her 'historical' character than on upholding cultural norms or stereotypes.

To begin with the more traditional model, Mary's female gender, as evidenced in her role as Virgin and mother of Christ, is central to the Byzantine Christian tradition. She was honoured from a very early period,

---

[125] See above, n. 1.
[126] Neville 2019, 27–30. Maria Evangelatou also suggests contradictory roles for the Virgin Mary in Byzantine texts; see Evangelatou 2014, 294–9.

as we have already seen, for her role as the virginal mother of Jesus Christ.[127] Festal liturgical texts, which began to be produced from the early fifth century onward, primarily celebrated Mary's role in the incarnation.[128] Although preachers and hymnographers viewed this role as divinely preordained, they began to be interested in her personal (and female) response to this world-changing event. Christian exegesis of the annunciation story (Lk 1:26-38) shifted its focus during the late antique period from Mary's docile acceptance to more thoughtful consideration of Gabriel's message.[129] The latter approach built on Mary's role as 'Second Eve': preachers and hymnographers began to stress the importance of free will in each case, with the first Eve making the disastrous choice to disobey God while the second (Mary) undid this betrayal by accepting his command.[130]

Greek liturgical texts, following the Syriac tradition,[131] began to include dramatic dialogues between Gabriel and Mary or Mary and Joseph, which revealed her gradual shift from doubt to belief and acceptance.[132] It is nevertheless puzzling that the same liturgical writers remained reticent about when the conception of Christ actually took place. The view that Mary was impregnated through her ear, at the moment when the archangel first addressed her, persisted until the end of our period.[133] It appears that various theological considerations pulled the narrative one way or the other: whereas preachers and hymnographers wished to emphasise Mary's free consent to the incarnation, they also aimed to preserve the miraculous nature of the conception and to remain faithful to the Gospel of Luke. Even so, such invented dialogues offered an opportunity for exploring Mary's feminine traits, including modesty, humility and openness to influence. She was portrayed as a pious virginal girl who was willing to obey, but appropriately cautious in her reception of an unknown stranger with a life-changing message.

[127] The most complete survey of patristic and medieval doctrine concerning the Virgin Mary remains Graef 1963 (2009). See also Gambero 1999; Boss 2007; Rubin 2009; Reynolds 2012; Maunder 2019.

[128] See Chapters 1 and 2.   [129] Constas 2003, 273–313; Allen 2011, 72–8; Arentzen 2017, 46–86.

[130] Constas 2003, 282–90.   [131] Brock 1994 (2010), 125–38; Brock 2011, 9–47.

[132] See, for example, (ps-)Proklos of Constantinople, *Homily VI, On the Theotokos* ed. Leroy 1967; Romanos the Melodist, *Kontakion on the Annunciation*, ed. Maas and Trypanis 1963 (1997), 280–89; Germanos I of Constantinople, *Homily on the Annunciation*, ed. Fecioru 1946.

[133] Nicholas (Fr Maximos) Constas demonstrates that this problem only began to be dealt with in the later Byzantine period; see Constas 2003, 294–5.

Liturgical writers also described and invoked the Theotokos in metaphorical and typological language.[134] This symbolic message must have
developed slowly, perhaps from well before the beginning of the fifth
century, and become recognisable to late antique and Byzantine church-
goers.[135] Types such as Jacob's ladder, the burning bush, Gideon's fleece,
mountain, cloud and many others are not expounded or 'unpacked' in
festal homilies and hymnography; however, they act as prophetic, or
typological, signs of the Virgin in the Old Testament, also linking her
with the creation that God has blessed and chosen to enter.[136] This is
a language which not only works across time and text, but which actually
signifies a reality that 'God has stamped' on creation.[137] Many Marian types
allude to the 'feminine' qualities of the Theotokos: her absorption of fire or
water in the cases of the burning bush and Gideon's fleece, for example,
refer metaphorically to her conception and gestation of Christ, the Word
of God. Such signs reflect ancient ideas about childbirth: another common
type, the 'unploughed field' or paradise, produces Christ after being
implanted with divine seed.

Mingled with such imagery in ways that are more often implicit than
explicit, are allusions to other aspects of feminine activity. Nicholas (now
Fr Maximos) Constas analyses the ways in which Proklos of
Constantinople used imagery that was associated with weaving – a job
that was normally performed by women – in relation to the incarnation.[138]
This metaphor, according to which Mary's womb is the 'workshop'
(*ergasterion*) in which the flesh of God is woven together from divine and
created material, has further symbolic associations with the temple and its
veil – for which the Virgin spun the purple thread at the time of the
annunciation.[139] Turning to Romanos the Melodist's treatment of the
scene of Christ's nativity, Thomas Arentzen shows how Marian types
and metaphors are used to depict an erotic and expectant state of

---

[134] Cunningham 2004; Olkinuora 2015, 65–113.
[135] Krastu Banev suggests that biblical types for the Virgin Mary originated as types for the Church; see
Banev 2014.
[136] Young 1997, 152–7; Ladouceur 2006; Reynolds 2019.
[137] Michel Foucault describes this process as follows: 'in the treasure handed down to us by Antiquity,
the value of language lay in the fact that it was the sign of things. There is no difference between the
visible marks that God has stamped upon the surface of the earth, so that we may know its inner
secrets, and the legible words that the Scriptures, or the sages of Antiquity, have set down in the
books preserved for us by tradition. The relation to these texts is of the same nature as the relation to
things: in both cases there are signs that must be discovered.' See Foucault 1989, 37.
[138] Constas 1995; Constas 2003, 315–58.
[139] Proklos of Constantinople, *Homily I.1*, ed. Constas 2003, 136–7. On the symbolism of both the
temple and its veil, see Barker 1991; Barker 2004, 27–32.

motherhood. Romanos creates, for example, a 'Marian space' in the cave of Bethlehem with imagery that evokes darkness, secrecy and fecundity.[140]

The Virgin Mary plays an active but also problematic role in connection with the passion of Christ in some liturgical texts. Here both preachers and melodists stretch the boundaries of acceptable female behaviour, allowing Mary to break out of her more normal, or passive, response to the playing out of God's dispensation for salvation. Romanos the Melodist was the first Greek writer to describe the Virgin as an entirely human and grief-stricken mother, in his kontakion on her lament at the cross.[141] According to the melodist, she followed Christ on his journey to the cross, expressing sorrow, disbelief and fear at what was happening; he responded by telling her the reasons for his acceptance of death and assuring her that she would be the first person to witness his resurrection. Following Romanos, the theme was picked up by middle Byzantine preachers and hymnographers, becoming the focus of hymns intended for Good Friday, as well as for Wednesdays and Fridays throughout the year.[142] It featured in a tenth-century version of the apocryphal *Gospel of Nikodemos* and became the central preoccupation of the (probably) twelfth-century play, *Christos Paschon*.[143] The particular qualities of female grief are elaborated in all of these texts: women, including Mary, weep, cry out, let down their hair and tear at their faces with their nails.[144] Whereas patristic and Byzantine tradition deplores such behaviour on the part of most women, however, an exception is made in the case of the Mother of God. She acts out, or embodies, the meaning of divine *kenosis*; with her help, Christians are encouraged to participate fully in the pain that this entailed for him, but also in that which those who loved him were made to feel. There is also a paradoxical aspect to Mary's grief at the sight of Christ's crucifixion. Whereas liturgical writers and poets continue to stress the inviolability of Mary's virginity, they also describe her vulnerability as a grieving mother.[145]

---

[140] Arentzen 2017, 95.

[141] Romanos the Melodist, *Kontakion on Mary at the Cross*, ed. Maas and Trypanis 1963 (1997), 142–9; trans. Lash 1995, 141–50.

[142] For texts and analysis of this tradition, see Tsironis 1998.

[143] *Gospel of Nikodemos (Byzantine recensions)* 10.1–2, 10.1.3c–4a, ed. Gounelle 2007, 226–41 and discussion, 56–8, 63–4 (I am grateful to Dr Gounelle for bringing this passage to my attention); *Christos Paschon*, ed. Tuilier 1969.

[144] The classic study of this tradition is Alexiou 1974 (2002).

[145] As Fr Maximos Constas points out, a passage in one of the rhetorical exercises of the twelfth-century teacher Nikephoros Basilakes (an *ethopoiia* in which Mary laments the death of Christ on the cross) supports this point: see Constas 2014, 127. Mary cries, 'No longer am I the unconsumed bush; for I have been consumed entirely by the intelligible fire of your burial'; trans. Beneker and Gibson

As I mentioned above in connection with the topic of literary genre, middle Byzantine hagiography contains further surprises concerning the gendered behaviour of the Mother of God. Most of the surviving *Lives* of the Virgin emphasise Mary's dedication to the ascetic life; she carries out a life of seclusion, unceasing prayer and night vigils especially during the period that she spends in the Jewish temple between the ages of three and twelve and after the resurrection and ascension of Christ. This strand of Marian reflection became a preoccupation of writers such as Epiphanios of Kallistratos, John Geometres and the likely author of the Georgian *Life*, Euthymios the Hagiorite; however, it revived ideas that also appeared in letters that the fourth-century bishop sent to communities of virgins in Alexandria.[146] The virtues that Mary displayed as 'monastic' saint are ungendered in that they would apply to both female and male members of Byzantine communities. However, Athanasios, followed by the middle Byzantine writers, stresses aspects of asceticism that seem specifically associated with the female gender, including modesty, obedience, seriousness and others. The tenth-century hagiographers add unexpected aspects of Mary's monastic demeanour to this list, however: in addition to dedicating her life to prayer, the Virgin becomes a teacher and leader of the other apostles. This narrative, especially in the later hagiographical works as opposed to the *Life* by Epiphanios, is forthright and unequivocal, as we see in the following short passage of Euthymios the Athonite's Georgian *Life of the Virgin*:

> And she was a leader and a teacher to the holy apostles, and when anything was needed, they would tell her. And they received direction and good counsel from her, to the extent that those who were near the environs of Jerusalem would return. One after the other they went before her and reported everything that they were doing and how they were preaching, and they accomplished everything according to her direction.[147]

Although it is possible that this narrative reflects increasingly influential roles for women in middle Byzantine monasticism,[148] it may have a purely symbolic meaning: once again, the Virgin Mary extends the boundaries of

---

2016, 213. This text is incorrectly ascribed to Symeon the Metaphrast in PG 114, 209–18. I am grateful to Fr Maximos for informing me of the re-attribution of this text to Basilakes.

[146] Athanasios of Alexandria, *First Letter to Virgins* 12–17, ed. Lefort 1955, 73–99; trans. Brakke 1995, esp. 277–9.

[147] Georgian *Life of the Virgin* 99, ed. and trans. Shoemaker 2012, 126.

[148] Phil Booth (2015, 197) hints at the possibility of female authorship for a lost prototype of this text; however, if we accept Simelidis' thesis that the surviving version was written by Euthymios the Athonite with John Geometres' *Life of the Virgin* as its base, such influence becomes less likely; see Simelidis 2020, 128–9. For further discussion of the text, see Chapter 5, 197–9.

accepted male and female behaviour. The author intends his readers to see the Mother of God as an exceptional person who embodied the virtues and gifts of both genders.

The greatest stretch in this direction occurs in the depiction of Mary as invincible warrior who fought on the walls of Constantinople during the Avar siege of 626.[149] Although the texts (which belong to various genres) that are associated with this momentous event seem to construct this image of Mary for the first time, there are in fact some literary precedents.[150] The most important of these is the late fifth or early sixth-century *Akathistos Hymn*.[151] Although its second prologue is traditionally thought to have been composed just after, and in honour of, the siege of 626,[152] some of its stanzas, which were composed much earlier, provide a basis for Mary's celebration as protector of Constantinople. Following the typological and metaphorical imagery that denotes the Virgin's important role in the incarnation of Christ in earlier stanzas, the anonymous hymnographer suddenly invokes her as follows:

> Hail, immovable tower of the Church;
> Hail, impregnable wall of the kingdom;
> Hail, through whom trophies are raised up;
> Hail, through whom enemies fall . . .[153]

It is difficult to imagine that the Virgin Mary was not, along with many of other roles, viewed as the patron of Constantinople at the time that this hymn was written. The events of 626 may have impelled Constantinopolitan Christians to interpret such protection in a more literal way, with sightings of her active role in battle being recorded for posterity.

If we consider all of the aspects of the Theotokos that have so far been described, it is clear that she embodied and acted out qualities that were traditionally associated with both the female and male genders, according to religious writers of the early and middle Byzantine periods. Since we are dealing with a largely symbolic, as opposed to historical, figure in this

---

[149] Pentcheva 2006, 61–103.

[150] The contemporary texts that describe this event are the *Chronicon Paschale*, Theodore the Synkellos' *De obsidione*, and George of Pisidia's *Bellum Avaricum*.

[151] *Akathistos Hymn*, ed. Trypanis 1968; for analysis, see Peltomaa 2001 and below, Chapter 1, 53–8.

[152] The second prologue reads: 'To you, our leader in battle and defender, O Theotokos, I, your city, delivered from sufferings, ascribe hymns of victory and thanksgiving. Since you are invincible in power, free me from all kinds of dangers, that I may cry to you: "Hail, bride unwedded"'; *Akathistos Hymn*, trans. Peltomaa 2001, 3. On the date at which this prologue was added to the *Akathistos Hymn*, along with discussion of its possible composition by the early eighth-century patriarch Germanos of Constantinople, see Huglo 1951; Simić 2017, 19; Hurbanič 2019, esp. 276.

[153] *Akathistos Hymn* 23, trans. Peltomaa 2001, 18–19.

literary tradition, it only remains to be asked why she needed to encompass such diverse – indeed paradoxical – roles. I suggest that such portrayals reflect various didactic aims on the part of both liturgical writers and chroniclers. First, these writers wished to emphasise Mary's connection with the whole of humanity: she represented the community of believers, that is, the Church, which comprised male, female and eunuch members. Second, not only did Mary represent all people, but she served as a model of the best, or strongest qualities, that characterise both women and men, according to the Byzantines. Male virtues, such as strength, courage and active agency, were revealed in Mary's protective and intercessory roles; female ones, which included chastity, obedience and maternal love, could be seen in her birth-giving and ongoing relationship with Christ. Paradox played a part here too, however: male strength could be augmented by female virginity or chastity, as had been the case with the ancient goddess Athena. Mary, the Theotokos, thus became the quintessential exponent of human virtue, offering a perfect example of the ideal relationship between God and his human image.

Devotion to the Mother of God in the middle Byzantine period was widespread, as homilies, hymns and hagiography, including collections of miracle stories, all attest. The question whether Mary attracted more female than male followers, however, remains to be proved. Most sources suggest that all three genders, including women, men and eunuchs, appealed to the Virgin for help, as did every class in society. Processions and rites that led to, or took place at, the major Marian shrines in Constantinople involved the rulers on a weekly or annual basis.[154] It is this universal appeal of the Mother of God that leads me to doubt the suggestion that pictorial cycles of her infancy, such as that which appears in the narthex of the early twelfth-century church of Daphni near Athens, were intended especially for female viewers.[155] It is more likely that the Christological meaning of her story, combined with her widespread personal appeal, made this cycle an appropriate choice for this male monastic community. The Virgin went on to become patroness of the entirely male monasteries on Mt Athos during the middle Byzantine period, where she

[154] Constantine Porphyrogennetos, *Book of Ceremonies*, ed. Leich and Reiske 1935 and 1939, trans. Moffatt and Tall 2012, 762, 779, 781.
[155] Brubaker 2019, esp. 132–7. This is nevertheless an intriguing hypothesis; Brubaker also agrees that, 'As a male monastic church, Daphni resoundingly negates any lingering assumptions that veneration of the Virgin was the singular reserve of women'; see Brubaker 2019, 146. For another gendered approach to the decoration of Byzantine churches, see Gerstel 1998; on the location of women in church, see Mathews 1971, 130–4; Taft 1998; Talbot 2010.

was (and continues to be) venerated as intercessor and model of ascetic virtue.[156] Mary's female gender, along with the powers and virtues that this implies, was an important part of her popularity; however, I remain unconvinced that it was valued more by women than by men.

Some literary and material evidence does, however, suggest women's special involvement in the cult of the Virgin Mary. This includes Greek amulets that are preserved in Egypt, dating between approximately the fifth and seventh centuries. Some of these short prayers, which were written down on pieces of papyrus or parchment, folded and carried close to one's person, name their owners as women who seek help or healing from the Theotokos.[157] There are also tales in the *Pege* collection of miracle stories, compiled in tenth-century Constantinople, that involve gynaecological medical problems. Noble or imperial women, including Eudokia, sister-in-law of the emperor Maurice (582–602), and Zoe, mother of Constantine VII (913–59), were healed of breast cancer and infertility, respectively, at this important shrine.[158] These are balanced, however, by miracles that involve men and their particular ailments.[159] Overall, we gain the impression from this and other sources that women and men appealed to the Theotokos for help in equal numbers; she was too important for either sex to be excluded from her care.

To conclude this section, it appears that Mary's female gender, although theologically and culturally significant, did not inhibit the involvement of both men and women in her cult. She became a universal symbol of the Church, or of humanity, in relationship with its incarnate God. Certain aspects of Mary's gender contributed to this symbolic role: these included her virginity, motherhood and even female leadership. Jane Baun perceives a 'majestic, militant grandmother' in the middle Byzantine *Apocalypse of the Theotokos*;[160] if her role in this text occasionally seems subversive, this is counteracted by the Church's ability to accommodate the importunities of a mere woman – even if she is the Mother of God. Perhaps this helps to explain the development of the cult from about the late fifth century onward: the Virgin Mary is powerful because she exists both within, but also outside, a predominantly male celestial and ecclesiastical hierarchy.

---

[156] Talbot 1996; Tsironis 2000, 33; Speake 2002, 17–18, 21–5.   [157] De Bruyn 2015, 122–6.

[158] *Miracles of the Pege* 7 and 26, ed. and trans. Talbot and Johnson 2012, 218– 21, 266–7. According to Talbot, the sister of Maurice's wife Constantina was in fact named Charito. This appears to be an error on the part of the hagiographer; see ibid., 430, n. 11.

[159] *Miracles of the Pege*, for example, 2 (Leo I), 3 (Justinian) and many others, ed. and trans. Talbot and Johnson 2012, 208–13.

[160] Baun 2007, 275.

Like the 'holy man' described in Peter Brown's classic study,[161] she is thus able (like other social outsiders) to intercede fearlessly before the Righteous Judge in heaven.

The Purpose and Structure of This Book

Having provided an outline of the development of the Marian cult during our period (*c.* 400–1000) and introduced the topics of literary genre and gender, it is now time to explain the purpose and structure of the present study. I stated at the beginning of this chapter that, as demonstrated by numerous scholarly studies, the Virgin Mary in Byzantium remains a multifaceted and paradoxical figure. Since it is not possible to cover all of the surviving literary and material evidence concerning the Virgin in one book, I have chosen to focus on three distinct (although interactive) literary forms: homiletics, hymnography and hagiography. All three genres can be described as 'religious' in their purpose and content: unlike more 'secular', or classicising, genres such as histories, novels or epigrams, they employ Christian (although not always biblical) narratives, teach the essential truths, or doctrines, of this religion, and aim to involve their audiences or readers emotionally in this message. Homiletics and hymnography were intended primarily for liturgical contexts, while hagiography was employed in a wider variety of literary (although sometimes liturgical) contexts. However, as I attempted to show in the section on literary genre, there was much overlap between the three forms in terms of structure, content and rhetorical method.

In spite of the many similarities that exist in the portrayal of the Virgin Mary according to these separate literary forms, some differences are perceptible. Whereas homiletics and hymnography, which enjoyed a symbiotic relationship throughout the middle Byzantine period, especially stress Mary's importance in the Christological mystery, hagiography displays greater interest in her intercessory function in Byzantine society. This is not to say that homilies and hymns do not also contain such material; however, they appeal to the Virgin in particular structural or liturgical contexts, usually placing this emphasis after that of the didactic message. The *Lives* of the Virgin, collections of miracle stories and scattered accounts of miracles that occur in other hagiographical texts meanwhile reveal a variety of preoccupations. The tenth-century *Lives*, for example, are interested in the legendary narrative of Mary's whole life,

---

[161] Brown 1971.

which they glean from the *Protevangelion of James* and accounts of her dormition, along with other – sometimes lost – apocryphal texts. Although there is considerable variation between the four surviving Greek *Lives*, they all revive the dormant idea of the ascetic, or monastic, Virgin Mary and also stress her role as leader of female disciples and even, in the case of the Georgian *Life*, of the apostles.

This rich array of Marian portrayals, when combined with others such as that found in the *Apocalypse of the Theotokos*, suggests that Byzantine audiences and readers were able to accept multiple messages, depending on the contexts in which these were delivered. I build here on Margaret Mullett's and Martin Hinterberger's definitions of literary genre, which suggest that the intended reception of texts helped to determine the particular forms which authors chose to employ.[162] The context, whether liturgical, didactic, or for entertainment, also helped audiences to discern the intended meaning. I suggest that most Byzantines, even if they were not highly educated in letters, were capable of understanding the various symbolic or practical roles of the Theotokos, according to the separate settings in which she could be found. A supplicant at the shrine of the *Pege* in Constantinople, for example, expected to find a tall woman 'robed in purple',[163] whereas a congregant in Hagia Sophia (the church of Holy Wisdom) or any other Byzantine church pictured her as 'burning bush', 'Gideon's fleece', 'tabernacle' or 'temple'. The multiple ways in which the Virgin Mary was visualised, in both texts and images, suggest that her cult went far beyond those of most saints in that she represented at once the 'birth-giver of God', symbol of the incarnation, mediator and intercessor.

Although this book does not explore every aspect of the Mother of God in Byzantine culture or even address the majority of surviving literary genres, I hope that it provides an approach to the subject that will inspire future studies. The place of the Virgin Mary in Byzantine art and material culture still awaits full treatment. In short, Mary, the holy Virgin and Mother of God, reflects many aspects of Byzantine religious belief, culture and social structure. As the preacher Andrew of Crete stated in the early eighth century, 'She is the great world in miniature, the world containing him who brought the world from nothingness into being, that it might be a messenger of his own greatness.'[164]

---

[162] See above, n. 103.

[163] *Miracles of the Pege* 13, ed. and trans. Talbot and Johnson 2012, 234–5.

[164] Andrew of Crete, *Homily II on the Dormition*, PG 97, 1069B; trans. Daley, *On the Dormition of Mary*, 133.

CHAPTER I

Praise of Mary in Song: The Early Hymnography

Song was an integral part of both Jewish and Christian worship, according to the earliest written records of each religious tradition. Moses, along with his band of Israelites and Aaron's sister Miriam, sang songs of victory after the crossing of the Red Sea, according to Exodus 15:1–21. The other Old Testament canticles, along with the entire book of Psalms, not only reflect the historical experience of the Jews, but may also have been sung in temple and synagogue worship through to the beginning of the Christian era.[1] According to the younger Pliny (c. 61 - 113 CE), the followers of Jesus 'met regularly before dawn on a fixed day to chant verses alternately among themselves in honour of Christ as if to a god . . . '[2] Pagan tradition also involved the singing of sacred songs. Early Christians thus inhabited a world in which believers were accustomed to invoke, describe and praise their deities with words and music. Scholars do not agree about the precise ways in which Egyptian monasteries and urban churches organised the singing of the Old Testament psalms and responses in late antiquity; however, it is likely that this practice flourished especially in cathedral settings.[3] Psalmody, along with the nine biblical canticles, thus played important roles in the formation of early Christian hymnography. That hymns could be used to attract converts was also recognised from at least as early as the early fourth century.[4]

---

[1] Note, however, Bradshaw's reservations in this regard, owing to the lack of documentary evidence; see Bradshaw 2002, 38–9; McKinnon 1986 (1998).

[2] Pliny the Younger, *Letters* x. xcvi.7, trans. Radice 1975, vol. 2, 288–9: 'stato die ante lucem convenire, carmenque Christo quasi deo dicere secum invicem . . . ' It is interesting to note, assuming that Pliny's information is correct, that these early Christians used some kind of antiphonal or responsive singing.

[3] See Frøyshov 2000; Taft 2005, 188–97; Frøyshov 2007a; Krueger 2014, 5–6.

[4] Arkadiy Avdokhin has recently argued that Church leaders including Athanasios of Alexandria began to suppress more heterodox examples of hymnography in the course of the fourth century; see Avdokhin 2016. The power of religious song is also evidenced in the official reaction to Arius' methods of teaching prior to the Council of Nicaea in 325 CE; see Young 1983, 60–1; Williams 1987, 62–6. Extracts of Arius' *Thalia* are translated in Stevenson 1987, 330–2.

The question of genre, or literary form, is particularly complicated in the case of hymnography. To begin with, there is a close relationship between hymns and prayers – to the extent that it is misleading to separate them as independent forms. Although the psalms were composed as songs, for example, they also functioned as prayers. Many late antique and Byzantine hymns further performed a didactic role in ritual or liturgical settings. According to Matthew Gordley, this is indicated by direct address to the audience, by the expression of theological doctrine in ways that can be easily assimilated, and by vivid or dramatic use of narrative.[5] Early Syriac and Greek hymns contain in varying degrees all of the above qualities, from direct invocation of Christ, his mother Mary, or the saints, to concise or narrative theological formulations.

This chapter deals with liturgical hymnography that placed the Theotokos at the centre of its praise or teaching, focusing on texts that were intended for church settings.[6] It includes not only the earliest Greek examples of the genre, but also some Syriac and Georgian compositions that either influenced or transmitted such early works. Hymns that were intended mainly for public liturgical contexts began to be produced in eastern regions of the Roman empire or in Persia, where Syriac was spoken both inside and outside the Church, from at least as early as the fourth century. The earliest Greek examples survive mainly in Georgian translations that reflect liturgical practices in Jerusalem or Palestine. Hymnography that specifically praised or expounded the Theotokos began to be produced in Constantinople from the early fifth century onward. All of the surviving works, whether Syriac, Georgian or Greek, assumed particular forms according to their place within the developing offices or divine liturgies. They may be described as formal prayers to the Christian God, usually set to music, which were designed to invoke, praise and offer thanksgiving to God, the Theotokos or the saints, on behalf of the whole community. In addition to this, they taught the paradoxical doctrine of Christ's incarnation, which depended so materially on his mother Mary.

As a possible exception to this rough chronological outline, a short Greek prayer to the Theotokos, called by its Latin title, *Sub tuum*

---

[5] Gordley 2011, 5.
[6] Some songs, or poems, such as those that were composed by Gregory Nazianzen and Synesios of Cyrene in the late fourth and early fifth centuries, followed classical conventions in their vocabulary and metre; they may have been intended for small groups of friends rather than for larger congregations. However, none of these early hymns chose the Virgin Mary as their primary subject. See Wellesz 1961, 146–56.

praesidium, survives in a papyrus that now belongs to the John Rylands Library in Manchester. It is sung to this day in Oriental and Orthodox Christian liturgical services and may be translated as follows:

> Under your mercy we take refuge, Theotokos. Do not overlook our petitions in adversity but rescue us from danger, uniquely holy one and uniquely blessed one.[7]

The text is frequently cited as one of the earliest examples of a prayer that appeals to Mary's intercessory power; however, its date remains controversial.[8] Whereas Stephen Shoemaker suggests that it belongs to the fourth or even third century CE,[9] Theodore de Bruyn prefers a later context for the prayer, for two main reasons.[10] First, H. Förster has questioned the fourth-century dating of the palaeography that was suggested by its first editors, suggesting instead that it belongs to the sixth or seventh century.[11] Second, and perhaps more incontrovertibly, de Bruyn demonstrates that appeals to the mediating or intercessory powers of the Theotokos are largely absent in Egyptian liturgical texts before the sixth century.[12] Even 'paraliturgical' evidence, which consists of short prayers or amulets,[13] can be dated no earlier than the fifth century.[14] Such fragments, many of which appear to have had healing powers and to have been intended for female owners, testify to belief in the intercessory power of the Theotokos in Egypt from at this date, but probably not earlier.[15] This fascinating material, which cannot be classed as liturgical hymnography,

---

[7] John Rylands Papyrus III 470; trans. Price 2007, 56.

[8] See, for example, Price 2007, 56–7; Price 2008, 89–90; Shoemaker 2008b, 72–3.

[9] The original editors of the text suggested a fourth-century date for the *Sub tuum praesidium* prayer; see Hunt, Johnson and Roberts 1911–52, vol. 3, 46. Shoemaker hints in his latest study that the papyrus may date to as early as the third century; see Shoemaker 2016a, 68–73. For further discussion, see Stegmüller 1952; Giamberardini 1969; Starowieyski 1989; Johnson 2008, 62–3.

[10] De Bruyn 2015, 116–17.

[11] Förster 2005. In response to this study, Shoemaker cites Römer 1998, 138 and Luijendijk 2014, 30. The palaeographical question remains controversial, thus making the argument that is based on the religious context of the papyrus more important.

[12] De Bruyn 2015, 121–2; with regard to early Egyptian church dedications to 'holy Mary', see Papaconstantinou 2000, 93. Both are cited in de Bruyn 2015, 116–17.

[13] Scholars define 'amulets' as folded sheets of papyrus or parchment that were used to obtain protection, healing, or other kinds of help. See Förster 1995, 185; de Bruyn 2015, 122.

[14] De Bruyn 2015, 122–7.

[15] See, for example, the fifth- or sixth-century papyrus, which, when unfolded, 'revealed a few leaves of a plant, identified as trefoil, used for menstrual periods, intermittent fever, and three-day fever' and which contained the text, 'O Theotokos, incorruptible, undefiled, unstained mother of Christ, remember that you have said these things. Again heal her who wears this. Amen.' PGM P15b.8–10; de Bruyn 2015, 124–5, n. 123.

testifies to the development of personal devotion to the Virgin in fifth- and sixth-century Egypt.[16]

Other early examples of hymnography that describe or invoke the Virgin Mary include, as we shall see below, Syriac poetic homilies and early Palestinian hymns that were written in Greek but survive in tenth-century Georgian translations. All of this evidence is important when we reconstruct the origins of Marian praise in the Eastern Churches; most of it belongs to the sphere of collective liturgical worship. As stated above, this material represents theology in verse, which helped to teach congregations the important role that the Theotokos played in the incarnation of Christ. Whereas earlier examples, dating from the fourth century or before, confined themselves to Christological themes, hymns that were produced from about the late fifth century onward began to invoke Mary's intercessory power. An important example that probably belongs to this period is the *Akathistos Hymn*, which alludes repeatedly – and with the help of metaphorical imagery – to the Virgin's protective qualities. It is only in the course of the sixth century, however, that the Virgin became human and even maternal, according to both Syriac and Greek liturgical poets. The kontakia of Romanos the Melodist, which were sung in the course of all-night vigils in the churches of Constantinople, represented a turning point in Marian liturgical writing. Not only did this hymnographer combine Greek and Syriac models in order to create a three-dimensional and human image of the Mother of God, but his work influenced both hymnographers and preachers in the centuries that followed. The fourth to the sixth centuries were thus pivotal in the history of Eastern Christian hymnography. After this period, as we shall see in Chapter 4, a multitude of Marian hymns were added to liturgical services, including not only those that were intended for newly instituted feast-days, but also many for ordinary Sundays and weekdays. Christological Councils of the fifth century may not have provided the only impetus for growing public recognition of the Theotokos; however, they allowed Church leaders to endorse this tendency and to place it at the centre of their didactic efforts. Mary acted as a link between the divine and created worlds. Not only did she guarantee the humanity of Christ by means of her divine motherhood, but she also offered humanity a way to approach and influence the judgement of the heavenly Saviour.

---

[16] See Introduction, 33.

Syriac Liturgical Poetry

Whereas poetic homilies dominated the Greek and Latin liturgical traditions in the fourth and fifth centuries, hymns, in the form of prayer songs (*madrashe*), dialogue poems (*soghyatha*) and verse homilies (*mêmrê*) were favoured in the Syriac-speaking areas of Christendom during this period and beyond.[17] No proper assessment of Greek hymns and homilies that honour the Virgin can be made without taking into account the Syriac contribution.[18] Because Marian liturgical poetry developed early in the Syriac-speaking world – and because this probably influenced the Greek liturgical tradition – I have chosen to include some early examples in this section of the chapter.[19]

Praise of the Virgin Mary, especially for her role in the incarnation of Christ, began early in the Syriac context. Although it lies beyond my rough chronological limits, it is worth mentioning here the remarkable work known as the *Odes of Solomon*, which probably dates from the late second century.[20] This set of hymns, which may have emerged from a Judaeo-Christian – if not gnostic – background,[21] adopts a daring approach to gender: not only is the Holy Spirit, as is customary in early Syriac poetry, described by means of feminine imagery, but so is the Father. Ode 19 portrays Trinitarian involvement in Christ's conception in the following way:

> The Son is the Cup,
> And the Father is He who was milked;
> And the Holy Spirit is She who milked Him;
> Because His breasts were full,
> And it was undesirable that His milk should be ineffectually released.
> The Holy Spirit opened Her bosom,
> And mixed the milk of the two breasts of the Father.
> Then She gave the mixture to the generation without their knowing,
> And those who have received (it) are in the perfection of the right hand.
> The womb of the Virgin took (it),
> And she received conception and gave birth . . .[22]

---

[17] Brock 1994 (2010), 12–15.   [18] For an excellent recent study of this material, see Horn 2015.

[19] The parallels between Syriac and Greek liturgical poetry, especially the kontakia of Romanos, has been much discussed in scholarly literature. See, for example, Grosdidier de Matons 1977, 16–27; Petersen 1985; Brock 1989 (1999). For good background to the whole tradition, see Murray 1975 (2004); Brock 1994 (2010).

[20] *The Odes of Solomon*, ed. and trans. Charlesworth 1973. See also Harvey 1994 for discussion of the feminine elements in the hymns.

[21] Murray 1971, 378.   [22] *Odes of Solomon* 19, trans. Charlesworth 1973, 82.

The hymn goes on to describe Mary's labour, which is said to be without pain; however, she gives birth 'like a strong man with desire'. The author's willingness to play with gender imagery in this ode, as in others within the same collection, indicates a creative approach to the attributes and gifts of the divine Being; these works challenge listeners or readers to see God, along with those who acknowledge him, as manifesting both masculine and feminine qualities.

The fourth-century teacher (and possibly deacon) Ephrem the Syrian, who flourished in Nisibis and Edessa between about 307 and 373 CE,[23] devoted considerable attention to the Virgin Mary in his prayer songs (*madrashe*) and verse homilies (*mêmrê*). She takes on a largely symbolic role in Ephrem's poetry, representing the 'Second Eve', the container or material of the incarnate Christ, the Church, and a transfigured creation. As Sebastian Brock notes in his introduction to Syriac Marian liturgical poetry, 'The Syriac poets – and above all St Ephrem ... have a theological vision which might be described as holistic: for them everything in both the material and the spiritual world is mysteriously interconnected: nothing, and nobody, exists in isolation.'[24] Mary is the quintessential link in this interconnected universe; she provides the physical body whereby God enters creation as God-man and restores it to the prelapsarian – and also eschatological – state that he intended. Ephrem also emphasises, however, the importance of Mary's freely given consent to this event; here, with focus on the human ear as the receptacle of God's purpose, he describes the Virgin as the 'Second Eve'.[25] Whereas the original Eve listened to the words of the Devil and thereby brought about the Fall, Mary listened to the words of the archangel Gabriel and initiated salvation for humankind.

It is striking, in comparison with the works of contemporary Greek Fathers, that Ephrem focuses so consistently on the role of the Theotokos in his elaboration of God's dispensation for salvation. His theological position is nevertheless in line with Nicene views on the Trinity, with some of his statements about Christ's two natures echoing those of Alexandrian theologians such as Athanasios:

---

[23] Much has been written on the conflicting hagiographical accounts of Ephrem's life. For a recent summary, see his *Hymns on Faith*, trans. Wickes 2015, 5–14; for the earliest contemporary source concerning Ephrem's occupation, see Jerome, *On Illustrious Men* 115, trans. Halton 1999, 149.

[24] Brock 1994 (2010), 2.

[25] For extensive discussion, with background on the historical and theological development of Mary's conception through hearing, see Constas 2003, 273–313.

He was lofty but He sucked Mary's milk,
and from His blessings all creation sucks.
He is the Living Breast of living breath;
by His life the dead were suckled, and they revived . . .
As indeed He sucked Mary's milk,
He has given suck – life to the universe.
As again He dwelt in His mother's womb,
in His womb dwells all creation.[26]

We see echoes here of the lactic imagery that featured in the second-century *Odes of Solomon*. The important point for us to note, however, is Ephrem's antithetical treatment of Christ's two natures. Although the Son of God suckled Mary's milk as an infant, he was simultaneously engaged in providing life to the universe. In portraying the Virgin as Christ's birth-giver, Ephrem provides her with passages of direct speech towards her son, in which she meditates on his divine and human natures. Although such hymns are affecting, in that they seem to give Ephrem's audiences access to Mary's inner thoughts, he does not reveal much about her character or emotions – apart from her experiences of awe, astonishment and the effort to understand the momentous event that she was experiencing. These are highly Christological works, which lack the human portrayal of the Virgin Mary that would appear in both Syriac and Greek liturgical poetry a century or two later. Nevertheless, she occupies a central place in Ephrem's meditations on the mystery of the incarnation. In several of his *Hymns on Faith*, for example, Ephrem applies womb imagery not only to Christ's conception and birth from Mary, but also to his generation from God.[27] And in *Hymn 28*, Mary's womb is juxtaposed with the tomb in which Christ was laid after death: whereas these small and restricted spaces confined the uncontainable God, he also 'bound' – or gained power – over them in his incarnation.[28]

According to Ephrem, the Virgin Mary is the antitype for a wealth of Old Testament personages, places and objects, besides symbolising every-day aspects of creation such as palace, ship and the clothing Christ put on in his incarnation.[29] Each of these images conveys in some way the Christological message: Mary is the container, material, or vehicle for God's entrance into creation. In contrast again with his Greek

---

[26] Ephrem the Syrian, *Hymn on the Nativity* 4, trans. McVey 1989, 100. 149–50, 153–4.
[27] Ephrem the Syrian, *Hymns on Faith* 3.13, 18.10, trans. Wickes 2015, 70, 149. For a thoughtful appraisal of Ephrem's exegetical methods in the *Hymns on Faith*, see Wickes 2019.
[28] Ephrem the Syrian, *Hymn on Faith* 28.6, trans. Wickes 2015, 182.
[29] Brock 1994 (2010), 10–11.

contemporaries, Ephrem frequently emphasises the centrality of the Eucharist in Christian life. In this context, Ephrem describes the Virgin Mary as the purveyor, or container, of the body and blood of Christ.[30] In addition to being his mother, Mary is Christ's sister, bride, handmaid and daughter; her relationship with him is replicated in that with the Church, or the people who are members of Christ's body.

Although Ephrem alludes to Mary's mediating role, as the locus and agent of human salvation, he never describes her as intercessor, according to the definition that I provided in the Introduction.[31] As in the case of the fifth-century Greek preachers whose works we examined above, Ephrem's emphasis is always Christological. He does, however, suggest in some hymns that women have become special recipients of Christ's saving power, as a result of Mary's role in the incarnation:

> Women heard that, behold, a virgin indeed
> would conceive and bring forth. Well-born women hoped
> that He would shine forth from them, and elegant women
> that He would appear from them . . .[32]

Mary, the Theotokos, helped to bring about salvation for all Christians; however, her female gender, which recapitulated that of Eve, offers special hope to women. This theme, which also appears in fifth-century homilies that celebrate the Virgin Mary, perhaps gains extra meaning in the light of Ephrem's well-known pastoral care for women and establishment of all-female choirs of singers.[33]

In addition to Ephrem the Syrian's writings, many of which place Mary at the centre of their Christological teaching, numerous anonymous works survive in the Syriac liturgical tradition. Sebastian Brock dates many of these to the fifth or early sixth century. They include both *madrashe* and *soghyatha* that survive in both early manuscripts and later compilations.[34] Although T. J. Lamy published some of these works under the name of Ephrem, it appears that these attributions are untenable; they belong to a tradition which the latter helped to establish, but which continued to flourish a century or two later, thanks to many anonymous writers.[35] The prayer songs that are included in Brock's excellent translation of Marian

---

[30] He writes, for example, 'The Church gave us the living Bread,/ in place of the unleavened bread that Egypt had given./ Mary gave us the refreshing bread,/ in place of the fatiguing bread that Eve had procured for us.' See Gambero 1999, 115–16.
[31] See Introduction, 8–9. [32] *Hymn on the Nativity* 8, trans. McVey 1989, 123. 20.
[33] Ephrem the Syrian, *Hymns on Faith*, trans. Wickes 2015, 14; Harvey 2005; Harvey 2010, 17–39.
[34] Brock 1994 (2010), 12–13. [35] Brock 1994 (2010), 13–15.

writings, *Bride of Light*, were intended for the feast of the Commemoration of the Virgin which, as in Constantinople, was celebrated on 26 December in the West Syriac calendar and on the second Friday after Christmas in the East Syriac one.[36]

The emphasis in all of these prayer songs,[37] as in the authentic works of Ephrem, is Christological. One of the most extensive works, *Hymn 10*, provides antithetical statements about Christ that juxtapose his status as a tiny infant, crying and suckling milk, with that of King and Creator of the universe. The following stanza sums up this paradox concisely:

> Behold, You are in Your Father, in Mary,
> and on the Chariot,
> in the manger, and in every place!
> In truth You are in Your Father, without any doubt,
> You are in Mary, upon the Chariot,
> and in the lowly manger,
> You are in every place, for You are the Maker,
> You are in all, for You are the Fashioner.
> You are from the Father,
> Yet You are from Mary too . . .[38]

The Virgin Mary gains holy status from this association, as all of the hymns make clear. She is invoked with typological and metaphorical epithets, as 'a source of wonder to all the world'.[39]

In addressing the Theotokos as 'spring that provides the fountain', 'ship that bears joy from the Father', 'young dove . . . [that] carried the Eagle', along with many other images,[40] these poets built on a rich typological tradition that was by now well established in the Syriac liturgical tradition. However, we also find some elements in the hymns that appear to be new, perhaps reflecting developments within this tradition that took place sometime between the fourth and fifth centuries. One such development is the hymnographers' emphasis on Mary's chaste and modest character, which makes her a perfect model for ascetic women:

> Holy is her body, resplendent her soul, pure her mind,
> her understanding most luminous;

---

[36] *Bride of Light*, trans. Brock 1994 (2010), 36.
[37] I have based the following analysis on sixteen anonymous *Hymns on Mary*, which are translated in Brock 1994 (2010), nos. 6–21, 36–73. These were edited (and attributed to Ephrem the Syrian) in Lamy 1886, vol. 2, 519–90; see Brock 1994 (2010), 17.
[38] Anonymous, *Hymn on Mary* 10.5, trans. Brock 1994 (2010), 56.
[39] Anonymous, *Hymn on Mary* 5.3, trans. Brock 1994 (2010), 45.
[40] See, for example, Anonymous, *Hymn on Mary* 7.1–3, trans. Brock 1994 (2010), 49.

her thought is most perfect,
chaste, temperate, pure,
well proved, and full of beauty.

Let the entire band of virgins rejoice in Mary,
seeing that one of their number has knelt down and given birth
to that Hero who bears up all creation . . .[41]

Another hymn addresses the young girls who may have been members of the women's choir for whom the work was intended, instructing them to 'leap for joy' and marvel at the wise and holy Virgin Mary.[42] A second shift in emphasis, which differs from Ephrem's portrayal of Mary as the holy – but remote – Mother of God, is the attention which some hymnographers give to her maternal love for Christ. To cite just one example out of many, we find the following portrayal of the Nativity scene in *Hymn 10* on Mary:

She fondled Him and sang to Him;
as she kissed Him, He leapt up to meet her;
He gazed at her, smiling as a baby
as He lay in the manger, wrapped in swaddling clothes.
When He began to cry she got up and gave Him milk;
she embraced Him as she sang to Him,
swaying her knees until He became still.[43]

The theological purpose of passages such as this is to emphasise the paradox of Christ's incarnation. This stanza contrasts with those in which he is celebrated as King and Only-Begotten Son of God. However, the poet also portrays the Virgin Mary as a motherly figure with whom his audience may identify and feel empathy. Such passages presage a development in the Greek liturgical tradition that would only reach full expression by about the middle of the ninth century.[44]

Increasing interest in Mary as a human mother, who experiences both rational and emotional reactions to the incarnation, is also apparent in the dialogue hymns (*soghyatha*), which belong to the fifth or sixth century but build on a tradition of dispute literature that began in ancient Mesopotamia.[45] These hymns, which are mostly anonymous, may in

---

[41] Anonymous, *Hymn on Mary* 1.4–5, trans. Brock 1994 (2010), 36–7.

[42] Anonymous, *Hymn on Mary* 4.1, trans. Brock 1994 (2010), 42.

[43] Anonymous, *Hymn on Mary* 10.3, trans. Brock 1994 (2010), 56.

[44] Scholars have argued that emphasis on Mary's 'motherly' qualities emerged first in texts and later in images in response to iconophile theologians' interest in Christ's humanity; see Kalavrezou 1990; Kalavrezou 2000; Tsironis 2000. As I shall argue later, this theory should be adjusted in relation to the contribution of the sixth-century hymnographer Romanos the Melodist. See below, 58–65.

[45] Brock 1991; Brock 1994 (2010), 12–13.

turn have influenced the dialogic homilies that began to be composed in Greek from about the fifth century onward. They focus on biblical scenes, including the annunciation, nativity of Christ, his presentation at the temple, and others, adding long passages of direct speech between the main protagonists – as if in an attempt to create a form of liturgical mystery play. It appears, however, that dramatic hymns and homilies in both the Syriac- and Greek-speaking worlds were, like other liturgical compositions, sung or preached by the clergy within the normal offices or even eucharistic celebrations. Their purpose was didactic as well as dramatic: by emphasising the human thought processes and emotions of the Virgin Mary and other biblical characters, Eastern Christian liturgical writers conveyed the reality of the incarnation. The emphasis remained on Christ, whose simultaneous divinity and humanity were revealed through Mary, the all-pure Virgin and human mother.

The portrayal of the Virgin Mary in the dialogue hymns exhibits the full range of qualities that these two categories imply. We continue to see her more 'motherly' aspect in passages such as the following:

> As she cuddled Him
> she sang lullabies with loving words;
> she worshipped her child and said,
> 'Allow me, dear Lord, to embrace You ... '[46]

However, it is the scene of the annunciation that offers the greatest scope for developing Mary's character by means of dramatic dialogue. In a long hymn that elaborates the encounter between Gabriel and the Virgin, the hymnographer introduces a section of dialogue after ten stanzas of narrative introduction. Following the archangel's greeting, according to Luke 1:28, we witness Mary's doubt and distrust of this unexpected visitor, followed by gradual acceptance of his message. Her response, in which she describes what she sees (a being who is 'made of flame' and 'wrapped in coals of fire'),[47] reveals not only an awareness of mystery, but also a healthy scepticism as she seeks to distance herself from the unfortunate credulity of Eve. Mary is also modest, however; she is 'but a girl and cannot receive a man of fire'.[48] Audiences listening to this dramatic dialogue would thus have been introduced to an entirely human young woman, who experienced a variety of reactions to this momentous encounter and who eventually understood – and agreed to – the conception of God (who is 'all

---

[46] Anonymous, *Soghitha* 2.5, trans. Brock 1994 (2010), 83.
[47] Anonymous, *Soghitha* 41.16, trans. Brock 1994 (2010), 127.
[48] Anonymous, *Soghitha* 41.28, trans. Brock 1994 (2010), 129.

flame') in her womb.[49] It is difficult to believe that this genre, which appears to have flourished first in the Syriac liturgical tradition, did not influence Greek homiletic and hymnographic dialogic works. A few homilies, such as (ps-)Proklos of Constantinople's *Homily VI*, followed by Romanos the Melodist's dramatic kontakia, bear a close resemblance to these Syriac prototypes.[50] The form would also be picked up later, from about the early eighth century, in Germanos of Constantinople's homily on the Annunciation, as well as in kanons composed for the same feast.[51]

One other important figure in the early Syriac liturgical tradition was the late fifth- and early sixth-century preacher Jacob of Serugh. Born in the village of Curtam, on the Euphrates, around the middle of the fifth century, Jacob became bishop of Serug in 519 CE. He composed more than seven hundred verse homilies (*mêmrê*), many of which remain unpublished.[52] English translations of Jacob's works remain less numerous than those of his famous predecessor, Ephrem, but are gradually appearing, along with interpretative studies of his contribution to Syriac liturgical poetry.[53] A collection of homilies on the Mother of God displays the same interest in her role in the incarnation that we have observed throughout this tradition, combined with attention to her ascetic and maternal qualities. Jacob stresses the mystery of this holy figure, which scarcely allows him to imagine her beauty and splendour.[54] Like his anonymous contemporaries, however, he also emphasises her motherly tenderness towards the infant Christ, as we see in the following passage:

> Blessed is that one who carried, embraced, and caressed like a child
> God mighty forever more, by whose hidden power the world is carried.[55]

Or, in even more paradoxical language:

> Blessed is she who placed her pure mouth on the lips of that One, from whose fire, the Seraphim of fire hide themselves.
> Blessed is she who nourished as a babe with pure milk the great breast from which the worlds suck life.[56]

From the *Odes of Solomon* to this late fifth- and early sixth-century liturgical writer, the Syriac tradition embraces the feminine gender, with

[49] Anonymous, *Soghitha* 41.40, trans. Brock 1994 (2010), 130.
[50] For discussion of these works, see below, 58–65 (Romanos), 101 ([ps-] Proklos).
[51] For this material, see Chapters 3 and 4.
[52] For a helpful list of Jacob's works and their current editions, see Golitzen 2007, 180–1, n. 2.
[53] Jansma 1965; Chestnut 1976; Alwan 1986.
[54] Jacob of Serugh, *Homily I on the Mother of God*, trans. Hansbury 1998, 20.
[55] Ibid., trans. Hansbury 1998, 41.   [56] Ibid., trans. Hansbury 1998, 42.

all its attributes, not only in association with the Virgin Mary, but also with the Trinity itself.

In concluding this short section on the treatment of Mary in early Syriac liturgical hymns and homilies, it is worth repeating my view that subtle changes occurred between the time that Ephrem was writing (during the first three quarters of the fourth century) and that in which a number of anonymous writers and Jacob of Serugh flourished (fifth and sixth centuries). We have noticed increasing interest in Mary's personal qualities, as a model of asceticism, virginal girl and tender mother among the later liturgical writers. Although such details may have occurred sporadically in Ephrem's hymns, he portrayed the Virgin above all as a symbolic theological figure who stood between the divine and created worlds. She used her free will and provided Christ with human nature but remained somewhat remote from the rest of humanity in this capacity. What appears to be lacking in all of these writers, however, is an awareness – or attention to – Mary's intercessory power.[57] The only exception to this rule, which is – perhaps significantly – associated with the feast of the Dormition, is Jacob's homily on this subject. Here, after providing a narrative of Mary's death that omits many of the miraculous elements that were by this time circulating in other Syriac sources, the homily concludes by invoking the Virgin Mary's intercession on behalf of the faithful:

> O Son of God, by her prayers make your peace to dwell in heaven, in the depths, and among all the counsels of her sons.
> Make wars to cease, and remove trials and plagues; bestow calm and tranquility on seafarers.
> Heal the infirm, cure the sick, fill the hungry; be a Father to orphans whom death has left destitute . . .[58]

On the basis of this evidence, it is worth asking whether prayers to the Virgin Mary as intercessor before Christ, which were slow to emerge in Syriac liturgical writing, appeared in connection with speculation about her death and assumption into heaven. Narratives concerning this process appeared in written form only around the end of the fifth and beginning of the sixth century; can it be accidental that appeals to Mary's intercessory power appeared in liturgical texts at about the same time?[59] I shall return to

---

[57] The same conclusion is reached in Horn 2015.
[58] Jacob of Serugh, *Homily V on the Mother of God*, trans. Hansbury 1998, 99.
[59] Norelli and Shoemaker both suggest that belief in Mary's power to intercede on behalf of humanity inspired the narratives about her dormition and assumption into heaven; see Norelli 2009, 133–6 and Shoemaker 2015, 23.

this problem later, confining myself now to pointing out the circumstan-
tial – and highly suggestive – evidence that might support such a theory.

The Georgian *Ancient Iadgari*: A Witness to Early Palestinian Hymnography?

The *Ancient Iadgari*, which was edited from seven manuscripts in 1980 and
is still in the course of being translated into Western European languages, is
a precious source for early liturgical celebrations in the churches and streets
of Jerusalem and its surroundings.[60] This liturgical collection, or
Tropologion, which contains hymns for the entire year (including fixed
and movable feasts, as well as ordinary weekdays and Sundays), survives in
a number of Georgian manuscripts, most of which are preserved at the
Monastery of St Catherine in Sinai.[61] Although the Georgian scribes were
active in the tenth century (in some cases working at the Monastery of St
Sabas in Palestine), they compiled and copied Georgian translations of
a body of Greek hymnography that had been composed much earlier and
which is now lost. These manuscripts include elements that would later be
divided into separate books, such as the *Menaion*, the *Triodion*, the
Oktoechos and others, in the Byzantine liturgical tradition.[62]

The date of the material that appears in the various versions of the
Ancient Iadgari can be narrowed down to approximately the fifth (or
possibly even the fourth) through to the early seventh century. Charles
Renoux, who provides translations and commentaries of some of the texts
that make up the *Tropologion*, shows that the Georgian scribes sometimes
created composite works that were made up of 'layers' of individual
stanzas, collected from a variety of earlier sources.[63] Some of the earlier
layers reveal the influence of fourth-century Christological formulations or
early fifth-century liturgical homilies.[64] Stig Frøyshov has shown that, in
the case of the hymns known as kanons, the earliest examples may contain

---

[60] *Ancient Iadgari*, ed. Metreveli, Čanķievi and Hevsuriani 1980. The hymnody for Dominical feasts is
translated in *Schneider* 2004 (German); that for the Sunday *Oktoechos* hymnography, called the
'Resurrection Hymns' is translated in Renoux 2000, 2010, vols. 1–3 (French).

[61] For a review of the edition and an overview of the manuscripts, see Wade 1984; cf. Jeffery 1991;
Frøyshov 2012, 233–8; Galadza 2018, 52–6. A list of the manuscripts used for this edition is provided
in Frøyshov 2012, 234, n. 37. The manuscripts differ considerably in their content – to the extent that
the editors provide separate texts in their edition, arranged sequentially on each page for the purpose
of comparison; in short, this is a compilation of versions, not simply an edition of the text.

[62] Galadza 2018, 54.

[63] These layers are called 'sxuani' (Georgian) or ἄλλοι ('others' in Greek). See *Ancient Iadgari,
Resurrection Hymns*, vol. 1, trans. Renoux 2000, 16–17; vol. 2, ed. Renoux 2010, 11.

[64] *Ancient Iadgari, Resurrection Hymns*, vol. 1, ed. Renoux 2000, 16–17, 42–9; Frøyshov 2007b, 166.

only two or three canticles (usually the eighth and ninth odes or, alternatively, the seventh to the ninth) or of four, rather than eight, tones for
particular works.[65] Other archaic elements include the presence of
the second ode, which began to be omitted from kanons especially after
the early eighth century, along with the omission of theotokia at the end of
many odes.[66] According to Frøyshov, a terminus ante quem for the
Georgian *Ancient Iadgari* is provided by the omission of texts by seventh-
and eighth-century hymnographers including Sophronios of Jerusalem,
John of Damascus and Kosmas of Maïuma.[67]

One of the final sections of the *Ancient Iadgari* is a hymn collection
arranged in eight modes, intended for the Resurrection services of Vespers,
Matins and the Eucharist that are celebrated on Sundays. The structure is
roughly the same as that of the *Oktoechos*, a liturgical book that is used to
this day in Orthodox churches for Sundays throughout the fixed
liturgical year.[68] For reasons of space, I focus in the following discussion
only on the so-called 'Resurrection Hymns' in the *Ancient Iadgari*, which
contain a number of different forms of praise to the Theotokos.[69] Much of
this hymnography uses metaphorical and typological imagery to invoke
and praise the Virgin Mary.[70] Some verses also address her as intercessor,
employing language that is similar to that found in the *Akathistos Hymn*.
One of the most interesting sections of the *Ancient Iadgari Resurrection
Hymns* is a series of Marian 'Praises' which appear in just a few manuscripts. These are added – at least in some manuscripts – at the end of the
morning service (*Orthros*), accompanying the singing of Psalms 148–50.
However, they also constitute a Mariological corpus of stanzas that could
be used at various points in liturgical celebration. Many of these texts
appeal to the Virgin as intercessor on a collective and personal basis.[71]

Sinai Georg. 18, like most of the other witnesses to this tradition, was
copied in the tenth century. It contains (in addition to its festal and paschal
material) the *Resurrection Hymns* of the *Ancient Iadgari*. It is fragmentary,

---

[65] Frøyshov 2007b, 167.

[66] *Ancient Iadgari, Resurrection Hymns*, vol. 1, ed. Renoux 2000, 19–20; 72–6.

[67] Frøyshov 2012, 237–8.

[68] *Oktoechos*, ed. Papachrone 1988. For further discussion of the *Oktoechos* in the Byzantine period, see Chapter 4, 164–6.

[69] I thus leave out of this discussion – in the hope that they will be analysed by future researchers – the hymns for Lazarus Saturday through Pentecost (see *Hymnal of St Sabas*, ed. Renoux 2008), as well as those for other feasts, with their attendant theotokia and other Marian additions.

[70] *Ancient Iadgari, Resurrection Hymns*, vols. 1–3, ed. Renoux 2000, 2010.

[71] Ibid., vol. 2, ed. Renoux 2010, 20–1 (I have provided English translations on the basis of Renoux's French version of this and the following quoted hymns).

in that it contains only six of the eight tones, two of which are plagal, in this section of the codex.[72] Neither the theotokia of the first eight odes of the kanons (which are not always included), nor even the ninth, which is based on the Magnificat in Luke 1: 46–55, focus consistently on the Virgin Mary. Christological references to her nevertheless permeate this hymnography and she is sometimes invoked as intercessor, as we see in Ode Three of the kanon in the first plagal tone:

> Virgin, unwedded Mother,
> Who gave birth to Christ the Saviour,
> Do not stop praying,
> But intercede for us, your servants.[73]

The *Resurrection Hymns* contained in Sinai Georg. 18 and 40 use high-flown Mariological imagery in their invocation of the Virgin, addressing her, for example, as 'Theotokos', 'Mother of the Emmanuel', 'Mother of the King', 'Mother of Light', 'Cloud of Light' and 'Bride of Heaven', along with other poetic or biblical epithets.[74] The authors of these hymns also frequently stress the physical nature of the incarnation, as we see in the following kanon, Tone Three, Ode Five:

> We praise you, who were of David's seed,
> Since you received the Son of God in your womb,
> You bore him in a corporeal way
> And you remained, without reproach, a Virgin.[75]

Another witness to the *Resurrection Hymns*, which was also compiled in the tenth century, is Sinai Georg. 34. This 'vast liturgical encyclopedia'[76] contains not only the *Ancient* and *New Iadgari* (*Tropologia*), but also a *Horologion*, a Calendar and other elements.[77] Renoux, who has translated a part of the *Ancient Iadgari* section in his second volume of the *Resurrection Hymns*, suggests that its tenth-century scribe, Iovane Zosime, conceived of the whole manuscript as a compendium of ancient and new material, probably not intending all of its hymnography for contemporary liturgical

---

[72] Ibid., vol. 1, ed. Renoux 2000, 7–8.

[73] Ibid., vol. 1, ed. Renoux 2000, 263: 'Vierge, Mère inépousée,/ Qui enfantas le Christ Sauveur,/ Ne cesse pas de le prier,/ Mais intercède pour nous, tes serviteurs.'

[74] Ibid., vol. 1, ed. Renoux 2000, 60–1.

[75] Ibid., vol. 1, ed. Renoux 2000, 191 (8): 'Toi qui germas de David (cf. Is 11:1; 45: 8), nous te louons,/ Car tu reçus en ton sein le Fils de Dieu,/ Tu l'enfantas corporellement,/ Et tu restas vierge irréprochablement.'

[76] Ibid., vol. 2, ed. Renoux 2010, 11 ('une vaste encyclopédie liturgique').

[77] Frøyshov 2012, 254–5; Galadza 2018, 89–90, 101.

purposes.[78] Sinai Georg. 34 shares with Sinai 18 the poetic compositions known as the 'Praises of the holy Theotokos', which I mentioned above. A passage of intercessory invocation, taken from the Plagal Fourth Tone in both Sinai Georg. 41 and 34, celebrates the Virgin Mary in the following way:

> Rejoice, Theotokos, all-holy Virgin,
> Since because of you and through you, thanks to your child-bearing,
> All the ends of the earth celebrate you today . . .
> Who would not pray to you?
> For you save those who were owed to death,
> And, for those who were destined for torments,
> You made yourself audacious,
> At the right-hand of the One who is enthroned, your Son.
> We have no one who intercedes [for us] like you
> Besides you, yourself.
> Day and night, intercede for us,
> Before the One to whom you gave birth, God,
> For the salvation of our souls.[79]

This stanza pictures the Virgin Mary sitting at the right hand of Christ in heaven and begging him day and night to save her supplicants. It could only have been written in response to early dormition legends according to which her physical, as well as emotional, proximity to her Son could be envisioned.[80] This means that the Marian 'Praises', unlike earlier material included in the *Resurrection Hymns*, may belong to a later – but still 'ancient' – stage of hymnographic composition.[81]

The hymnographic material contained in the Georgian *Ancient Iadgari* thus represents a rich, but diverse, repository of texts that reflects liturgical

---

[78] *Ancient Iadgari, Resurrection Hymns*, vol. 2, ed. Renoux 2010, 14.

[79] Ibid., vol. 2, ed. Renoux 2010, 219–20: 'Réjouis-toi, Mère de Dieu, toute sainte Vierge,/ Car de toi et par toi, grâce à ton enfantement,/ Se réjouissent aujourd'hui toutes les extrémités du monde/ . . . Qui ne te prierait?/ Car tu sauves ceux qui étaient voués à la mort,/ Et, pour ceux qui étaient destinés aux tourments,/ Tu te fais audacieuse,/ À la droite de celui qui siège, ton Fils./ Nous n'avons personne qui intercède comme toi,/ En dehors de toi-même./ Jour et nuit, intercède pour nous,/ Auprès de celui que tu as enfanté, Dieu,/ Pour le salut de nos âmes.'

[80] For outlines of the various early families of dormition traditions, see Mimouni 1995, 37–172; Shoemaker 2002, 9–77.

[81] The *terminus ante quem* for this material of course remains the mid tenth century, when Sinai Georg. 41 and 34 were copied; see *Ancient Iadgari, Resurrection Hymns*, vol. 2, ed. Renoux 2010, 10–14. However, in using the term 'ancient' for this version of the *Georgian Iadgari*, I refer back to Frøyshov's case for a pre-seventh-century date for the hymnbook (see above, n. 67). Whereas Renoux notes an absence of references to the dormition traditions in much of this material, we see their influence on the hymnographer's understanding of the Virgin's intercessory power. On the issue of dating the 'Praises', see *Ancient Iadgari, Resurrection Hymns*, vol. 2, ed. Renoux 2010, 20–3.

celebration in Jerusalem before the beginning of the seventh century.[82] Renoux correctly stresses the importance of these early hymns, some of which might have been sung during the offices and stational processions which Egeria saw taking place in late fourth-century Jerusalem.[83] Their connection with homiletic and hymnographic development not only in the holy city, but also in the wider Byzantine – and especially Constantinopolitan – world awaits further study; it is also clear that this source is highly significant in the history of hagiopolite Marian devotion.

The *Akathistos Hymn*

Turning from the Syriac and Georgian traditions, the rest of this chapter covers developments in Greek hymnography from about the fifth century onward. The *Akathistos Hymn* is probably the earliest example of Marian hymnography to belong to this category.[84] The hymn, which is sometimes described as a kontakion,[85] is one of the most important literary works of the Byzantine period, as well as being a masterpiece of Marian liturgical praise. It consists of twenty-four stanzas to which three *prooemia* (prologues), the second of which may have been composed in a later century, are attached. Each stanza begins with a narrative or didactic section, which might be described as the kontakion sections of the hymn. These are followed by strings of salutations in the form of litanies, which address the Theotokos with a multitude of poetic images and biblical types. An alphabetical acrostic runs through the whole hymn, affirming its completeness and also perhaps acting as a mnemonic device for singers. The salutations to the Virgin employ the word 'Hail' or 'Rejoice' (*Chaire*) for each invocation, according to the rhetorical device of *anaphora* – or the repetition of the same word at the beginning of successive lines. This practice was imitated in numerous Marian homilies and hymns in the centuries that followed. The *Akathistos Hymn* is sung to this day in Chalcedonian Orthodox churches of every jurisdiction. Its full delivery takes place in Matins of the fifth Saturday in Lent, but sections of the hymn are also sung on the four Fridays leading up to that date and on some other days of the liturgical year.[86] The name that is assigned to the hymn, 'Akathistos', simply

---

[82] For further discussion, with emphasis on the early (possibly fourth- to early fifth-century) dating of this material, see Shoemaker 2016a, 186–94.

[83] *Ancient Iadgari, Resurrection Hymns*, vol. 1, ed. Renoux 2000, 28–40.

[84] *Akathistos Hymn*, ed. Trypanis 1968, 29–39; trans. Peltomaa 2001, 2–19.

[85] Wellesz 1961, 192; *Akathistos Hymn*, ed. Trypanis 1968, 17.

[86] *Triodion katanyktikon*, trans. Mother Mary and Ware 1978, 54–5; 422–46. According to Wellesz, the *Akathistos Hymn* may originally have been intended for the feast of the Annunciation; he deduces this on the basis of the titles that are assigned to it in later manuscripts known as *kontakaria*.

means, 'Not sitting down'. The instruction that congregations should stand as
the *Akathistos Hymn* is sung testifies to the importance and solemnity of this
liturgical work.

Leena Mari Peltomaa, in her recent study of the *Akathistos Hymn*,[87]
dates it to the period between the Third and Fourth Ecumenical Councils,
that is, to between 431 and 451 CE – and preferably to a date as close to the
Council of Ephesus (431) as possible.[88] Her adoption of this date, which
challenges a scholarly consensus that has tended to place the hymn in the
sixth century or even later,[89] is supported by the Christological language
and doctrine that it contains. Peltomaa suggests that this teaching reflects
the theological context of the Council of Ephesus and that it shows no
influence from that of Chalcedon, held twenty years later.[90] In opposition
to this argument (which is made largely on the basis of the hymn's
theological content rather than its generic form), it is worth pointing out
that no hymnographic parallels, which might explain the refined and
apparently fully fledged structure of the hymn, exist in early fifth-century
Constantinople. Although the *Akathistos Hymn* is more declamatory than
Romanos the Melodist's kontakia, its metrical and poetic structure resembles the latter corpus more closely than any homilies that can be dated
definitively to the fifth century.[91]

My inclination to adopt an early sixth- rather than fifth-century date for
the *Akathistos Hymn*, mainly on the basis of its highly developed poetic
form, is reinforced by the presence of elements which, as we shall see in the
following chapter, are lacking in the homilies of Proklos, Hesychios and
other early panegyrists of the Theotokos. Most fifth-century liturgical

---

According to the important Patmos kontakarion, Ms. P. 212 (late tenth century), the hymn was sung
either during the Saturday vigils in the middle of Lent; see Wellesz 1961, 191. For further discussion
of this manuscript, see Arentzen and Krueger 2016; Arentzen 2017, 175.

[87] Peltomaa 1997; Peltomaa 2001.   [88] Peltomaa 2001, esp. 49–114.

[89] Maas 1910; Wellesz 1956; Trypanis 1968, 24–5; Mitsakis 1971, 483–509; Grosdidier de Matons 1977,
32–6; Constas 2005 (a review of Peltomaa 2001).

[90] Peltomaa 2001, 85–101. Although Peltomaa 2001, 49, claims the support of Trypanis 1968, 24–5, for
her argument, she has in fact misinterpreted the latter, who writes: 'I am inclined to agree with the
scholars who attribute it (with the exception of Prooemium II) to the days of Justinian I. So fully
finished a kontakion can hardly belong to an earlier period in the development of this literary genre,
even though the insistence on the Virgin as the Mother of God (Θεοτόκος) and the triumphant
expression of this suggests a date closer to the Council of Ephesus (431 A.D.)'. In other words,
according to Trypanis, although the theological content of the hymn might suggest a relationship
with the third Ecumenical Council, its literary structure and style place it in the sixth century,
during the reign of Justinian.

[91] Peltomaa bases her argument for a mid-fifth-century date mainly on its similarities in Christological
terminology with sources including (ps-)Basil of Seleucia's *Homily XXXIX, On the Annunciation*,
Proklos of Constantinople's *Tomus ad Armenos* and the latter's five Marian homilies. See Peltomaa
2001, 77–114.

homilies focus on Mary's Christological importance, but not on her protective or intercessory power. The *Akathistos Hymn*, perhaps reflecting the
Virgin's growing importance as patron or defender of the imperial city of
Constantinople, offers striking witness to this development. As we saw in the
Introduction, appeals for protection from the Virgin appear not only in the
famous second prologue, which was added to the hymn after 626 CE
(possibly as late as in the early eighth century), but also in some of its original
stanzas.[92] Stanza 23, for example, invokes the Virgin Mary as follows:

> . . . Hail, immovable tower of the Church;
> Hail, impregnable wall of the kingdom;
> Hail, through whom trophies are raised up;
> Hail, through whom enemies fall;
> Hail, healing of my body;
> Hail, protection of my soul,
> Hail, bride unwedded.[93]

The second prologue, which builds on this foundation with even more
explicit reference to the plight of a besieged capital city and its subsequent
deliverance, adds the following lines:

> To you, our leader in battle and defender,
> O Theotokos, I, your city, delivered from sufferings,
> ascribe hymns of victory and thanksgiving.
> Since you are invincible in power,
> free me from all kinds of dangers,
> that I may cry to you:
> 'Hail, bride unwedded.'[94]

Such invocation of the Virgin's intercessory and protective functions
suggests a later date of composition than that in which Proklos of
Constantinople or Cyril of Alexandria was preaching. The *Akathistos
Hymn* celebrates above all, as they did, Mary's mysterious role in Christ's
incarnation, but it also recognises her intercessory power.

In addition to its appeals for help in 'all kinds of dangers', the *Akathistos*
teaches Christological doctrine with the help of metaphor, typology and
dramatic narrative. Such didactic methods reveal the hymnographer's
awareness and assimilation of earlier Greek – and possibly Syriac – liturgical texts that celebrate the Theotokos. The parallels with homilies by
Proklos of Constantinople and (ps-)Basil of Seleucia are particularly

---

[92] See Introduction, 31 and n. 152.   [93] *Akathistos Hymn*, stanza 23, trans. Peltomaa 2001, 19.
[94] Ibid., Prooemium II, trans. Peltomaa 2001, 3.

striking, as Peltomaa has shown.[95] Whereas most scholars agree that the homilies provided inspiration for the *Akathistos Hymn*,[96] Peltomaa takes a different view, arguing that they may all have emerged from the same religious setting and have been mutually influential. Such a process would place the composition of the *Akathistos Hymn* during the three years that led up to the Council of Ephesus in 431 CE or shortly thereafter. In my view, however, (ps-)Basil of Seleucia's *Homily XXXIX* belongs to a slightly later period, as we shall see in the following chapter. Its intercessory content suggests a date after the end of the fifth century, which perhaps brings it closer to the likely date of the *Akathistos Hymn*.[97]

The Christological teaching of the *Akathistos* is remarkable both for its adherence to the terminology of the Council of Ephesus and for its poetic and typological epithets for the Theotokos. Evidence of the hymn's strict 'orthodoxy' can be found, for example, in the first prologue:

> Having secretly received the command,
> The bodiless one went with haste to Joseph's dwelling,
> And said to her that knew not wedlock:
> 'He who bowed the heavens and came down
> is contained unchanged but whole in you.
> I see him take the form of a servant in your womb;
> I stand in amazement and cry to you:
> Hail, bride unwedded.'[98]

The emphasis on the unchanged nature of Christ, the Word, when he entered Mary's womb and took on the 'form of a servant', reflects the teaching of such Alexandrian or Alexandrian-influenced bishops as Cyril and Proklos. The hymnographer presents complex doctrine here in the form of dramatic narrative: the archangel Gabriel (or 'bodiless one') hastens to Joseph's house, finds the Virgin Mary, and discloses his paradoxical message. Gabriel also expresses his astonishment at the sight of the mystery; his reaction will be felt by every member of the congregation who joins in the refrain, 'Hail, bride unwedded'.

Poetic or typological approaches to the role of the Virgin in this mysterious process are employed in other stanzas of the *Akathistos Hymn*, always in the form of acclamations or 'chairetismoi':

> Hail, vine-twig of unfading bud;
> Hail, treasure of undying fruit;

[95] Peltomaa 2001, 77–114.
[96] Maas 1910, 306; Trypanis 1968, 25; Grosdidier de Matons 1977, 35–6.   [97] See Chapter 2, 78–82.
[98] *Akathistos Hymn*, Prooemium 1, trans. Peltomaa 2001, 3.

Hail, you who till the tiller who loves humankind;
Hail, you who cultivate the cultivator of our life;
Hail, earth that flourishes with a fertility of compassion;
Hail, table that bears a wealth of mercy . . .[99]

Such rich imagery is not only evocative in metaphorical terms, but it also has typological connotations. Fifth-century preachers including Hesychios of Jerusalem, Proklos of Constantinople and Cyril of Alexandria compared Mary to the untilled earth out of which God created Adam.[100] Christ, as the Second Adam, thus recapitulated this divine act, allowing humanity to be restored to its original – but now deified – state. But the Virgin could also assume a range of other natural guises: she was the twig from which the 'unfading bud' would bloom, the tiller of the fertile field, the table that (in a eucharistic sense) would hold the body and blood of Christ, and so on. Such symbolism is never restricted to just one meaning in Byzantine liturgical texts such as this; it offers layers of possible interpretation, thereby suggesting the limitless qualities of the human container and nurturer of Christ. The natural imagery that appears in the *Akathistos Hymn* is also effective in its sensuality. Singers or listeners are induced to visualise lush and fertile landscapes in their mind's eye. This is the original and undefiled creation that God created and saw as 'good'. Mary thus stands for the receptive, but also productive, creation that was intended for salvation.[101]

Peltomaa is correct, however, in her assertion that neither the fifth-century homilies nor the *Akathistos Hymn* 'describe Mary as a personality'.[102] In other words, the Virgin is treated more as a theological concept than as a real person, with female and motherly qualities, in these liturgical works.[103] This aspect of the hymn suggests that it may have been composed earlier than the time at which our next important hymnographer, Romanos the Melodist, was active. The latter, as we shall shortly see, developed an image of the Mother of God that was both human and maternal – in fact, as Sarah Gador-Whyte has memorably put it, she became in the hands of Romanos 'a suburban mum'.[104]

---

[99] Ibid., stanza 5, trans. Peltomaa 2001, 7.
[100] For further discussion of these preachers, see Chapter 2, 70–7.
[101] For an interesting new approach to the *Akathistos Hymn* that examines especially its use of nature imagery, see Arentzen 2021.
[102] Peltomaa 2001, 76.
[103] I. Kalavrezou echoes this view, writing, 'Mary is still the Theotokos defined at the council, a concept'; Kalavrezou 1990, 166, quoted in Peltomaa 2001, 73 and 76.
[104] Gador-Whyte 2013, 87. In fact Gador-Whyte attributes this expression to Roger Scott in her analysis.

Nevertheless, as I argued above, the sophisticated structure of the *Akathistos Hymn* suggests to me, like numerous other scholars but *pace* Peltomaa, a date towards the end of the fifth or beginning of the sixth century. This would allow time for the hymnographer, along with other liturgical writers whose work may not survive, to have fully absorbed the doctrinal and rhetorical developments of the first half of the fifth century. The absence of references or allusions to the Council of Chalcedon in the *Akathisthos Hymn* may reflect diplomacy rather than ignorance on the part of its author, since appealing to a wide range of religious opinions was more important in the post-conciliar period than propagating a divisive – if officially accepted – doctrinal definition.[105]

Romanos the Melodist

This sixth-century hymnographer was, as many scholars acknowledge,[106] the greatest liturgical innovator of his period; I shall therefore focus on his work for the remainder of this chapter.[107] Romanos was probably born in Syria and became a deacon in Berytus (modern Beirut); he moved to Constantinople during the reign of Anastasios I. He worked as a deacon in a church that was located in a district of the imperial city called *tou Kyrou* where he composed numerous kontakia that expounded biblical (both Old and New Testament) narratives.[108] The Virgin Mary occupied a central place in Romanos' understanding of the divine dispensation. Scholars have not yet determined whether Romanos was inspired to develop such a dramatic portrayal of the Virgin by Greek or Syriac liturgical sources – or even, as later legend suggested, by the Mother of God herself.[109] Nevertheless, it is clear that Romanos visualised, probably in response to strong popular devotion in Constantinople during the reign of Justinian, a Virgin Mary who was entirely human and maternal while remaining mysteriously virginal.[110] According to Romanos, Mary spoke for and as one

---

[105]   N. Constas offers this solution, which I find convincing, in his review of Peltomaa 2001; see Constas 2005, 358.
[106]   See below, nn. 113–14.
[107]   For complete editions of Romanos' works, see Maas and Trypanis 1963 (1997); Grosdidier de Matons 1964–81, 5 vols. For ease of reference, I refer only to the Maas and Trypanis edition in this book.
[108]   Maas 1906, 29; Grosdidier de Matons 1977, 178–89; Arentzen 2017, 1–6; Gador-Whyte 2017, 7–9.
[109]   The legend that the Mother of God gave Romanos a scroll to eat, after which he was inspired to write kontakia, appears in the tenth-century *Synaxarion of Constantinople*; see *Synax. CP*, 95–6; the story is also told in the the *Menologion of Basil II* and several other *menaia* or *synaxaria* on Romanos' feast-day, 1 October. See Barkhuizen 2012, 5.
[110]   Arentzen 2014; Arentzen 2017.

of the congregation, while also occupying a privileged position as mother of Christ.[111] The richness of this characterisation, which managed to incorporate all of the elements in the Marian liturgical tradition that we have noted so far while also inventing new ones, would have an impact on Greek preachers and hymnographers for centuries to come.[112]

Romanos the Melodist has attracted a huge amount scholarly interest since the beginning of the twentieth century.[113] This has gained momentum in recent years, with various new studies of the sixth-century hymnographer, along with translations of his kontakia, appearing in a variety of languages.[114] However, as Thomas Arentzen noted in 2013, there were – until quite recently – surprisingly few investigations into the role of the Virgin in the Melodist's kontakia.[115] The problem is slowly being rectified, not only thanks to Arentzen's work on the subject, but also to contributions from Leena Mari Peltomaa and Sarah Gador-Whyte. Peltomaa, who notes that out of about sixty authentic works, nine kontakia give Mary a central role in their narratives, examines their portrayal of her as virgin, 'Second Eve', mother and intercessor.[116] A second article, published five years later, provides focused analysis of Mary's role as intercessor according to various kontakia by Romanos.[117] Gador-Whyte has meanwhile examined the Virgin Mary's various aspects in a more gendered way, contrasting her 'motherly' characteristics with more masculine ones, as defender of Constantinople.[118] Following this work, Arentzen contributed a rich and provocative doctoral thesis on Romanos's treatment of the Virgin Mary,[119] which has now been revised and published as a monograph.[120] While not denying the various categories that both Peltomaa and Gador-Whyte identified, Arentzen urges against the impression that Romanos presents a 'schizophrenic' Virgin; he argues that she appears in various kontakia as a fully integrated human being, rather than as a theological or civic symbol.[121]

In the discussion that follows, I largely accept this analysis on the grounds that the chief purpose of Romanos the Melodist's kontakia

---

[111] For a thoughtful assessment of Mary's relationship to the congregation, both through words and silence, see Frank 2019.
[112] Cunningham 2008a.
[113] See, for example, Maas 1906; Carpenter 1932; Grosdidier de Matons 1977; Grosdidier de Matons 1980–1; Wellesz 1961, 179–97.
[114] For example, Lash 1995; Schork 1995; Maisano 2002; Krueger 2004, 159–88; Frank 2005; Koder 2005; Frank 2006; Krueger 2006; Koder 2010; Barkhuizen 2012; Krueger 2014, 29–65; Arentzen 2017; Gador-Whyte 2017.
[115] Arentzen 2014, 21.   [116] Peltomaa 2010.   [117] Peltomaa 2015.
[118] Gador-Whyte 2013, esp. 80–1 and 87; see now Gador-Whyte 2017, esp. 70–1.
[119] Arentzen 2014.   [120] Arentzen 2017.   [121] Arentzen 2014, 21–2.

appears to be the dramatic engagement of congregations with the Virgin Mary as a sympathetic – albeit powerful – human mother. Her transition from a state of fecund or expectant (as opposed to ascetic) virginity to one of protective motherhood is one with which lay audiences (especially women) could identify.[122] However, the deeper Christian symbolism of these dramatic narratives would not have been lost on sixth-century Constantinopolitan congregations either. Romanos portrays the transformation of humanity, or the Church, in its ongoing encounter with Christ through the agency of his mother Mary. This, I would argue, is framed within a 'high' or neo-Chalcedonian Christology that stresses both the divinity of Christ and his condescension in assuming human nature. The Theotokos thus acts preeminently as the person through whom Christians gain access to her Son; this role works simultaneously in her historical acceptance of the incarnation, but also in personal or collective devotion. Above all, however, Romanos portrays this process in a dramatic way, engaging his listeners dynamically with his interpretation of biblical (and sometimes apocryphal) narratives.

To begin with the Christological framework within which Romanos worked, it is worth recalling Aloys Grillmeier's assessment that this hymnographer 'systematically avoids speaking of Christ's humanity. The accent is always on the divinity.'[123] This position is illustrated, for example, in the kontakion on the marriage at Cana when Christ delivers a short homily to his inquisitive mother, reminding her not only that he created the universe, but that he also planned human salvation by taking flesh from her:

'Lift up your mind to my words and understand, incorruptible woman,
    what I will say. For when from what did not exist
I created heaven and earth and the universe,
I was able immediately
To adorn at that time all that I created ...

Revered woman, listen clearly to this: I could in another way have liberated
    those who have fallen,
By not taking on the form of a poor servant.
But nevertheless, I endured first to be conceived
And then to be born as man
And draw milk from your breasts, O virgin ...'[124]

---

[122] Cf. Arentzen 2013; Arentzen 2014; Arentzen 2017, esp. 46–86.
[123] Grillmeier, trans. Allen and Cawte, 1995, 521.
[124] Romanos the Melodist, *Kontakion on the Marriage at Cana*, strophes 13–14, Maas and Trypanis 1963, 53–4, trans. Barkhuizen 2012, 60 (with adjustments).

Romanos also follows earlier liturgical writers, both Greek and Syriac, in describing Christ's simultaneous divinity and humanity by means of antithetical statements, as we see in his kontakion on the Hypapante (Presentation of Christ into the Temple) :

> ... for the One who created Adam is being carried as a babe.
> The uncontainable is contained in the arms of the elder.[125]

Although Romanos portrays Christ, in accordance with Chalcedonian doctrine, as both God and man, he 'retains a Christology from above' while avoiding the one-nature theology of Severos of Antioch and his followers.[126] It is now worth examining how this influenced the poet's understanding of the Virgin Mary, as virginal birth-giver and mother of Christ.

Romanos portrays Mary, as the first witness of Christ's incarnation, reflecting on this mystery as she cradles the infant Christ in her arms. She struggles to comprehend Christ's simultaneous divinity and humanity, as we see in another stanza of the kontakion on the *Hypapante*:

> While the angels sang in praise of the Lover of mankind, Mary was walking, carrying him in her arms,
> and pondering how she had become a mother yet remained a virgin.
> Realising that the birth was beyond nature, she was afraid and trembled.
> Reasoning to herself she said,
> 'What title can I find for you, my Son?
> For should I call you, as I see you, man, you are more than man,
> who kept my virginity unsullied, only Lover of mankind.
>
> Should I call you perfect man? But I know your conception was divine.
> None of humankind is ever
> conceived without union and without seed, as you were, sinless One.
> And if I call you God, I marvel as I see you like me in all things,
> for you have nothing which differentiates you among humans,
> even though without sin you were conceived and born.
> Shall I suckle you or give you glory? For the facts proclaim you
> God without time, even though you have become man, only Lover of
> mankind.'[127]

---

[125] Romanos the Melodist, *Kontakion on the Presentation in the Temple*, strophe 1, Maas and Trypanis 1963, 27, trans. Lash 1995, 28.

[126] Grillmeier, trans. Allen and Cawte, 1995, 520.

[127] Romanos the Melodist, *Kontakion on the Presentation in the Temple*, strophes 3–4, Maas and Trypanis 1963, 28–9, trans. Lash 1995, 28–9.

The Virgin also recognises the consequences for herself of this miraculous birth. In the less well-known second kontakion on the Nativity of Christ, she exclaims:

> 'I do not deny your grace, which I experienced, O Master,
> nor do I discount the rank which I attained on giving birth to you;
> for I rule over the world
> since I have carried your power in my womb, I have power over all . . .'[128]

Romanos occasionally goes so far as to call Mary 'Queen', implying that ordinary people may approach her as long as they address her with appropriate respect and deference.[129] A high Christology thus implies a high Mariology in the works of Romanos. However, it is precisely within this theological context that the hymnographer describes the Virgin's essential role as mediator and intercessor for Christians.

Romanos the Melodist, perhaps building on the imagery of the *Akathistos Hymn*, refers frequently to Mary's role as intercessor before Christ. Such passages, as in later Byzantine hymnography, frequently appear in the closing strophes of the kontakia; they reflect the homiletic convention of closing speeches with respectful invocation of the holy subject or subjects. In the last three strophes of his first kontakion on the Nativity of Christ, Romanos has the Virgin herself pray to Christ on behalf of the rest of humanity. An extract of this speech reads as follows:

> 'For I am not simply your mother, compassionate Saviour;
> it is not in vain that I suckle the giver of milk,
> but for the sake of all I implore you.
> You have made me the mouth and the boast of all my race,
> and your world has me as a mighty protection, a wall and a buttress.
> They look to me, those who were cast out
> of the Paradise of pleasure, for I bring them back.'[130]

Romanos more often invokes either Christ or the Virgin in his own voice, speaking for the rest of humanity as he seeks their help:

---

[128] Romanos the Melodist, *Kontakion on the Nativity* II, strophe 2, Maas and Trypanis 1963, 10 (my own translation).

[129] This occurs, for example, in Romanos' *Kontakion on the Annunciation* I, strophe 1: 'Come, let us accompany the archangel Gabriel to the Virgin Mary,/ and greet her as mother and nourisher of our life./ For it is not fitting only for the general to greet the queen,/ but it is also permitted for the lowly to see her and address her,/ whom all the generations proclaim blessed . . . '; Maas and Trypanis 1963, 281; trans. Barkhuizen 2012, 29.

[130] Romanos the Melodist, *Kontakion on the Nativity* I, strophe 23, Maas and Trypanis 1963, 8; trans. Lash 1995, 11.

We implore you, O All-Holy, Long-Suffering, Life and Restoration, Source
of goodness,
look down from heaven and visit all those who ever trust in you;
rescue our life, Lord, from all constraint and affliction,
and, in the faith of truth, guide us all,
at the prayers of the immaculate Mother of God (Θεοτόκου) and Virgin.
Save your world, and those in the world, and spare us all,
you who, for us, became man without change, only Lover of mankind.[131]

The kontakion on Mary at the cross, which must have been intended
for the vigil on Good Friday, invites congregations to share her doubt
and extreme grief at the impending crucifixion of her son. Niki Tsironis
correctly notes the influence of this powerful hymn on subsequent
Byzantine treatments of this theme, both in hymnography and
homiletics.[132] As in his other kontakia, Romanos portrays the dynamic
encounter between Christ, as like a lamb he is 'being dragged to
slaughter',[133] and his mother, who is apparently following the procession to Golgotha. The kontakion contains a prologue, in which the
hymnographer calls to the congregation to 'praise him who was cruci-
fied for us',[134] followed by seventeen strophes. The latter present
a dramatic dialogue between Mary and Christ, with the former speaking
for seven strophes and the latter for nine. The seventeenth strophe is
voiced by Romanos who, by means of direct address to Christ, sums up
soteriological meaning of his incarnation and crucifixion – also
acknowledging his gift of 'freedom of speech' (parresia) to the 'honoured Lady' (tē semne).[135]

Christ remains in this kontakion, as in the others that we have examined, the God and Creator who knows exactly why he must undergo such
suffering and how the story will end. When the Virgin asks why (when he
could perform miracles and give life to corpses such as Lazarus) he does not
simply give an order for Adam and the rest of humanity to be raised up
from Hades, she does not receive a direct reply. Instead Christ explains,
using medical imagery, that Adam and Eve need healing:

[131] See for example, Romanos the Melodist, Kontakion on Presentation at the Temple, strophe 18; Maas
and Trypanis 1963, 33– 4; trans. Lash 1995, 34. Cf. Kontakion on the Marriage at Cana, strophe 21,
Maas and Trypanis 1963, 56; Kontakion on Mary at the Cross, strophe 17, Maas and Trypanis 1963,
148–9.
[132] Tsironis 1998, 114–18; see also Cunningham 2008a, 259.
[133] Romanos the Melodist, Kontakion on Mary at the Cross, strophe 1; Maas and Trypanis 1963, 142;
trans. Lash 1995, 143.
[134] Ibid., Prologue; Maas and Trypanis 1963, 142; trans. Lash 1995, 143.
[135] Ibid., strophe 17; Maas and Trypanis 1963, 149; trans. Lash 1995, 150.

> By intemperance, by gluttony,
> Adam became ill and was borne down to the lowest hell.
> And there he weeps for the pain of his soul.
> While Eve, who once taught him disorder,
> groans with him, for with him she is ill,
> that together they may learn to keep the physician's order.
> Have you now understood? Have you grasped what I say?
> Once again, Mother, cry out, 'If you pardon Adam,
> forgive Eve also, my Son and my God.'[136]

It is possible that by focusing on the need to 'heal' Adam and Eve, rather than providing a detailed theological explanation of Christ's crucifixion, Romanos wishes to shift the focus towards Mary's intercessory role in human salvation. Alternatively, this may simply reflect his awareness that contemporary congregations were more interested in the human, rather than the theological, impact of this world-changing event. In any case, the emphasis shifts in the next two strophes to whether or not Mary will see her son again. Christ reassures her, following a long-standing patristic tradition, that she will be the first to see his resurrected body:

> When he heard this, the One who knows all things
> before their birth answered Mary, 'Courage, Mother,
> because you will see me first on my coming from the tomb . . .'[137]

Although courage is restored in the fifteenth strophe, the Virgin reveals her inner doubts and sorrow in all of her preceding speeches. She is a fully human mother, who shouts, protests and sheds tears in her efforts to dissuade Christ from his tragic purpose. She mourns the fact that she alone is faithful since the disciples, including Peter, have all abandoned their teacher. But above all, she weeps because this is her child who is on the way to unjust slaughter. The contrast between Mary's ignorance, which causes such lament, and Christ's calm understanding of the reason for his crucifixion is conveyed mainly, as we have seen, by means of direct speech. This drama, which is resolved when Mary is taught the truth and declares that she is 'conquered by love',[138] depicts an emotional transition from doubt to belief in the resurrection of Christ. But above all, it is worth noting an element that would survive into later Byzantine liturgical treatment of this theme: namely, that the pain and suffering which Christ experienced on the cross can best be expressed through the experience of his

---

[136] Ibid., strophe 10; Maas and Trypanis 1963, 146; trans. Lash 1995, 147.
[137] Ibid., strophe 12; Maas and Trypanis 1963, 146; trans. Lash 1995, 148 (with one small adjustment).
[138] Ibid., strophe 15; Maas and Trypanis 1963, 148; trans. Lash 1995, 149.

mother. This helps to explain the emphasis not only in hymnography for Good Friday, but also in the short hymns known as stavrotheotokia which are sung throughout the year, on the suffering of the Virgin Mary. Whereas Western medieval theologians, liturgical writers and iconographers shifted focus to a suffering Christ, their Byzantine counterparts preferred to show the depth of this pain through the experience of his mother.[139]

The most striking innovation in Romanos the Melodist's portrayal of Mary thus consists in his literary development of her character by means of dramatic dialogues and monologues according to the rhetorical device of *ethopoiia*. Such treatment is not confined to the Theotokos; as Georgia Frank and others have shown, the hymnographer explores the thoughts and reactions of many other biblical and even apocryphal characters in his effort to bring their narratives to life for sixth-century congregations.[140] In the case of the Virgin Mary, we join her at the scene of the nativity, reflecting in solitude or welcoming three exotic visitors, at the meeting with Symeon in the temple, at the marriage at Cana, on the way to the cross and in many other settings. Romanos skilfully draws his listeners into an empathetic relationship with Christ's mother, encouraging them to enter into her state of awe, tender love for her divine Son, fear, and perplexity. The underlying purpose of such teaching is of course to convey the paradoxical doctrine of Chalcedonian Christianity. However, what appears to be new is the liturgical poet's interest in engaging his audience fully in this mystery, which is not merely remembered as biblical narrative but is also experienced sensorially in liturgical and sacramental ceremony.

Conclusion

Although Byzantine Marian hymnography may have been slow to develop, it had earlier roots in the Syriac and Jerusalem liturgical rites, as evidenced by later Georgian compilations of hymnbooks. Such praise was inspired in the first place by Christological reflection on Mary's important role in the incarnation of Christ. She is described in the Syriac hymns of Ephrem and other melodists as the 'bridge' between God and humanity. However, the Theotokos also represents a microcosm of the universe, embodying the transfigured creation into which God chose to enter in his human incarnation. Intercessory content, which reflected growing belief in Mary's own

---

[139] For vivid discussion of the Virgin Mary's lament at the foot of the cross, as depicted in Byzantine texts and icons, see Constas 2014, 124–8.

[140] Frank 2005; Krueger 2005; Krueger 2006; Arentzen 2017, 14–16; Gador-Whyte 2017, 1–11.

transition to heaven after death and her consequent 'freedom of speech' with her Son, began to appear in the course of the fifth, but especially in the sixth century in both Oriental and Byzantine Christianity. It is witnessed in short prayers, or amulets, that have been discovered in Egypt, in many of the sung homilies and hymns of the Syriac churches, and in the early Byzantine *Akathistos Hymn*. The early stichera and kanon stanzas that appear in the Georgian *Ancient Iadgari*, or hymnbook, which reflect the Jerusalem rites before the seventh century, are more difficult to date. However, they offer ample witness to growing devotion to the Theotokos in this region. Although Mary thus has both doctrinal and intercessory importance before the middle of the sixth century, she remains, in the words of Ioli Kalavrezou, 'a concept' rather than a human, and above all, maternal person.[141] It is finally in the hymns of Romanos the Melodist that we see a truly rounded portrayal of the Mother of God. This creative hymnographer used narrative, dramatic dialogue and direct address in order to bring biblical stories, along with their chief protagonists, to life for Constantinopolitan congregations.

The reception of the various hymnographic traditions that I have described in this chapter varied, according to time, place and liturgical setting. Some aspects of this hymnody are universal: regardless of their place in divine liturgies, offices or private prayer, such texts offer praise, invocation and theological instruction. The choirs or individuals who sang the hymns would obviously have absorbed such content the most, whereas listening congregations – even if they joined in refrains or 'alleluias' – might not have heard every phrase or nuance. Susan Ashbrook Harvey has shown that not only men, but also women, participated in the singing of hymns in the Syriac churches.[142] There is no evidence for such a practice in the Greek-speaking world, apart from the likelihood that female monastics sang the psalms and their responses, along with other hymnography, in their monasteries. What we can say is that kontakia such as those composed by Romanos the Melodist were intended to be understood. This hymnographer uses relatively simple koine Greek, lively narrative, dialogue and apostrophe in order to engage his audiences. Hymnography remained one of the most important ways in which theology was taught in the Byzantine Church – as it continues to be today in modern Orthodox Churches. It also provided an opportunity for direct address and supplication to the Theotokos, who represented the meeting place of humanity and divinity in both theological and intercessory terms.

---

[141] Kalavrezou 1990, 166.   [142] See above, n. 33.

CHAPTER 2

From Theotokos to Intercessor: The Early Homiletic Witness (c. 400–600)

Early homilies on Mary, the Theotokos, seem remarkably well developed when they burst into view at about the beginning of the fifth century.[1] Many of these works were composed in honour of a new feast in memory of the Virgin. This was celebrated throughout the eastern territories of the Christian Roman empire either on 15 August (in Jerusalem) in connection with the feast of Christ's Nativity, either on a Sunday before or the day after 25 December, in Constantinople.[2] Judging by the content of the homilies that were written in honour of this feast – some of which will be studied below – it was an occasion on which Mary's role in the incarnation was recognised. She helped to inaugurate a new creation by means of her virginal conception and birth of Christ, the Son and Word of God. Mary is praised in exalted terms in the surviving orations, which were composed and delivered in Jerusalem, Antioch, Constantinople, and other cities and parishes in the Eastern Roman empire. However, her role as protector and intercessor of believing Christians would not be celebrated for another century. That element of Marian devotion seems to have developed more slowly than did the Christological emphasis. This is not to say that individual Christians did not yet venerate the Theotokos as a figure of power in her own right.[3] It is possible either that Church leaders viewed this aspect of her cult as unsuitable for festal preaching or that they sought to rein in the burgeoning cult. To put this in another way, early Byzantine bishops and presbyters channelled popular devotion to the Virgin into

---

[1] A useful assessment of the fifth-century and later Greek homilies that deal with the Virgin Mary can be found in Caro 1971–3. For studies of individual preachers who delivered sermons on the Theotokos, see Leroy 1967; Aubineau 1969; Aubineau 1978; Aubineau 1988; Constas 2003.

[2] See Introduction, 9 and n. 38; Jugie 1923b; Jugie 1944, 172–212, esp. 175–7; Capelle 1943; Leroy 1967, 66; Constas 2003, 135.

[3] Shoemaker 2015; Shoemaker 2016a; Kateusz 2019. Although I do not agree with all of the claims of both scholars, they offer much food for thought regarding the early cult of the Virgin. See further discussion in Introduction, 6–8.

a doctrinal framework that received further endorsement at the Councils of Ephesus and Chalcedon, in 431 and 451, respectively.[4]

Festal homilies from this period onward adopted a form that was closely related to the great theological orations of Gregory Nazianzen in the fourth century.[5] The basic structure of such orations includes an opening section (*exordium* or prologue) in which the preacher alludes to the event that is being honoured on this day. In Proklos of Constantinople's first homily on 'the holy Virgin Theotokos', for example, he begins by inviting his audience to 'the Virgin's festival', which 'has benefits to bestow on those who assemble to keep it'.[6] This is followed by development of the theme of the festival, which in this case is the incarnation of Christ in the womb of the Virgin. Much of the text, as in so many other festal orations, adopts a hymnic style, with short 'Asianic' phrases,[7] rhythmic patterns and an array of metaphorical and typological imagery to describe the Virgin Mary. The preacher ends with a short section (the *conclusio*) in which he sometimes propounds ethical teachings or, in later Marian homilies, appeals to her intercessory power on behalf of the congregation.

We know more about the delivery and reception of homilies in these early centuries than we do for the middle Byzantine period.[8] Scholars including Ramsay MacMullen, Pauline Allen, Wendy Mayer and Jan Barkhuizen have studied the liturgical contexts for which homilies were intended and what kinds of people attended church in Antioch, Jerusalem, Constantinople and elsewhere.[9] Both internal and external evidence can be employed in order to build up a picture of such reception. Preachers such as John Chrysostom (who delivered many exegetical and festal homilies – but none that focused specifically on the Virgin Mary) recorded the reactions of their audiences, which included clapping, cheering, or

---

[4] Extensive scholarly literature exists on the relationship between the Council of Ephesus and Mary's growing importance in Christian doctrine and devotion. See, for example, McGuckin 1994 (2004); Constas 1995; Price 2004. In his latest study, however, Richard Price casts doubt on the centrality of Mary, as 'Theotokos', in the Acts of the Council of Ephesus; see Price 2019. Studies that posit political influence, and especially that of the empress Pulcheria, on the proceedings at Ephesus include Holum 1982; Limberis 1994; Cooper 1998; McGuckin 2001b.

[5] Gregory's festal orations cover certain feasts such as Theophany (Christmas) and Pascha, but they also provide a wealth of Trinitarian teaching. See Gregory Nazianzen, *Orations*, ed. Bernardi 1978, Moreschini 1990, trans. Vinson 2003; Daley 2006; Harrison 2008.

[6] Proklos of Constantinople, *Homily I*, ed. and trans. Constas 2003, 136–7. For a useful discussion of Proklos of Constantinople's festal orations, see Barkhuizen 2001, 12–13.

[7] On the Asianic style in Greek rhetoric, see Kennedy 1994, 95–6.

[8] For an excellent introduction to early Byzantine homiletics, see Mayer 2008. Further bibliography on early Christian preaching includes Cunningham 1990; Olivar 1991; Allen and Cunningham 1998; Stewart-Sykes 2001; Harrison 2013, 133–68.

[9] MacMullen 1989; Allen 1998; Mayer 1998; Barkhuizen 1998.

expressing boredom or disapproval.[10] Proklos of Constantinople also referred to people in the congregation, identifying different groups, genders or ages.[11] However, it is not always clear whether such references are rhetorical or real: remarks *ad hominem*, especially in polemical contexts, were common in early Christian homiletics.[12]

As for the location in which homilies were delivered, we again have some information for particular preachers or orations. We know, for example, that Hesychios of Jerusalem delivered homilies both at the church of the Anastasis in Jerusalem and at the site of the Kathisma, between Jerusalem and Bethlehem, in the early fifth century.[13] Proklos' first homily, *On the Holy Virgin Theotokos*, was delivered in the Great Church of Constantinople, Hagia Sophia, on the feast of the Memory of the Virgin, 430.[14] The current patriarch Nestorios, who disagreed with Proklos' use of the epithet 'Theotokos', is known to have been present; thus this highly ornate panegyrical sermon must have been received with enthusiasm by some members of the congregation, but disapproval by others – along with their bishop. Some of the homilies of the sixth-century bishop of Antioch, Severos, are also documented as to time and place of delivery, which helps us to assess their possible impact on congregations that might have been urban or rural, large or small, and so on.[15] Many of the surviving homilies of this period remain mysterious, however, not only with regard to their place and time of delivery, but even to their authorship and date. We can only hypothesise about the place of such works, which include (ps-)Basil of Seleucia's *Homily XXXIX, On the Annunciation*, in the history of Marian doctrine and devotion.[16]

This chapter examines a selection of Marian homilies that date between the early fifth and the sixth centuries. It would be impossible to cover every example that survives, many of which still lack critical editions and secure attributions; however, those that I have chosen all demonstrate growing interest in the Virgin during this period. As in the case of hymnography, there is a slow shift from purely doctrinal to more devotional content between about the end of the fifth and the beginning of the sixth century. The difficulties of dating some homilies makes it impossible to chart this process exactly; however, a trend is broadly visible. Aside from this, it is

---

[10] MacMullen 1989; Mayer 1998; Harrison 2013, 144–6.
[11] Barkhuizen 1998; Barkhuizen 2001, 35–41.   [12] Uthemann 1998; Harrison 2013, 159–60.
[13] See below, n. 19.   [14] Constas 2003, 135; Barkhuizen 2001, 4, n. 16.
[15] Allen 1996; Allen 1998, 218–20; Allen and Hayward 2004, 49–52, 107–8; for the Marian homilies, see especially Allen 2011, 72–3.
[16] For extensive discussion of this homily, see Peltomaa 2001, 77–85.

fruitful to examine the ways in which these preachers praise the Theotokos, teach the paradoxical doctrine of the incarnation in which she played such a vital role and call on their audiences to participate in the liturgical celebrations. This was an experience that involved both the intellect and the emotions, as scholars including Carol Harrison, Derek Krueger, Andrew Mellas and Robert Taft have shown.[17] Preachers were aware of their rhetorical power and used it to full effect, attempting to place the Virgin Mary, along with Christ, at the centre of the Christian narrative.

Mary as Theotokos: Early Fifth-Century Homilies

According to the ninth-century chronicler Theophanes, a monk and presbyter called Hesychios was active as a preacher in Jerusalem at least a decade before Nestorios became bishop of Constantinople in 428.[18] Four homilies that focus especially on the Virgin Mary survive, including two on the feast of the *Hypapante* ('Meeting' or Presentation of Christ in the temple), celebrated in Jerusalem during this period on 14 February (forty days after the Nativity celebration on 6 January), and two which were probably intended for the main feast-day on which Mary was commemorated in this region during the fifth century, namely, 15 August. The association of that date with the Virgin's 'dormition' (or 'falling asleep' – a euphemism for death) would only come a century or two later. The feast at this time, which was celebrated with a synaxis at the site of the Kathisma, a rock three miles from Bethlehem where Mary was believed to have rested on her way to register for the census and give birth in that city, was concerned with her virginity and divine motherhood. According to Michel Aubineau, the two homilies on the *Hypapante* were preached in the church of the martyrium in Jerusalem during the early years of Hesychios' presbyterate. All but one of the homilies may therefore predate the Council of Ephesus; the latter (*Homily V*) has a more 'triumphal' quality, which may indicate the deposition and condemnation of Nestorios in 431.[19]

Hesychios of Jerusalem explored the role of the Virgin Mary in relation to her divine Son, Christ, especially in the two homilies that were dedicated to her feast. He described her most often as 'Virgin' (*parthenos*) , but he also

---

[17] Taft 2006, 79–87; Harrison 2013, 133–68; Krueger 2014; Mellas 2020.
[18] Theophanes Confessor, *Chronicle*, ed. De Boor 1963, 83, trans. Mango and Scott 1997, 129; Aubineau 1978, xv.
[19] Aubineau 1978, LXII–LXVI.

used the more technical term 'God-bearer' (Theotokos) seven times –
especially in *Homily V* which may have been pronounced after the conclusion of the Council of Ephesus.[20] Hesychios employed a rhythmic 'Asianic'
rhetorical style, displaying a fondness for devices such as *anaphora, antith-
esis, exclamatio* and others. Hesychios also described Mary by means of
poetic metaphor and biblical typology, most of which expressed her
virginal fecundity – as we see in the epithets 'unseeded, fertile, and
uncultivated garden', 'lamp without an orifice', 'ark of life' and others.[21]
Aubineau has noted possible influence from Cyril of Alexandra and
Proklos of Constantinople – especially after the crucial period of the
early 430s – in *Homily V,* on the Theotokos.[22] Hesychios expressed
a Christology that was close to the Alexandrian, as opposed to the
Antiochene, tradition, celebrating the conception and birth of the Logos
who condescended to take flesh from a pure virgin while remaining
consubstantial and co-eternal with God the Father. Like Proklos and
Cyril, he linked Mary's virginity with Christ's divinity, declaring, for
example, 'If you had known a man, you would not have given birth to
God.'[23]

It is likely that congregations in Jerusalem were able to appreciate at least
the rhythmic and poetic flow of Hesychios' preaching – even if they did not
understand every word of his elevated koine Greek. Variations between
discursive, dialogic and exclamatory passages would also have helped to
retain their attention. It is noticeable that Hesychios frequently focused on
the importance of the Virgin Mary for female Christians in his homilies.
She was 'a Virgin who surpassed all women' but who also 'enveloped the
sisters of her race in joyful light'.[24] We seek in vain, however, for references
to the Virgin's intercessory power in these homilies; nor is her maternal
stance with regard to her divine son emphasised in any way that is not
Christological. Hesychios of Jerusalem's Marian homilies thus reflect the
theological importance of this subject – at least in festal preaching – at the
beginning of the fifth century. Such restraint is also visible in the even more

---

[20] Aubineau 1978, XLIV.
[21] See especially Hesychios of Jerusalem, *Homily V, On the Theotokos Mary* 1, ed. and trans. Aubineau
1978, 158–61.
[22] Aubineau 1978, 145–7.
[23] Hesychios of Jerusalem, *Homily V, On the Theotokos Mary* 5.12–13, ed. and trans. Aubineau 1978,
166–7.
[24] Hesychios of Jerusalem, *Homily VI, On the Theotokos Mary* 1.5–6, 19, ed. Aubineau 1978, 194–5:
παρθένου ... ἥτις τοσοῦτον ὑπερέβαλε πάσας ...; καὶ τὰ τῆς χαρᾶς τὰς ὁμοφύλους περιήστραψε
φῶτα ...

acclaimed homilies of his contemporaries, Proklos of Constantinople and Cyril of Alexandria, to whom I turn next.

Nicholas (Fr Maximos) Constas has traced the controversial circumstances in which Proklos of Constantinople preached his celebrated first homily, which was widely disseminated later and acquired almost canonical status.[25] This oration was probably delivered in the church of Hagia Sophia in Constantinople on the day after Christmas in 430. Preaching in the presence of his main theological opponent, the archbishop Nestorios, Proklos, who was then titular bishop of Kyzikos, presented an extravaganza of poetic metaphors and biblical types in order to demonstrate Mary's role as virginal 'birth-giver' of Christ. The point of such rhetoric is to illustrate the way in which divinity came to reside physically in the created world, as we see in the following passage:

> She who called us here today is the Holy Mary; the untarnished vessel of virginity; the spiritual paradise of the second Adam (cf. Rom 5:14; 1 Cor 15:21–2, 45–9); the workshop for the union of natures; the market-place of the contract of salvation; the bridal chamber in which the Word took the flesh in marriage; the living bush of human nature, which the fire of a divine birth-pang did not consume (Ex 3:2); the veritable swift cloud (Is 19:1) who carried in her body the one who rides upon the cherubim; the purest fleece drenched with the rain which came down from heaven (Judg 6:37–8), whereby the shepherd clothed himself with the sheep (cf. Jn 10:11); handmaid and mother (cf. Lk 1:38, 43), virgin and heaven, the only bridge for God to mankind; the awesome loom of the divine economy upon which the robe (Jn 19:23) of union was ineffably woven. The loom-worker was the Holy Spirit; the wool-worker the overshadowing power from on high (Lk 1:35). The wool was the ancient fleece of Adam; the interlocking thread the spotless flesh of the Virgin. The weaver's shuttle was propelled by the immeasurable grace of him who wore the robe; the artisan was the Word who entered in through her sense of hearing.[26]

This rich array of imagery, which is inspired by both biblical and nonbiblical sources, builds on a tradition of Marian praise that had already been established by Hesychios of Jerusalem, Attikos of Constantinople and others. However, Proklos went further in his poetic exploration of the paradoxical mystery, always emphasising Mary's central role in the joining of the divine and human natures in Christ. Four other homilies, which were probably all intended either for the single Marian feast that was celebrated in Constantinople in this period (26 December) or for

---

[25] Constas 2003, 56–71, 128.
[26] Proklos of Constantinople, *Homily I.1*, ed. and trans. Constas 2003, 137. 15–31.

Christmas itself,[27] and which were delivered in the course of four or five years before and after the Council of Ephesus in 431, display similar didactic and rhetorical methods.

It is likely that controversy surrounding the Virgin Mary's growing importance in the lives of Constantinopolitan Christians began well before the Council of Ephesus – and perhaps even before Nestorios was appointed to this archiepiscopal see in 428. Constas suggests that debate may have arisen around the establishment of the new feast, probably celebrated on 26 December, which focused especially on Mary's role as virginal mother of Christ.[28] The rise of a female figure within a celestial hierarchy that was by this time visualised in masculine terms may have shocked some bishops within the Eastern Church.[29] Proklos defended the Virgin's holy status especially in his fifth homily, which may have been delivered several years before the Council of Ephesus, perhaps during the episcopate of Attikos of Constantinople (406–25).[30] The oration opens by describing the splendour of the stars, saints, relics and other created entities, which reflect the glory of God that permeates the universe. Proklos goes on to declare that

> ... there is nothing as exalted as Mary the Theotokos, for the [same] one whom all [the prophets] beheld enigmatically in their visions, she carried incarnate in her womb.[31]

The preacher then celebrates the paradoxical nature of the incarnation, contrasting the swelling and changing of Mary's belly with the unchanging nature of God the Word, the pollution that is normally associated with childbirth with the incorruptibility of both Christ and the Virgin, and so on.[32] Such emphasis recalls a standard Christian response to perceived Jewish criticism of the incarnation on the grounds of impurity, an example of which may be found in Proklos' second homily, 'On the Incarnation and on the Lampstand of Zechariah':

[27] Constas 2003, 135, 160, 193–5, 214, 247–8.
[28] Proklos' first homily on the Theotokos may in fact represent the earliest witness to the existence of this feast in Constantinople. See Constas 2003, 57. For shifting scholarly views on the exact date when it was celebrated, but wide current consensus that it fell on the day after Christmas (26 December), see Introduction above, n. 38. In fifth-century Palestine, the commemoration of Mary occurred on 15 August. The feast was celebrated at Mary's place of rest ('kathisma') between Jerusalem and Bethlehem; it was not originally associated with the dormition or death of the Virgin. See Shoemaker 2002, 79–98; Avner 1999; Avner 2011.
[29] Proklos of Constantinople, *Homily I.1*, ed. and trans. Constas 2003, 245.
[30] Constas 2003, 248.
[31] Proklos of Constantinople, *Homily V.2*, ed. and trans. Constas 2003, 259. 47–9.
[32] Proklos of Constantinople, *Homily V.2*, ed. and trans. Constas 2003, 259–61.

Let then the children of the Jews be ashamed, those who disparage the virgin birth saying: 'If a virgin gave birth she is no longer a virgin.' You miserable wretch! Adam was brought into the world and labour did not disgrace his birth, but when God was born according to the flesh his birth was subject to corruption?[33]

By distancing both the birth of Christ, along with his 'birth-giver', from the normal process of conception and childbirth,[34] the preacher describes a unique mystery while also exalting its instrument or receptacle, that is, the Virgin Mary. She is thus revealed as a figure who is greater and holier than all other created beings, including patriarchs, prophets, and saints, because she, a female human being, contained the God who is uncontainable.

It is interesting to note, not only in the five homilies that are attributed to Proklos, but also as we saw earlier in those of Hesychios, a consistent emphasis on women and virgins as recipients of Mary's redemptive power. Proklos writes, for example, in his fourth homily, as follows:

Let women come running, for a woman has brought forth, not the flower of death, but has given birth to the fruit of life. Let virgins also come running, for a virgin has given birth, not by disgracing her virginity, but by sealing her incorruptibility. For the child came forth without ruffling the bed-chambers of the womb; leaving behind, as he grew in grace, the workshop of nature just as he found it. Let mothers come running, for through the Tree of Life a virgin mother has set aright the tree of disobedience. Let daughters also come running, for the obedience of a daughter has avenged the offence of maternal disobedience.[35]

Passages such as this could be interpreted as having little to do with preachers' awareness or interaction with contemporary women, since they usually develop the long-standing theological juxtaposition of Eve and Mary, as female initiator and healer, respectively, of the original Fall from grace. Such invocation of all women in fact became a *topos* in later

---

[33] Proklos of Constantinople, *Homily II.4*, ed. and trans. Constas 2003, 169. 78–82. Cf. *Homily II.9*, ed and trans. Constas 2003, 171–3; *Homily IV.3*, ed. and trans. Constas 2003, 233.

[34] Rather oddly, however, Proklos frequently refers to Mary's 'birth-pangs' (ἡ ὠδίν) in his homilies. See *Homily I.3*, ed. and trans Constas 2003, 138.40; 152 (note); *Homily II.4*, ed. and trans. Constas 2003, 166. 40–1; *Homily IV.1*, ed. and trans. Constas 2003, 226.12. Most Patristic and Byzantine theologians denied Mary the normal process or pangs of birth; see, for example, John of Damascus, *On Orthodox Faith* IV.14, ed. Kotter 1973, vol. 2, 201.75–84; trans. Chase 1958, 364–5. Early exceptions to this rule (probably in order to counter Gnostic or docetic ideas about Christ's birth) include the Latin writers, Tertullian and (possibly) Hilary of Poitiers. See Graef 1963 (2009), 33–4, 43. For thoughtful reflection on Patristic nuance with regard to this subject, see Frost 2019, 38–42.

[35] Proklos of Constantinople, *Homily IV.2*, ed. and trans. Constas 2003, 229. 31–8.

Byzantine homilies and hymns – to the extent that any reference to real women in congregations is difficult to discern. Nevertheless, early fifth-century preachers such as Hesychios and Proklos consistently mentioned women, especially mothers and virgins, in their sermons, suggesting that, thanks to Mary, they were blessed and fulfilled as Christian believers.[36] It is possible that ordinary women, along with powerful ones such as the empress Pulcheria, were perceived as playing an important (albeit non-clerical) role in the Church in this period; the association of such prestige with growing devotion to the Virgin remains to be fully explored.

It is noteworthy too that Proklos, like Hesychios, did not invoke the Theotokos as intercessor anywhere in his surviving sermons. Although he praised her in exalted language, employing a wealth of typological and metaphorical imagery, as we have seen, this was always linked to the role of the Theotokos in the Christological mystery. The emphasis in these orations, whether poetic or discursive, remained on Mary's association with creation, holy spaces or passages to the divine world, and human nature; she was rarely described as 'queen' or mistress of heaven. Proklos, like other bishops who preached in defence of the Virgin's role as Theotokos before, during or just after the Council of Ephesus, wished to defend the Alexandrian understanding of the incarnation, according to which the Logos and Son of God assumed human flesh while remaining fully divine.

One other important theologian and preacher of this period, Cyril of Alexandria, should be mentioned in association with the growth of Marian praise around the time of the Council of Ephesus. Cyril, who joined Proklos in opposing the teachings of Nestorios and who played a key role in the latter's deposition, delivered a sermon at the church of St Mary at Ephesus during the same summer that the Council took place.[37] This work was another landmark in the history of rhetorical praise of the Virgin Mary, as we see in the following famous extract of the homily:

> We hail you, O Mary Mother of God (Θεοτόκε), venerable treasure of the entire world, inextinguishable lamp, crown of virginity, scepter of orthodoxy, imperishable temple, container of him who cannot be contained, Mother (μήτηρ) and Virgin, through whom it is said in the holy Gospels: 'Blessed is he who comes in the name of the Lord' (Mt 21: 9).[38]

---

[36] Constas 2003, 247.

[37] Cyril of Alexandria, *Homily IV, On the Virgin Mary* (*CPG* 5248). Quasten calls this 'the most famous Marian sermon of antiquity' in Quasten 1994, vol. 3, 131. See also seven others, all delivered in Ephesus in the summer of the Council (431), according to Quasten. Further bibliography includes Caro 1972, vol. 2, 269–83; Santer 1975; Peltomaa 2001, 68–71.

[38] *ACO* I. I. 2, 102; trans. Gambero 1999, 247–8.

Cyril, like Proklos, sought to convey a precise theological message, namely, that God, the Word, had taken flesh in Mary's womb while remaining eternally of one substance with the Father. The implications of this teaching for the Virgin, who 'contained the uncontainable' from the moment of his conception, were immense, both for her and for the rest of humanity. In an earlier (second) letter to Nestorios, dated to February 430, Cyril had elaborated this position more fully:

> Scripture, after all, has not asserted that the Word united a man's role (ἀνθρώπου πρόσωπον) to himself but that he has become flesh. But the Word's 'becoming flesh' is just the fact that he shared flesh and blood like us, made our body his own and issued as man from woman without abandoning his being God and his being begotten of God the Father but remaining what he was when he assumed flesh as well ... This is the key to the holy fathers' thinking. This is why they dare to call the holy Virgin 'Theotokos' – not because the Word's nature, his Godhead, originated from the holy Virgin but because his holy body, endowed with life and reason, was born from her and the Word was 'born' in flesh because [he was] united to this body substantially (καθ' ὑπόστασιν).[39]

Several other fifth-century bishops or presbyters appear to have delivered homilies in praise of the Theotokos. These include Theodotos of Ankyra[40] and Chrysippos of Jerusalem.[41] Some variation in the theological and poetic treatment of the Theotokos is visible in this period,[42] but her place, as the link between God and his creation, is mostly expressed throughout these liturgical texts by means of a rich array of typological and metaphorical images. The most significant shared feature of these homilies, which serves to distinguish them from works composed about a century later, is their lack of focus either on Mary's human qualities – as revealed, for example, in her maternal care for the infant Christ – or on her intercessory power.[43] From Jerusalem to Constantinople, as the surviving

---

[39] Cyril of Alexandria, *Second Letter to Nestorios* 7, ed. *ACO* I.I.1, 28.12–22, trans. Wickham 1983, 9–11, repr. Russell 2000, 37 (with one adjustment).

[40] *CPG* 6128, *BHG* 1966, PG 77, 1389–1412. See also Aubineau 1969, 7–8; *CPG* 6136, *BHG* 1143g, ed. Jugie 1925 (1990), 318–35; Aubineau 1969, 8.

[41] *CPG* 6705, *BHG* 1144n, ed. Jugie 1925 (1990), 336–43.

[42] For example, Chrysippos states in his homily on the Theotokos that she will rise on the final day of judgement with everyone else from the fallen state that she shares with the rest of humanity. See Jugie 1925, 338. 28–9.

[43] Exceptions to this rule, especially with regard to the former category, can of course be found in the fifth-century corpus. Chrysippos, for example, writes about Mary's motherhood of Jesus in the following passage – which has as its primary emphasis the antithetical contrast between Christ's vulnerability as a baby and his power as God: ' ... she became a mother without losing her virginity; she produced milk, without having experienced marriage; she nursed the infant, and there was no

homilies of Hesychios and Proklos testify, fifth-century preachers emphasised the Christological importance of the Theotokos. Such preoccupation
with doctrine, as opposed to Marian devotion, does not necessarily indicate
the absence of such feeling among fifth-century Christians; it is possible
that church leaders avoided open veneration of the Virgin in their sermons
so as to promote a theological message that had gained prominence during
the controversies that led up to the Council of Ephesus. These preachers
thus succeeded in channelling Marian devotion towards a more intellectual – or mystical – understanding of the Virgin's central role in the
incarnation of Christ.

A Transitional Phase: Focus on Mary as 'Mediator' in Late Fifth- and Early Sixth-Century Greek Homiletics

One of the greatest problems in assessing the homiletic and hymnographic
traditions of late antiquity and Byzantium lies in our inability to date or
place many texts – sometimes even within several centuries. Pauline Allen,
Theodora Antonopoulou and other scholars have repeatedly alerted us to
this problem;[44] it is unlikely ever to be fully resolved, owing to the wealth
of material (both published and unpublished) and lack of scholarly per-
sonnel and resources that would be necessary to tackle it. For the period
between about the middle of the fifth and the end of the sixth century,
there exist a number of pseudonymous or wrongly attributed homilies.[45]
Roberto Caro has gone some way towards untangling this complicated
tradition, but the attribution and dating of many works remain
controversial.[46] In the discussion that follows, I intend to apply certain
criteria which have been noted so far in this chapter, including the
portrayal of Mary as a remote theological or more personal – indeed

---

father for the infant on earth.' See Chrysippos of Jerusalem, *Homily on the Holy Theotokos Mary* 3,
ed. Jugie 1925 (1990), 341. 4–7.

[44] Allen 1998, 202; Allen 2011, 70–1; Antonopoulou 2013, 186.

[45] Cunningham 1996; Allen 1998; Allen 2011; *CPG*, vol. 3.

[46] Caro 1971–3; but see also Marx 1940; Allen 1998. Other sixth-century (or possibly late fifth-century)
preachers who focused on the Theotokos in their sermons include Anastasios of Antioch (d. 599;
CPG 6948–9 [on the Annunciation], 6950 [on the Hypapante]); various pseudonymous authors
including (ps-)Gregory Thaumatourgos (*CPG* 1775–6 [on the Annunciation]); (ps-)John
Chrysostom (*CPG* 4519 [on the Annunciation]); (ps-)Athanasios (*CPG* 2268 [on the
Annunciation]); (ps-)Gregory of Nyssa (*CPG* 3214) [on the Annunciation]; and Theoteknos of
Livias, who may have flourished in Palestine sometime between 550 and 650 (see Wenger 1955, 96–
110; *CPG* 7418). I am unable, for reasons of space, to deal with all of these writers in detail in the
present study; Theoteknos' homily on the Dormition will be treated in Chapter 6 along with other
early and middle Byzantine orations on this subject.

maternal – figure, in order to argue a late fifth- or sixth-century date for two controversial but important works, namely, (ps-)Basil of Seleucia's *Homily XXXIX, On the Annunciation*[47] and (ps-)Proklos of Constantinople's *Homily VI, On the Theotokos.*[48] Scholarly debate concerning the dating and attribution of problematic homilies has previously focused largely on their Christological content; this ignores the larger question of literary and theological emphasis on the Virgin Mary as a figure of importance in her own right. I believe that Mariological developments did occur between approximately the end of the fifth century and the middle of the sixth and that these may help to situate disputed works. Other considerations, such as the literary form – and especially the use of dramatic dialogue in connection with, for example, the Annunciation scene – may also play a part in this process. Although such dating remains hypothetical (and risks circular argumentation), I suggest that it helps us to sketch the broader picture of a developing Marian cult in the course of the early Byzantine centuries.

(Ps-)Basil of Seleucia's *Homily XXXIX, On the Annunciation* has attracted considerable notice in recent years, partly because its acclamations of the Theotokos resemble some of those that appear in the *Akathistos Hymn.*[49] Arguments concerning the authenticity of this oration have focused mainly on the possible circumstances of its delivery, Christological content and rhetorical style.[50] Whereas B. Marx argued against Basil's authorship of the homily, mainly because its theological content and style are uncharacteristic of this bishop's Antiochene background and homiletic oeuvre, suggesting that it might instead have been composed by Proklos, Caro defended its authenticity. The association of the homily with the feast of the Annunciation, which was not added to the liturgical calendar until 560,[51] has long been ruled out;[52] a number of early homilies were composed on this theme, owing to its

---

[47] *CPG* 6656. 39, *BHG* 1112p, PG 85, 425–52.

[48] *CPG* 5805, *BHGa* 1110, *BHGn* 1126e, ed. Leroy 1967, 298–324.

[49] (ps-)Basil of Seleucia, *Homily XXXIX, On the Annunciation* (*CPG* 6656. 39). L.-M. Peltomaa (2001, 77–85) provides an excellent analysis of the homily; cf. Caro 1972, vol. 2, 285–308. For the *Akathistos Hymn*, see Chapter 1, 53–8. Whereas most scholars believe that the (ps-)Basil homily influenced the *Akathistos Hymn*, Peltomaa argues the reverse.

[50] B. Marx (1940, 84–9) argued that the homily was composed by Proklos of Constantinople. This view is followed by J. Quaston, G. Godet, A. Kreuz, R. Laurentin and F. Diekamp; see Peltomaa 2001, 78, n. 145. Caro, however, challenges this attribution, reaffirming Basil of Seleucia as the author of the homily; see Caro 1972, vol. 2, 288–305.

[51] van Esbroeck 1968–9; Allen 2011, 72.

[52] Lenain de Tillemont argued against the early date (and authenticity) of this homily on these grounds, but later scholars, including especially Marx, have since pointed out that preachers and hymnographers celebrated the Annunciation as a theme long before the feast had been added to the Constantinopolitan liturgical calendar. Such celebrations usually took place in association with the

importance in the biblical account of Christ's incarnation.[53] However, there are features which suggest that it belongs not to the middle of the fifth century, as has previously been argued, but rather to the later part of this century or even to the early sixth. Before discussing this possibility, however, it is worth briefly describing the work and highlighting its importance as a link between the primarily Christological material that was associated with the Council of Ephesus or its immediate aftermath and the more devotional – although still highly theological – homilies that appeared slightly later.

The homily begins with protestations of humility, which are in line with the rhetorical conventions of the genre and thus reveal little about the orator.[54] After an excursus in which discovery of Mary's role in the incarnation is compared with Moses' journey out of Egypt and up Mt Sinai, as the purified Christian believer begins to take in the mystery of this exalted subject, the oration proceeds to unfold its Christological message. Scholars have noted a careful use of theological language in the work, which avoids both the extreme Apollinarian and Nestorian positions.[55] The term 'Theotokos' is used nine times in the homily, although Mary is also called 'all-holy Virgin' and 'holy Mother of the Lord'. On the basis of its discursive theological passages and choice of epithets for the Virgin, we may conclude that the homily on the Annunciation displays a primarily Alexandrian Christological position. Some anomalies, such as the statements that the Logos 'puts on flesh' (περιβάλλεται σάρκα) and that 'he truly bore an ensouled body' (σάρκα ... ἀληθῶς εψυχωμένην ἐφόρεσε),[56] evoke a more Antiochene understanding of theology; overall, however, this work expresses a high Christological position, with regard to both the Son of God and his mother.[57]

---

feast of the Nativity of Christ. See Lenain de Tillemont 1637–98, vol. 15, 344–7; Marx 1940, 85; Caro 1972, vol. 2, 288.

[53] See Caro 1971, vol. 1, 241–55 (Antipater of Bostra); Caro 1972, vol. 2, 285–308 ([ps-]Basil of Seleucia, *Homily XXXIX*); 309–44 ([ps-]Proklos of Constantinople, *Homily VI*); 468–577 (numerous other writers).

[54] This has not prevented some scholars from drawing conclusions about the homily's authorship on this basis; whereas Marx, who wishes to assign the work to Proklos of Constantinople, argues that the author's modesty reflects his unfamiliarity with the congregation at Ephesus, in or just before 431 CE, L. M. Peltomaa responds that such a humble attitude does not fit with Proklos' well-known reputation as a panegyrist of the Virgin Mary; see Marx 1940, 86; Peltomaa 2001, 82.

[55] Caro 1972, vol. 2, 292–3, 298–308; Peltomaa 2001, 78.

[56] (ps-)Basil of Seleucia, *Homily XXXIX, On the Annunciation*, PG 85, 432C, 433B, 445C (τὴν ὁμοούσιον ἐμοὶ σάρκα περιβαλλόμενος); 437C–D (σάρκα ... ἀληθῶς εψυχωμένην ἐφόρεσε). Cf. Peltomaa 2001, 79.

[57] See, for example, the following passage: 'For the One born was not merely human but God the Logos, made incarnate of a virgin and assuming flesh of the same essence as me, so that he might save like by means of like', PG 85, 445C; quoted and translated by Peltomaa 2001, 81.

Although most scholars have dated the homily to the mid fifth century,
sometime between the first and second Councils of Ephesus (431 and 449)
on the basis of its highly Christological content, it contains a few elements
which cause me, as noted above, to suspect a slightly later date. To deal
with the Christological question first, it seems likely on the basis of
homilies that can securely be dated to the sixth century (such as those of
Severos of Antioch) that such preoccupations did not cease after the
conciliar debates of the first half of the fifth – in fact preachers continued
to emphasise this aspect of Marian devotion throughout the sixth and
subsequent centuries, as we shall see in the course of this book.
Controversy concerning the Chalcedonian definition may indeed have
caused preachers including Severos to employ Mary as a means of proving
their theological position: whereas her virginity proved the divinity of
Christ, her humanity demonstrated the reality of his incarnation. Thus
the highly Christological content of (ps-)Basil's homily does not, to my
mind, necessarily indicate an Ephesine context for its delivery; that it fails
to employ specifically Chalcedonian vocabulary may reflect a conciliatory
position that is also visible in the *Akathistos Hymn* – assuming, as I do, that
this important work was also composed in the late fifth or early sixth
century.[58]

More telling, in my view, are various features in the (ps-)Basil homily
that do not correlate with the works of Hesychios, Proklos and other early
fifth-century Marian preachers. First, and most importantly, it is worth
noting this homilist's focus on Mary as his primary subject of praise or, as
he puts it, as 'the great mystery of the Theotokos that is above understanding and language'.[59] Although this author's predecessors praised the Virgin
in exalted language, they were always careful to place her within
a Christological context.[60] (Ps-)Basil incorporates such didactic considerations, as we have seen, but he also – unlike his homiletic forerunners –
includes some elements that appear to be new. For example, as noted
already by Peltomaa and others, this preacher describes the Virgin as one
who 'mediates between God and humans' (μεσιτεύουσα Θεῷ καὶ
ἀνθρώποις).[61] He further reveals his belief in Mary's exalted position in
relation to Christ when he instructs his congregation later in the homily to

[58] N. Constas also adopts this argument in his criticism of Peltomaa's early dating of the *Akathistos
Hymn*, suggesting that 'the language of Chalcedon was deliberately avoided in the interest of church
unity' during the period following its promulgation; see Constas 2005, 358.
[59] (ps-)Basil of Seleucia, *Homily XXXIX, On the Annunciation*, PG 85, 429B.   [60] See above, 70–7.
[61] (ps-)Basil of Seleucia, *Homily XXXIX, On the Annunciation*, PG 85, 444B; Caro 1972, vol. 2, 307;
Peltomaa 2001, 80–1.

pray to the 'all-holy Virgin' that she may lead them towards a merciful reception at the Throne of Judgement.[62] Such a vision of Mary's intercessory role at the Last Judgement does not appear anywhere in the earlier fifth-century liturgical works that I have surveyed; it also seems likely that it reflects the various apocryphal traditions on her dormition that were circulating in the Greek-speaking world by about the end of the fifth or early sixth century.[63]

One other aspect of this homily deserves comment, namely, its focus on Mary as a human mother in a passage that follows a brief dialogic treatment of the Annunciation. The preacher visualises the Virgin holding the infant Christ in her arms, inventing a monologue in which she addresses him with some bemusement, as follows:

> 'What then shall I do for you? Shall I nurse you or shall I theologise? Shall I care for you as a mother or shall I worship you as a servant? Shall I embrace you as a son or shall I pray to you as God? Shall I give milk or offer incense . . . ?'[64]

Such dramatic treatment of this subject, which foreshadows that which Romanos the Melodist would employ in relation to various biblical scenes and characters, gives the audience a glimpse into Mary's thoughts and emotions on giving birth to a divine son. However, it also plays an important didactic role, using antithetical statements in order to demonstrate Christ's divine and human natures. Above all, however, such vivid portrayal of the scene, with the help of the rhetorical device of *ethopoiia*, changes the Theotokos from the 'flat', or primarily theological, treatment of earlier fifth-century liturgical texts to a fully human character with whom congregations – and perhaps particularly women – could identify.[65]

Taken together, these theological and literary preoccupations seem to indicate a late fifth- or early sixth-century date for this pseudonymous homily. Although I am inclined, for the reasons stated above, to place the work somewhat later than has so far been suggested,[66] it is also possible to establish a *terminus ante quem*. On the grounds that the preacher cites only the 'Memory of Mary' as the occasion for his oration, with the

---

[62] (ps-)Basil of Seleucia, *Homily XXXIX, On the Annunciation*, PG 85, 452B; Caro 1972, vol. 2, 307–8.
[63] Shoemaker 2002, 26–7.
[64] (ps-)Basil of Seleucia, *Homily XXXIX, On the Annunciation*, PG 85, 448B (my translation).
[65] Here I differ from Peltomaa, who uses the adjective 'flat' to describe the portrayal of the Virgin Mary in this homily, as in other authentic works of the period of Ephesus; see Peltomaa 2001, 82.
[66] Caro 1972, vol. 2, esp. 300–5; Peltomaa 2001, 82 (who concludes first that the homily was influenced by the *Akathistos Hymn*, rather than vice versa, and second, that it was delivered after the Council of Ephesus).

Annunciation being a thematic rather than a festal preoccupation, it is likely that he delivered it before the latter feast was added to the Constantinopolitan liturgical calendar in 560.[67] It remains impossible to determine exactly where and when the homily was first composed and delivered, but it thus contains elements both of more ancient Marian panegyrics (in its lack of festal or 'biographical' content) and of post-fifth-century preoccupations, such as emphasis on the Virgin's intercessory power and human response to the archangel Gabriel's message.

Another oration, which has attracted considerable scholarly attention with respect to its attribution and date, is (ps-)Proklos' *Homily VI* entitled 'An *Enkomion* on the Theotokos'.[68] This is a long and complex work, which includes sections of panegyrical prose that frame two alphabetical acrostic dialogues: the first is between Joseph and Mary, while the second embroiders Luke's dramatic account of the encounter between Mary and the archangel Gabriel. Scholars including La Piana, Marx, Leroy (who produced a critical edition of the text), Aubineau and Caro have debated not only the authenticity of this homily, but also whether it is actually a composite work consisting of an early fifth-century core to which the dialogic sections were later added.[69] There is not space here to summarise all of these arguments in detail; suffice it to say that the strongest case against Proklian authorship lies in the structure of the homily. First, it is much longer than any of the fifth-century bishop's other orations and second, the dramatic dialogues do not belong to his normal style of homiletic delivery.[70] Leaving aside the question whether the work is composite (which may never be definitively proved), the dialogues suggest at least a late fifth- or sixth-century date, but the lack of reference to Mary's intercessory function or personal qualities, as a human being who is capable of intellectual and emotional transformation, seem to predate either the *Akathistos Hymn* or the kontakia of Romanos. It is worth adding that the highly theological and rhetorical nature of the entire text suggests

---

[67] For discussion of six early homilies that address the theme, rather than the feast, of the Annunciation, see Allen 2011, 72–4.

[68] *CPG* 5805, (ps-)Proklos, *Homily VI, On the Theotokos*, ed. Leroy 1967, 298–324 (see above, n. 48).

[69] La Piana 1912 (1971), 128–52; Marx 1940, 90–3; Leroy 1967, 273–92; Aubineau 1972, 589–92; Caro 1972, vol. 2, 308–44.

[70] Leroy, who defends the authenticity of the homily, argues that although other examples of dialogue do not appear in contemporary Greek homiletics, Proklos might have derived the idea from Syriac dialogue homilies (*soghyatha*). Aubineau dismisses this idea as too hypothetical; it is worth adding that Sebastian Brock dates most Syriac *soghyatha* to the fifth or sixth centuries. Whether mutual influence might have taken place in the early fifth century thus remains open to question. See Leroy 1967, 275–6; Aubineau 1972, 590–1; Brock 1994 (2010), 12–13.

that it was composed for a well-educated audience. Leroy, along with other scholars including La Piana, noted some peculiar – possibly early fifth-century – exegetical elements, including references to death and the Devil (as important protagonists in the playing out of God's dispensation for salvation) and emphasis on Joseph's doubt, which threatened (if an angel had not intervened) to persist until the actual birth of Christ from the Virgin Mary.[71]

Owing to the fact that dramatic dialogues came to feature so importantly in later Byzantine homilies and hymns on the Annunciation, it is worth briefly considering the ones that appear in this (ps-)Proklian homily. As in the case of the later examples, both sections of the oration present these dialogues in direct speech, although the preacher occasionally interjects extradiegetical remarks (which depart from the alphabetical acrostic that governs the speeches of the two protagonists).[72] The purpose of both dialogues is primarily theological. In the first dialogue, Mary responds gently to Joseph's opening accusations by invoking the prophets, testifying to the miraculousness of Christ's conception, and urging her betrothed husband to believe and thereby participate in the promised salvation. This dialogue, which is expressed in rhyming iambic couplets, thus resembles a lawsuit: the Virgin asks for a chance to plead her defence (*apologia*), but only secures Joseph's promise to wait and see at the birth of the infant. Following Matthew's account (Mt 1:20–1), the preacher then explains that Joseph was satisfied of the truth of Mary's story after he received a visitation from an angel. A string of antithetical statements follows, in which the Virgin's suspected shamelessness is contrasted with her actual purity and holiness. The second dialogue begins with Mary expressing her disbelief and lack of understanding of the miracle, on the basis of her speech in Luke 1: 34. In the ensuing conversation, Gabriel instructs the Virgin about the paradoxical event that is taking place in her womb: Christ remains eternal, majestic and divine even as he assumes the earthly state of human nature. Although she asks for reassurance, Mary does not experience the intellectual and emotional transformation that is described by later liturgical writers such as Romanos or Germanos of Constantinople. There is a static quality to this dialogue, which helps to emphasise the theological

---

[71] Leroy 1967, 279–81.

[72] The terms 'intradiegetical' and 'extradiegetical' refer to the direct speech which may be used either between characters who exist within the narrative framework of a homily or hymn or to that which the preacher or hymnographer directs to his own audience; for further discussion of these terms, see Cunningham 2003 (where the terms 'intratextual and extratextual' are used for the same phenomena); Eriksen 2013, esp. 100–8.

rather than personal drama of the Annunciation scene. As in earlier homilies, such as the genuine works of Proklos, the preacher implies that the incarnation took place at the time that Mary heard Gabriel's greeting. He also stresses, like most patristic writers, her passive role in this event; addressing the Virgin himself at the end of the dialogue, (ps-)Proklos instructs her to 'cast off doubt and eagerly accept the greeting'. For she does not know about the divine plan that lies behind the event or the meaning of Gabriel's name, that is, 'man of God'.[73]

Whereas the use of dialogues, for dramatic and didactic effect, may suggest a somewhat later date for this homily than the early or middle part of the fifth century, it remains firmly in line with the primarily theological approach to the Theotokos that characterised the liturgical sermons of that period. Unlike (ps-)Basil's *Homily XXXIX, On the Annunciation*,[74] there are no allusions here to Mary's intercessory power or human qualities. A number of other homilies, some of which also became associated with the feast of the Annunciation (although in fact they only dealt with this thematically in connection with their celebration of Christ's incarnation), remain uncertain in their attributions and dates.[75] These include a lively homily that is attributed to Gregory Thaumatourgos, but which more probably belongs to the late fifth or early sixth century.[76] Its celebration of a feast, ostensibly the Annunciation but more likely the Nativity of Christ, suggests a date before the former feast was adopted by Justinian in 560.[77] Caro has also pointed to its use of unusual vocabulary in relation to Christ's incarnation, which may suggest Arian influence or else a provincial lack of awareness with regard to the Christological definitions of Chalcedon.[78] Various other homilies, some of which were also associated with the Annunciation, remain to be studied carefully with respect not only to their dogmatic content, but also their place in the Marian homiletic tradition.[79] The lack of intercessory invocation, combined with apparent unawareness of individual Marian feasts or allusions to apocryphal texts concerning her infancy and death, suggest that they belong to an intermediate period between the first burst of her liturgical celebration

---

[73] (ps-)Proklos, *Homily VI, On the Theotokos* XII.1, ed. Leroy 1967, 313. In the next line, the author tells Mary to 'lay aside feminine humility and to assume a manly purpose'; see my comments on the ambiguity of gender categories with regard to the Virgin in the Introduction, 25–34.

[74] See above, n. 49.   [75] See Caro 1972, vol. 2, esp. 345–577.

[76] (ps-)Gregory Thaumatourgos, *Homily I, On the Annunciation*, PG 10, 1145–56.

[77] Although the homily begins by celebrating the Annunciation, even including a short dialogic section in the middle, it ends with praise of the Nativity of Christ, juxtaposing in a rather unusual way the manger in which the infant's body lay with the altar on which the heavenly bread would be placed in the eucharistic offering. See ibid., PG 10, 1153C.

[78] Caro 1972, vol. 2, 487–91.   [79] See Caro 1972, vol. 2, 468–577.

and the more devotional and festal praise that would develop from about the middle of the sixth century onward – especially in the kontakia of Romanos the Melodist. Further studies, to complement the work of Roberto Caro and others, however, will help to situate these important homiletic texts. In my view, one other text, the *Akathistos Hymn*, may also be dated to this transitional period on the basis both of its unique formulation of Marian imagery and its use of mediatory and intercessory language.[80] With regard to the latter category, however, the *Akathistos Hymn* seems to reflect a later stage than do some of the homilies that I have just been discussing. Could this indicate an even later date of composition than theirs – perhaps during the first decades of the sixth century?

Sixth-Century Developments: Severos of Antioch and Other Preachers

We turn now to the sixth-century liturgical texts, which reflect an exceptionally creative phase of Marian liturgical expression. Pauline Allen has identified and analysed most of the surviving Byzantine Marian homilies of the sixth century.[81] Her various studies help to situate these works within the larger tradition; in line with my own conclusions, Allen sees this as a period in which preachers' focus shifted gradually from purely Christological considerations to more Mariological praise and devotion. Even if we take into account the problems of date and attribution, which afflict this corpus as much as any other in the Byzantine homiletic tradition,[82] we are left with some remarkable examples of Marian preaching by figures including Severos of Antioch and Abraham of Ephesus. Such preachers flourished not only in Constantinople, but also in Asia Minor and Palestine. Their works display an ongoing preoccupation with Christological controversies, especially between adherents of Chalcedon and those who opposed it because they upheld 'one nature' in Christ, but also growing attention to Mary as a figure of importance in her own right. It is also possible to trace in these homilies the addition of feasts such as the Annunciation and the Dormition in the course of the sixth century. Whereas Severos preached on the subject of the Annunciation in the context of the pre-Nativity celebrations that were still observed in Antioch at the beginning of the century,[83] Abraham mentioned the recent institution of the feast of the Annunciation in a homily that may have been

---

[80] *Pace* Peltomaa 2001.   [81] See Allen 1996; Allen 1998; Allen 2011.   [82] See Chapter 3, n. 13.
[83] Allen 2011, 72.

delivered between 560 and 563.[84] Although many sixth-century preachers
directed panegyrical praise towards the Theotokos, it is also noticeable that
some, such as Leontios of Constantinople, appear to have ignored her in
their festal or exegetical homilies.[85] In evaluating the contributions of those
homilists who did compose orations in honour of Mary, I will begin with
the important proponent of one-nature Christology who also became
patriarch of Antioch, Severos.

Severos of Antioch was a prolific writer whose oeuvre includes 125
cathedral homilies, as well as nearly 300 letters.[86] The most important
sermons for our purposes are those on the Annunciation (mentioned
above), the Nativity of Christ and two on the memory of the Virgin
Mary.[87] One of the remarkable aspects of Severos' homiletic works, as
opposed to those of most Byzantine preachers, is that these can sometimes
be dated and even placed with regard to the circumstances of their delivery.
Homily XIV, 'In memory of the holy Mother of God', for example, is
known to have been delivered in the church of the Theotokos in Antioch
on 2 or 3 February 513 on the feast of the *Hypapante*.[88] Severos delivered his
homilies in churches in and around Antioch when he served as the anti-
Chalcedonian patriarch of that city between 512 and 518.[89] Following the
death of the Miaphysite emperor Anastasios in 518, the patriarch Severos
was condemned and expelled from his seat; however, he managed to escape
and spent most of the rest of his life in Egypt.[90] His surviving homilies,
which were originally delivered in Greek, survive only in Syriac translations
that were produced by a contemporary bishop, Paul of Callinicum, and
revised by Jacob of Edessa in 701 CE.[91]

---

[84] Abraham of Ephesus, *Homily on the Annunciation*, ed. Jugie 1922 (2003), 443.2.14–20. On the date of
      the feast's introduction into the liturgical calendar of Constantinople, see Introduction, n. 57.
[85] Leontios of Constantinople, *Homilies*, trans. Allen with Datema 1991, 10. According to Allen and
      Datema, the Virgin Mary features only rarely in Leontios' homilies. She is called 'Virgin', 'Virgin
      Mary' or 'Mary', but never 'Theotokos'. It is also noteworthy that there are no surviving homilies by
      Leontios on feasts or themes related to the Virgin Mary.
[86] Allen and Hayward 2004, 39–55.
[87] Severos of Antioch, *Homily II, On the Annunciation*, ed. Brière and Graffin 1976, PO 38.2, 272–91;
      Homily XIV, On the Memory of the Theotokos, ed. Brière and Graffin 1976, 400–15; *Homily XXXVI,
      On the Nativity of Christ*, ed. Brière, Graffin and Lash 1972, PO 36.3, 458–73; *Homily LXVII, On the
      Holy Mother of God and Ever-Virgin*, ed. Brière 1912, PO 8.2, 349–67.
[88] Downey 1961, 659; Allen and Hayward 2004, 107.   [89] Allen and Hayward 2004, 4–5.
[90] Allen and Hayward 2004, 24–30. After about 530, Justinian and Theodora attempted reconciliation
      with exiled anti-Chalcedonian bishops, including Severos; however, such progress was rescinded in
      536 at a synod in Constantinople and Severos was again condemned.
[91] Fragments of the original Greek versions survive in *catenae* (chains of quotations), *Homily LXXVII*
      (transmitted under the name of Gregory of Nyssa or Hesychios of Jerusalem), or in writings of
      Severos' opponents. See Allen and Hayward 2004, 31.

Although Pauline Allen has already treated Severos of Antioch's Mariological homilies in several wider studies, it is possible to add a few observations to her findings.[92] First, it is noticeable that the early sixth-century patriarch tends to avoid the poetic imagery and typology that was so widely used in fifth-century Greek homilies on the Theotokos. He refers to her for the most part as 'Virgin' or 'Theotokos' – branching out in his *Homily XIV, On the Memory of the Theotokos*, to describe her also (and with careful justification) as 'prophetess', 'apostle' and 'martyr'.[93] In general, Severos prefers discursive to poetic methods of teaching Christological theology. He devotes large sections of each homily to expounding the doctrine of Christ's incarnation, as we see somewhat later in the same work:

> Therefore the one who was born was also named Emmanuel, since he is one indivisible and without confusion, out of two natures, both divinity and humanity. This one who, since he possesses all the unique and indivisible qualities, namely, his incorporeal generation from the Father and the very same divinity (for he alone was begotten of the only One, even God from God) and his birth from the Virgin (for he alone was born in the flesh of a woman not joined in marriage and the only one of her kind), did not violate his mother's virginity – how was this one, after the inexpressible union, prepared to be divided and broken by the duality of the natures, as the Synod of Chalcedon has taught since it followed the foolish teachings of Nestorius? But he is in all respects one and unique . . .[94]

Severos stresses here and elsewhere in his homilies that Christ, although condescending to be born of the flesh of a virginal woman and thus assuming human nature, remained fully divine, in one hypostasis, one person and one nature (out of two, the divine and the human).[95] Such teaching is also frequently combined with polemical invective against the Council of Chalcedon and its supporters, as we also see in the passage quoted above.

The implications of Severos' one-nature doctrine for Mary, the Theotokos, are significant, but it is noticeable that he does not focus on her – even in the homilies that were delivered largely in her honour – to the same extent as did Proklos of Constantinople or Hesychios of Jerusalem.

---

[92] Allen 1996, esp. 165–70; Allen 1998, 207–8; Allen 2011, esp. 72–3.

[93] Severos of Antioch, *Homily XIV, On the Memory of the Theotokos* 3, ed. Brière and Graffin 1976, PO 38.3, 400; trans. Allen and Hayward 2004, 112; cf. Allen 1996, 168.

[94] Severos of Antioch, *Homily XIV, On the Memory of the Theotokos* 17, trans. Allen and Hayward 2004, 116–17.

[95] Cf. Severos of Antioch, *Homily II, On the Annunciation* 6, ed. Brière and Graffin (with Lash and Sauget) 1976, PO 38.2, 274–5.

Nevertheless, we do find a few references to her role as mediator in these homilies, in contrast to the more theological focus of the fifth-century works. Following the didactic Christological section that we just noted in his *Homily XIV, On the Memory of the Theotokos*, Severos writes as follows about Mary:

> This is why we honour also the holy Mother of God and ever-virgin Mary with honours which are surpassing great, inasmuch as she is the one who is able, more than all the other saints, to offer up supplications on our behalf, and since we too make our boast of her as having acquired her as the adornment of our race – the rational earth from whom the second Adam, who is neither fashioned nor made, fashioned himself in flesh (cf. 1 Cor 15:44–5) – the plant of virginity from which Christ the heavenly ladder was prepared in flesh by the Spirit, so that we ourselves might be able to ascend to heaven when we fix our footsteps firmly upon it (cf. Is 9:36) . . .[96]

It is also worth highlighting Severos' treatment of the Annunciation, in which he adds to a growing tradition of elaborating rhetorically the dialogue between the Virgin and the archangel Gabriel, as recounted in Luke 1:26–38. Like most patristic commentators, the patriarch allows Mary only a minor role in accepting, or even understanding, her miraculous virginal conception.[97] He explains that the incarnation occurred in 'this brief instant and in this indivisible space of time' during which 'the word of the archangel was proffered and the Word of God was found in Mary's womb'.[98] Although the Virgin doubts and is persuaded only gradually by the archangel's arguments, it is clear that she has little say over the outcome of this interview. We also find scant interest in Mary's inner feelings or thoughts in this homily, compared with later treatments of the subject, for example, in Romanos the Melodist's kontakia or the eighth-century dialogic homily on the Annunciation by Germanos of Constantinople.

Severos of Antioch thus occupies a transitional position between the more theological orations of the fifth century, in which Mary was celebrated above all as the all-pure Bearer of God, and those of the mid sixth, when she became intercessor and human mother. His cathedral homilies offered opportunities for the teaching of Christological faith, expression of

---

[96] Severos of Antioch, *Homily XIV, On the Memory of the Theotokos* 18, trans. Allen and Hayward 2004, 117.

[97] For comprehensive discussion of this issue, see Constas 2003, 273–313.

[98] Severos of Antioch, *Homily II, On the Annunciation* 11, ed. Brière and Graffin (with Lash and Sauget) 1976, PO 38.2, 278–9. Allen comments that this notion of an instantaneous conception, which was shared in most patristic exegesis on this subject, may have derived from anti-Origenist polemic; see Allen 2011, 72.

praise to God, his mother and his saints, and ethical direction. There is some invocation of the mediating role of the Theotokos here, as we have seen, but this does not take centre stage. One other aspect, which I have not yet mentioned, is the preacher's apparent lack of awareness of major feasts. This is surprising in some cases, such as that of the *Hypapante* which had been observed in Jerusalem since at least the late fourth century; on at least one of these occasions, as we have seen, Severos chose to deliver an *enkomion* on the Theotokos without any clear reference to the event of Christ's Presentation in the Temple. As for the Annunciation, Severos treated this topic from a thematic rather than a festal point of view. As mentioned above, the feast was not officially added to the Byzantine liturgical calendar until 560 CE – long after Severos delivered his homily during the period leading up to the Nativity of Christ.[99] Finally, it is noticeable that Severos of Antioch only rarely celebrates the Theotokos as a figure of importance in her own right. He mentions the Virgin Mary in his homilies most often in connection with her role as birth-giver of Christ, the Son and Word of God.

In the decades that followed Severos' deposition from the patriarchate of Antioch in 518, during which the emperors Justin I and Justinian embraced Chalcedonian rather than Miaphysite Christological doctrine, we see a steady growth in the cult of the Virgin Mary. Pauline Allen suggests that this was a period in which two separate but parallel paths, of doctrine and liturgy, began to converge in the Mariological tradition.[100] Not only did Justinian (527–65) institute important new liturgical feasts in which Mary played a central role (including the *Hypapante*, the Annunciation and possibly her Nativity),[101] but he also dedicated new churches to her throughout the empire.[102] Cyril Mango argues that belief in the Virgin's role as protector of Constantinople was already flourishing during the reign of Justinian, with her main relic, a robe, being celebrated in literary texts from either the sixth or early eighth century onward.[103] The Virgin's cult

---

[99] According to Allen, the homily was delivered between 18 November and 16 December 512; this was therefore one of the earliest of Severos' episcopal homilies. See Allen 2011, 72.

[100] Allen 1996, 169.   [101] See Introduction, 11–12.

[102] Prokopios, *Buildings*; for a list of precise references, see Introduction, n. 55; cf. Peltomaa 2015, 136, n. 66.

[103] Mango 2000, 19. On an early (either sixth- or early seventh-century) kontakion to the Holy Fathers which mentions the Virgin's 'garment' (*esthes*), see Mango 2000, 23. For other homilies that celebrated the robe and the belt, see below, 129–33. Another writer who mentions the Virgin's garment or 'mantle' is the late sixth-century Latin writer, Gregory of Tours. On Gregory's use of Byzantine sources, see Cameron 1975. I am grateful to Andrea Olsen Lam for reminding me of Gregory's narratives concerning the miraculous power of the Virgin's robe; see also Chapter 5, 182–3.

appears to have begun in association with healing shrines that were located within or just outside the imperial city; although such shrines often had modest origins, they attracted increasing imperial or aristocratic patronage in the course of the sixth century. It is also worth mentioning the use of an image of the Theotokos, who replaced that of the goddess Victory ('Nike') , on imperial lead seals during the last years of Justinian's successor, Justin II (565–78).[104] This may reflect, as Mango has also argued, the Virgin's secure position in this era both as guarantor of imperial victory and defender of Chalcedonian Christological doctrine.[105]

There was no lack of theological justification for Byzantine emperors who wished for political and ecclesiastical reasons to endorse an already flourishing popular cult of the Virgin Mary. From being affirmed as 'Theotokos' at the Councils of Ephesus and Chalcedon (431 and 451, respectively), Mary came to be viewed as the guarantor of Christ's simultaneous humanity and divinity. Such focus on the human, but also pure and virginal, body of the Theotokos led to interest not only in her birth and way of life, but also the manner of her death. Accounts of the Virgin's dormition and assumption into heaven began to circulate, first in Syriac and then in Greek, around the end of the fifth and beginning of the sixth century. Such a role was as important to Chalcedonian – and Neo-Chalcedonian – theologians as it was to those who endorsed one nature in Christ. While it may be an overstatement to argue that the two parties could agree on the importance of the Theotokos (along with aspects of her cult including feasts, relics and intercession) – and thus came to view her as a point of unity in the midst of real or potential schism – it does seem clear that she played a key part in the Christology of both factions.

Scholars continue to debate the relationship between popular devotion and doctrinal affirmation of the Virgin Mary, searching for the origins of both in the history of the universal Church, as well as for the impact of each aspect of the Marian cult on the other.[106] Although, as I argued in the Introduction, devotion to the Virgin existed well before the Council of Ephesus, it is likely that the affirmation of her role as Theotokos in that context gave impetus to the development of her cult. What appears to have

---

[104] Seibt 1987, 36–7.

[105] Whereas Mango suggests these explanations for the imagery of Justin II's seals as alternative models, I see no reason why both could not have been operative; see Mango 2000, 21. The theological model is also argued tentatively in Mango 1993–4, 168.

[106] It is worth remembering here what P. Allen calls the 'caveats in the secondary literature' with regard to the term 'popular': we are referring to 'phenomena with wide appeal, rather than to those which were prevalent among the illiterate masses'; see Allen 1996, 164. Cf. Momigliano 1972; Cameron 1979a.

occurred from the second half of the fifth century onward – but to have gathered pace especially in the course of the sixth – was the imperial and ecclesial acceptance of Mary, not only as theological symbol, but also as protector of the imperial capital, Constantinople, mediator for Christians before Christ, and defender of the faith. We find evidence of this development not only in the proliferation of Marian churches and shrines and official imagery, as mentioned above, but also in the many homilies and hymns that can be securely dated to this period. In contrast to the highly Christological liturgical texts of the previous century, which, as we have seen, contained little or no intercessory invocation of the Virgin, some sixth-century homilies and hymns appealed for her help and protection.

Abraham of Ephesus was a Chalcedonian bishop who lived during the reign of Justinian. His two surviving homilies, on the Annunciation and the *Hypapante*,[107] reflect both a more developed liturgical calendar and possibly a higher Mariology. As we saw earlier in this chapter, Abraham considered himself the first Byzantine preacher to mention – and celebrate – the newly instituted feast of the Annunciation on 25 March.[108] Since we know (thanks to a letter written by Justinian I which was published in 560) that the feast was added to the calendar at about this time,[109] it is possible to place Abraham's homiletic compositions soon after that date. Pauline Allen has again provided us with some analysis of Abraham's two homilies; she notes that his homily on the Annunciation, while strong on Chalcedonian doctrine and polemical attacks on various heresies as well as Judaism, focuses only minimally on the Virgin's response to Gabriel's message.[110] Like most of his predecessors, including Severos, Abraham envisions the conception of Christ as an instantaneous event that took place as soon as the archangel uttered his greeting to the unsuspecting girl.[111] The homily on the *Hypapante*, which is faithful to the Lukan narrative of Christ's presentation in the Temple, provides more extensive celebration of the Theotokos in its second half. Allen, following Jugie, states that this hymn of praise is 'so high-flown in contrast to the rest of the sober piece that it has to be a later addition'. She also notes that Mary is addressed as intercessor in this section of the homily; again, this may be part of the later interpolation.[112] Here we encounter once again the difficulty of tracing a clear line of development in Marian devotion in the course of the sixth century. If Jugie and Allen are correct in asserting that

---

[107] *CPG* 7380–1; ed. Jugie 1922 (2003), 442–54.   [108] See above, n. 84.
[109] van Esbroeck 1968–9.   [110] Allen 2011, 73.
[111] Abraham of Ephesus, *Homily on the Annunciation* 4, ed. Jugie 1922 (2003), 445, lines 24–30.
[112] Allen 2011, 81; cf. Jugie 1922 (2003), 433.

this section of Abraham's homily is inauthentic, then this preacher may be described as a traditionalist who aligned himself with the more theological approaches to the subject that were characteristic of fifth- and early sixth-century Marian homiletics. If, however, the homily was transmitted in its original form, then we see in its final paragraph a precursor of the full-fledged Marian praise that would appear in homilies and hymns from the early seventh century onward. The passage also includes a clear allusion to Mary's intercessory power, as the preacher appeals to her 'not to stop mediating (πρεσβεύουσα) on behalf of all of us' before Christ 'who was well pleased to be born and made flesh from you'.[113]

Conclusion

I have attempted to trace in the course of this chapter a developing homiletic tradition in honour of Mary, the Theotokos, in the fifth and sixth centuries, which received stimulus both from Christological debates and from growing popular devotion. The relationship between these two forces is difficult to determine; it is possibly even misleading to disentangle them since they were closely related. What is clear, however, is that the universal Church, in both East and West, effectively harnessed this move-ment by placing Mary, the Theotokos, at the heart of the Christological mystery. She became the link whereby God became man or, to adopt the poetic and typological imagery that fifth-century liturgical writers favoured, the place, or receptacle, in creation that God entered and transfigured. As Christ himself inexorably – and even after Chalcedon – became more divine on the basis of Cyril of Alexandria's influential vision, Mary's role as mediator and intercessor grew more essential.

The developments that we have seen between early fifth-century and mid-sixth-century homilies seem clear, even if some (especially dubious) works remain difficult to categorise. We noted in the earliest period, in the works of Hesychios of Jerusalem and Proklos of Constantinople for example, a tendency to celebrate Mary in purely Christological terms. She is certainly a figure of importance in this period, but is viewed more as a theological symbol than as a human woman. By about the end of the fifth and beginning of the sixth century – and here the dating of liturgical works including (ps-)Basil of Seleucia's homily on the Annunciation becomes problematic – we see an increase in allusions to Mary as mediator, although she remains a rather two-dimensional figure. It is finally in the

---

[113] Abraham of Ephesus, *Homily on the Annunciation* 9, ed. Jugie 1922 (2003), 454, lines 19–21.

kontakia of Romanos the Melodist, as we saw in the previous chapter, that a more personal characterisation of the Virgin begins fully to appear. Her Christological role remains important, but she is also, as scholars have recently stressed, protector of Constantinopolitan Christians, intercessor and mother.[114] These various aspects of the Theotokos could be experienced by ordinary Christians by means of civic and liturgical celebration, devotion at holy sites and healing shrines, and with the help of narrative or panegyrical texts and images.

The sixth century thus represents, as both Mango and Cameron have argued, an important stage in the developing Byzantine cult of the Virgin Mary.[115] Most elements of this cult were in place by the end of Justinian's reign in 565, having been promoted by a an active policy of church building, the addition of Marian feasts to the liturgical calendar, and the composition of hymns and homilies for these feasts by writers such as Romanos and Abraham of Ephesus. Further stimulus would be provided in the seventh through to the ninth centuries, partly in response to external challenges such as Persian or Avar invasions, as we shall see in subsequent chapters. However, the depiction of Mary as a fully human – and motherly – figure in the kontakia of Romanos during this period can scarcely be described as an aberration in a literary tradition that would only reach fruition in response to Iconoclasm in the course of the eighth and ninth centuries. It is important to acknowledge that such emphasis on Mary's human qualities, which was interpreted in accordance with Chalcedonian Christology, had surfaced by the fifth century in the Syriac liturgical tradition and was fully explored by Romanos the Melodist in the sixth. This background was fundamental to the development of Marian festal homilies from the late sixth century onward, as well as to that of hagiography and miracle stories, which also began to circulate in the middle Byzantine centuries.

---

[114] Gador-Whyte 2013; Arentzen 2017.   [115] Cameron 1978; Cameron 1979a; Mango 2000.

CHAPTER 3

Panegyrics and Supplication: Homilies from c. 600 to 1000

> The body of the God-bearer, then, is a source of life because it
> received into itself the entire life-giving fullness of the Godhead;
> it is the precious treasury of virginity, the heaven above us, the earth
> that produces God, the first-fruits of Adam's dough that was divinised
> in Christ, exact image of [creation's] original beauty, divinely sealed
> guardian of God's ineffable judgements, dwelling-place of virtues ...[1]

This remarkable passage, preached by the eighth-century preacher Andrew of
Crete in a homily on her Dormition, expresses succinctly the importance of
the Virgin Mary in Byzantine theology. She symbolised the receptive creation
that Christ, the Word of God, chose to enter through his incarnation. But
Mary also played a prophetic role in this tradition, as the 'messenger' that bore
witness to the 'greatness' of divinity. In both ontological and ethical terms, the
Virgin thus enabled her son to recreate the fallen world, including humanity,
according to his preordained dispensation. In addition to virginal motherhood
and discipleship, intercessory power became – especially after about the
beginning of the sixth century – a distinguishing quality of the Theotokos.
Preachers addressed all of these topics in their festal, exegetical and occasional
homilies on the Mother of God. However, as we shall see in the course of this
chapter, they could be woven together differently in response to the purpose,
context and audience of each occasion.

From approximately the beginning of the seventh through to the end of
the ninth century, the production of homilies in honour of the Mother
of God entered its most productive phase. The reasons for such a flowering
of panegyrical and exegetical writing are unclear, but it is possible that the
relatively recent introduction of feasts honouring important events in the
Virgin's legendary life was a stimulus. As we saw in the Introduction, these
festivals were mostly added to the liturgical calendar – first in Jerusalem
and then in Constantinople – in the course of the sixth through to the early

[1] Andrew of Crete, *Homily I on the Dormition*, PG 97, 1068C (my translation).

eighth centuries.[2] After the ninth century, homilists (who could include bishops, priests, and lay men such as emperors or court officials) continued to preach in honour of the Theotokos; however, judging by the surviving texts and manuscripts, they were not as prolific as their predecessors. This may reflect the fact that a corpus of sermons (now acting as readings) for individual Marian feasts had become so popular that new works were only rarely allowed to replace them.[3]

Preachers of the earlier period, including Andrew of Crete, Germanos of Constantinople, John of Damascus and George of Nikomedia, sometimes produced 'trilogies', or series of sermons in three parts, which were delivered in the course of single all-night vigils.[4] Such sermons were transmitted for the most part in liturgical collections intended for use in cathedrals, parish churches and monasteries.[5] The Marian works appeared especially in panegyrical collections for the fixed liturgical year; the sermons were assigned to the feasts of Mary's Nativity (8 September), the Commemoration of Joachim and Anna (9 September), the Entrance into the Temple (21 November), Conception (9 December), Annunciation (25 March) and Dormition (15 August) . Additional celebrations included the feast of Christ's Presentation in the Temple or 'Meeting' with Symeon (*Hypapante*), celebrated on 2 February, and the commemoration of the deposition of Mary's robe at Blachernai (2 July) and of the belt at Chalkoprateia (31 August). Preachers who composed new works from the end of the ninth century onward included such important figures as the patriarch Euthymios,[6] the emperor Leo VI,[7] Neophytos the Recluse,[8] Michael Psellos,[9] John Geometres[10] and James Kokkinobaphos.[11]

---

[2] See Introduction, 11–12.
[3] Theodora Antonopoulou observes that whereas the smaller number of later homilies in liturgical collections reflects the fact that well-established feasts were already provided with readings, this evidence does not necessarily reflect a reduction in new compositions. Nevertheless, 'the prescription of set sermons indicates a reluctance for the majority of preachers to compose new speeches'. See Antonopoulou 1997, 111–12.
[4] Chevalier 1937.   [5] Ehrhard 1936–52; Cunningham 2011b.
[6] Euthymios of Constantinople, *Enkomion on the Holy Belt*; *Homilies I, Ia, II on the Conception of the Virgin Mary* (*BHG* 1138, 1134a–c), ed. Jugie 1922 (2003); ed. Jugie 1926 (1990).
[7] Leo VI, *Homilies I, XII, XV and XX, On the Annunciation, Dormition, Nativity and Entrance of the Virgin Mary*, ed. Antonopoulou 2008.
[8] Neophytos the Recluse, *Homilies on the Nativity and the Entrance into the Temple of the Virgin Mary*, ed. Jugie 1922 (2003).
[9] Michael Psellos, *Sermons on the Annunciation, the Entrance into the Temple, and the 'Usual Miracle'*, ed. Jugie 1922 (2003); Fisher 1994.
[10] John Geometres, *Homily on the Annunciation* (*BHG* 1158), PG 106, 811–48.
[11] James Kokkinobaphos, *Homilies on the Virgin Mary*, PG 127, 543–700; a critical edition is currently being prepared by E. Jeffreys.

Sometimes such authors' works would be gathered into 'special' collections or volumes devoted exclusively to their oeuvre, as in the case of Leo VI and John Xiphilinos;[12] for the majority of such Middle Byzantine texts, however, space would be made in the evolving liturgical collections where they would sometimes displace more famous earlier models.

The problems associated with the study of middle Byzantine homiletics (like those of the earlier period) remain acute, as Theodora Antonopoulou has repeatedly emphasised.[13] When attempting to identify the extant corpus, scholars remain dependent on older studies of Byzantine religious literature, such as those by Karl Krumbacher and Hans-Georg Beck.[14] There is no extension – at least to date – of the invaluable catalogue of patristic texts (extending through the eighth century), which Maurice Geerard published between 1974 and 2003.[15] In addition to this, not only do some homilies remain unedited or wrongly identified in manuscript catalogues, but the attribution of many others is uncertain. The highly conventional nature of Middle Byzantine Marian preaching means that it is often difficult to be sure of the authenticity of individual works; in some cases, sermons may even be attributed in manuscripts to more than one author. Such problems undoubtedly hinder our study of the development of doctrinal, literary and devotional themes in Marian festal sermons; nevertheless, as I shall argue in this chapter, it is possible to discern unique qualities in the work of individual preachers as well as theological and literary developments throughout our period. It would be misguided, as in the case of earlier Marian homilies, to delay further study on the grounds that critical editions, secure attributions and even modern translations do not yet exist.

In the course of this chapter, I will examine seventh- to tenth-century Marian sermons according to their subject matter, thus dividing the discussion into sections based on the festal or occasional nature of the surviving orations. With regard to the festal sermons, I have followed the order of feasts according to the Byzantine liturgical calendar which begins on 1 September. Thus we begin with homilies composed for the feast of the Nativity of the Virgin (8 September), then the Entrance into the Temple (21 November) and so on, up to the Dormition (15 August). Although it is impossible to be comprehensive in my coverage, I shall attempt to provide as

---

[12] Ehrhard 1938, vol. 2, 208–42; 1939, vol. 3, 523–722; Antonopoulou 1997, 95, n. 4, 111.

[13] Antonopoulou 1998; Antonopoulou 2011; Antonopoulou 2013.

[14] Krumbacher 1897; Beck 1959. However, see also Kazhdan 1999 and 2006 for useful discussions of homiletics, as well as other genres of Byzantine literature.

[15] *CPG*, with revised versions.

much detail as possible in the analysis of separate categories within the genre as a whole. Homilies on the Virgin Mary range from high-style panegyrical works (called 'logoi' or 'enkomia' in the manuscripts that transmit them) to exegetical homilies that focus more on biblical or apocryphal narratives. 'Occasional' homilies, such as those on the sieges of Constantinople in 626 (attributed to Theodore Synkellos) and 860 (by Photios), adopt a more discursive literary style than the festal orations, although they may offer even more opportunities for displaying the authors' classical training and rhetorical eloquence. The various genres – to the extent that they can be formally determined – offer different insights into Marian doctrine and devotion in the middle Byzantine period.[16] They thus testify to the various aspects of Mary's Christological and intercessory roles, which depended so much on the contexts in which she was invoked both in Constantinople and elsewhere in the medieval Christian world.

The Virgin Mary's role in the Christological mystery that lies at the heart of Christian revelation remained a central preoccupation for preachers in both festal and occasional contexts.[17] As we saw in the Introduction, this doctrine, which had been elaborated especially at the Councils of Ephesus and Chalcedon in 431 and 451 CE, respectively, defined Mary as the one who had been preordained to conceive and bear Christ, the Son and Logos who was co-eternal with the Father, when he became incarnate. The Virgin's essential part in this process inspired growing theological reflection, especially after the Council of Ephesus, on her purity, holiness and capacity, as one who was 'higher than the heavens and wider than the whole of creation ... [since] no one dwelt in [her] except the Craftsman and Creator and Maker of heavenly and earthly things'.[18] Festal preachers describe this doctrine discursively, but also resort frequently to typological or metaphorical language in order to express the way in which a human being could contain, convey or otherwise offer access to divinity itself. Such signs (for example, types involving

[16] As discussed in the Introduction, 20–5, the classification of Marian sermons remains problematic: the boundaries between 'festal' and 'occasional' homilies are porous, with considerable variation in structure, content and style existing within each category; see Cunningham 2008c; Mayer 2008. However, the distinctions that do exist – at least in theory – between these groups are significant enough to justify my decision to treat them separately. Similarly, I regret the omission (for reasons of space) of homilies on Dominical feasts (such as the Nativity of Christ), which also deal with the Theotokos, in this study. I hope that future studies of Mary's role in the homiletic genre as a whole will succeed in filling these gaps.

[17] For an excellent new study of Christological developments in Marian sermons of the seventh and eighth centuries, see Iverites 2019.

[18] John of Euboea, *Homily on the Conception of Mary*, PG 96, 1488A–B; trans. Cunningham 2008b, 188–9.

the tabernacle or temple and its furniture) may also refer subtly to the various ways in which God revealed himself both before and after his incarnation – whether in the words of prophecy or scripture or in sacraments such as baptism and the Eucharist.

Marian sermons frequently open with summaries of God's whole dispensation of salvation, beginning with creation and leading towards the final resurrection, as they describe how Mary reversed Eve's sin and enabled the restoration of God's image in humanity by giving birth to the second Adam, Christ.[19] In addition to celebrating the Virgin's exalted role as Theotokos and Mother of God, however, preachers consistently point to her humanity, stressing the genealogy that led to her legendary parents, Joachim and Anna, the physical nature of her birth and death, and (with some variation among individual homilists) her maternal qualities vis à vis Christ and the rest of humanity. Although typology played an important role in Marian festal sermons from the seventh century onward, I shall save detailed discussion of this topic for the chapter on hymnography since it is in that liturgical genre that this method of exegesis is fully refined.[20] I will confine myself in this chapter to tracing changes in the Christological depiction of Mary in festal and occasional sermons, also seeking to determine whether variations in dogma that have been noticed by some scholars (for example, with respect to her conception and death) are visible in the writings of individual preachers.[21]

Another aspect of Marian preaching that developed noticeably from the seventh century onward was a willingness to accept apocryphal, as well as biblical, sources as a basis for celebrating the Virgin's conception, birth, life and death.[22] Some feasts, including the Virgin's Nativity, Entrance into the Temple, Conception and Dormition, depended on such sources since the canonical New Testament provides scant information about these aspects of Mary's life. As several scholars have recently noted, liturgical writers from the early eighth century onward began openly to cite the *Protevangelion of James*, the late second- to early third-century gospel that contained a narrative concerning the Virgin's conception from an elderly

---

[19] On the use of Adam/Eve and Christ/Mary typology, which had been used since at least the second century by Christian writers including Justin Martyr and Irenaeus of Lyons, see Graef 1963 (2009), 29–31; Reynolds 2012, 55–6.

[20] See Chapter 4, 146–9.

[21] See, for example, Jugie 1952 (with regard to homilies on Mary's Conception); Jugie 1944; Wenger 1955; Mimouni 1995 (homilies on Mary's Dormition).

[22] For general introductions to the apocryphal sources concerning the infancy, life and death of the Virgin Mary that circulated in the Greek-speaking Byzantine world, see Shoemaker 2002; Norelli 2009.

(and previously sterile) Jewish couple, Joachim and Anna, her dedication to the temple at the age of three, betrothal to Joseph, annunciation and birth-giving of Christ, and the flight into Egypt.[23] Whereas patristic writers including Clement of Alexandria and Gregory of Nyssa were aware of this source, they avoided alluding to it by name.[24] Suddenly, in the eighth-century sermons on the Conception, Nativity and Entrance of the Mother of God into the Temple, we find this text being openly quoted and interpreted – often in an intertextual way that combined its narrative with that of the canonical Old and New Testaments.

Further strands of the apocryphal traditions surrounding the 'dormition', or death, and assumption of the Virgin Mary influenced Greek homilies on this subject even earlier, with John of Thessalonike and Theoteknos of Livias employing various versions of the story from as early as the beginning of the seventh century.[25] I shall explore in the course of this chapter the responses of individual preachers to the Marian apocryphal traditions during the middle Byzantine centuries. Whereas most of these orators accept and elaborate these narratives enthusiastically, a few also allude to reservations in some (unidentified) circles concerning their veracity or orthodoxy while others appear to employ them with more care than did others.

Finally, I am interested in the expression of devotion towards Mary, the Mother of God, as intercessor in the middle Byzantine period, on the basis of the homiletic evidence. We will examine the form and manner of preachers' invocation of the Virgin Mary as protector and advocate of the rest of humanity before her Son, Jesus Christ. Scholarly attention has focused in recent years on the development of a more 'maternal' image of the Virgin in texts and art during the iconoclastic centuries: Ioli Kalavrezou and Niki Tsironis have argued that this process was linked to iconophile defence of the reality of Christ's incarnation according to the Chalcedonian definition of two natures in one hypostasis.[26] Eighth- and ninth-century Marian sermons provide ample evidence to substantiate this theory, suggesting that ideas about Mary's (as well as her mother Anna's) motherly qualities developed much earlier in texts than they did in art. However, it is worth looking more closely at such literary passages in order

---

[23] *Protevangelion of James*; for discussion of this text, see Introduction, n. 27. On its reception by eighth-century homilists, see Panou 2011, 139–43; Cunningham 2011a.

[24] Elliott 1993, 49; Panou 2011, 66–71.

[25] Daley 1998, 7–9; for background on the various traditions concerning Mary's Dormition, see below, 116–19; cf. Mimouni 1995; Shoemaker 2002.

[26] Kalavrezou 1990; Tsironis 2000; Kalavrezou 2000.

to provide nuance to this argument. As Annemarie Weyl Carr has recently argued, the Virgin's *eleos*, or 'mercy', was not always associated with personal affect in this period, nor was it directed towards the Christian faithful, as opposed to Christ.[27] It is also noticeable that the term 'Mother of God' (whether appearing in Greek as *Meter Theou*, *Theometor* or other forms) remained a formal and dogmatic term in this period, being used synonymously with 'Theotokos' and other epithets. More affective invocation of the Virgin, combined with indications that she enters into the feelings of her supplicants, appeared consistently in homiletic writing only after the end of Iconoclasm.[28] Writers including George of Nikomedia, John Geometres and Euthymios the Athonite envisaged Mary as a tender, sorrowing mother who suffered unendurable pain at Christ's death on the cross.[29] However, the extent to which post-iconoclast preachers focused on Mary's human and maternal qualities continued to vary. It is important to consider the liturgical context, intended audience and purpose of individual sermons when assessing their content, since such factors could influence the manner in which homilists chose to portray the Virgin.

The corpus of sermons written for various feasts – as well as for occasional celebrations – of the Mother of God between the seventh and tenth centuries is surprisingly diverse in spite of an increasingly conventional repertoire of theological teachings, typology and narrative or intercessory content. Such diversity seems to depend more on the creative contributions of individual preachers than on the historical development of Marian veneration. Nevertheless, as I hope to demonstrate, it is possible to discern some doctrinal and devotional trends in the course of this period. Progress from an exalted and remote 'Theotokos' to a more human and maternal 'Mother of God' continued to grow between the seventh and tenth centuries in liturgical texts as well as in art; in addition to this, we are able to discern an increasingly personal aspect in Marian devotion, which reflects changes in Byzantine Christian spirituality during this period. Iconoclasm played a role in this process, but it remains unclear

[27] Weyl Carr forthcoming. I am very grateful to the author for showing me a draft of this article, which was originally delivered at a Colloquium on emotion at Dumbarton Oaks Research Library in Washington, DC.

[28] One exception to this rule, as we shall see later, is (ps-)John of Damascus' *Homily on the Nativity of the Virgin Mary*, ed. Kotter 1988. This employs more affective language in relation to the Virgin than is found in most eighth-century Marian festal sermons.

[29] On the theme of Mary's lament at the cross, as handled in Byzantine liturgical hymns and homilies, as well as in art, see Alexiou 1974 (2002), 62–131; Maguire 1981, 91–108; Tsironis 1997; Tsironis 1998; Shoemaker 2011c; Tsironis 2011.

how much the iconophile understanding of the Virgin Mary differed from that of the iconoclasts. In any case, it is probably liturgical changes, including the addition of homiletic and hymnographic texts within a variety of new settings throughout the liturgical year, which contributed most to this process.

The Conception, Nativity and Entrance of the Theotokos into the Temple

Elaboration of the narrative of the Virgin Mary's conception, birth and childhood, as recounted in the second-century *Protevangelion of James*, began, as I suggested above, only from about the eighth century onward in liturgical homilies and hymns.[30] Some eighth-century writers referred to both events in the same text (either prose or verse) – whether this was intended for the feast of the Nativity or that of the Entrance of the Virgin into the Temple.[31] This suggests that these festivals had only recently been accepted into the calendar and were not yet being celebrated consistently throughout the empire.[32] The narrative about Mary's infancy did, however, form part of the accepted repertoire of liturgical tradition from about this time onward. Many preachers elaborated the apocryphal story in the same way that they did the New Testament accounts: they interpreted the theological meaning of the narrative, showed its relationship with canonical books of the Old and New Testaments, and sought to involve their congregations in a dramatic re-enactment of the events that it described. The last of these endeavours could be enhanced by means of the rhetorical device of *ethopoiia* (dramatic characterisation). Preachers sometimes invented pensive monologues for Joachim and Anna, along with dialogues between the latter and Zacharias, the high priest who received the three-year-old Mary in the temple, the archangel Gabriel, Joseph, and other characters who featured in the apocryphal story of Mary's infancy.[33]

Official acceptance of the *Protevangelion* narrative from the first half of the eighth century onward reflected growing theological emphasis on the

---

[30] See above, n. 23. [31] Cunningham 2008b, 32–3.

[32] It is interesting to note, for example, that John of Euboea, writing in the middle of the eighth century, lists the main Marian feasts, but omits those of the Entrance into the Temple and the Dormition. Later in the same homily, however, he adds the latter to his 'decalogue', or list of ten feasts, emphasising its importance as 'the last and great one': John of Euboea, *Homily on the Conception of the Virgin Mary*, PG 96, 1473C– 1476B, 1497B–1500A; Cunningham 2008b, 24, 182–3, 194–5.

[33] On the use of dialogue in Byzantine homiletics, see La Piana 1912 (1971); Kecskeméti 1993; Cunningham 2003.

Virgin Mary's human nature, which guaranteed that of Christ. Mary's genealogical roots were traced through her parents, Joachim and Anna, to the Old Testament king David – although sometimes Anna was described as belonging to the priestly lineage of the Levites.[34] Preachers also stressed the righteousness and good standing of this holy couple within the Jewish community, which made the rejection of Joachim's offering to the temple all the more humiliating. Sermons celebrating the Conception, Nativity or Commemoration of Joachim and Anna on 9 September adhered to the narrative found in the *Protevangelion of James* in asserting that the former went out into the wilderness to pray and fast for forty days while Anna remained at home, lamenting both her own sterility and the absence of her husband.[35] It is also noticeable that preachers frequently used this opportunity to celebrate the harmony of Joachim's and Anna's marriage. John of Euboea, probably writing in the early eighth century on the Conception of the Virgin, vividly describes Anna's distress at the absence of her 'dearest husband', inventing a monologue in which she questions whether he is even still alive.[36] The eighth- or ninth-century lay preacher Kosmas Vestitor also stresses this pious partnership, which he contrasts with the more dysfunctional relationship of Adam and Eve:

> [Anna was] a woman who rejected all evil; a woman who lived faithfully before God with her husband; a woman who regularly attended the temple of God along with her own spouse, with prayers, fasts, and pleasing, bountiful gifts; a woman who in unanimity of soul and bodily chastity always possessed constancy of understanding with her husband.[37]

---

[34] See, for example, John of Euboea, *Homily on the Conception of the Virgin Mary*, PG 96, 1489C: '[The Jews] accepted that it was he who advanced in wisdom from God and men (cf. Lk 2:52), and that Mary, the holy Theotokos, was from a royal and priestly tribe, according to how they reckoned this customarily among themselves', trans. Cunningham 2008b, 189–90; Kosmas Vestitor, *Homily on Holy Joachim and Anna*, PG 106, 1012A: 'For the righteous progenitors of the Theotokos were truly perceived in advance as worthy of being related to Christ in flesh and of being honoured as belonging to a famous family, by which I mean a kingly and priestly one. For the Theotokos takes her genealogy from both, since the two tribes became intertwined in different ways from the beginning . . . ', trans. Cunningham 2008b, 143. For discussion of traditions (including Syriac) concerning the Virgin Mary's genealogy, see Brock 2006.

[35] This contrasts with the narrative found in four middle Byzantine *Lives of the Virgin* (to be discussed in Chapter 5, 191–205): according to those texts, Joachim prayed in the temple instead of retreating into the wilderness. See Epiphanios of Kallistratos, *Life of the Virgin*, ed. Dressel 1843, 16, PG 120, 189C; Symeon the Metaphrast, *Life of the Virgin* 2, ed. Latyshev 1912, 348. 10–15; John Geometres, *Life of the Virgin*, Vat. gr. 504, fol. 173v, col. 1; Georgian *Life of the Virgin* 3–4, ed. Shoemaker 2012, 38–9.

[36] John of Euboea, *Homily on the Conception of the Virgin Mary*, PG 96, 1472B–C, trans. Cunningham 2008b, 180–1 (8).

[37] Kosmas Vestitor, *Oration on Joachim and Anna*, PG 106, 1005–6, trans. Cunningham 2008b, 140 (3).

Euthymios of Constantinople, preaching towards the end of the ninth century, further praises the couple's blessed marriage, which he envisions in terms of 'piety, ascetic endeavour, and every godly virtue'.[38] Such emphasis on the holiness of this marriage is noteworthy since, according to Jugie, the sermon was probably delivered in the first instance to a male monastic audience.[39]

As Eirini Panou has recently shown, preachers of our period also emphasised the ascetic qualities of Joachim and Anna, which rendered them worthy of divine favour.[40] They identified the typological connection between the elderly couple's conception of Mary and that of the prophet Samuel from Hannah and Elkanah (1 Kgs 1-2 [1 Sam 1-2]). However, some of the earlier orators also emphasise the fact that conception, when it did take place due to God's miraculous intervention, occurred in an entirely natural way. Andrew of Crete, after recounting the story of their sterility and prayers to God to be granted a child, describes the fulfilment of the elderly couple's request in detail:

> [The divine power] stimulated [Joachim] into fruitfulness and [Anna] into producing a child; and having meanwhile sprinkled the withered passages of the reproductive organs with the juices of sperm production, it brought them from infertility into productivity.[41]

John of Euboea describes the same phenomenon, more metaphorically, in the following way:

> ... blessed is the descendant and daughter of David who comes forth from your loins and belly. For you are earth while she is heaven. You are of clay, but through her those who are of clay become heavenly.[42]

(Ps-)John of Damascus is explicit about the Virgin Mary's physical conception from both parents, but also explores the emotional bond between parents and child, as we see in one passage of his homily on the Nativity of the Theotokos:

> Blessed are the loins and the womb from which you sprouted forth! Blessed are the arms that carried you and the lips which tasted your pure

---

[38] Euthymios of Constantinople, *Homily I on the Conception of the Virgin Mary* 2, ed. Jugie 1926 (1990), 442. 40–1.
[39] Jugie 1922 (2003), 479.   [40] Panou 2011, 111–17.
[41] Andrew of Crete, *Homily I on the Nativity of the Virgin Mary*, PG 97, 816C–D, trans. Cunningham 2008b, 80 (6).
[42] John of Euboea, *Homily on the Conception of the Virgin Mary*, PG 96, 1477B, trans. Cunningham 2008b, 184 (12).

kisses – the lips only of your parents that you might always be a virgin in every way![43]

In contrast to such graphic – and sometimes affective – accounts of the conception of the Virgin Mary, however, some later preachers became more circumspect. Late ninth- and early tenth-century preachers such as George of Nikomedia, Euthymios of Constantinople and Leo VI emphasised the prayerful supplications of Joachim and Anna to God before they conceived Mary, avoiding any mention of the physical nature of the reproductive process.[44] Panou has argued that some middle Byzantine preachers went so far as to teach that Mary's conception took place as a result of prayer, rather than through sexual intercourse;[45] however, I am not fully convinced by this theory. Theodore of Studios, as Panou herself records, wrote between 809 and 811/12 to correct a hermit named Theoktistos of his mistaken – even heretical – notion that the Virgin Mary had been conceived without physical union taking place between her parents.[46] The fact that such discussions took place at all indicates that some uncertainty surrounded this subject, probably inspired by increasing emphasis on Mary's purity and status as the one who had been chosen by God – from the very beginning of his saving dispensation – to bear his Son. Nevertheless, middle Byzantine preachers remained committed to the theological doctrine that the Virgin represented Christ's physical link with the rest of humanity. If she had escaped the normal methods of conception and birth, along with death, the reality of his incarnation would have been undermined.

Interest in Mary's family background, physical conception and emotional bonds with her parents reflected, according to Niki Tsironis, an iconophile campaign to reinforce – in opposition to a perceived dualist tendency in iconoclast theology – the human nature that Christ received directly from his mother.[47] Such dualism consisted in the alleged denial by iconoclasts that any aspect of the created world, including not only Christ's human body but also physical reminders of him, such as relics or icons,

---

[43] (ps-)John of Damascus, *Homily on the Nativity of the Virgin Mary* 6, ed. Kotter 1988, 175. 13–15, trans. Cunningham 2008b, 61. For further commentary on this passage, see Tsironis 2011, 192.

[44] George of Nikomedia, *Homily on the Conception of St Anna*, PG 100, 1365C–1369D; Euthymios of Constantinople, *Homily II on the Conception of St Anna* 2, ed. Jugie 1925 (1990), 451–2; Leo VI ('the Wise'), *Homily XV, On the Nativity of the Virgin Mary*, ed. Antonopoulou 2008, 221–6.

[45] Panou 2011, esp. 114–17.

[46] Theodore of Studios, *Letter 490*, ed. Fatouros 1992, 16–20; Panou 2011, 113.

[47] Tsironis 1998, 180; Tsironis 2000; Tsironis 2005; Tsironis 2010; Tsironis 2011.

could be transfigured or infused with divine power. Tsironis has also shown how preachers of this period attempted by rhetorical methods to involve their audiences in the sensual and emotional aspects of both biblical and apocryphal stories. Congregations were invited metaphorically to see, hear, smell, touch and taste the narrative of the incarnation; this should be assimilated not simply by means of text and hearing, but by full physical participation in the liturgical celebration.[48] Such experience could also now be reinforced by emphasis on an apocryphal narrative that seemed to have both biblical and theological foundations – even if it lacked full canonical credentials based on patristic or conciliar endorsement. The Virgin Mary, according to eighth-century and later liturgical writers, possessed a biography that linked her, and therefore Christ as well, to a royal and righteous lineage that had been foretold by prophets and implicitly accepted by earlier Christian tradition.

There is evidence to suggest that, in spite of liturgical writers' acceptance of the Marian apocryphal tradition by the middle of the eighth century, some individuals or groups within the Church remained opposed to this trend.[49] Such material is difficult to interpret since it takes the form of polemic, which was a common feature in Byzantine homiletics;[50] nevertheless, it appears often enough to suggest that eighth- and ninth-century preachers were not always sure that their message would be received enthusiastically. Germanos I of Constantinople, preaching before 730, referred to 'those who are moving their tongues against' Mary in his second homily on her Entrance into the Temple, and rebuked them for failing to acknowledge the events that he described.[51] Tarasios, who was patriarch of Constantinople from 784 to 806, inveighed against those Christians who claimed that Anna gave birth to Mary after seven, rather than nine, months of pregnancy. He accused them of having learned such teachings from 'heretics', who had 'fallen from truth and rectitude.'[52] Just over a century later, Photios, who was also patriarch of Constantinople, attacked unnamed people who did not accept the story of Anna's miraculous conception of Mary at an advanced age.[53] It is unclear whether Photios was criticising these opponents merely for doubting the truth of the miracle or for

---

[48] Tsironis 2011, esp. 183–8.   [49] This issue is discussed in Panou 2011, 117–43.
[50] See Cunningham 1999. On the wider issue of polemic in Byzantine literature, see Cameron 1991b; Déroche 1991; Cameron and Hoyland 2011; Cameron 2014.
[51] Germanos of Constantinople, *Homily II on the Entrance*, PG 98, 312A, trans. Cunningham 2008b, 164.
[52] Tarasios of Constantinople, *Homily on the Entrance* 6, PG 98, 1485D. According to Eirini Panou, John of Damascus, Andrew of Crete, the *Synax. CP* and the *Synaxarion* of Basil II also defended Anna's nine-month pregnancy; see Panou 2011, 127.
[53] Photios, *Homily IX, On the Birth of the Virgin* 5, ed. Laourdas 1959, 91. 26–92. 12; trans. Mango 1958, 167–8; cf. Panou 2011, 118.

rejecting the witness of the apocryphal narrative. Nor is it evident, as in the case of earlier preachers' adversaries, just who they were, especially when Photios associated them later in the same sermon with pagans or, possibly, classicising intellectuals.[54] All of the above examples suggest that the acceptance of Marian apocryphal texts continued to be questioned by some prominent Christians throughout the eighth and ninth centuries. Such opposition may have been directed for the most part against the non-canonical nature of such texts; however, it also seems to have focused occasionally on particular aspects of these narratives.

Any opposition to apocryphal texts, along with other aspects of the Marian cult, would appear to have been weak and short-lived, however, judging by the extent to which they featured in many sermons that are dated both to this period and later. Popular preachers such as Andrew of Crete, John of Damascus and George of Nikomedia relied extensively on the *Protevangelion of James*, along with apocryphal accounts of the dormition, in their sermons. Increasingly, as we saw earlier, such material attracted as much exegesis and dramatic elaboration as did the canonical biblical texts.[55] Coverage of the Virgin Mary's Entrance into the Temple was also based entirely on the narrative of the *Protevangelion*, which relates that, having reached the age of three, the holy child was taken by her parents to the temple in Jerusalem and dedicated to God as a gift of thanksgiving. The second-century text relates how, following a procession to the temple with 'the undefiled daughters of the Hebrews', the priest placed Mary on the third step of the altar where 'she danced for joy with her feet and the whole house of Israel loved her'.[56] The child then remained in the temple until she reached the age of twelve, being 'nurtured like a dove' and receiving 'food from the hand of an angel'.[57]

Although the date when the feast of the Virgin Mary's Entrance into the Temple (21 November) was added to the Constantinopolitan liturgical calendar remains unclear, most scholars accept that this must have

---

[54] Mango suggests in his introduction to this sermon that Photios may have been directing his tirade against a rival school of intellectuals in ninth-century Constantinople, which possibly leaned towards the study of Plato and the Neoplatonist philosophers more than he liked. See Mango 1958, 163–4.

[55] Panou suggests that George of Nikomedia represented the culmination of this process, since he treated apocryphal texts such as the *Protevangelion of James* with as much reverence as scripture in his homilies on the Mother of God. See Panou 2011, 110.

[56] This image is inspired by David dancing before the Lord, as recounted in 2 Kgs 6:14 [2 Sam 6:14] (although the Greek text of the LXX says that David 'struck upon tuned instruments before the Lord'; see Pietersma and Wright, trans., 2007, 281).

[57] *Protevangelion of James* 7.3–8.1, Elliott 1993, 60.

occurred around the beginning of the eighth century – or possibly even later.[58] As I suggested above, flexibility about full-scale celebration of the feast in different regions may be indicated both by its absence in earlier liturgical sources, such as the Morcelli calendar,[59] and by some eighth-century preachers' tendency to celebrate Mary's dedication to the temple in sermons on her Conception or Nativity.[60] As the apocryphal narrative of this event already suggests, the acceptance of this female child into the Jewish temple in Jerusalem was replete with theological significance. According to the *Protevangelion of James*, Mary was even received into the innermost sanctuary, or 'holy of holies', of the temple.[61] Middle Byzantine preachers developed the typological meaning both of the temple and of its innermost sanctuary. The Virgin was thus described as the 'living temple' that superseded the lifeless temple of stone: she was being prepared to contain, as the temple's sanctuary had done before her, the limitless and eternal God who would become incarnate in her womb.[62] Preachers, along with hymnographers, developed a typology in connection with the Jewish temple that expressed succinctly the sacred nature not only of the temple itself, but also of the objects and furnishings within its precincts, which had conveyed or revealed the living God to his chosen people. Mary, as

---

[58] See Cunningham 2008b, 24–6; Krausmüller 2011, 228–30; Panou 2018, 46–7. Some scholars believe, however, that the feast was introduced earlier than the early eighth century, arguing that it was related to the inauguration date (20 November) of the sixth-century (Justinianic) church of the Nea in Jerusalem; see Carlton 2006, 103–5; cf. Harrison 2006, 150. Earlier discussion of this question occurs in Vailhé 1901–2; Chirat 1945. The absence of pre-eighth-century hymnography, homilies and other liturgical evidence for the feast suggests that, whereas the dedication of the Nea church may have influenced the eventual choice of date for the feast, this process may have occurred several centuries later. The difficulty of authenticating early eighth-century homilies for the feast, including those that are attributed to Germanos of Constantinople and Andrew of Crete, is addressed in Chirat 1945, 128–30. On three spurious unpublished homilies that are attributed in manuscripts to Andrew (Cod. Athon. Laurae E147 (*CPG* 8201); Cod. Athon. Esphigmenou 76; Cod. Panteleimon 300), see Brubaker and Cunningham 2007, 243, nn. 49–50. Another homily on the Entrance that is listed as unpublished among Andrew of Crete's works (*CPG* 8202) and which is contained in two twelfth-century manuscripts (Athen. 2108 and Hierosol. Sab. 60) is in fact excerpted from Andrew's *Homily I on the Nativity of the Virgin*; see Brubaker and Cunningham 2007, 244. For a recent summary of the questions surrounding the institution of the feast of the Entrance, see Kishpaugh 1941, 30–6; Olkinuora 2015, 34–8.

[59] *Morcelli Calendar*, vol. 1, 33–4. This calendar probably dates to around the early eighth century; see Krausmüller 2011, 229.

[60] For example, Andrew of Crete, *Homily I on the Nativity of the Virgin Mary*, PG 97, 820B–C; John of Euboea, *Homily on the Conception of the Virgin Mary*, PG 96, 1481B–1489A. John also fails to mention the feast of the Entrance into the Temple in his list of ten great feasts; see above, n. 32.

[61] Although the *Protevangelion of James* does not mention this detail in its narrative of Mary's upbringing in the temple, it is mentioned later in the text, at Chapter 13.2; see Elliott 1993, 62.

[62] See, for example, Andrew of Crete, *Homily IV on the Nativity of the Virgin Mary*, PG 97, 877D–880B; (ps-)John of Damascus, *Homily on the Nativity of the Virgin Mary* 10, ed. Kotter 1988, 180; Germanos I of Constantinople, *Homily I on the Entrance*, PG 98, 293, 301.

Theotokos, became the antitype of Moses' tabernacle, the ark of the covenant, the jar that contained manna, the seven-branched candlestick and, as we have seen, the temple itself. The theological meaning of the apocryphal narrative, which contained rich intertextual association with the Old and New Testaments, dominated most homiletic discourse. Such a preoccupation, which is visible in both sermons and hymns, was concerned above all with the Christological aspect of Marian veneration; the Virgin's preparation for her future role as 'birth-giver of God' was associated above all with the ritual purity of a sacred precinct belonging to the Jews that would give way to a new covenant, namely, God's physical entrance into creation through her flesh.

Although middle Byzantine preachers thus focus above all on the theological and typological symbolism of this feast, they sometimes seek to engage their audiences in the human and dramatic aspects of the narrative. The two sermons that are ascribed to Germanos of Constantinople, for example, both invent dialogues when describing the encounter between Mary's parents, Joachim and Anna, and the high priest Zacharias.[63] Such direct speech is used in order to expound the theological meaning of the events that are unfolding, as the parents express their thankfulness to God and the nature of their gift while the priest acknowledges his own understanding of its significance – obviously informed by his awareness of the typological and prophetic background of the offering. However, the preacher also used this trope in order to convey dramatically the human dimension of the story. The second sermon on the Entrance, for example, has Anna confess to the priest the range of emotions that she experienced, first in sterility and then in receipt of God's favour and the miraculous gift of a child.[64] Congregations, on hearing these words, might have been moved to sympathise with Anna and to follow her example in seeking God's help for problems such as sterility, childbirth or any form of emotional distress. Like all other feasts, that of the Entrance into the Temple thus conveyed not only a Christological message, but also a human dimension that was directly associated with this theological teaching. That women played a major role in the story may have added to its appeal for many lay Christians throughout the Byzantine period and beyond.

To stray slightly beyond our period, it is worth noting that, alone among middle Byzantine preachers, the twelfth-century preacher, James of

---

[63] Germanos I of Constantinople, *Homilies I–II on the Entrance*, PG 98, 300A–304B, 312D–316B.
[64] Germanos I of Constantinople, *Homily II on the Entrance*, PG 98, 313A–316B.

Kokkinobaphos, comments on the unusual aspect of the narrative of Mary's Entrance into the Temple – namely, that a female child should have been admitted into a Jewish precinct that had so far been frequented only by priests. James is aware of the gender barrier that is deliberately being overturned in the apocryphal narrative when he comments that it was an 'innovation' (*kainotomian*) for a girl to enter a place that was normally occupied only by men.[65] After some close exegesis of the relevant passage in the *Protevangelion of James*, the preacher concludes that Mary's unique purity and future role as birth-giver of God justifies her presence in the temple. It is possible that his awareness of a female patron, for whom this 'desk' homily may have been specially composed, also influenced James Kokkinobaphos' treatment of gender issues in this story.[66]

Christ's Presentation in the Temple or 'the Meeting' (*Hypapante*)

Pauline Allen provides a useful overview of the early and middle Byzantine homiletic tradition associated with the feast of Christ's 'Meeting' in the temple with Symeon, which had been celebrated in Jerusalem since as early as the fourth century.[67] As Allen notes, the feast was marked by both a stational liturgy and the use of lighted candles in both Jerusalem and Constantinople, where it was introduced into the liturgical calendar either in 527 or 542.[68] Although the feast of the Presentation began as a purely Christological celebration, marking the transition of the old covenant (symbolised by the prophet Symeon) to the new, it moved in the course of the sixth and seventh centuries towards a more Mariological focus. This was based on two factors: first, the celebration of Mary's purification forty days after giving birth to Christ and second, remembrance of the biblical passage in which Symeon predicted that a sword would pierce her heart (Lk 2:35); the latter passage, following rather negative reception by early theologians such as Origen,[69] came to be interpreted by later preachers as

---

[65] James of Kokkinobaphos, *Sermon III*, PG 127, col. 621 A–B.

[66] On James's female patron, see Jeffreys 2014; Jeffreys 2019, 282–3.

[67] Allen 2007, esp. 3–8; Allen 2011, 78–84. On the feast, see further Leclercq 1948; Aubineau 1978, 2–4. Although originally celebrated on 14 February (forty days after the earlier feast of the Nativity of Christ on 6 January), the feast of the Presentation was moved forward to 2 February after that of Christ's Nativity had moved back to 25 September. This occurred towards the end of the fourth century. See Talley 1986, 134–41.

[68] Allen 2007, 2–3. George Kedrenos recorded the introduction of the feast during the reign of Justin I. See Kedrenos, *Historiarum compendium*, ed. Bekker 1838, vol. 1, 641.

[69] See Introduction, n. 66.

referring to the sorrow that the Virgin Mary would experience on witness-
ing her son's death on the cross. It is also likely, however, that emphasis on
the Theotokos in later homilies on the feast of Christ's Presentation in the
Temple reflected her increasing importance, in both Christological and
devotional terms, in the Byzantine Church.

The attribution and dates of post-sixth-century homilies on the feast of
the Presentation remain especially problematic. Two sermons, attributed
to Leontios of Neapolis and Sophronios of Jerusalem, belong to the
seventh century, a dubious work which has been excluded from John
Damascene's authentic works may be dated to the eighth, and a sermon
that is attributed variously to Athanasios, Proklos and George of
Nikomedia, along with one by Leo VI, may belong to the ninth or early
tenth centuries.[70] Emphasis on the purification of Mary (as well as of the
infant Christ) appears in both seventh-century works. Leontios provides
intertextual discussion of the sanctification that she experienced when the
Holy Spirit came upon her and the power of the Highest overshadowed her
at the conception of Christ (Lk 1:35), stressing the divine nature of this
birth and the purity of the virginal mother. The focus here remains
Christological, reinforced by antithetical statements that describe the
infant being embraced by motherly arms even while having the cherubim
as his throne.[71] Both Leontios and Sophronios interpret Symeon's prophecy to Mary as referring to her pain at the passion: they acknowledge the
uncertainty and doubt that not only she, but also the myrrh-bearers and
apostles, will experience, but point forward towards the resurrection,
which will release them from this fear.[72] The two seventh-century
preachers use this festal opportunity to emphasise orthodox doctrine
concerning the two natures of Christ; the Virgin Mary's role in this
mystery, as 'God-bearer' yet human mother, thus receives attention more
for dogmatic than devotional reasons.

The sermon that is attributed to the eighth-century monk and preacher,
John of Damascus, characterised by Allen as a 'dry composition . . . [which]
could well be a desk homily',[73] explores at some length Symeon's statement
to Mary about the sword piercing her soul.[74] Like his predecessors, this

[70] See Allen 2007, 7–8, for a list and descriptions of these sermons.
[71] Leontios of Neapolis, *Homily on the Presentation*, PG 93, 1569D.
[72] Leontios of Neapolis, *Homily on the Presentation*, PG 93, 1580C–D; Sophronios of Jerusalem,
Homily IV, On the Presentation, ed. Duffy 2020, 102–47.
[73] Allen 2007, 7.
[74] (ps-)John of Damascus, *Sermon on the Presentation of Christ into the Temple* 10, ed. Kotter 1988,
390–1.

homilist interprets Symeon's words as referring to the Virgin's doubt and pain at Christ's future passion, which he describes in vivid language. She will suffer in her heart what Christ experienced in physical terms. However, the following biblical phrase, 'that the thoughts of many may be revealed', is understood to refer to the enlightenment that will follow the resurrection. The homily ends with praise for the Theotokos in the form of *chairetismoi*, invoking her intercessory and protective role in relation to the rest of humanity.[75]

The homily on the Presentation that is attributed variously to Athanasios, Proklos and George of Nikomedia, offers a straightforward, exegetical approach to the feast.[76] The preacher expounds the Lukan pericope verse-by-verse, endeavouring by means of exclamations and direct questions to bring the event to life for his congregation. He praises Mary's purity and virginity, which reveals the divinity of her Son, but also emphasises her humanity as she mourns his death on the cross.[77] The sermon expresses less overt praise for the Mother of God, however, which perhaps suggests an earlier – possibly seventh-century – date. Leo VI's sermon on the same subject, which is dated to the period 894–6,[78] begins with Christological focus; however, the preacher emphasises Mary's role as Christ's virginal mother throughout the oration in order to underline the mystery of the incarnation. The overturning of the old covenant, which is nevertheless met in the person of Symeon – as well as typologically in the Theotokos – leads up to celebration of Mary's role in initiating a new creation. The sermon ends with praise for the 'Virgin and Mother' who made possible this saving dispensation and who also acts as protector and intercessor for the empire and its faithful inhabitants.[79]

The focus of the feast of the Presentation thus remained Christological, but preachers increasingly – especially from the seventh century onward – stressed its Marian content. Most homilies allude to Mary's purification after forty days only in order to show how her virginal birth bore witness to Christ's divine and human natures. Symeon's prophecy concerning the sword that would pierce the Virgin's soul is understood to refer to her suffering at Christ's passion; this reveals her close association (in both

---

[75] (ps-)John of Damascus, *Sermon on the Presentation of Christ* 14, ed. Kotter 1988, 394–5.

[76] Allen discusses the date of the (ps-)Athanasian sermon (*CPG* 2271), noting that it shares four passages (practically verbatim) with the sermon by Sophronios and arguing that it must be dated to a period well after the Council of Chalcedon (451). Owing to the well-developed Marian emphasis in this homily, it seems likely that it is dated to the seventh century or later; see Allen 2007, 7–8.

[77] (ps-)Athanasios, *Homily on the Presentation*, PG 28, 996D.   [78] Antonopoulou 1997, 69.

[79] Leo VI, *Homily XXVIII, On the Presentation of Christ*, ed. Antonopoulou 2008, 400–1.

physical and emotional terms) with her Son and it would be overturned when he was resurrected from the tomb.

The Annunciation

As we saw in Chapter 2, homilies on the Annunciation began to appear long before the feast was added to the Constantinopolitan liturgical calendar during the reign of Justinian.[80] The theme of the archangel Gabriel's announcement to the Virgin Mary and her acceptance of the incarnation of Christ (Lk 1: 26–38) was recognised early as initiating God's dispensation for the overturning of the consequences of the Fall and bringing about human salvation. Early homilies on this subject, which were not always associated with any formal celebration of a feast, include works by Hesychios of Jerusalem,[81] (ps-)Proklos of Constantinople[82] and others. Many of these works contain dialogic sections incorporating direct speech – both between Gabriel and the Virgin Mary and between the latter and Joseph. It is not known why this topic became so associated with the rhetorical device of *ethopoiia*, that is, characterisation through invented speech (either monologue or dialogue), but it may reflect influence from the Syriac liturgical tradition. Byzantine preachers, as well as hymnographers, used dialogue in order to help congregations identify, on a personal and emotional level, with the Virgin Mary. Building on the brief, but also dialogic, narrative of Luke's Gospel, liturgical writers revealed dramatically her initial fear and doubt, followed by gradual acceptance of the integrity of the divine messenger and the saving content of his news. It is nevertheless puzzling that Byzantine liturgical tradition neglected both the Virgin's *fiat* and the question of the moment at which Christ was actually conceived in its portrayal of the Annunciation. Building on a long-standing tradition that Mary was impregnated by means of her ear, as soon as the archangel Gabriel addressed her, preachers, hymnographers and iconographers often implied that the incarnation took place at the moment of their encounter.[83] Such an interpretation is contradicted, however, by another strand in the tradition, namely, the dialogue between Mary and Gabriel in which the

---

[80]   See Chapter 1, 11–12. For discussion of the earlier homiletic tradition, along with sixth- and seventh-century preaching on the Annunciation, see Allen 2011, 72–8.

[81]   Hesychios of Jerusalem, *Homilies I and II, On the Hypapante*, ed. Aubineau 1978, 24–43, 61–75; Caro 1971, vol. 1, 40–53.

[82]   (ps-)Proklos of Constantinople, *Homily VI, On the Theotokos*, ed. Leroy 1967.

[83]   Constas 2003, 294–9.

former is slowly persuaded to accept her role in the incarnation, thereby allowing the process to begin.[84]

The dialogic qualities of two long sermons on the Annunciation that were composed by the eighth-century bishops Andrew of Crete and Germanos of Constantinople have been explored at length elsewhere. Scholars have shown how the former preacher emphasises the theological meaning of the Virgin Mary's dialogue with Gabriel, whereas the latter creates a lively and personal re-enactment of their encounter.[85] It is difficult to imagine how this homily would have been performed in church – either when it was first delivered or in subsequent public readings – since long sections of the text are composed entirely of direct speech. The moment at which Mary finally gives her assent to the incarnation serves not only to portray her acceptance of this news, but also to express recognition of her own role in the mystery and joy at its outcome:

> I shall sing psalms and praise the Lord 'for he has looked upon the humility of his servant; for behold, from now on all generations will call me blessed' (Lk 1:48). And the people of the nations will praise me without ceasing.[86]

Later sermons for this feast, including works by Photios, John Kyriotes Geometres, Leo VI, Michael Psellos and James Kokkinobaphos, abandoned such extensive use of dialogue. They focused instead, like many of their precursors, on the inaugural nature of the feast (although the Conception and Nativity of the Virgin could also be treated in this way), its witness to the reality of the incarnation, and the entrance of God, as Son and Logos, into the created world. Many of these homilists employed high-flown language in their panegyrical orations: the beauty of the natural world in springtime was seen as reflecting God's entrance into his creation.[87] Photios, for example, who probably preached his oration in Hagia Sophia in the presence of the emperor,[88] used bridal imagery when describing the Virgin Mary's encounter with the archangel. She was chosen by God as a pious and virginal girl to become his bride and initiate salvation for the human

---

[84] This apparent contradiction, which has important theological implications, does not worry early Byzantine preachers such as Germanos of Constantinople or Andrew of Crete.

[85] Kazhdan 1999, 61–4; Cunningham 2003, 110–12; Arentzen 2019.

[86] Germanos I of Constantinople, *Homily on the Annunciation*, PG 98, 329D, ed. Fecioru 1946, 91, trans. Cunningham 2008b, 234 (4).

[87] For parallels between textual and visual imagery of springtime in relation to the Annunciation, see Maguire 1981, 42–52.

[88] Photios, *Homily VII, On the Annunciation*, ed. Laourdas 1959, 74–82; trans. Mango 1958, 139–49; on the context of this homily, see Mango 1958, 138.

race.[89] John Geometres provided a striking contribution to the genre with his oration on the Annunciation complementing his longer *Life*, or set of orations, on the Mother of God.[90] Geometres offers throughout this sermon a masterly juxtaposition of opposites: earthly and heavenly, virgin and mother, old and new – all of which reveal not only the beginning of a new dispensation, but also the paradox of the incarnation. He focuses not only on the physical role of the Theotokos, but also on her feelings, thoughts and eventual acceptance of God's will. This portrait depends on earlier accounts, such as that by Germanos, but raises the subject to an even higher theological level. This tenth-century writer works within a long tradition, employing for example a well-established repertoire of types and metaphors for the Virgin Mary; however, he also underlines her essential roles both in guaranteeing Christ's humanity and in revealing his unchanging divinity. It is also noticeable, as in the case of Photios, that John Geometres portrays the Virgin's personal virtue and modesty (which are monastic ideals) to a greater extent than did his eighth-century predecessors. She is envisioned as a real and pious person who plays an essential role in God's dispensation for salvation.

Mary's Lament at the Cross

Like the feasts of Christ's Presentation in the Temple and the Annunciation, the Virgin Mary's lament at the foot of the cross, which was commemorated on Good Friday, was inspired by a biblical rather than an apocryphal source. The Gospel of John, which describes briefly Mary's presence at the foot of the cross and Christ's words both to her and to 'the disciple standing by' (Jn 19:26–7) (who was understood in later tradition to be John the Evangelist) led liturgical writers, including the sixth-century hymnographer Romanos, to develop the theme of the Virgin's lament at the death of her Son. Her maternal pain, as we saw earlier, could be connected with Symeon's prophecy to her when he encountered Christ in the temple and said that 'a sword shall pierce your soul' (Lk 2:35). Niki Tsironis has argued that, following Romanos' development of the subject in a kontakion on Mary at the cross, Germanos of Constantinople – or perhaps a contemporary preacher – elaborated this theme in a sermon on the same subject. The text includes an emotional monologue in which the Virgin addresses her Son, asking why his death is necessary and how it fits

---

[89] Photios, *Homily VII, On the Annunciation* 7, ed. Laourdas 1959, 80–2; trans. Mango 1958, 146–8.
[90] John Geometres, *Homily on the Annunciation*, PG 106, 811–48; John Geometres, *Life of the Virgin*, ed. Constas and Simelidis, forthcoming. See Chapter 5, 197–9.

into God's plan for salvation.[91] This sermon may represent a link between the hymn by Romanos and an oration for Good Friday by George of Nikomedia, in which the emotional response of the Virgin Mary to her Son's death is developed even more fully. According to Tsironis, George's oration for Good Friday represents the first example of a Marian homily on the crucifixion of Christ. The orator uses Mary's involvement in the passion in order to emphasise Christ's full humanity as he died on the cross. Her pain, which she experiences as a burning fire within her entrails,[92] reveals the Virgin's physical, as well as emotional, relationship with her Son. It is likely, as both Tsironis and Kalavrezou have argued, that such emphasis on Mary's human emotions reflected iconophile insistence on the humanity of Jesus Christ, which he gained from the physical nature of his mother. There is also, however, a theological symmetry in her involvement in his life, from conception to death and resurrection. Whereas she experienced no pain in conceiving and giving birth to her divine Son, Mary was vulnerable or, to speak metaphorically, torn apart – like the veil of the temple – at his death. Her life thus mirrored his, in that she experienced the full pain of his mortality but also saw him resurrected from the dead three days later. It is striking, as Tsironis and Constas have both suggested, that post-iconoclastic liturgical writers chose to emphasise this paradox, thus illustrating the full *kenosis*, or divine self-emptying into humanity, not only of Christ, the Word of God, but also (metaphorically) of his mother Mary.[93]

Although the Virgin Mary's lament at the foot of the cross was only treated by a few Byzantine preachers, it was developed further in hymnography – especially in the so-called 'enkomia' (in fact laments)[94] for Good Friday matins and the short stavrotheotokia ('cross or crucifix hymns in honour of the Theotokos') that were sung throughout the liturgical year especially on Wednesdays and Fridays. We shall examine this hymnography in the next chapter; for now, it is worth commenting merely that the relationship between the homiletic and hymnographic treatment of this theme awaits further study. It is interesting to note that the Virgin's lament appeared also in non-liturgical contexts, such as hagiography in her honour and even in the Byzantine recensions of the apocryphal *Gospel of*

---

[91] (ps-)Germanos of Constantinople, *Homily on the Burial of the Lord's Body*, PG 98, 269C–277B. Tsironis suggests an eighth- or ninth-century date for the homily, although it is attributed in some manuscripts to Germanos II; Tsironis 1998, 223–8. See also Taft 1990 (1995), 83, who attributes the homily to Germanos II (1222–40); Beck 1969, 668.

[92] George of Nikomedia, *Homily on Good Friday*, PG 100, 1468A; cf. Constas 2014, 127.

[93] I am indebted to the work of Fr Maximos Constas in presenting this argument: see Constas 2014, esp. 124–8; cf. Tsironis 1998, 286–8.

[94] For bibliography, see Introduction, n. 12.

Nikodemos.[95] A more maternal aspect of the Virgin Mary appears in all of these literary genres, expressing a close and fully engaged relationship with her divine Son.

The Dormition and Assumption

Before looking at the homilies that were composed for the feast of Mary's Dormition (15 August), it is worth summarising briefly the literary accounts that inspired them. The legend has no biblical foundations but is based on various apocryphal narratives concerning the Virgin's life, death and afterlife. There can be no doubt that these stories helped to justify Mary's growing importance in both Christological and intercessory terms within the late antique Church. They affirmed, in ways that are similar to the witness of Christ's passion and resurrection to his divine and human natures, both her humanity and her miraculous (or deified) qualities.

The legends concerning the death and assumption of the Virgin Mary into heaven appeared first in texts dating from the end of the fifth or beginning of the sixth century – although it is likely that they circulated, perhaps orally, in the Eastern Christian world for several centuries before this time.[96] Different traditions survive in a variety of languages, with two main versions circulating in the Byzantine empire as well as in the regions that it influenced, including the West. Stephen Shoemaker, following the attempts of Antoine Wenger and Michel van Esbroeck to establish 'families' of texts,[97] classifies these as the 'Palm of the Tree of Life' and the 'Bethlehem' versions; there are also versions to which Shoemaker assigns titles including 'Coptic' and 'A-Typical'.[98] The prototype for the 'Palm of the Tree of Life' version is preserved only in a set of Syriac fragments known as the *Obsequies of the Holy Virgin*, which belongs to the earliest period of Marian dormition accounts.[99] These fragments contain scattered episodes belonging to a longer narrative of Mary's death and assumption, including an account of a heavenly tour that she experienced immediately after her translation to heaven.[100] A sixth-century Greek version of this narrative became the basis for John of Thessalonike's early seventh-century

---

[95] *Gospel of Nikodemos (Byzantine recensions)* 10.1–2, 10.1.3c–4a, ed. Gounelle 2007, 226–41 and discussion, 56–8.

[96] See Mimouni 1995; Shoemaker 2002; Shoemaker 2015.

[97] Wenger 1955, 66; van Esbroeck 1981.   [98] Shoemaker 2002, 25–77.

[99] Shoemaker 2002, 33; trans. Wright 1865, 42–51.

[100] Shoemaker 2002, 34. According to Shoemaker, a complete version of this earliest narrative survives only in an Ethiopic translation, called the *Liber Requiei*. He provides a translation of the latter, along with its Syriac counterparts, in his Appendix A, 290–350.

homily on the Dormition. The 'Bethlehem' version of Mary's dormition circulated in a Syriac text known as the *Six Books*,[101] as well as in a Greek *Discourse on the Dormition* that was attributed to John the Evangelist.[102] Either one or both of these two sources influenced most of the subsequent homiletic treatment of the Virgin Mary's dormition in the Greek-speaking Byzantine world.

The 'Palm of the Tree of Life' version of Mary's dormition begins with her meeting on the Mount of Olives with an angel who informs her of her approaching death and gives her a palm branch from the Tree of Life. The Virgin then returns to her house in Jerusalem, where she begins to prepare herself for this event, informing her female servants and arranging her affairs. The apostles are then transported miraculously from their various missions around the inhabited world, with John arriving first at the house. The rest of the apostles arrive shortly after this, followed by Christ with a company of Old Testament prophets and angels. Mary then dies and Christ receives her soul, handing it to the archangel Michael who takes it directly to heaven. The apostles prepare a bier and process with Mary's body to the tomb at Gethsemane. During this procession, however, a Jew (sometimes described as a high priest) named Jephonias attempts to upset the bier. An angel cuts off his arms at the elbows, however, as he grasps the bier; he then repents and is healed. The apostles then continue to the tomb and place Mary's body inside, sealing it with a stone. They keep watch outside the tomb, waiting for Christ to return. After three days, he reappears and takes the body, along with the apostles, up to heaven where the body and soul are joined together again. The apostles then return to earth in order to fulfil their missions while the Virgin Mary remains in paradise, seated next to the Father and the Son.[103]

The 'Bethlehem' version is meanwhile transmitted in several Syriac versions including the *Six Books* narrative, some of which survive in ancient palimpsest manuscripts. The most influential text to emerge from this family, as we saw above, is the Greek *Discourse on the Dormition*, which was attributed to St John the Theologian (or Evangelist). According to van Esbroeck, this was a medieval 'best-seller', which survives in over 100 Greek

---

[101] The *Six Books* survives in a number of Syriac manuscripts; see the edition by Wright 1865. For discussion, see Shoemaker 2002, 46–57.

[102] *Transitus of (ps-)John the Evangelist*, ed. Tischendorf 1866; trans. Elliott 1993 (2004), 701–8.

[103] This abbreviated summary is based on that provided in Shoemaker 2002, 37–8. Certain details, such as the apostles' conversation concerning Christ's 'mysteries' as they wait outside the tomb and the tour of heaven and hell after the Virgin's resurrection, appear in some early versions but are not picked up in the later homiletic tradition.

manuscripts, as well as in Georgian, Arabic, Latin and Church Slavonic versions.[104] The 'Bethlehem' version of the narrative differs from the 'Palm of the Tree of Life' story in that it places Mary in Bethlehem, whence she visits Jerusalem in order to pray at Christ's tomb. She receives her angelic visitation, informing her of her approaching death, at the tomb. The Virgin then returns to Bethlehem where she is joined by the apostles (who are transported miraculously to her house from their various missions). After this, she performs some miracles and then prepares to die. As Shoemaker has suggested, this version of the dormition story contains a distinctly anti-Judaic aspect: the Jews obstruct or even attack the Virgin Mary at various points in the narrative, with the story about Jephonias being elaborated to an even greater degree than in the 'Palm' version.[105] Whereas some narratives belonging to this version omit any mention of Mary's bodily assumption into heaven or resurrection, others do include this element of the story.[106]

There has been scholarly controversy concerning the possibility that some of the Bethlehem narratives reflect an earlier tradition (sometimes called 'Dormitionist'), which has not yet taken the step (as in the case of the 'Assumptionist' tradition) of affirming the Mary's early resurrection in heaven following her bodily assumption.[107] In addition, whereas Mimouni, Daley and a few other scholars have argued for the association of the earliest legends of Mary's assumption with an anti-Chalcedonian doctrinal position,[108] Shoemaker maintains that there is no such connection. He prefers to see the separate literary traditions surrounding the legend of Mary's dormition as reflecting diverse – and sometimes even gnostic – Christian perspectives in the late antique world. According to him, variations in the narratives concerning the Virgin Mary's death and assumption did not reflect particular doctrinal positions; rather, they emerged from a growing Marian devotion that was common to both 'orthodox' and 'heterodox' Christian communities in the Near East.[109] Whereas Mimouni acknowledges that direct evidence for a connection between Miaphysite belief and interest in the Virgin Mary's fate after death is lacking, he points to the coincidence of the discussions leading

---

[104] Van Esbroeck 1981, 269; Mimouni 1995, 118–27; Shoemaker 2002, 51.
[105] Shoemaker 1999; Shoemaker 2002, 51–2.   [106] Mimouni 1995, 125–7. Shoemaker 2002, 52.
[107] The main proponents of the two sides of the argument are Mimouni 1995, 18–21 (who argues for the chronological priority of the 'Dormitionist' legend) and Shoemaker 2002, 20–5 (who contests any chronological development – or organic relationship – between the two traditions).
[108] Cothenet 1961; Mimouni 1995, esp. 1–21, 664–6; Daley 1998, 7–12. Mary Clayton (1998, 25–6) also takes up this theory.
[109] Shoemaker 2002, esp. 15–25, 256–62.

up to – and following – the Council of Chalcedon in 451 and the first emergence of Syriac texts on the dormition.[110] In my view, this subject requires further investigation, with focus on both internal and external aspects of the surviving texts, for an answer to be reached.[111]

The third important source for middle Byzantine preachers was one which they regarded as apostolic – as opposed to the apocryphal sources that provided the outlines of the story. This was the short passage in (ps-) Dionysios the Areopagite's *Divine Names*, which had circulated widely since its probable composition in late fifth- or early sixth-century Syria.[112] The author, who was believed by Byzantine commentators to be the apostle who is mentioned in Acts 17: 34, was invoked reverently by Andrew of Crete, as 'a man learned in sacred doctrine ... to whom hints of the mysterious representations of super-celestial minds were revealed, in a way worthy of the angels'.[113] The significant passage in the *Divine Names* is in fact phrased so ambiguously that some modern scholars have suggested that the 'life-giving and God-receiving body' (ζωαρχικοῦ καὶ θεοδόχου σώματος) – which the author claims to have witnessed along with the other apostles – refers to the Eucharist rather than to the recently deceased Virgin Mary.[114] Whatever its author may originally have meant, the text was interpreted as a witness to Mary's deathbed scene by Byzantine liturgical writers from about the seventh century onward. (Ps-)Dionysios expresses this vision (whether eucharistic or Marian) in mystical terms, describing how the apostles – including especially his 'teacher', Hierotheos – experienced an ecstatic 'communion with the things praised' as they met together in the holy place.[115]

The feast of the Virgin Mary's *Koimesis* or Dormition('falling asleep') was first celebrated in Jerusalem, probably in connection with her tomb near Gethsemane and its associated church.[116] It was added to the Constantinopolitan liturgical calendar at the end of the sixth century,

---

[110] Mimouni 1995, 665.

[111] It is also worth noting in this context that some ambiguity concerning Mary's actual death exists in the Roman Catholic Church; see Jugie 1944, 506–82; cf. Shoemaker 2002, 9–17.

[112] (ps-)Dionysios the Areopagite, *The Divine Names* III.2, ed. Suchla 1990, 141. 1–17; trans. Luibheid 1987, 70.

[113] Andrew of Crete, *Homily II on the Dormition*, PG 97, 1060D, trans. Daley 1998, 127 (9).

[114] (ps-)Dionysios the Areopagite, *On the Divine Names* III.2, ed. Suchla 1990, 141. 6; for discussion, see Jugie 1944, 99–101; Andreopoulos 2016, 80– 2. This theory is strongly contested in Shoemaker 2002, 29–30.

[115] καὶ τὴν πρὸς τὰ ὑμνούμενα κοινωνίαν πάσχων ..., (ps-)Dionysios the Areopagite, *The Divine Names* III.2, ed. Suchla 1990, 141. 12; trans. Luibheid 1987, 70.

[116] The church, which was built around a first-century necropolis, was probably built in the fifth century. It is not mentioned in the Jerusalem *Armenian Lectionary*, but appears to have featured in

but may not have been celebrated consistently in churches throughout the empire until about a century later. The earliest surviving homilies, including those by John of Thessalonike, Theoteknos of Livias and possibly (ps-) Modestos of Jerusalem, date from the seventh century. However, a flowering of liturgical sermons for the feast, including several 'trilogies' or three-part homiletic series, took place in the course of the eighth century. These include the series of Dormition sermons that are attributed to Germanos of Constantinople, John of Damascus, Andrew of Crete and Kosmas Vestitor. Some preachers, including Theodore of Stoudios, Leo VI and John Geometres, continued to compose sermons in honour of the feast in subsequent centuries; however, their output was less prolific (although of equal theological and devotional importance) than that of their eighth-century counterparts.

The introduction of the feast of the Virgin Mary's Dormition into the Western (Latin) church calendar took place during the papacy of Sergius (687–701), who was a Syrian by birth.[117] According to Wenger, however, the reference in the *Liber Pontificalis* may refer merely to a procession on 15 August, not to the feast itself. He suggests that the feast was already in use by the middle of the seventh century (perhaps under Pope Theodore, 642–9), after which the need for appropriate homilies and readings on this subject began.[118] It was during the following centuries that Latin compilers of homiliaries and other liturgical collections began to translate the orations of Andrew of Crete, John of Damascus, Germanos of Constantinople and Kosmas Vestitor. Latin preachers themselves were constrained by earlier condemnation of apocryphal texts such as the *Transitus* attributed to (ps-)Melito of Sardis that were circulating in the West.[119] Nevertheless, the eighth and ninth centuries saw the beginnings of preaching on this subject, much influenced by Byzantine prototypes, by figures such as Paul the Deacon[120] and Ambrosius Autpertus.[121]

In the discussion that follows, I shall focus primarily on Greek homilies that were produced in Thessalonike, Constantinople and Palestine between the seventh and tenth centuries. This is a body of material that

---

the fifth-century Patriarch Juvenal's plan to promote the Chalcedonian definition of Christ's two natures after 451. See Bagatti, Piccirillo and Prodomo 1975, 11–82; Shoemaker 2002, 98–107.

[117] *Liber Pontificalis*, ed. Duchesne, vol. 1, 376; Jugie 1944, 196, n. 1. See Dell'Acqua 2019, 239–41; Dell'Acqua 2020, 262.

[118] Wenger 1955, 141.

[119] This occurred in response to the Gelasian Decree. See Dobschütz 1912, 334–57. For discussion of the reception of the Dormition tradition in the West after the ninth century, see Jugie 1944, 360–88.

[120] Paul the Deacon, *Homilies I–II on the Assumption*; Lambot 1934; Wenger 1955, 144, nn. 2–3.

[121] Ambrosius Autpertus, *Homily on the Assumption of Mary*; see also Dell'Acqua 2020, 103–5, 262–4.

was produced in honour of the feast especially after it became well established in churches from the beginning of the eighth century. As in the case of other Marian festal sermons, this analysis attempts to trace variations in doctrine, literary or theological themes, and devotional aspects, such as Mary's intercessory role or maternal qualities. It will become clear on the basis of this discussion that whereas doctrinal consensus concerning this important event in the Virgin's life was established early, preachers could be innovative in their theological emphasis, rhetorical method and devotional response to the feast. It is possible to discern not only variation between individual preachers, but also the development of certain preoccupations, such as Mary's human or maternal relationship with her Son, in the course of these centuries.

With regard to the narrative of the dormition story itself, small differences appear between the various Byzantine homilies. Shoemaker has noted, for example, the emphasis on some 'gnostic' elements in seventh-century texts such as John of Thessalonike's influential homily on the Dormition.[122] When the evangelist John (Christ's 'beloved' disciple) returns to the house on Mount Zion in Jerusalem, Mary addresses him as follows:

> 'Remember that [Christ] loved you above all the Apostles; remember that you, rather than any of the others, leaned on his breast. Remember that it was to you alone, as you reclined on his breast, that he spoke the mystery that no one knows except me and you, since you are the chosen virgin, and since he did not wish me to grieve, for I was his dwelling place. For I said to him, "Tell me what you have said to John", and he gave you a command and shared it also with me.'[123]

Passages such as this suggest that Christ conveyed secret knowledge to certain disciples or even to his mother Mary; the recipients vary according to different gnostic traditions, but the elements of exclusivity and mystery are always present. A detail which was not mentioned by John of Thessalonike, but which may reflect earlier – and possibly heterodox – accounts of the dormition is the *charta*, or leaf of papyrus, which Mary passes on to the evangelist John, according to the eighth-century preacher Kosmas Vestitor. This text, according to Kosmas, contained mysteries which Jesus had revealed to his mother when he was still a small child.[124] The relationship between the apostles, who sometimes

---

[122] Shoemaker 2002, 54, 205, 210–11, 217, 251.

[123] John of Thessalonike, *Homily on the Dormition* 6, ed. Jugie 1925 [1990], 384.5–13, trans. Daley 1998, 53.

[124] Kosmas Vestitor, *Homily II on the Dormition*, ed. Orbán 2000, 108.123–109.143; see also Wenger 1953, 287 – 89.

vie with each other when presiding over Mary's death-bed, the inclusion or not of the incident involving Jephonias and, above all, the manner in which the deceased Virgin is placed in the tomb and how soon she is assumed into heaven may also vary in the separate homiletic accounts. It is striking, for example, that the early eighth-century patriarch Germanos of Constantinople diverges from other Byzantine preachers in suggesting that Mary's body disappeared almost immediately after the apostles placed her reverently in the tomb at Gethsemane. Before they could even seal the tomb, 'as all looked on . . . the Virgin's pure body was taken away'.[125] Such variation could perhaps be justified on the grounds that these events were associated with apocryphal, rather than canonical, sources. However, homilists were also frequently motivated, as we shall see below, by theological or literary considerations. Above all, Byzantine preachers emphasised the mysterious nature of the Virgin Mary's death and assumption into heaven, as they developed what Brian Daley calls 'a cultivated vagueness' with regard to the events that they were celebrating.[126]

Another aspect of these sermons that could vary from writer to writer was the extent to which they displayed interest in, or knowledge of, the topographical features of the scenes that they described. Most of the Byzantine preachers believed, according to the 'Palm of the Tree of Life' version of the legend, that Mary was living in the highest (and most ancient) part of the city of Jerusalem, known as Mount Zion, at the time when their story began. She occupied the house that included an upper room where Jesus had presided over the last supper with his disciples (Mt 26:17-30; Mk 14:12-25; Lk 22:7-38; Jn 13:1–17: 26) and appeared to his disciples at the time when Thomas doubted his resurrection (Jn 20:26-9). Of the preachers who might be expected to know the holy city well, (ps-) Modestos of Jerusalem displayed little awareness of its topography.[127] Theoteknos of Livias, Andrew of Crete and John of Damascus, all of whom either originated or worked in the region of Palestine, meanwhile revealed their knowledge of the location of the house on Zion and the

---

[125] Germanos I of Constantinople, *Homily II on the Dormition*, PG 98, 369C, trans. Daley 1998, 177.

[126] Daley 1998, 27.

[127] Daley notes that the ninth-century patriarch, Photios, doubted the authenticity of this homily. See Photios, *Bibliotheca*, Cod. 275, ed. Henry 1977, vol. 8, 119; PG 104, 244C; Daley 1998, 42, n. 41. It is noteworthy that the author refers to the doctrine of Christ's two wills (divine and human), which was affirmed at the third Council of Constantinople (680–1); Daley 1998, 15. M. Jugie is also sceptical of the homily's authenticity, assigning it to the end of the seventh or beginning of the eighth century; see Jugie 1944, 214–23.

tomb, with its associated church, in the garden of Gethsemane. Andrew, although probably preaching either in Constantinople or on Crete at later stages in his ecclesiastical career, remembered the marble slabs in the upper room on Zion on which pilgrims could still see imprints of the Virgin's continuous kneeling prayers.[128] Both preachers also described the church at Gethsemane either literally or in terms that were intended to evoke its allegorical meaning.[129] It appears that John may even have been preaching during the vigil of the Dormition in that location, as he addressed his congregation in following words: 'You see, dear fathers and brothers, what this illustrious tomb has to say to us . . .'[130]

Mention of the Virgin's relics in the homilies on the Dormition, especially the robe (or robes) and the grave clothes, occurred frequently, perhaps indicating an interest in promoting veneration of these objects. It is puzzling that some preachers who lived between the early seventh and tenth centuries (including John of Thessalonike, Kosmas Vestitor and John Geometres) described Mary offering two robes to a pair of faithful widows who served her. If we consider the fact that one robe, housed at the church of the Blachernai at least from the early seventh century onward, attracted devotion in Constantinople, it is difficult to see why these Byzantine orators felt the need to mention two garments.[131] The grave clothes, which either remained in the tomb or were assumed into heaven along with the Virgin's body according to different preachers, were some-times mentioned in the closing sections of the Dormition homilies.[132] One other object received emphasis in many sermons, namely, the palm branch that the angel gave to the Theotokos at the beginning of the narrative and

---

[128] Andrew of Crete, *Homily I on the Dormition*, PG 97, 1073A, trans. Daley 1998, 104. [J.-P. Migne erroneously printed this homily as the second in the trilogy; see Daley 1998, 115, n. 1.]

[129] Andrew of Crete, *Homily II on the Dormition*, PG 97, 1064C–1065D, trans. Daley 1998, 129–30. [This homily is printed in PG as the first in the series, according to Daley 1998, 135, n. 1.] John of Damascus, *Homily III on the Dormition*, ed. Kotter 1988, 550.16–551.45; trans. Daley 1998, 233.

[130] John of Damascus, *Homily II on the Dormition*, ed. Kotter 1988, 536.1–4, trans. Daley 1998, 222; see also Daley 1998, 230, n. 35.

[131] See, for example, John of Thessalonike, *Homily on the Dormition* 6, ed. Jugie 1925 (1990), 385.26; Daley 1998, 54. Two robes are also mentioned in the Georgian *Life of the Virgin* 105, ed. and trans. Shoemaker 2012, 132.

[132] See, for example, John of Thessalonike, *Homily on the Dormition* 14, ed. Jugie 1925 (1990), 401.34–402.2, trans. Daley 1998, 67 (John says that the shroud remained in the tomb after Mary's body was assumed into heaven; however, he does not relate what happened to it after that); Germanos I of Constantinople, *Homily II on the Dormition* 9, PG 98, 369C, trans. Daley 1998, 177 (Germanos says that 'the shroud was then gently taken up into the air from the Apostles' hands in a light cloud . . .'); John of Damascus, *Homily II on the Dormition* 17, ed. Kotter 1988, 535.11–12 (John suggests here that the burial cloths were left behind, after the Virgin's body was assumed into heaven); (ps-)John of Damascus, *The Euthymiac History*, ed. Kotter 1988, 536.5–539.68; trans. Daley 1998, 224–6.

which she then entrusted to her caretaker, the apostle John. Some preachers, such as John of Thessalonike, suggested that this object would later become a miracle-working relic, as we see in the following passage:

> When the holy Theotokos, Mary, was about to lay aside her body, the great angel came to her and said, 'Rise, Mary, take this branch of palm, which he who planted Paradise gave to me, and give it to the Apostles so that they may carry it as they sing before you, for after three days you will lay aside your body ... And do not be concerned about the palm branch; for by it many shall be healed, and it shall be a norm of testing for all who live in Jerusalem.'[133]

That veneration of the tomb itself, along with any objects that were associated with the life or death of the Virgin Mary, continued even after the Muslim occupation of Jerusalem is attested by John of Damascus, in the final section of his first homily on the Dormition:

> Just as if one should store up costly ointment in his clothes or in some other place, and later remove it, some trace of the fragrance would remain when the ointment is gone, so now, too, that holy, sacred, and spotless body, full of divine fragrance, that boundless spring of grace ... still did not leave that tomb without honor: it gave it a share of divine fragrance and grace, and left it as a source of healing and of all good gifts for those who approach it in faith.[134]

Another feature of most Dormition homilies was anti-Judaic polemic, which often featured in the section of the narrative concerning Jephonias, the doubting Jew who lost his hands when attempting to overturn the Virgin Mary's bier as it was being carried from the house on Zion to the tomb.[135] Although preachers took the opportunity to castigate the Jews, blaming them for their unbelief and responsibility for Christ's passion, they also suggested that the miraculous restoration of Jephonias' hands, after touching the bier, caused them to believe in the sanctity of the Virgin.[136] John of Thessalonike stated that, following the miracle, Peter allowed Jephonias to remain alone with Mary's body for three hours, blessing her and reading out witness texts from 'the holy books of Moses

[133] John of Thessalonike, *Homily on the Dormition* 3, ed. Jugie 1925 [1990], 378.21–379.13; trans. Daley 1998, 49–50 (with adjustments).

[134] John of Damascus, *Homily I on the Dormition* 13, ed. Kotter 1988, 499.12–19, trans. Daley 1998, 198.

[135] Shoemaker 1999. The anti-Judaic element is even stronger in narratives associated with the 'Bethelehem' tradition; see Shoemaker 2002, esp. 51–2.

[136] See, for example, Theoteknos of Livias, *Homily on the Dormition* 19–20, ed. Wenger 1955, 280.20–282.9; trans. Daley 1998, 75–6.

and the other prophets'.[137] This offered what would have been regarded as a positive interpretation of an ancient – but undeniably polemical – section of the narrative, while also linking it to the kind of typology that was especially associated with liturgical praise of the Theotokos. John of Damascus also attempted a more optimistic spin on this story, concluding his version with the words, 'So a crisis can often be the mother of decisions that are for our good.'[138]

The doctrinal position of the various preachers, as regards Mary's death and assumption into heaven, was largely consistent, although it could be expressed in different ways. From the seventh through to the tenth century, Byzantine homilists emphasised the reality of the Virgin's death although they also stated that her body was incorruptible. The seventh-century Palestinian preacher Theoteknos of Livias wrote, for example:

> And even though the God-bearing body of that holy one did taste death, it was not corrupted; for it was kept incorrupt and free of decay, and it was lifted up to heaven with her pure and spotless soul by the holy archangels and powers . . .[139]

Andrew of Crete, in the early eighth century, stated that the Virgin Mary 'obeyed the laws of nature and reached the end of life',[140] while John Geometres, at the end of the tenth, affirmed more graphically that 'she went to the earth, complying with the common law of nature'.[141] Even as they recognised the reality of Mary's death, however, the various preachers stressed the incorruptibility of her body – even after three days in the tomb. This miraculous aspect of her person was linked with her perpetual virginity, before, during and after the birth of Christ, as John of Damascus stated succinctly in the following passage:

> It was fitting that she, who preserved her virginity undamaged by childbirth, should have her body preserved from corruption even in death.[142]

---

[137] John of Thessalonike, *Homily on the Dormition* 13, ed. Jugie 1925 [1990], 400.22–33, trans. Daley 1998, 66. This preacher also states that Jephonias had been a high priest in the Jewish temple before his conversion to Christianity.

[138] John of Damascus, *Homily II on the Dormition* 13, ed. Kotter 1988, 530.18–19; trans. Daley 1998, 217.

[139] Theoteknos of Livias, *Homily on the Dormition* 15, ed. Wenger 1955, 278.12–15, trans. Daley 1998, 74 (4).

[140] Andrew of Crete, *Homily I on the Dormition*, PG 97, 1073A–B, trans. Daley 1998, 104. Later in the same sermon, Andrew expanded on this statement, writing that 'the Mother of God, without altering anything of the laws of our nature, obeyed the law laid upon us and completed her life in the flesh under the same conditions as we do, though she entered and left this life in a wonderful way'; PG 97, 1085C, trans. Daley 1998, 112–13.

[141] John Geometres, *Life of the Virgin* 31, ed. Wenger 1955, 386–7.

[142] John of Damascus, *Homily II on the Dormition* 14, ed. Kotter 1988, 531.24–5, trans. Daley 1998, 218.

Reasoning such as this reflected a long-standing patristic belief in the connection between physical virginity and the eternal and incorruptible life of God, as Trinity, and the angels. In the same way that Christ's virginal birth from Mary revealed his divine, as well as human, nature, it also protected her from the dissolution after death that affects all other human beings. Andrew of Crete pursued this mystery somewhat further in his first homily on the Dormition, asking how the separate parts of Mary's body could be reassembled after her assumption into heaven. He ascribed this process to the Creator's inscrutable will, asserting that something entirely new and different must have taken place in the destiny of this otherwise mortal woman.[143]

Most Byzantine preachers preferred to remain apophatic with regard to what happened in heaven, once Mary's body and soul had been assumed separately and at different times, however. Such ambiguity has led Martin Jugie to suggest that certain later theologians, including John Geometres, developed an idea of Mary's 'double' assumption into heaven.[144] They argue that according to this tenth-century orator, Mary's body and soul remained separated after being assumed into heaven, awaiting there the day of general resurrection like all other human beings. After close inspection of the relevant passage, I am able to agree with Wenger that John did not deny that Mary's body and soul were reunited in heaven; he sought rather to distinguish the manner of her assumption from that of Christ's ascension.[145] Most earlier preachers, while avoiding clear statements

---

[143] Andrew writes as follows: 'For as her womb was not corrupted in giving birth, so her flesh did not perish in dying. What a miracle! The child put corruption to flight, and the tomb did not admit of corruption ... I do not know if the parts of her body were all immediately joined to form a single, composite whole – for I shall make little philosophical speculation on these things, since the Creator apparently saw fit, in his inscrutable mind, to honour his mother this way – or if each part emerged over the other, one taking its new position on the outside, the other on the inside, after they had all been separated from each other; or if the sequence [of reconstitution] which supernaturally ran its course in her was strange and different, and all happened in a truly new way in her, as she received beyond her own nature a supernatural structure that lies beyond all words and all knowledge of ours.' Andrew of Crete, *Homily I on the Dormition*, PG 97, 1081D–1084B, trans. Daley 1998, 110–11.

[144] Jugie 1944, 316–22. Antoine Wenger, however, asserts – on the basis of a close reading of Geometres' text – that whereas this author affirms (like all other Byzantine theologians) Mary's incorruptibility after death, he leaves the question of her early resurrection open – that is to say, as a mystery. See Wenger 1955, 197.

[145] John Geometres, *Life of the Virgin* 48, ed. Wenger 1955, 396.31–398.5: Καὶ τὸ παραδοξότερον· εἰς οὐρανοὺς ὑψομένη καθάπερ τὸ πνεῦμα δίχα τοῦ σώματος, οὕτω καὶ νῦν τὸ σῶμα δίχα τοῦ πνεύματος, ἵνα καὶ τὸ πρὸς τὸν υἱὸν ὁμοῦ καὶ τὸ πρὸς δούλους δείξῃ καὶ κοινὸν ὁμοῦ καὶ διάφορον· αἰρομένη μὲν εἰς οὐρανούς, ἀλλὰ καὶ ὅλη καὶ πρὸ τῆς ἀναστάσεως, καθάπερ ἡμεῖς μετὰ τὴν ἀνάστασιν, καὶ ὅλη μὲν καθάπερ καὶ ὁ ταύτης υἱός, ἀλλὰ διηρημένη καὶ μετὰ τὴν διάλυσιν. Wenger translates this passage as follows: 'et ce qu'il y a de plus merveilleux, c'est que, élevée d'abord jusqu'aux cieux comme l'esprit sans le corps, c'est maintenant le corps qui est élevé sans l'esprit, afin de montrer par là à la fois ce qu'elle a de commun et de différent tant avec son Fils

about the Virgin Mary's early resurrection, implied that this was the outcome of her miraculous assumption into heaven. To take one example, Germanos of Constantinople (after breaking with tradition by suggesting that Mary's body flew up to heaven before the tomb could even be sealed) described her heavenly destiny in the following words:

> In this way, when you had suffered the death of your passing nature, your home was changed to the imperishable dwellings of eternity, where God dwells; and becoming yourself his permanent guest, Theotokos, you will not be separated from his company.[146]

Germanos further indicated that by entering heaven in body and soul, the Virgin Mary joined Christ in allowing human nature (in its deified form) to be eternally present in heaven. As John Geometres put it, two centuries or so later, 'in this manner, it is not only by the Son, but also by her, that our nature was introduced into heaven and rules over all visible as well as invisible things'.[147]

The importance of the dormition narrative for the Virgin Mary's role as protector and intercessor thus rests on belief in her proximity to Christ in heaven, following her death and assumption. It is no surprise therefore that the various sermons that honoured the feast of the Dormition frequently stressed this aspect of Marian devotion. Such emphasis was present in the seventh-century homilies as much as in the later works. If any development can be detected, it lies in the ways that Mary's intercessory function tended to be invoked. Whereas the early seventh-century works often stressed Mary's role as 'queen', 'fortification', 'protector' or 'ambassador', sermons dating from the early or middle of the eighth century onward mentioned more frequently her role as 'God-bearer' or 'mother', suggesting that her close relationship with Christ offered hope of intercession, or even salvation, for the human race. Germanos of Constantinople in fact went further than some of his contemporaries in attributing (perhaps hyperbolically) all salvation to the agency of the Mother of God:

> No one is filled with the knowledge of God except through you, all-holy One; no one is saved but through you, God-bearer (Θεοτόκος); no one is free of danger but through you, Virgin Mother (Παρθενομῆτορ); no one is

---

qu'avec nous. En effet, elle est élevée aux cieux mais tout entière, et avant la résurrection, comme nous le serons nous-mêmes après la résurrection. Elle est élevée tout entière comme son Fils, mais divisée et après la disjonction.'

[146] Germanos of Constantinople, *Homily I on the Dormition*, PG 98, 348B; trans. Daley 1998, 159 (with one adjustment).

[147] John Geometres, *Life of the Virgin* 41, ed. Wenger 1955, 392.32–4.

redeemed but through you, Mother of God (Θεομῆτορ); no one ever receives mercy gratuitously except through you, Container of God (Θεοχώρητε) .[148]

Byzantine preachers employed affective language to varying degrees in their descriptions of the relationship between Mary and Christ, or between either of these figures and their faithful followers. Although some increase in such language is noticeable in Marian sermons after the end of Iconoclasm, it is not entirely absent from the works of earlier preachers. Theoteknos of Livias, (ps-)Modestos of Jerusalem and Germanos of Constantinople all described Mary's nurturing of Christ as a baby in vivid terms.[149] John of Damascus, when describing his own love for the Mother of God, was even more prone to rhetorical – even erotic – outbursts of emotion:

> Having come to this point in my discourse, I am – if I may express my inner feelings – on fire with hot and restless yearning, I am seized with a thrill of awe and bathed in joyous tears, imagining that I could embrace that blessed and beloved bed, so full of wonders ... I pressed my eyes, my lips, my forehead, my neck, my cheeks to her limbs, rejoicing in these sensations as if her body were present and I could touch it, even though I knew full well that I cannot see the one I long for with these eyes.[150]

However, it was from the ninth century onward that emotional expressions of love and devotion, expressed by preachers on behalf of their audiences, were manifested most fully. George of Nikomedia's sermon on the lament of the Mother of God at the foot of the cross set a precedent for the kind of language that appeared in John Geometres' oration on the Dormition.[151] The artistry with which the latter contrasted Mary's joy at her 'falling asleep' with her grief at the foot of the cross shows the extent to which such panegyrists were able to adapt rhetorical methods to the task of expounding a theological message.[152]

---

[148] Germanos of Constantinople, *Homily I on the Dormition*, PG 98, 349C, trans. Daley 1998, 160–1 (8) (with adjustments).

[149] Theoteknos of Livias, *Homily on the Dormition* 5, ed. Wenger 1955, 274.4–8, trans. Daley 1998, 71–2; (ps-)Modestos of Jerusalem, *Enkomion on the Dormition*, PG 86, 3297C–3200A, trans. Daley 1998, 93; Germanos I of Constantinople, *Homily I on the Dormition*, PG 98, 348A–B, trans. Daley 1998, 159 (6).

[150] John of Damascus, *Homily II on the Dormition* 5, ed. Kotter 1988, 522.1–523.4; trans. Daley 1998, 209.

[151] George of Nikomedia, *Homily on Great Friday*, PG 100, 1457–89; see Tsironis 1998, 279–89.

[152] John Geometres, *Life of the Virgin* 21, ed. Wenger 1955, 378.32–380.9. Both emotions reveal Mary's human nature as well as her unconditional love for Christ. The orator seeks to show in an exaggerated way the extent to which both grief and happiness draw human beings closer to God.

Byzantine sermons on the Dormition thus present the Virgin Mary as a human being who was destined for a miraculous end. They emphasise the reality of her death, like that of Christ, but also the incorruptibility of her pure and virginal body. The manner of her death, which was painless and involved no physical dissolution, bore witness to her role as the container and birth-giver of God. Thus Mary's virginity was connected with – or indeed led to – the miraculous state of her body after death. The assumption into heaven, which most authors (following the dominant apocryphal tradition) describe as happening three days after Mary's burial, led to the mysterious reunion – indeed resurrection – of her body and soul in heaven. This destiny also allowed the Virgin to play an ongoing role as intercessor *par excellence* in Byzantine society. Although she occasionally manifested herself on earth in visions or dreams, Mary was more often pictured at the right hand of Christ in heaven. Her maternal relationship with him, which preachers described in relation either to his infancy or to his death on the cross, allowed the Virgin to enjoy a unique *parresia*, or 'freedom of speech' with her divine Son.

Occasional Homilies

This category includes a group of sermons that were composed for special, or occasional, events, such as the celebration of victory against enemy attacks, the consecration of Marian churches or translation of her relics, or the dedication of an icon of the Mother of God. The choice to analyse these homilies as a group is my own; their classification as 'occasional homilies' does not reflect a systematic generic concept on the part of Byzantine writers. Nevertheless, it is clear that orations celebrating Constantinopolitan victories over enemies including Persians, Avars, Arabs and Slavs share certain characteristics. Many of these texts attribute the city's deliverance from danger to the Virgin Mary. Unlike the festal homilies that we have examined so far, the emphasis falls more on Mary's intercessory and protective roles and less on her Christological importance. Although the seventh- and eighth-century texts refer to her as 'Virgin', 'Theotokos', 'Theometor' or even 'Mother of God', the figure that they portray is strong and intimidating; she displays few of the maternal or affective qualities that are described in post-iconoclastic festal sermons. The occasional orations also emphasise that the salvation of the imperial city depends on the Virgin Mary's favour. They enjoin their audiences to undertake prayer and vigils, seeking her intercession especially at times of military danger.

Two orations, which might also be described as narrative treatises, are ascribed in manuscripts to the early seventh-century synkellos Theodore.[153] This figure, who was an ecclesiastical assistant to the patriarch Sergios, appears to have been an eyewitness both of the translation of the Virgin's robe from Hagia Sophia to the Blachernai shrine after an attack on Constantinople by the Avars in 623 and of the devastating siege by both Avars and Persians in 626. The homily is divided into two parts: the first describes the theft of the robe by Galbios and Kandidos and its translation to the church of the Blachernai during the reign of the late fifth-century empress Verina, while the second provides an account of the return of the relic to Blachernai after it was placed in the Great Church for safekeeping during the Avar attack of 623.[154] As Averil Cameron emphasised in a seminal article on the subject, this homily reveals a developed cult of the Virgin Mary by the beginning of the seventh century, while also bearing witness to the sanctity of the Blachernai robe.[155] Theodore Synkellos' homily on the siege of 626 represents one of three contemporary literary witnesses to this event.[156] The orator describes the day-to-day unfolding of events, showing at each stage how the Theotokos intervened in order to bring victory to the Byzantines. Scholars have worked to unravel conflicting historical accounts of this siege, especially since later Byzantine historians embroidered the narratives that were provided by contemporary eyewitnesses including Theodore Synkellos. Confusion has arisen, for example, over the role played by icons of the Theotokos in the course of the siege; according to Theodore Synkellos, these were placed on the western gates of the city, presumably for prophylactic reasons.[157] Elsewhere in the text, emphasis is placed on actions which the Mother of God initiated herself (although without making herself visible), including the entrapment of Avars near one of her churches outside the city walls,[158] sinking a fleet of the enemy's boats (*monoxyla*),[159] and eventually causing both the Avar khagan and the Persian emperor to give up hope and

---

[153] Theodore Synkellos, *Inventio*, ed. Combefis 1648, Loparev 1895; Theodore Synkellos, *De obsidione*, ed. Sternbach 1900.
[154] On the legend of the translation of Mary's robe to Constantinople, see Wenger 1955, 111–39; Weyl Carr 2001; Wortley 2005.
[155] Cameron 1979b.
[156] The other two are George of Pisidia's *Bellum Avaricum*, ed. Pertusi 1959, and the *Chronicon Paschale*, ed. Dindorf 1832. For more analysis of the siege of 626 and its literary sources, see Hurbanič 2019.
[157] Theodore Synkellos, *De obsidione* 15, ed. Sternbach 1900, 304.4–9; trans. Makk 1975, 18–19.
[158] Ibid. 19, ed. Sternbach 1900, 305.37–306.12; trans. Makk 1975, 21–2.
[159] Ibid. 33, ed. Sternbach 1900, 311.17–40; trans. Makk 1975, 31–2.

retreat.[160] Similarities between these two texts include a tendency to compare events in Christian history with Old Testament antecedents and an emphasis on Mary's role as chief defender,[161] or as intercessor before the Christian God, of Constantinople.

An oration with a similar agenda is that which is attributed to Germanos I of Constantinople, celebrating the deliverance of the imperial city from an Arab attack in 718.[162] This text, which adopts a similar style to that of Theodore Synkellos' sermon on the siege of 626, addresses praise to the Mother of God (*Theometor*) for protecting Constantinople from 'Saracens, enemies of the confession that proclaims the glory of Christ'.[163] The preacher describes how this alien army, which was huge and irresistible, launched itself against the city without realising that it was protected by in invincible 'rampart', the Mother of God herself. Similar use is made of Old Testament examples of victory as in Theodore Synkellos' sermon on the siege of 626: the preacher cites the Jews' flight from Egypt, led by Moses, as a precedent for the divine favour experienced by Byzantines in the course of this siege.[164] References to the Theotokos are framed in more Christological language than was the case in Theodore Synkellos' sermon; however, the author attributes victory and the successful defence of the imperial city entirely to her intercessory agency. He also states more than once that such favour must be maintained by annual celebration of events such as this, during which panegyrical praise to the Virgin should be offered throughout the night.[165]

The two orations which the patriarch Photios delivered in commemoration of a Russian attack on Constantinople in 860 display characteristics that are similar to the previous examples.[166] According to this

---

[160] Ibid. 39, ed. Sternbach 1900, 314.1–17; trans. Makk 1975, 35–6.

[161] See Wenger 1955, 117–18, who identifies an interest in Old Testament history as one of Theodore's defining characteristics as a Christian orator.

[162] Germanos I of Constantinople, *Homily on the Deliverance of Constantinople*, ed. Grumel 1958. Several scholars, including Speck 2003, Darrouzès 1987, 7–8, and Kazhdan 1999, 58, have expressed doubts about the authenticity of this homily. It is variously ascribed to an anonymous author who was active about a century later or to Germanos I's namesake and successor, Germanos II (patriarch of Constantinople, *c.* 1222–40).

[163] σαρακηνοῖς τοῖς ἀντιτασσομένοις τῇ ὁμολογίᾳ τῆς δόξης αὐτοῦ ..., Germanos I of Constantinople, *Homily on the Deliverance of Constantinople* 9, ed. Grumel 1958, 193.

[164] Ibid. 12–15, 19, ed. Grumel 1958, 194–7.

[165] Ibid. 17, 23, ed. Grumel 1958, 195–6, 198. It is passages such as these which may account for the assignment of the homily to the Friday on which the *Akathistos Hymn* is sung, during the fifth week of Lent. Other manuscripts assign the text to the feast of the Dormition (15 August); see Grumel 1958, 183–5.

[166] Photios, *Homilies III and IV*, ed. Laourdas 1959, 29–52; trans. Mango 1958, 82–110. For further bibliography both on the homilies and on the events that they describe, see Mango 1958, 74, n. 1.

contemporary account, followed by some later historians, an army of Rus'
had unexpectedly descended on Constantinople from the Black Sea, laying
waste to islands in the Bosphoros and the surrounding countryside, before
mounting a siege against the imperial city.[167] The emperor Michael III
happened to be absent on a military campaign, thus leaving the city in
a vulnerable position. Photios describes in the second sermon, delivered
after the sudden and apparently miraculous retreat of the Rus', how he
sought the protection of the Mother of God, leading the people in prayer
and processing around the walls of the city with her robe:

> Immediately as the Virgin's garment went round the walls, the barbarians
> gave up the siege and broke camp, while we were delivered from impending
> capture and were granted unexpected salvation.[168]

The patriarch attributes this victory directly to God, who has forgiven his
people, but also implies that their prayers to the Virgin Mary played a role
in this outcome. These orations, which are written in a classicising style
with reference to mythological as well as Christian imagery, express sound
doctrine with regard to Mary's Christological role while also addressing her
as intercessor and protector of Constantinople – sometimes with the help
of military language:

> We put you forward as our arms, our rampart, our shield, our general: may
> you fight for your people![169]

Sermons that commemorate relics or the consecration of churches in the
Virgin Mary's honour offer similar opportunities for invocation of her
intercessory power. For example, Germanos of Constantinople's homily
on the consecration of the Virgin's shrine (probably at the church of the
Chalkoprateia), her belt and the swaddling clothes of Christ expresses
unqualified praise for the Theotokos. Germanos understands the physical
objects associated with the Virgin and her Son as offering access to their
power and mercy; their enveloping properties can also be seen as protecting
(in metaphorical terms) the people, their church and the whole city.[170]
Employing affective language that is reminiscent of Theodore the
Synkellos' description of an earlier patriarch's emotion on seeing the

---

[167] For a summary of this narrative, along with critical evaluation of the literary sources including
Photios' homilies, see Mango 1958, 75–7.

[168] Photios, *Homily IV, On the Departure of the Russians* 4, ed. Laourdas 1959, 45. 23–31; trans. Mango
1958, 102–3.

[169] Ibid. 7, ed. Laourdas 1959, 52. 8–9; trans. Mango 1958, 110 (with adjustments).

[170] See, for example, Germanos I of Constantinople, *Homily on the Holy Belt*, PG 98, 377B–C.

Virgin's robe, Germanos describes the feelings of those who come to venerate the belt as follows:

> Who, having gazed earnestly and with faith on your honoured belt, Theotokos, is not filled at once with delight? Who, on fervently falling down before it, has left without his petition being granted? Who, on contemplating your token, does not immediately forget every affliction? Words cannot express the nature of joy, wellbeing, and happiness that have been enjoyed by those [people] who come and stand in your sacred church, in which you have been well pleased for your honoured belt to be placed ... ?[171]

Another sermon, which has been attributed variously in manuscripts to Germanos, Michael Synkellos and Niketas of Paphlagon, describes the physical and spiritual veneration of Mary's holy relics by devout Constantinopolitan Christians.[172] Material manifestations of holy personages inspire an emotional response on the part of middle Byzantine panegyrists. Although such language may be exaggerated for rhetorical reasons, it conveys the theological teaching that the incarnate God, along with his human mother, continued to manifest himself in creation through the sacraments, relics and even painted icons. Such points of contact demand in turn a physical and emotional response on the part of the Byzantine faithful.

Intercession

It should be evident, on the basis of the discussion so far, that allusions to the Virgin Mary's intercessory power in middle Byzantine homilies depends to a large extent on the context and subject matter of individual orations. Preachers who composed orations for the great Marian feasts did invoke the help and protection of the Mother of God, usually reserving such passages for their closing sections or epilogues; however, they tended to be more preoccupied in the body of the text with expounding her place in the Christological mystery that was being celebrated. Even feasts such as the Virgin Mary's Nativity or Entrance into the Temple, which were based on the *Protevangelion of James* rather than the canonical New Testament, were interpreted as events that led up to the incarnation of Christ rather

---

[171] Germanos I of Constantinople, *Homily on the Holy Belt*, PG 98, 381C, trans. Cunningham 2008b, 254–55 (10).

[172] Anon., *Homily on the Translation of the Belt of the Theotokos*, ed. Combefis 1648, vol. 2, 791. Dirk Krausmüller attributes the homily, which he edits and translates in a slightly different version, to a Studite monk and synkellos named Michael; see Krausmüller 2021. Another important late ninth-century homily is that by the patriarch Euthymios; see Euthymios, *Enkomion on the Holy Belt*, ed. Jugie 1922 (2003), 505–14.

than as Marian celebrations in their own right. Nor did the Virgin's relationship with Byzantine Christians represent the primary focus of such orations. Preachers would praise the Theotokos for her physical and moral purity, address her by means of an inexhaustible supply of biblical types and metaphors, and describe her essential role in the conception, birth and ministry of Christ; however, appeals for intercession – although occasionally present in festal homilies – were more often reserved for those which I have described as 'occasional'. One important exception to this rule, however, were the numerous sermons on the Dormition of the Virgin, which invoked her mediating power in relation to Christ. This must have to do with the narrative content of such sermons, which describe Mary's assumption into heaven and subsequent position of power and influence.[173]

It is worth reminding ourselves here of the shifting meaning of 'intercession' in the middle Byzantine period.[174] According to Byzantine orthodox doctrine, Mary did not wield power in her own right; rather, she sought to influence God on the basis of the *parresia* ('freedom of speech') which she possessed both as his mother and, following her death and assumption, companion in heaven. Nevertheless, some homilies and hymns convey the impression that the Virgin Mary herself was capable of working miracles or even 'saving' Christians.[175] It is possible that such passages represent either hyperbolic expressions (which should not be taken literally) or that liturgical writers actually did blur the boundaries between divine and mediated power. We should also distinguish, as Annemarie Weyl Carr points out, between the concepts of *eleos* ('mercy') as an active – but not necessarily affective – quality and as a more 'reactive', or descriptive, quality. Weyl Carr argues that hymnographic portrayal of Mary's intercessory aspect in the middle Byzantine period is based on the antique concept that mercy is primarily acted out: as a property of God, it manifests itself in benevolence and justice.[176] This may help to explain why some homiletic invocation of the Theotokos appears to be one-way: preachers, on behalf of their congregations, called on the Mother of God to help them, defend the city or work other kinds of miracles. Appeals to

---

[173] It is striking, however, that Byzantine iconography did not exploit this theme to the extent that Western artists did, with their depictions of the Virgin ascending in glory or being crowned by Christ. Byzantine icons instead portray the deathbed scene in which Christ receives Mary's soul, pictured in all its vulnerability as a swaddled baby, before transferring it to the care of the archangel Michael who will take it to heaven. See, for example, two tenth-century icons (in ivory and steatite) that are reproduced in Evans and Wixom 1997, 155–6 (Pls. 101–2).

[174] For recent discussion of this question, see Cunningham 2015.

[175] See, for example, Germanos of Constantinople's *Homily I on the Dormition*, quoted above, n. 148.

[176] Weyl Carr forthcoming.

her intercessory power did not always convey the sense that she would automatically respond or that, if she did, such action would be inspired by her personal (or even maternal) love for humanity.

Such an approach to the intercessory function of the Virgin Mary appears to have changed in response to iconophile emphasis on the humanity of Christ, as Kalavrezou and Tsironis have argued; by the second half of the ninth century, preachers such as George of Nikomedia drew their audiences closer to the Mother of God by emphasising her tender and maternal feeling as she stood at the foot of the cross.[177] The portrayal of an entirely human figure must have encouraged Christians to view Mary as a sympathetic and merciful recipient of their petitions for help. I would argue, however, that conventions of a long-standing liturgical tradition, which often upheld the formal – and above all Christological – view of the Theotokos, meant that variations in her portrayal as intercessor depended as much on the creative intentions of individual preachers as it did on changing perceptions over time. It remains important, when assessing this aspect of the homiletic tradition, to consider the variety of influences that may have played a part in preachers' portrayal of Mary as intercessor and advocate for the rest of humanity.

Conclusion

The various homiletic forms that have been examined in this chapter represent an important body of evidence concerning the Virgin Mary in the middle Byzantine period. The conventional nature of such texts, which often begin with flowery prologues that appear indistinguishable one from another, masks actual variation in their treatment of biblical or apocryphal narratives, didactic method and praise or invocation of the Mother of God. In analysing so many sermons in the course of one chapter, I have inevitably condensed important aspects of their content and manner of expression. Nevertheless, I hope that this study will offer a general interpretative framework from which future studies may begin.[178]

Development in Marian preaching between the seventh and tenth centuries may be traced in various ways. First, it is noticeable that Christological preoccupations – in other words, the didactic need to demonstrate the Virgin Mary's essential role in the incarnation of Christ,

---

[177] Kalavrezou 1990; Kalavrezou 2000; Tsironis 2000.
[178] It is worth noting again here Fr Evgenios Iverites' work on the theological content of early eighth-century Greek homilies; see Iverites 2019.

remained constant throughout our period. Seventh-century festal and occasional homilies already viewed the Theotokos as the guarantor of Christ's human and divine natures, as propounded at the Council of Chalcedon in 451. Such teaching developed further in the course of the eighth and ninth centuries, perhaps in response to Iconoclasm, with elaboration of biblical types that reveal Mary's role, as a created but also sanctified receptacle for God. Her Jewish lineage, as attested in the second-century *Protevangelion of James*, terrestrial life and actual death (even if this process was reversed after three days in the tomb) also served to demonstrate the Virgin's link with the rest of humanity. Second, as I suggested in relation to festal sermons on Mary's Conception, Nativity and Entrance into the Temple, preachers from about the early eighth century onward began openly to employ and expound the second-century apocryphal narrative known as the *Protevangelion of James*. However, sermons which were assigned in manuscripts to the separate feasts of Mary's Conception, Nativity and Entrance into the Temple still frequently strayed from one topic to another – sometimes including all three – perhaps in response to the fact that celebration of the three feasts remained variable in different parts of the empire during this period. A narrative concerning the Virgin's death and assumption into heaven, based on the Syriac *Obsequies of the Holy Virgin*, was accepted into the Greek homiletic tradition even earlier, with seventh-century preachers such as John of Thessalonike, Theoteknos of Livias and possibly (ps-)Modestos of Jerusalem contributing homilies on this subject. And finally, the progression from an impersonal, but powerful, intercessory figure to a more tender and motherly Virgin Mary may be traced through comparison of supplicatory sections in various festal and occasional homilies. I have argued that whereas such a development did occur between the seventh and mid ninth centuries, probably as a result of iconophile emphasis on the humanity of both Christ and his mother, variation remained, being determined either by generic conventions or by individual authorial approaches to the Virgin Mary.

The Marian homiletic tradition consisted of many strands, from which individual preachers wove images of this holy figure that suited their particular didactic or devotional purposes. The richness of this literary tradition, which remains to be fully appreciated by scholars, gave impetus to a richly allusive and intertextual process of liturgical preaching. Not only did existing sermons inspire others on similar or related subjects, but they also informed a growing hymnographic tradition, which will be explored in the following chapter.

CHAPTER 4

Theology in Verse: Middle Byzantine Hymnography

'Glory to God in the highest' (Lk 2:14), I hear from the bodiless ones in Bethlehem today, [as they sing] to him who was well pleased that there should be peace on earth. The Virgin is now wider than the heavens; light has shone upon those who are in darkness and has exalted the humble, who are singing like the angels, 'Glory to God in the highest'.[1]

Middle Byzantine hymns, which were sung either by cantors or choirs in churches throughout Constantinople, along with cities and provinces of the outlying empire, offer praise and thanksgiving to God. One of the predominant purposes of this genre, which includes texts and their musical settings, is to express joyful thanksgiving to God. As we see in the passage that opens this chapter, humanity joins the whole of creation in this activity: this is a cosmological event in which the divine and created realms are eternally joined in harmonious praise.[2] The Marian feasts, which were added to the Constantinopolitan liturgical calendar between about the middle of the sixth century and the beginning of the eighth, were adorned with hymns that celebrated the Virgin's essential role in bringing about the new dispensation.[3] Even her death, or dormition, offered hope to Christians since she was believed to have remained uncorrupted in her tomb for three days before being assumed bodily into heaven. A strong penitential strand also pervades Marian hymnography, however, especially in service books such as the *Triodion* and the *New Oktoechos* or *Parakletike*, which were probably compiled from the ninth century onward.[4] This material, which emerged from a mainly monastic background, appealed

---

[1] John the Monk, *Sticheron for the Lity at Great Compline for Christmas*, Tone 1, *Menaion*, vol. 2 (Nov.–Dec.), 659 (my translation). Hymns are not listed according to their attributions or authors in the notes for this chapter, but according to liturgical books in the bibliography (Primary Sources).

[2] Kallistos of Diokleia 1990, esp. 8–11; Taft 2006.

[3] On the addition of the Marian feasts to the Constantinopolitan liturgical calendar, see Introduction, 11–12; Cunningham 2008b, 19–28; Krausmüller 2011, 228–30.

[4] *Triodion katanyktikon*; *Paraklitike*; Krueger 2014, 130–221.

constantly to the Virgin as the merciful protector of Christians who could intercede on their behalf before her son, Jesus Christ.

Hymnography remained the most accessible way of teaching theology to Christian congregations throughout the Byzantine period. And Mary, the Mother of God, assumed a central position in liturgical services, including the offices and both ordinary and festal Divine Liturgies. Hymns in praise of the Virgin linked together the separate parts of liturgical services or stational liturgies. They often appeared at the end of offices such as Vespers and the morning service (*Orthros* or Matins) – reflecting in song what congregants would have seen depicted in the apses of most middle Byzantine churches: the benevolent, but always solemn, image of the Theotokos, presiding over the holy space of the sanctuary.[5] The reason for such centrality, which had evolved from about the fifth century onward, as we have seen in previous chapters, was primarily Christological. Mary represented the link between the divine and created realms of existence. She, as a human but also virginal mother, contained the uncontainable God within her womb. She was thus considered more holy even than the highest ranks of angelic beings, according to troparia that were regularly sung in the daily and festal offices and liturgies.[6] Christ's incarnation, which brought new life and salvation to humankind, was signified in the person of his holy mother. This aspect of the Virgin's role in Byzantine hymnography outweighs that of her intercessory or protective power – although the latter is important too. Many hymns, such as the following theotokion (or short hymn in honour of the Virgin Mary), express both forms of praise; however, it is usually the Christological one that comes first:

> You have contained, in your womb, O Virgin Mother, One of the Trinity, Christ the King, whose praises all creation sings and before whom the thrones on high tremble. O all venerable Lady, entreat him for the salvation of our souls.[7]

[5] Evangelatou 2019.
[6] See, for example, *Typikon of the Great Church*, vol. 1: 31 July, p. 354: Ἁγιωτέρα τῶν χερουβίμ, ὑψηλοτέρα τῶν οὐρανῶν, πανύμνητε, Θεοτόκον σε ἐν ἀληθείᾳ ὁμολογοῦντες, ἔχοντες ἁμαρτωλοὶ προστασίαν καὶ εὑρίσκομεν ἐν καιρῷ σωτηρίαν ('more holy than the cherubim, higher than the heavens, all-praised one; we sinners hold you as our protection and look for salvation at the opportune time while confessing you truly as birth-giver of God').
[7] Andrew of Crete, *Kanon for the feast of the Nativity of the Virgin Mary (8 Sept.)*, Ode Nine, Theotokion; *Menaion*, vol. 1 (Sept.–Oct.), 103; trans. M. Mary and Ware 1969, 124 (with adjustments).

This chapter examines the various types of hymn that were composed in honour of the Virgin between *c.* 600 and 1000 in Byzantium, taking into account their positions within the various services and feasts of the Christian church year. It should be stated at the outset that, for reasons both of space and expertise, I have chosen to focus on texts but not on their musical settings.[8] Even with this limitation, however, it is impossible to include more than a small part of this vast body of literature. I will therefore look first at a selection of Marian feasts and their appointed texts, which are found in the *Menaia* (service books for the fixed liturgical year). Such hymnography celebrated events in the Virgin's life, whether these were attested in biblical or apocryphal texts. It often used particular types or images in relation to this subject matter; however, much intertextual – or interfestal – reference is also visible in this material.[9] I turn in the second part of the chapter to hymnographic texts that were composed for the daily or weekly offices according to service books including the *Oktoechos* or *Parakletike*, along with some that were intended for books that covered the moveable liturgical year, such as the *Triodion* and the *Pentekostarion*. It is possible, at least to some extent, to trace literary and theological developments in a diachronic way on the basis of these rich collections.[10]

Byzantine audiences assimilated hymnography, like some of the other literary forms, or genres, that are studied in this book, in more than one context. The most obvious place for hearing hymns was in church, where this condensed – and also musical – form of theological teaching pervaded the liturgical services throughout the year. However, some important kanons, including especially those that were attributed to the eighth-century theologians and melodists John of Damascus and Kosmas, were quoted, paraphrased and analysed (in the form of exegetical commentaries) both during and beyond the middle Byzantine period.[11] The earliest complete commentaries of eighth-century kanons appeared towards the end of the ninth

---

[8] In doing so, I follow the example of some recent scholarship on Byzantine hymnography, including studies by Arentzen, Frank, Krueger and Mellas. For an innovative new study, which examines both texts and music in Marian hymnography for the feast of the Entrance into the Temple (21 November), see Olkinuora 2015.

[9] Jaakko (now Fr Damaskinos) Olkinuora argues in fact for 'intermedial' reference between the separate Marian feasts. By this, he means that texts, images and music refer to each other; this methodology for the study of various art forms has recently been used widely in Scandinavian scholarship. See Olkinuora 2015, 19–22.

[10] For a useful introduction to the Byzantine liturgical books, see Velkovska 1997.

[11] Skrekas 2008, xx–xxxiv.

century.[12] In the late eleventh century, Eustathios of Thessalonike composed one of the fullest and most erudite commentaries on an iambic kanon on Pentecost that is attributed to John of Damascus; it is likely that this was intended for a teacher who needed help in deciphering the meaning of this complicated hymn.[13] There is evidence that kanons were used as teaching tools in eleventh- and twelfth-century schools in major cities such as Thessalonike and Constantinople.[14] Hymns thus fulfilled not only a liturgical function in the Byzantine Church, but also assisted theological teaching in non-liturgical settings. I shall return to this question, which concerns the reception of hymnography, towards the end of this chapter, after considering the content and rhetorical style of the various hymn forms that were composed in honour of the Theotokos during the middle Byzantine period.

The field of Byzantine hymnography, perhaps even more than homiletics, presents numerous problems for researchers. Most of the texts that are published in modern service books for the Chalcedonian Orthodox Churches lack critical editions.[15] They also reflect choices that were made in the eleventh and twelfth centuries following a move to standardise the structure and content of liturgical services. Certain hymns were selected for the official collections: the process continued in the late Byzantine period and was more or less completed by the printing of liturgical books in Venice in the sixteenth century.[16] Behind this unified front lie numerous unpublished hymns which, like the published ones that await critical editions, need scholarly attention. Another problem in dealing with this material is that attributions to individual hymnographers are often tenuous: a text that is ascribed to a certain author in one manuscript may be attributed to another elsewhere. Reliable modern catalogues and compilations of Byzantine hymns are also lacking.[17] Fortunately, the field has been opening up in recent years, thanks to scholars' increasing interest in

---

[12] Glosses on iambic kanons attributed to John of Damascus written by one Theodosios (or Theodoros) are preserved in Cod. Paris. Coislin. 345 (ninth–tenth century); see Skrekas 2008, xxi, n. 60.

[13] Eustathios of Thessalonike, *Exegesis*. This text is now available in a critical edition; see Cesaretti and Ronchey 2014; review in Lauxtermann 2015; cf. Skrekas 2008, xxviii–xxxi.

[14] Demetracopoulos 1979; Skrekas 2008, xxix.

[15] Olkinuora 2015, 2–3; Simić 2017, 8–9. To note one exception to this rule, a recent critical edition of the iambic kanons of John of Damascus appears in Skrekas 2008.

[16] Frøyshov 2013, 'Byzantine Rite'.

[17] Researchers may nevertheless consult the dated, but still useful, compilations that include the *Anthologia graeca carmina*, ed. Christ and Paranikas 1871; Follieri 1960–6; Szövérffy 1978–9; *Analecta hymnica graeca*, ed. Gonzato and Schirò 1966–80.

both liturgical and hymnographic studies. Although the work of compar-
ing liturgical manuscripts, providing critical editions of individual hymns
and distinguishing the styles of individual hymnographers will take many
years, it is already underway on an international basis.[18]

In spite of the many gaps in our knowledge that remain, there is much
that can be said about the Marian hymns according to the Byzantine rite.
Following the example of most other scholars,[19] I have chosen to rely on
the published service books that are still used in modern Orthodox
churches.[20] If we accept that hymnography, even more than homiletics,
assumed a conventional – even formulaic – style during the middle
Byzantine centuries, then attribution to individual authors becomes less
important.[21] Like holy icons, Marian hymns were intended to convey the
incarnational theology that prevailed after the Council of Chalcedon,
followed by the Christological debates of the sixth through to the mid
ninth centuries. It was especially after the 'Triumph of Orthodoxy', or the
restoration of icons in 843, that Mary's place as the chief signifier of the
incarnation took hold in both images and texts.[22] This theology is
expressed in hymns with the help of prophecy, typology and other forms
of biblical exegesis. In fact, as Archimandrite Ephrem Lash has suggested,
the words of scripture are 'woven into the fabric of the Church's prayers
and hymns, many of which are in fact little more than mosaics of biblical
words and phrases'.[23] This is a distinctive message, which differs from
homiletics in its poetic, but precise, definition of the Virgin's central place
in God's dispensation. We also find here a more urgent appeal to her
intercessory power, which hymnographers express on behalf of their congregations. The two strands are woven seamlessly together in many hymns,
including especially the various forms of theotokion, which suggests that
hymnographers did not attempt to distinguish between the Christological
and intercessory aspects of their compositions.[24]

[18] For example, Gigante 1964; Antonopoulou 2004; Afentoulidou 2008; Skrekas 2008; Simić 2017. It is
worth noting, however, that Simić proposes a different approach in his recent study of the hymns
that are attributed to the early eighth-century hymnographer Germanos of Constantinople. He
suggests that 'date and authorship are not always of crucial importance'. It is possible to study
hymnography on a thematic basis, recognising that texts that are intended for congregational use are
in a sense 'timeless'; see Simić 2017, 11.
[19] See, e.g., Olkinuora 2015; Krueger 2014.
[20] For a good introduction to these books, see Getcha 2012.
[21] On problems relating to Byzantine authorship, see Krueger 2004; Papaioannou 2013; Pizzone 2014.
[22] Kalavrezou 1990; Tsironis 2000; Koutrakou 2005; Evangelatou 2019.   [23] Lash 2008, 35.
[24] In fact the two elements are closely linked; see Koutrakou 2005, 81.

Marian Hymns and Their Place in Liturgical Practice

The liturgical services that were celebrated in the Constantinopolitan churches of the middle Byzantine period reflected a synthesis of two main sources, called the 'Palestinian' (or sometimes 'Jerusalem' or 'hagiopolite') and 'Constantinopolitan' rites. The former, which included more elaborate hymnody for the daily offices, probably reached the imperial city in the course of the seventh century and began to be used in many Constantinopolitan churches and monasteries from that time onward.[25] The *Psalter* was the basis for both collective and private worship in the early Church.[26] Hymnography originated, especially in Palestinian churches and monasteries, as a set of responses to the reading or chanting of separate verses of the Psalms or of the biblical canticles.[27] Various hymn forms originated in the Palestinian setting but became part of the Byzantine synthesis; most of these, such as the 'stichera', were refrains that were sung in response to verses of Psalms such as 'Lord, I have cried' (Ps 140 [141]) that were read in the course of the daily or festal offices.[28] Such hymnography continued to be composed and added to the liturgical books that were in use in the Great Church of Hagia Sophia, as well as in smaller churches and monasteries in Constantinople and its environs in the course of the middle Byzantine centuries. The most important forms, for our purposes, were the kanon (a long hymn that was sung primarily in *Orthros*, the morning office) and the theotokion (a short troparion that was dedicated specifically to the Mother of God). I will therefore focus for the most part in this chapter on these two genres – not forgetting, however, that stichera, aposticha and other forms of hymnography also dealt frequently with Mary's place in the divine dispensation.[29]

The kanon replaced the singing of the biblical canticles in liturgical offices such as *Orthros*. Although it used to be thought that this hymn form emerged from a monastic context in Palestine, Georgian liturgical manuscripts that were discovered at the Monastery of St Catherine on Sinai in 1975 suggest that it developed in the cathedral of Jerusalem (known as the 'Anastasis'), with its surrounding churches and shrines.[30] The kanon was based on nine biblical odes, beginning with Moses' song of victory

---

[25] Frøyshov 2013, 'Byzantine Rite'; Frøyshov 2020.   [26] Frøyshov 2007a, 200–1; Parpulov 2010.
[27] Taft 1986, 31–56; Taft 2005; Frøyshov 2007a; Krueger 2014, 5–6.
[28] Taft 1986, 75–91, 273–91.
[29] For orientation on the various forms of Byzantine hymnography, see Wellesz 1961, esp. 171–245; Conomos 1984, 1–25.
[30] Frøyshov 2013, 'Rite of Jerusalem', citing the tenth-century manuscript, Sinai Georgian O.34; Xevsuriani 1978; Frøyshov 2020, 355.

following the crossing of the Red Sea (Ex 15:1–9) and ending either with the Magnificat (Lk 1:46–55) or the prayer of Zacharias (Lk 1:68–79). The second ode (Deut 32:1–43) began to be omitted from most kanons after about the middle of the eighth century; however, it was often included before that (as in the case of works composed by Andrew of Crete and Germanos of Constantinople).[31] Some kanons, especially the later ones, included theotokia after each ode. Scholars have recently noticed that these short troparia do not always reflect the subject matter of the kanons in which they are found; this may mean that they were sometimes added later, either by the original hymnographers or by scribes.[32] Nevertheless, the presence of both theotokia and the ninth ode (which is usually dedicated to praise of Mary) in kanons for both daily and festal use points to her importance both as Theotokos and as intercessor in the middle Byzantine period.

Festal Hymnography

As we have seen in previous chapters, four main feasts (the Nativity, Entrance into the Temple, Annunciation and Dormition of the Virgin) were probably in place – at least in Constantinople – by about the middle of the eighth century.[33] In addition to these, the commemoration of Mary's parents, Joachim and Anna (9 September), her Conception (9 December), and the Presentation of Christ in the Temple or *Hypapante* (2 February) can be classed as Marian (or in the case of the latter, partly Marian) feasts. The relics of the Mother of God, that is, her robe and belt, were honoured on the dates of their supposed translations to Constantinople, that is, 2 July and 31 August, respectively. Scholars continue to debate the dates at which all of these feast-days originated, along with the extent to which they may have been celebrated in various parts of the remaining Eastern Roman empire; however, they mostly appear in the eighth-century Morcelli calendar and are all found in the tenth-century *Typikon of the Great Church*.[34]

The hymnography that was composed for these Marian feasts focused, as in the case of homiletics, on the important role that the Virgin Mary

---

[31] Frøyshov 2013, 'Byzantine Rite'; Jeffery 1991, 58; Nikiforova 2013, 174–5.

[32] Cunningham 2012 (unpublished); cf. Krueger 2019, however, who offers an exception to this rule in the work of a ninth-century hymnographer named 'Christopher'.

[33] See Introduction, 11–12.

[34] The Morcelli Calendar, which reflects Constantinopolitan liturgical practices in the early eighth century, omits the feasts of the Entrance into the Temple and the Conception; see Morcelli 1788, vol. 1, 19, 38, 47, 49, 66. For the *Typikon of the Great Church*, see Mateos 1962, vol. 1, 18–23, 110–11, 220–5, 252–9, 328–31, 368–73, 386–7.

played in providing Christ with his human nature and thus helping to bring about the new dispensation of salvation for humanity. She was also, thanks to the gift of free will, the 'Second Eve', who reversed the disastrous choice of the first Eve by accepting God's dispensation at the moment of the annunciation. Liturgical writers, including preachers and hymnographers (who were often the same people), expressed this joyous message by means of narrative, which could often include dramatic monologue or dialogue, and exegetical teaching that employed more typological than allegorical imagery. These writers also used intertextual methods with regard not only to the biblical and apocryphal (or paracanonical) sources for the events that were being celebrated, but also to liturgical texts that belonged to other feasts in the Marian calendar.[35] In the following section, we will examine the theological, stational and intercessory content of the hymns that were composed in honour of the main Marian feasts, aiming to discover what is distinctive about each feast and how the various hymnographers chose to celebrate them. As in Chapter 3, on middle Byzantine homiletics, feasts are treated (as in Byzantine liturgical books) in order of their place in the fixed liturgical year, beginning on 1 September.

The Nativity of the Virgin Mary (8 September)

Hymnography, like homiletics, celebrated the feast of Mary's Nativity as a pivotal event in the history of God's dispensation for salvation, regardless of the fact that it is recorded only in the *Protevangelion of James* and not in the canonical Gospels.[36] Short hymns, or stichera, for the offices of Vespers and Matins remind congregations repeatedly of the importance of this turning point in history. Prophecy, in the form of Old Testament signs and types, was fulfilled in this birth: a hymn for Vespers, for example, alludes to the root and rod of Jesse (Is 11:1) from which salvation (the Theotokos) sprouted.[37] It is Mary, the daughter of a barren mother, Anna, who initiated salvation:

---

[35] J. Olkinuora has recently shown that in addition to such literary parallels, there were musical and iconographical correspondences between the feasts that helped to link them all together; see Olkinuora 2015.

[36] *Protevangelion of James* 5.2, trans. Elliott 1993, 59. The vigil for the feast was celebrated in the church of the Chalkoprateia in Constantinople; see the *Typikon of the Great Church*, ed. Mateos 1962, 18–21; Janin 1953, 249.

[37] Sticheron for 'Lord I have cried', Vespers, 8 Sept., *Menaion*, vol. 1 (Sept.–Oct.), 87; trans. M. Mary and Ware 1969, 98.

The soil which formerly was barren gives birth to fertile ground and nourishes with milk the holy fruit sprung from her sterile womb. Dread wonder: she who sustains our life, who received within her body the Bread of Heaven, feeds at her mother's breast.[38]

The anonymous hymnographer uses metaphorical language that suggests the Virgin's connection with the earth out of which God created the first human being (Gen 2:7), while also implying that the old, fallen or sterile, order has been replaced by the fertile one of the new dispensation. The reference to Anna's breast-feeding of the newborn Mary also provides a vivid picture of human motherhood. While thus emphasising Mary's humanity, this short hymn simultaneously reminds the congregation of her God-bearing capacity: she is the one who will '[sustain] our life . . . [and receive] within her body the Bread of Heaven', that is, Christ.[39]

Two kanons, which are attributed to the early eighth-century hymnographers John 'the Monk' (probably also of Damascus) and Andrew of Crete, were sung in the morning office.[40] These help to establish the links between Old Testament events and the birth of the Virgin, which herald the new dispensation, by their structured use of the biblical canticles. Both kanons also employ spoken and typological prophecy in order to reinforce such continuity. Whereas many later kanons allude only indirectly to the canticles on which each ode is based, these early examples are more explicit. John of Damascus, for example, echoes the language of the first canticle in his call to the faithful to 'honour in hymns the ever-Virgin maiden, who has come forth today from a barren woman for the salvation of mortal men'.[41] Following a first stanza in which the congregation is reminded that the same God who 'shattered the enemy with his mighty arm and made

[38] Sticheron for 'Lord I have cried', Vespers, 8 Sept., *Menaion*, vol. 1 (Sept.–Oct.), 87; trans. M. Mary and Ware 1969, 99.
[39] On breast-feeding as a symbol both of humanity and of eucharistic nourishment, see Bolman 2005.
[40] Scholars have expressed doubts concerning the attribution of some kanons to John of Damascus; among the hymns attributed to him are a few that were in fact written by John Mauropous (late eleventh century); Wellesz 1961, 237. For further evaluation of the authenticity of hymns attributed to John of Damascus, see Louth 2002, 253; Eustratiades 1931–3. The iambic kanon on Pentecost, on which Eustathios of Thessalonike and others commented (see above, n. 13), is variously attributed by commentators to John of Damascus, John the Monk and John Arklas; see Skrekas 2008, esp. xxxv–xxxvi; Cesaretti and Ronchey 2014, 40*–44*. For the purposes of this study, I use the name of this author, assuming that this particular kanon was composed by the eighth-century poet and theologian – until it is proved otherwise. It is also worth noting that other kanons, including one that is attributed to Germanos I of Constantinople, survive in manuscripts but are not included in modern Orthodox service books. Kosta Simić (2017, 45–55) provides analysis of a kanon on the Nativity of the Virgin that is ascribed to Germanos.
[41] John of Damascus, *Kanon for the Nativity of the Virgin*, Tone Two, Ode One, *Menaion*, vol. 1 (Sept.–Oct.), 94.

Israel pass through the Red Sea' has now initiated a new creation, Andrew of Crete then calls on everyone – not just humanity – to rejoice:

> Let all creation dance for joy and let David also be glad; for of his tribe and seed has come forth a rod that bears as a flower the Lord and Deliverer of all.[42]

Such emphasis on the continuity between the Old and New Testaments, as stages in God's plan for salvation, is characteristic of festal hymnography. The method of exegesis, which hymnographers inherited from early apologists and commentators such as Irenaeus of Lyons, is both historical and allegorical, as we shall see below. In liturgical contexts, both prophecy and typology remain grounded in literal readings of the Old Testament even as they lift events, such as those described in Exodus, out of their narrative contexts and show their prophetic meaning.

It is also worth noting that Andrew twice mixes references to the Virgin's infancy in the temple with his celebration of her birth. He writes, for example, in the first ode of his kanon, as follows:

> The Holy of Holies is placed as an infant in the holy sanctuary, to be reared by the hands of an angel. Let us all feast with faith the day of her nativity.[43]

Another reference to that event occurs in a stanza of the sixth ode:

> Your wise parents, O undefiled one, brought you, who are the Holy of Holies, as an offering to the house of the Lord, there to be reared in holiness and made ready to become his mother.[44]

These allusions to the Entrance into the Temple, which had been established as a separate feast on 21 November at least by the time that the *Typikon of the Great Church* was compiled in the tenth century, suggest that it was lacking in the order of service that Andrew was following – either in Constantinople or on Crete – in the early eighth. They also confirm the early date of this kanon, thus strengthening the likelihood that it was composed by the famous hymnographer from Jerusalem.

Both John and Andrew use numerous biblical types when invoking the Mother of God in their kanons on her Nativity. It is worth taking time to discuss this method of biblical exegesis, since it assumes such a prominent

---

[42] Andrew of Crete, *Kanon for the Nativity of the Virgin*, Tone Eight, Ode One, *Menaion* vol. 1 (Sept.–Oct.), 94; trans. M. Mary and Ware 1969 (with adjustments), 111.
[43] Ibid.
[44] Andrew of Crete, *Kanon for the Nativity of the Virgin*, Ode Six, *Menaion*, vol. 1 (Sept.–Oct.), 99; trans. M. Mary and Ware 1969 (with adjustments), 118.

role in both hymnography and homiletics of the middle Byzantine period. Typology is a method of interpretation that establishes links between Old Testament and New Testament events, objects or people.[45] As Frances Young suggests in her important contribution to this subject, typology goes beyond the historical correlation between type and antitype. Following Sebastian Brock's interpretation of the way in which the fourth-century Syriac poet Ephrem employs it, Young suggests that typology indicates 'a universal or eternal truth played out in time, time and again'.[46] Typology thus has an historical basis but, when sung in the context of a liturgical service, it is lifted out of that concept of time and into an eternal, or eschatological, present. Types and antitypes allow a more prophetic understanding of scripture, with types such as the burning bush representing a 'mimetic impress' of their antitype, the Virgin Mary. The early Fathers read the Old Testament with a view to finding the impression of Mary, the Theotokos, embedded in its narrative. As Andrew of Crete wrote in the eighth century:

> For there is not, indeed there is not, anywhere throughout the whole of the God-inspired Scripture where, on passing through, one does not see signs of [the Virgin Mary] scattered about in diverse ways; [signs] which, if you should disclose them for yourself in your industrious study of the words, you will find that a more distinct meaning has encapsulated so much glory before God.[47]

Numerous Marian types appear in the hymnography not only of the *Menaion*, but also in other service books such as the *Parakletike*, the *Triodion* and the *Pentekostarion*. They include well-known objects in the Old Testament such as Jacob's ladder (Gen 28:10–17), the burning bush (Ex 3:1–6), the east gate of the temple (Ezek 44:1–3), the dark, shaded, curdled or uncut mountain (Ex 19:18; Hab 3:3; Ps 67:16 [68:15];[48] Dan 2:34), the fleece drenched with dew (Judg 6:37–40), and those which were associated either with the tabernacle or the temple (Ex 25–40; 3 Kgs 6–7 [1 Kgs 6–7], etc.).[49] The latter include not only the holy structures

[45] As Frances Young points out, 'typology' is a modern construct. Patristic and Byzantine exegetes did not distinguish between typology and allegory, although they mostly used them for distinct purposes and in different settings; see Young 1997, 152. For modern studies of typology, see Daniélou 1960; Frye 1981; Goppelt 1982; Cunningham 2004.
[46] Young 1997, 154; cf. Brock 1985, esp. 53–84.
[47] Andrew of Crete, *Homily IV on the Nativity of the Virgin Mary*, PG 97, 868B–C; trans. Cunningham 2008b, 47 (the same translator's version differs slightly at ibid., 127).
[48] On the type of the 'curdled mountain', see Lash 1990, 70–2.
[49] On the use of the Old Testament (which was usually read in separate books according to the version of the Greek Septuagint [LXX]), see Magdalino and Nelson 2010, 1–38.

themselves, which God inhabited, but also their furniture, including the ark of the covenant in the holy of holies, the table, the jar of manna, the candlestand and other items. Such types express in allegorical terms the manner in which God inhabited or made himself felt in his own creation; whereas the places or objects were lifeless in the old dispensation, they were fulfilled in the living body of a virginal woman in the new one.

It is worth asking why typology, which is usually employed without any commentary throughout Byzantine hymnography and homiletics, came to be applied so extensively to the Virgin Mary. It is possible that her virginal conception and birth of Christ naturally evoked such theological treatment. Liturgical writers felt less able to express this paradoxical event in discursive terms and thus resorted to more poetic or typological methods. And, although typology 'is only distantly related to metaphor', as Hannick suggests,[50] it does evoke images of a deified creation – that is, a world in which God has made his presence felt. Mary, as a mortal human being, was embedded in that creation; she could thus be pictured as a shaded or curdled mountain, Gideon's fleece, or the temple in which God lived. The metaphors taken from daily life that fifth-century preachers such as Proklos of Constantinople and Hesychios of Jerusalem employed were largely replaced in the middle Byzantine period by biblical images. Typology was rich in the sense that it portrayed the Mother of God in both prophetic and poetic ways; it could also evoke more than one biblical reference, thus furnishing layers of meaning for theological reflection – at least for those singers and listeners who were able to assimilate hymns quickly.

The kanons by John of Damascus and Andrew of Crete employ types that refer more to Mary's future role as birth-giver of God than to the event that is being celebrated. She is thus invoked as the branch of the root of Jesse,[51] holy table (Ex 25:22–9),[52] and throne (Is 6:1; Ezek 1:26; Dan 7:9),[53] along with other types. In some cases, as in Ode Seven, which is inspired by the song of the three children in the fiery furnace (Dan 3:26–90 [LXX]), we find a direct correlation between the chosen type and this subject matter. Both John and Andrew cite the prefiguration of the Virgin Mary in the burning bush (Ex 3:1–6). This type, involving a flame that left a thorny bush intact, foreshadowed the way in which 'the flower of [Mary's] virginity was not withered by giving

---

[50] Hannick 2005, 73.
[51] Andrew of Crete, *Kanon for the Nativity of the Virgin*, Ode Three, *Menaion*, vol. 1 (Sept.-Oct.), 95; ibid., Ode Four, *Menaion*, vol. 1 (Sept.–Oct.), 97, etc.
[52] Ibid., Ode Five, *Menaion*, vol. 1 (Sept.–Oct.), 98.
[53] John of Damascus, *Kanon for the Nativity of the Virgin*, Ode Five, *Menaion*, vol. 1 (Sept.–Oct.), 98.

birth'.[54] Other types, such as the tabernacle or temple, were more appropriate to feasts that referred both to the historical second temple of Jerusalem (as in the cases of Mary's Entrance into the Temple and Christ's Presentation) and to the idea that God came to inhabit a holy space, first in human-made (or lifeless) structures and second in the womb of a living woman.[55]

It is also noteworthy that John of Damascus departs from the usual, more telegraphic, style of typological referencing to explain this symbol to his audience. He writes on the subject as follows:

> The bush on the mountain that was not consumed by fire, and the Chaldean furnace that brought refreshment as the dew, plainly prefigured you, O bride of God. For in a material womb, unconsumed, you have received the divine and immaterial fire . . .[56]

Such discursive explanation of this well-known type is unusual in Byzantine hymnography. It may reflect the didactic approach that John sometimes adopted in his liturgical poetry. He also revealed in this way the connection between the subject matter of the seventh ode (the furnace in which the Chaldean children were placed) and the Marian type of the burning bush. Both Old Testament objects prefigured the Virgin's miraculous conception of the divine Word since, as the hymnographer stated in the following stanza, Moses (like contemporary Christians) 'was taught through symbols not to think earthly thoughts'.[57]

Invocation of the Mother of God as intercessor appears infrequently in the hymns for the feast of her Nativity; this is again typical of festal hymnography as a genre. Feasts, as opposed to ordinary days of the week, were primarily occasions for joy and thanksgiving, as I suggested at the beginning of this section. Nevertheless, the common litanies and prayers that interspersed the 'proper' verses for the day included invocations of the Virgin and the saints. And some hymnographers, such as the early eighth-century patriarch Germanos, supplied short hymns of supplication, as we see in the aposticha that are attributed to him in the office of Great Vespers for this feast:

---

[54] Gregory of Nyssa, *Life of Moses* 11.19, ed. Mülenberg and Maspero at https://referenceworks .brillonline.com/browse/gregorii-nysseni-opera; ed. and trans. Daniélou 1955, 116–19; trans. Malherbe and Ferguson 1978, 59.

[55] For further discussion of the assignment of types to individual feasts, see Ladouceur 2006.

[56] John of Damascus, *Kanon for the Nativity of the Virgin*, Ode Seven, *Menaion*, vol. 1 (Sept.–Oct.), 100; trans. M. Mary and Ware 1969 (with adjustments), 119.

[57] Ibid.

The joy of all the world has shone forth upon us, the far-famed Virgin sprung from righteous Joachim and Anna. On account of her exceeding goodness she is become the living temple of God, and is in truth acknowledged as the only Theotokos. *At her prayers, O Christ our God, send down peace upon the world and on our souls great mercy.*

As foretold by the angel, you have today come forth, O Virgin, the all-holy offspring of righteous Joachim and Anna. You are a heaven and the throne of God, and a vessel of purity, proclaiming joy to all the world, O Protector of our life. You destroy the curse and give blessing in its place. Therefore on this feast of your birth, O maiden called by God, *intercede that our souls may be given peace and great mercy.*[58]

Such verses, if they are indeed the work of this important liturgical writer, reflect the presence of intercessory content in both hymnography and homiletics by at least the middle of the eighth century. Its presence or absence in festal hymnography thus reveals the overall aim of this poetry for any given day or hour of the year. Another slot, which typically although not always contains intercessory prayer, are the theotokia that follow the odes of the kanons in Matins. Thus John of Damascus praises Mary as 'Theotokos, protector and helper of us all' in the theotokion following Ode Three,[59] and declares that he is 'absolved of sin by your supplications', after Ode Four.[60] There are also numerous references to the Virgin Mary's role as mediator, or 'deliverer from the sharp punishment of old', which, as I suggested in the Introduction, represents a more theological concept than the practical job of supplication or intercession before Christ.[61] Andrew of Crete remains aloof throughout his kanon from the latter; this may reflect his tendency, according to Kazhdan, to adopt an 'impersonal and rational' tone in his liturgical writing.[62]

The Entrance into the Temple (21 November)

Hymns for this feast, which is also based on the narrative in the *Protevangelion of James*, focus on the theological meaning of Mary's sojourn between the ages of three and twelve in the holy precincts of the Jewish temple in Jerusalem. In historical terms, this would have been

---

[58] Germanos of Constantinople, *Aposticha*, Tone Four, *Menaion*, vol. 1 (Sept.–Oct.), 91–2; trans. M. Mary and Ware 1969, 106 (with adjustments and italicisations to show the intercessory content). For further discussion of these verses, see Simić 2017, 45.
[59] John of Damascus, *Kanon on the Nativity*, Ode Three, *Menaion*, vol. 1 (Sept.–Oct.), 95; trans. M. Mary and Ware 1969, 112.
[60] Ibid., Ode Four, *Menaion*, vol. 1 (Sept.–Oct.), 96; trans. M. Mary and Ware 1969, 114.
[61] See Introduction, 15; Reynolds 2012, 152–3.   [62] Kazhdan 1999, 53–4.

the second temple that Herod renovated in the intertestamental period but which the Romans destroyed in 70 CE.[63] The story of the Virgin Mary was in any case legendary. Byzantine hymnographers, preachers and hagiographers thus tended either to refer to the first temple of Solomon or to visualise it as a Christian church.[64] The innermost space, known as the 'holy of holies', could be imagined as the sanctuary of a middle Byzantine church. A screen (or curtain) separated it from the nave in which lay Christians were allowed to stand.[65] Unlike other human beings – and especially females – the juvenile Mary was received into this holiest of spaces as preparation for her own forthcoming role as the holy space that God would inhabit.[66] The hymns for the offices of the feast of the Entrance celebrate the event with the help of the same rhetorical and didactic devices that preachers used.[67] However, middle Byzantine hymnographers refined such methods so as to deliver precise theological teaching about this feast to their audiences.

The instruction that is delivered on the feast of the Entrance into the Temple includes various themes. One of these is Joachim's and Anna's offering of this female child as an 'acceptable sacrifice' to the high priest Zacharias.[68] Another such offering to the Jewish temple appears in the feast of Christ's Presentation or Meeting (*Hypapante*) on 2 February.[69] The narrative helps to reinforce continuity between the Old and New Testaments (cf. 1 Kgs 1:24–8 [1 Sam 1:24–8]); however, it may also imply Mary's eventual sacrifice at the loss of her son, Christ, at the cross. The ceremonious nature of this dedication is underlined by the procession of virgins that accompanies Mary and her parents to the temple – a scene that is vividly illustrated in the twelfth-century manuscripts of the homilies of James of Kokkinobaphos.[70] A sticheron that was sung at Vespers for the feast describes it as follows:

---

[63] Hayward 1996, 1–6; Edelman 2014.
[64] They visualised it, for example, with its furniture (including the ark of the covenant) in place, whereas these items did not survive in the second temple of Jerusalem. See Hamblin and Seely 2007, 48; Cunningham 2016, 153–4.
[65] Demus 1948, 14–22; Gerstel 1999, 5–14.
[66] On the location of girls and women in Byzantine churches, see Mathews 1971, 130–3; Taft 1998.
[67] Olkinuora 2015, 208–32.
[68] Sticheron for 'Lord I have cried', Tone One, Small Vespers; *Menaion*, vol. 2 (Nov.–Dec.), 216; trans. M. Mary and Ware 1969, 164.
[69] *Menaion*, vol. 3 (Jan.– Feb.), 468–89.
[70] Cod. Paris. Gr. 1208, fols. 80, 86; Cod. Vatic. Gr. 1162, fols. 59v, 62v. These two illustrated manuscripts are discussed in Omont 1928; Hutter and Canard 1991; Linardou 2004; Linardou 2007. They can be accessed online at https://gallica.bnf.fr/ark:/12148/btv1b55013447b/f171.image and https://digi.vatlib.it/view/MSS_Vat.gr.1162, respectively.

> The young girls rejoice today. With their lamps in hand, they reverently
> precede the spiritual Lamp, as she enters the holy of holies. They foreshadow
> the indescribable brightness that will shine forth from her and give light by
> the Spirit to those who sit in the darkness of ignorance (Is 9:2).[71]

There is a double, or intertextual, scriptural reference in this image of the
processing virgins holding torches: first, and most importantly, it refers to
Psalm 44 [45], which has special significance in relation to the Entrance of
the Virgin Mary into the Temple. Mary, according to patristic and
Byzantine commentators, is the 'princess [who] is decked in her chamber
with gold-woven robes . . . behind her the virgins, her companions, follow'.
She is taken to 'the palace of the king' in order to be his bride (Ps 44:12–15
[45:12–15]). Such nuptial imagery has echoes with the Song of Songs and,
when the psalm is interpreted allegorically, the princess, or Mary, stands
for all Christians who await the Bridegroom, Christ. The second potential
meaning of the procession, however, belongs to the New Testament. One
unpublished kanon for the forefeast of the Entrance associates the Virgin
Mary's companions with the parable of the ten wise and foolish virgins (Mt
25:1–13).[72] This story would also remind congregations of the eschatological significance of this feast, in the sense that Christian believers
await their Bridegroom, Christ, who will return at the Second Coming.

Hymnographers further suggest that the Virgin, on entering the holy
precincts of the temple, is being prepared to contain Christ, the Word of
God. Thus the material temple will be superseded by the living, human, one,
as the following verse suggests: 'The holy of holies [that is, the Theotokos] was
worthily brought to live in the holy places . . . '[73] This concept of a pure and
holy container or space, which God is pleased to inhabit, finds expression in
a whole range of biblical types for the Mother of God. The hymnography for
the feast of the Entrance tends to prefer those that involve the tabernacle, the
temple, as well as furniture or objects that are contained within these spaces.
Such types may be characterised as 'container' images, although a few, including the gate of the temple through which only the Lord could pass (Ezek 44:1–
3), have to do with the passage from one realm (created) to another (divine).
Paul Ladouceur has shown that the feast of the Entrance includes more
references to Mary as temple than do the other feasts.[74] The following example

[71] Sticheron for 'Lord I have cried', Tone Four, Great Vespers; *Menaion*, vol. 2 (Nov.–Dec.), 218.
[72] Cod. Sinait. Gr. 570; see Olkinuora 2015, 103.
[73] Sticheron for 'Lord I have cried', Tone One, Small Vespers; *Menaion*, vol. 2 (Nov.–Dec.), 216.
[74] Ladouceur 2006, 10.

shows how not only Ezekiel's gate, but also other types, may be combined in one verse:

> The Law prefigured you most wonderfully as tabernacle, jar of manna, strange ark, veil of the temple, rod of Aaron, temple never to be destroyed, and gate of God; and so it teaches us to cry to you: O pure Virgin, you are truly highest among all.[75]

Typology helps to illustrate the meeting of the old and new dispensations in the person of the Virgin Mary. She simultaneously represents the holy spaces that God, or Christ, comes to inhabit (tabernacle, jar, ark and temple), but also the place of transition – or passageway – from the created to the divine realm (veil and gate).

It is also worth looking briefly at the way in which some hymnographers incorporate dialogic elements into their songs for this feast.[76] Although this rhetorical method is used more sparingly here than in festal homilies, it is still present – perhaps in imitation of the longer passages of dialogue that appear in the spoken genre. Two kanons are sung in the morning service, which are attributed to the ninth-century hymnographers George of Nikomedia and Basil the Monk. Both alternate between panegyrical and narrative approaches to the feast in their kanons, using a variety of rhetorical devices including *exclamatio, prosopopoia* and *ethopoiia*.[77] Basil, for example, addresses Joachim and Anna directly, exhorting them to rejoice as they present their daughter as 'a three-year old victim of sacrifice, holy and utterly without spot'.[78] And, in his fourth ode, the same hymnographer calls on the prophets Habakkuk and Isaiah, the virgins of Psalm 44 [45], Joachim and Anna, and finally the 'holy of holies' (or Virgin Mary) herself. All are reminded of their various roles in the story (to prophesy, accompany, offer, or live in the temple) and urged to celebrate the feast.[79] George of Nikomedia provides some dialogue in sections of his kanon, which may reflect homiletic treatment of the theme. In Ode Eight, for example, he invents a dialogue between Anna and Zacharias, as the former leads her child into the temple:

[75] George of Nikomedia, *Kanon for the Entrance of the Virgin into the Temple*, Tone Four, Ode Nine; *Menaion*, vol. 2 (Nov.–Dec.), 233–4; trans. M. Mary and Ware 1969, 191 (with adjustments).

[76] Olkinuora 2015, 229–32. For background on dramatic dialogue in Syriac and Byzantine homilies and hymns, see Brock 1983; Brock 1987; Cunningham 2003; Arentzen 2019.

[77] Kennedy 1994, 202–8; Rowe 1997, 143–4 (under 'affective' figures).

[78] Basil the Monk, *Kanon on the Entrance of the Virgin into the Temple*, Tone One, Ode Three; *Menaion*, vol. 2 (Nov.–Dec.), 225; trans. M. Mary and Ware 1969, 177.

[79] Basil the Monk, *Kanon on the Entrance of the Virgin into the Temple*, Ode Four; *Menaion*, vol. 2 (Nov.–Dec.), 226–7; trans. M. Mary and Ware 1969, 180.

As Anna led the undefiled temple into the house of God, she cried aloud and said with faith to the priest, 'Take the child that was given to me by God and lead her into the temple of your Creator, and sing to him with joy: "All you works of the Lord, bless the Lord"'.

When he saw Anna, Zacharias said to her in spirit, 'You are leading the true Mother of life here, whom the prophets heralded from afar as the Theotokos. And how will the temple contain her? Therefore I cry in wonder, "O all you works of the Lord, bless the Lord"'.[80]

The dialogue continues, with Anna expressing her sense of renewed faith and Zacharias his recognition of the importance of this event. It is interesting to note the presence of a refrain in this ode, which may have been intended for audience participation.[81]

The hymnography for the feast of the Entrance into the Temple thus portrays this event as a point of transition between the old and new covenants. The Jewish temple stands for the law-givers and prophets who awaited the coming of the Lord into his own creation. It will be fulfilled in the person of the Theotokos, who is being prepared as the holy space that will contain God. Elizabeth Theokritoff sums up this feast, on the basis of its hymnography, as follows:

> The whole point of this feast is that [Mary] fulfills the meaning of the temple: 'The living temple of the holy glory of Christ is offered in the temple of the Law' (Lord, I have cried, 3). She is to be brought up in the tabernacle, in the place of propitiation, in order to become the 'tabernacle' – the dwelling place of him who was begotten of the Father before all ages, for the salvation of our souls (cf. Vespers, Lity, 1) . . . The three-year-old Mary, then, is being prepared to be the starting point for the fulfilment of this whole process of God's covenant with his people.[82]

Prophecy, typology and even dramatic narrative pervade the hymns for the offices and vigil of the feast. In spite of its apocryphal, rather than biblical, basis, this event was viewed as an important stage in the history of God's dispensation for salvation.

---

[80] George of Nikomedia, *Kanon on the Entrance of the Virgin into the Temple*, Ode Eight; *Menaion*, vol. 2 (Nov.–Dec.), 231–2; trans. M. Mary and Ware 1969, 187–8 (with adjustments).

[81] On the singing of refrains by congregations, see Frank 2006, 63; Taft 2006, 60– 7; Krueger 2014, 19; Arentzen 2016; Arentzen 2017, 13; Frank 2019.

[82] In a footnote to this passage, Theokritoff adds that elsewhere in the hymnography for the feast, Mary is called 'the immaculate heifer who has conceived the divine calf' (Basil the Monk, Kanon, Ode 5.3); 'cf. the parable of the prodigal son. She is a sacrifice preparing the way for greater sacrifice'; Theokritoff 2005, 82, 87, n. 20.

The Annunciation (25 March)

If the Nativity of the Virgin Mary was interpreted by hymnographers as inaugurating a new creation, then the Annunciation celebrated this event to an even greater degree. This day, as both melodists and preachers proclaimed, recalled – but also re-enacted – the moment at which Christ, the Word of God, became incarnate in Mary's womb. Although it celebrated the Virgin's role in this process, the Annunciation was primarily a Christological feast.[83] Liturgical writers celebrated the mystery that lies at the heart of Christian doctrine, namely, the entrance of God into his own creation as the incarnate Christ. Elizabeth Briere (Theokritoff) suggests that whereas Christmas, or the Nativity of Christ, 'is the feast of Nicene dogma, the Annunciation is the feast of the dogma of Ephesus. Christmas stresses that the Virgin's newborn child is the Father's uncreated Son, while Annunciation stresses that this same Son entered the Virgin's womb.'[84] As I indicated in earlier chapters of this book, the feast of the Annunciation was added to the Constantinopolitan liturgical calendar in the middle of the sixth century; however, homilies and hymns that celebrate this event survive from at least a century earlier.[85] Early Christian liturgical writers thus saw the story of the archangel Gabriel's appearance to Mary and her acceptance of his message (Lk 1:26–38) as a significant moment in the story of the new dispensation well before this event came to be celebrated in a separate feast.

The feast of the Annunciation is based on a biblical, as opposed to an apocryphal, narrative, which is dramatic in its very nature.[86] Both hymnographers and preachers (as we have already seen) elaborated the dialogue between Gabriel and Mary that appears in the Gospel of Luke, sometimes also adding an additional (and imagined) dialogue between Mary and Joseph.[87] Although this device is developed further in homiletics, it also plays a part in hymns that were composed for the offices of the Annunciation, including especially the kanon that was sung in the morning service.[88] Another important element in hymns (just as in homilies)

---

[83] Briere 1983, 181; but contrast Pauline Allen's view that homilies on the Annunciation assumed a more Mariological character, especially after the work of Sophronios of Jerusalem in the early seventh century: see Allen 2011, 74–8.

[84] Briere 1983, 181.   [85] See above, 12, 78–9, n. 53.

[86] See Luke 1:26–38, but also the *Protevangelion of James* 11, which provides an abbreviated narrative; trans. Elliott 1993 (2004), 61.

[87] Significant examples of homilies containing both dialogues are (ps-)Proklos, *Homily VI, On the Theotokos*, and Germanos I of Constantinople, *Homily on the Annunciation*.

[88] *Menaion*, vol. 4 (March–April), 176–81. Individual odes in the kanon are attributed variously to John the Monk (probably the Damascene) and Theophanes Graptos; see M. Mary and Ware 1969, 448, n. 2. According to Kosta Simić, several other eight- and nine-ode kanons for this feast survive,

that were written for this feast is the extensive use of typology and poetic epithets for the Virgin Mary. This often takes the form of salutations, based on the archangel's greeting, 'Hail' or 'Rejoice' (*Chaire*), as recorded in Luke (Lk 1:28). Although the long sequences of salutations in some hymns and homilies might appear to have a lyrical purpose, they in fact express precise theological teaching. Biblical types, such as those discussed above, proclaim the Virgin's role as container of or gateway to divinity while poetic images, which are usually drawn from earlier texts such as the *Akathistos Hymn*, perform a similar function. A further aspect of this feast, which made it a complicated affair to organise in liturgical terms, was that it usually took place during the period of Lent – but sometimes during Holy Week or even over Easter.[89] The Byzantine *typika* explain in detail how the fixed and moveable elements for the day should be intercalated; however, the hymnography for the Annunciation usually took precedence (except if it coincided with Easter itself) over that of the moveable calendar. According to the *Typikon of the Great Church*, the vigil of the Annunciation was celebrated in Hagia Sophia, followed by a procession to the forum and then to the church of the Chalkoprateia, where the Divine Liturgy took place.[90]

As I suggested above, the hymnography for all of the offices for the Annunciation has a dialogic aspect; this reflects a long-standing dramatic tendency in the liturgical treatment of this feast. Stichera, aposticha and other hymns refer immediately to the encounter between the archangel Gabriel and Mary, assuming knowledge of this story on the part of Byzantine congregations:

> Taking pity on that which he has made and bending down in his great mercy, the Maker hastens to dwell in the womb of a maiden, the child of God. To her the great archangel came, saying to her: 'Hail, favoured one; the Lord is with you. Do not be afraid of me, the chief commander of the armies of the King. For you have found the grace that your mother Eve once lost; and you will conceive and bring forth him who is of one substance with the Father.'

but are not included in the published *Menaion*. The various kanons are attributed to Andrew of Crete, Germanos I of Constantinople, George of Nikomedia and Theophilos; see Simić 2017, 59–76, who also provides detailed analysis of the kanon that is attributed to Germanos.

[89] See the instructions for how to celebrate the feast according to the day on which it falls in the lunar (or moveable) calendar in the *Menaion*, vol. 4 (March–April), 146–70; *Typikon of the Great Church*, ed. Mateos 1962, vol. 1, 256–9.

[90] *Typikon of the Great Church*, ed. Mateos 1962, vol. 1, 252–5; cf. Constantine Porphyrogennetos, *Book of Ceremonies* I. 35, ed. Vogt 1935, vol. 1, 172–3 (Bk 1. 44), trans. Moffatt and Tall 2012, 184–5.

Mary said to the angel, 'Your speech is strange, as is your appearance; your words and disclosures are also strange. I am a maiden, uninitiated into marriage; do not lead me astray. You say that I will conceive him who remains uncircumscribed; how will my womb contain the One whom the wide spaces of heaven cannot contain?' 'O Virgin, let the tent of Abraham that once contained God teach you: for it prefigured your womb, which now receives the Godhead.'[91]

Details of this scene that are familiar from earlier or possibly contemporary hymns and homilies are immediately visible. Mary is described as a 'maiden' (ἡ κόρη); she is thus the timid and virginal girl whom we also encounter in Syriac dialogue hymns, Romanos the Melodist's kontakion on the Annunciation and Germanos of Constantinople's famous homily for the same feast.[92] The archangel is 'chief commander of the armies of the King' – a formidable and even frightening figure who suddenly bursts in on the girl. The Virgin's reaction to this appearance is also typical of earlier liturgical treatments of the scene. She is taken aback and finds this male intruder 'strange'; she uses the same adjective to describe his message and manner of speech. But above all, it takes Mary time to assimilate the theological significance of the event that is about to take (or indeed has already taken) place. She needs to receive some additional teaching, which comes in the form of a typological reference – in this case (rather unusually) the tent from which Abraham entertained three 'men' or angels, who were understood in Byzantine tradition to represent the Trinity (Gen 18:1–16).[93]

As we saw above, the dialogic kanon that is sung in the morning office is attributed, according to the *Menaion*, to John the Monk, although some service books ascribe only its eighth and ninth odes to John and the remainder to Theophanes 'Graptos'.[94] John 'the Monk' is in this case assumed to be John of Damascus, although this epithet sometimes refers to the eleventh-century bishop of Euchaita John Mauropous.[95] The kanon opens with praise not of Mary the 'maiden' but of the 'queen and

[91] Stichera in Tone Four for 'Lord I have cried', Small Vespers for the Annunciation, *Menaion*, vol. 4 (March–April), 145 (my own translation, based on M. Mary and Ware 1969, 437).
[92] *Bride of Light*; *Dialogue Poems on Mary*; Romanos the Melodist, *Kontakia I–II on the Annunciation*, ed. Maas and Tripanis 1963, 280–93; Germanos I of Constantinople, *Homily on the Annunciation*.
[93] Earlier Greek fathers were somewhat slow to make this connection, preferring to view at least two of the young men as angels; see *ACCS*, vol. 2 (Gen 12–50), 60–6. The idea that one of the three men was Christ, the second Person of the Trinity, appears in Eusebios of Caesarea's *Proof of the Gospel* V.9, ed. Heikel 1913, 232; this text is excerpted in John of Damascus, *On the Divine Images* III, ed. Kotter 1975, 171; trans. Louth 2003, 121.
[94] See above, n. 88.
[95] Wellesz 1961, 237. For further evaluation of the authenticity of hymns attributed to John of Damascus, see Louth 2002, 253; Eustratiades 1931–3.

mother'.[96] As Thomas Arentzen has recently shown, regal epithets for the Mother of God had become commonplace by the middle of the sixth century when Romanos composed his kontakion on the Annunciation. Although it may not have featured in Byzantine iconography, such imagery was used in both homilies and hymns to express the high status that Mary enjoyed in the celestial hierarchy.[97] And, as with many other aspects of the Virgin's multifaceted nature, this could be juxtaposed with her image as a humble girl; the paradox reflected that of Christ's divine and human natures in the incarnation.

The dialogue between Gabriel and the Virgin Mary in John's kanon is somewhat compressed in comparison with those provided in Romanos the Melodist's kontakion and Germanos of Constantinople's homily on the Annunciation. And, since it is embedded in a kanon, it loosely follows the structure of the odes and their basis in the biblical canticles. The hymnographer, using his own voice on behalf of the congregation, sings praises either to Christ or to his mother in the first stanza of each ode, with dialogic stanzas following these salutations. Although there is some dramatic play on Mary's transition from doubt and fear to acceptance of the archangel's message, such dialogue also provides an opportunity for theological teaching. Mary asks Gabriel to explain the meaning of Old Testament prophecy or typology that foretold the virgin birth. In Ode Four, for example, she asks the following question:

> 'I have learned from the prophet, who foretold in times of old the coming of Emmanuel, that a certain holy Virgin would bear a child (Is 7:14). But I long to know how the nature of mortal men will undergo union with the Godhead.'[98]

The archangel proceeds to explain this mystery, using types including the burning bush and Gideon's fleece as illustrations. The transition from doubt to faith, which appears to occur in association with the conception itself, is thus a process more of learning theology than of emotional development for Mary in this kanon. This contrasts with the dramatic dialogues that appear in the homily and kontakion by Germanos and Romanos, respectively, on which various scholars have commented.[99]

---

[96] John the Monk, *Kanon on the Annunciation,* Tone Four, Ode One; *Menaion,* vol. 4 (March–April), 176; trans. M. Mary and Ware 1969, 448–9.

[97] Arentzen 2019, 167–9, with commentary on Herrin 2000.

[98] John the Monk, *Kanon for the Annunciation,* Ode Four; *Menaion,* vol. 4 (March–April), 177; trans. M. Mary and Ware 1969, 451.

[99] Arentzen 2019, 167–9; Cunningham 2003, 110–12; Kazhdan 1999, 61–4.

The kontakion that appears after Ode Six is in fact a stanza of the *Akathistos Hymn*, which hails Mary's role as Second Eve 'through whom the creation is made new'.[100] More epithets and types follow, with both Gabriel and the Virgin herself describing her role in poetic, but theologically precise, terms. Here, as in earlier examples of homilies and hymns on the Annunciation, there is no interest in Mary's *fiat*, that is, the free choice that caused her to accept God's will and conceive Christ. The hymnographer sees her instead as destined to bear the Word of God in her womb. Thus the exact moment at which this world-changing event took place is unimportant – although it is understood to have taken place at some point during the conversation between Gabriel and the Virgin Mary.[101]

In view of the emphasis that hymnographers and other liturgical writers placed on Mary's role as mediator of salvation, it is perhaps to be expected that appeals to her intercessory role occur infrequently in the hymnography for the feast of the Annunciation.[102] There are a few exceptions to this rule, however, as in an apostichon for the lity (procession) in the vigil, which is ascribed to Andrew of Crete. After describing once again the story of the Annunciation in which 'things below are joined to things above',[103] Andrew concludes with a prayer:

> We are saved in him and through him; let us cry aloud with Gabriel to the Virgin, 'Hail favoured one, the Lord is with you.' Christ our God, who is our salvation, has taken human nature from you and raised it up to himself. Pray to him that our souls may be saved.[104]

It is the theological content that predominates in this hymnography, however, including even in the ninth ode of John the Monk's kanon. The initiation of Mary's role as Mother of God is too important a subject for melodists to waste time seeking her assistance on behalf of Christian congregations.

---

[100] John the Monk, *Kanon for the Annunciation, Kontakion; Menaion*, vol. 4 (March–April), 179; trans. M. Mary and Ware 1969, 454; cf. *Akathistos Hymn*, stanza 1, trans. Peltomaa 2001, 4–5.

[101] For an excellent discussion of patristic and Byzantine treatment of the Virgin Mary's conception of Christ *through her ear*, see Constas 2003, 273–313 ('The Poetics of Sound').

[102] For the distinction between the Virgin's role as mediator and intercessor, see Introduction, 8–9; Reynolds 2012, 152–3.

[103] This phrase is typical of Andrew's thought, which is influenced by that of Gregory Nazianzen. Compare, for example, his homily on the Nativity of the Virgin in which he writes: 'She mediates between the height of divinity and the humility of flesh . . . ', PG 97, 808C; trans. Cunningham 2008b, 73.

[104] Andrew of Crete, *Apostichon in Tone Four* at the Lity, *Menaion*, vol. 4 (March–April), 174 (my own translation).

The Dormition (*Koimesis*)

This feast, which was probably established in the late sixth or early seventh century by the emperor Maurice (582–602), is one of the great Marian celebrations in the Byzantine liturgical calendar.[105] Its hymnography, not all of which is precisely dated, addresses the Virgin with such extravagant epithets as 'queen', 'throne of heaven' and 'source of life'. The stichera, aposticha, kanons and other hymns include some narrative concerning the translation of the apostles to Mary's tomb, her death, burial and assumption into heaven; however, they devote more space to theological expressions of praise for this holy person. Like the preachers whose orations we examined in the previous chapter, hymnographers focus their attention on the paradox that Mary presents: she is a fully human being who, as a virgin, gave birth to God; she thus truly died, but must also have remained incorruptible.[106] As in the case of the other festal hymns that we have so far examined, moral exhortation is absent and intercessory content is minimal. However, there are allusions to the Virgin Mary's presence at the right hand of Christ, following her dormition and assumption, and to her ability to intercede on behalf of faithful Christians before the Righteous Judge and King.

In the discussion that follows, I will focus on two kanons that were composed for the feast of the Dormition which are ascribed to Kosmas the Melodist and John of Damascus. If these attributions are correct, the two works are thus examples of kanon writing from the first half of the eighth century.[107] They both show signs of such early composition: for example, the kanons both refer explicitly to the canticles on which each ode is based – a quality that is not present in every later composition. Since the kanons are entirely devoted to the subject of the Mother of God, it is

---

[105] According to the fourteenth-century historian, Nikephoros Kallistos Xanthopoulos, the feast was added to the Constantinopolitan liturgical calendar, as 15 August, by the emperor Maurice (582–602): *Ecclesiastical History* 17.28, PG 147, 292B. This institution reflected the commemoration of the Theotokos on that date in Jerusalem since about the middle of the fifth century; see van Esbroeck 1988a; Shoemaker 2002, 78–141.

[106] There has been much scholarly coverage of the theological meaning of the death and assumption of the Virgin Mary, both for Eastern and Western medieval Christendom. See especially Jugie 1944; Wenger 1955; Mimouni 1995; Van Esbroeck 1995; Shoemaker 2002. As regards the actual death, but bodily incorruption, of the Virgin Mary, there has been some variation of scholarly opinion; such ambiguity also characterises the papal pronouncement, called the 'Munificentissimus Deus', which was issued on 1 November 1950. See Boss 2007, 281–3. For further discussion, see Chapter 3, 116–29.

[107] The kanons were intended for the morning office (*Orthros*) and appear in the *Menaion*, vol. 6 (July–Aug.), 412–19. Andrew Louth, following Nikodemos the Hagiorite, provides commentary on the kanon that is ascribed to John of Damascus in Louth 2002, 274–82.

difficult to distinguish theotokia that stand out from the other stanzas of
each ode. They each combine some narrative elements with passages of
eulogy or invocation. And little distinction between the thought or style of
the two melodists can be detected; these hymns belong already to a well-
established genre in which structure to some extent dictates the content of
each ode. Nevertheless, it is possible to discern original – or striking –
elements that may reflect the separate approaches of the two Palestinian
hymnographers.

As in all other festal hymnography, time collapses in the context of the
present celebration. Kosmas therefore begins with a reference to the
'spiritual hosts', along with the 'multitude of apostles, coming together
suddenly from the ends of the earth', that attended the deathbed of the
Theotokos. In the next stanza, however, he celebrates her abode in heaven
where she lives eternally with her son.[108] John of Damascus, after uttering
praise throughout his first ode to the 'Queen and Mother' who now stands
beside Christ, describes in the final stanza of the third ode how the apostles
were miraculously taken to Zion in order to assist at the Virgin's burial.[109]
Narrative passages thus mix with panegyrics throughout both kanons. The
rhetorical intention was to transport congregations simultaneously to the
Virgin's bed-chamber in the house on Zion, the tomb at Gethsemane and
(at least obliquely) her final throne in heaven.

Both hymnographers also provide concise theological teaching concerning the death and assumption of the Virgin. Kosmas, for example,
expresses the paradox in a stanza that is addressed directly to the
Theotokos:

> O pure Virgin, you have won the honour of victory over nature by bringing
> forth God; yet, like your son and Creator, you have submitted to the laws of
> nature in a manner above nature. Therefore, in dying, you have risen to live
> eternally with your Son.[110]

In what way did this death, which occurred 'in a manner above nature',
take place? The melodist provides further explanation in Ode Six:

> The Lord and God of all gave you, as your portion, the things that are above
> nature. For just as he preserved you as a virgin in childbirth, so did he

---

[108] Kosmas the Melodist, *Kanon on the Dormition of the Virgin*, Tone One, Ode One; *Menaion*, vol. 6
(July–Aug.), 412–13; trans. M. Mary and Ware 1969, 514–15.
[109] John of Damascus, *Kanon on the Dormition of the Virgin*, Tone Four, Odes One and Three;
Menaion, vol. 6 (July–Aug.), 413–14; trans. M. Mary and Ware 1969, 515–16.
[110] Kosmas the Melodist, *Kanon on the Dormition of the Virgin*, Ode One; *Menaion*, vol. 6 (July–Aug.),
413; trans. M. Mary and Ware 1969, 515.

preserve your body incorrupt in the tomb; and he glorified you by a divine translation, showing you honour as a son to a mother.[111]

We find here the juxtaposition between Mary's virginal birth and her preservation from corruption in the tomb that is also made in contemporary homilies on this subject.[112] In both cases, however, liturgical writers stress the idea that this holy woman, like Christ, did indeed die. The language that refers to 'incorruption' thus means merely that her body was not submitted to the normal process of decay that affects all other human beings. As for the process by which the Theotokos reached her position on a 'throne' at the right hand of Christ in heaven, the hymnographers are reticent. They, like preachers, speak metaphorically of this process, with expressions such as 'divine translation' (θείᾳ μεταστάσει),[113] departure to 'the heavenly mansions' (εἰς οὐρανίους θαλάμους)[114] and others.

Typology abounds in Kosmas the Melodist's kanon and it always conveys precise theological meaning. References to the ark of the covenant, the tabernacle and the temple are frequent since Mary's body, which had contained God and remained incorruptible in death, fulfilled both prophetic types. A more metaphorical link exists between Mary's womb and the tomb in which she was laid, both of which are antitypes for the containers described in the Old Testament. Their incorruptible qualities are ascribed to Christ, as we see in the following verse:

> The Lord and God of all gave you, as your portion, the things that are above nature. For just as he kept you a virgin in childbirth, so did he preserve your body incorrupt in the tomb . . .[115]

There are also frequent references to Mary as the antitype of the queen or princess in Psalm 44 [45] in the hymns for the feast of the Dormition. This probably reflects her exalted position in heaven, following the assumption. A sticheron that is sung at the beginning of Vespers suggests that Mary, the Queen, will be accompanied to heaven by virgins; although this may refer metaphorically to all faithful Christians who have died and been

---

[111] Ibid., 415; trans. M. Mary and Ware 1969, 519.
[112] For example, Andrew of Crete, *Homily I on the Dormition*, PG 97, 1081D; trans. Daley 1998, 110: 'For as her womb was not corrupted in giving birth, so her flesh did not perish in dying. What a miracle!'
[113] Kosmas the Melodist, *Kanon on the Dormition of the Virgin*, Ode Six; *Menaion*, vol. 6 (July–Aug.), 415; trans. M. Mary and Ware 1969, 519.
[114] Kosmas the Melodist, *Kanon on the Dormition of the Virgin*, Ode Nine; *Menaion*, vol. 6 (July–Aug.), 419; trans. M. Mary and Ware 1969, 524.
[115] Kosmas the Melodist, *Kanon on the Dormition of the Virgin*, Ode Six; *Menaion*, vol. 6 (July–Aug.), 415; trans. M. Mary and Ware 1969, 519.

transported to heaven, it also evokes the virgins of the Psalm.[116] A third example is the 'holy mountain of the Lord', which Kosmas uses in the fourth ode with reference to its canticle, the prayer of Habakkuk (Hab 3:1–19). Kosmas calls to his listeners, as follows:

> Come, O people, and gaze in wonder: for the holy mountain of the Lord, in the sight of all, is exalted above the hills of heaven. The earthly heaven takes up her dwelling in a heavenly and imperishable land.[117]

The type of the mountain, which is based on the biblical verse, 'God will come out of Temen, and the Holy One from a shady, densely wooded mountain' (Hab 3:3), has associations with other mountains in the Old Testament (Ex 19:18; Ps 67:16 [68:15], Dan 2:34). All of these suggest in different ways the manner in which Christ emerged mysteriously, or without rupture, from a fully human mother. In the case of Habakkuk, the mountain is covered with a storm cloud. This 'overshadowing' cloud refers to the way in which the 'power of the Most High [overshadowed]' the Virgin according to Luke (Lk 1:35).[118] The various biblical references, which also have metaphorical value in that they suggest Mary's human qualities by associating her with physical creation, add layers of meaning to individual types such as this. Composers such as Kosmas employed a well-known stock of types and images but combined them in new ways in their festal hymns.

References to contemporary audiences, along with their collective or personal relationships with the Virgin Mary, are less easy to find in festal hymnography. A few examples can be found, however, as in the hypakoe that follows the third ode of the second kanon:

> From all generations we call you blessed, O Virgin Theotokos, for Christ our God who cannot be contained was pleased to be contained in you. Blessed also are we in having you as our help. For you intercede for us by day and by night, and the sceptres of kings are strengthened by your supplications. Therefore, singing your praises, we cry aloud to you: 'Hail, favoured one, the Lord is with you.'[119]

---

[116] Sticheron for 'Lord I have Cried', Great Vespers, Tone One; *Menaion*, vol. 6 (July–Aug.), 406; trans. M. Mary and Ware 1969, 506.

[117] Kosmas the Melodist, *Kanon on the Dormition of the Virgin*, Ode Four; *Menaion*, vol. 6 (July–Aug.), 414; trans. M. Mary and Ware 1969, 517.

[118] Ladouceur 2006, 34.

[119] *Hypakoe after the third ode*, Tone Five, Matins for the Dormition of the Virgin; *Menaion*, vol. 6 (July–Aug.), 414; trans. M. Mary and Ware 1969, 516 (with adjustments).

It is possible that the congregation would have joined in with the final verse (which is of course Gabriel's salutation to the Virgin in Luke 1:28). There are further supplications to the Mother of God, combined again with the *chairetismos*, in the stichera for Psalm 140 [141] in Vespers. However, the emphasis in most hymns for the offices that made up the vigil for this feast remains Christological.

Hymnographers of the middle Byzantine period thus drew on an accepted body of biblical interpretation, which included literal and typological (but not allegorical) methods, in order to express the manner in which Mary, the Mother of God, enabled God to fulfil his saving dispensation. She symbolised the physical creation that he inhabited and from which he took his human nature in the incarnation. Feasts including the Nativity of the Virgin, the Entrance into the Temple and the Annunciation were celebrated as events that initiated this dispensation. They also helped to reveal the doctrine of two natures that had been defined at the Councils of Ephesus and Chalcedon: Mary was the 'workshop' in which the two natures were woven together.[120] The feast of the Dormition revealed both the humanity and the divine holiness of this virginal mother. The pure body that had contained and given birth to God died a real death but remained uncorrupted in the tomb. And, as a premonition of the resurrection that good Christians would experience after the Final Day, Mary was assumed bodily into heaven and allowed to sit at the right hand of her Son. It is somewhat surprising that the hymnography for this feast does not celebrate her consequent influence as intercessor to a greater extent; however, the melodists preferred to emphasise Christological teaching at the expense of supplication to the Mother of God.

Daily Services: the *Oktoechos* or *Parakletike*

Turning from festal to daily hymnography, it is necessary to introduce another service book, which came into existence at an early date. The *Oktoechos*, whose composition has traditionally (and mistakenly) been ascribed to the eighth-century theologian John of Damascus,[121] was replete with hymnography for the eight-week cycle of tones on which the fixed liturgical year was based. It contained the basic services for the daily offices,

---

[120] The classic expression of this metaphor, as we saw in Chapter 2, occurs in Proklos of Constantinople's *Homily I*; see Constas 2003, 136–7.
[121] See Louth 2002, 252–3.

beginning each day with Vespers, providing different texts (along with their musical settings according to the tones) for each of the eight weeks in the cycle. The *Oktoechos* was already in use by the early sixth century but continued to grow with contributions from famous hymnographers including Andrew of Crete and John of Damascus. Ninth-century monastic hymnographers, and especially Joseph the Hymnographer, expanded the book further, providing kanons for each day of the week according to the eight tones.[122] Hereafter it came to be called the *New* or *Great Oktoechos* or, more commonly, the *Parakletike*.[123] Particular honour was paid to the Theotokos, along with the cross, in the more penitential services for Wednesdays and Fridays. This is the context in which we find a rich collection of stavrotheotokia (hymns that honour Mary's lament at the foot of the cross) to which I shall turn shortly. It is possible that such emphasis reflects the monastic contexts in which much of this hymnography was composed.

The Virgin Mary plays a central role throughout the other daily services, however, not only in kanons and their theotokia, but also in other short hymns or prayers. We have only to look at the beginning of the *Parakletike*, for example, to find the dogmatic theotokion that is sung at Great Vespers for Sunday:

> Let us sing in praise of Mary the Virgin, the glory of the whole world, who was made from human seed and bore the Master, [she] who was the gate of heaven, the song of the bodiless ones, and the adornment of the faithful. For she was revealed as heaven and temple of the Godhead. Having torn down the wall of enmity, she substituted peace and opened up the Kingdom. Holding fast therefore to her, as the anchor of faith, we have as our defender the Lord who was born from her. Let the people of God then take courage, take courage![124]

The hymnographer praises the Virgin as the vehicle of salvation. She is described in typological terms, with images such as gate (Ezek 44:1–3) and temple (3 Kgs 6–7 [1 Kgs 6–7]). However, praise of Mary leads to celebration of Christ, who defends his people from both external and internal enemies. Since it links this section of the office (the singing of Ps 140 [141]) with the next (the entrance of the bishop or priest from the sanctuary, followed by the singing of the evening hymn known as *Phos Hilaron* or

---

[122] For discussion of Joseph the Hymnographer's role in the production of the 'Nea Oktoechos' or *Parakletike*, see Ševčenko 1998 (2013), 110; *Parakletike*, trans. Guillaume 1977, 5–18.

[123] Wellesz 1961, 139–40.

[124] Theotokion for Great Vespers on on Saturday in Tone One, following 'Lord I have cried', *Parakletike*, 3 (my translation).

'Joyful Light'), the placement of this theotokion perhaps reflects, in liturgical terms, the Mother of God's role as 'gate of heaven'.

The offices that follow, including those for midnight and for the morning (*Orthros*), each contain two – or sometimes three – kanons. Thus the *Parakletike* offers at least four different kanons for each day of the year in an eight-weekly cycle; these would be accompanied by the kanons for both the fixed and movable years that appear in other liturgical books including the *Menaion*, the *Triodion* or the *Pentekostarion*.[125] As we contemplate this group of kanons (not to mention all of the other hymnodic forms that appear in the various liturgical books), we are struck by their sheer quantity. Nancy Ševčenko is probably correct in suggesting that this material was intended mainly for monastic audiences.[126] She writes that the intercessory kanons of the *Parakletike* are 'especially penitential and personal . . . [the poet] appeals to the saint both to rescue him now from various sorts of troubles, the troubles of daily life, and to intercede for him at the end of time'.[127]

If we choose the kanons for Sunday Matins in the *Parakletike* in the first tone, for example, we find that the Theotokos features especially in the theotokia that follow each ode, and to some extent also in the ninth ode. The theme for Sunday is the resurrection of Christ whereas other days of the week focus in turn on the archangels (Monday), John the Baptist (Tuesday), the cross and the Theotokos (Wednesday and Friday), the apostles and St Nicholas (Thursday), and the martyrs (Saturday). The kanons for Sunday are carefully structured, using heirmoi (the opening verses, along with their melodies, for each ode) that evoke the canticles on which they are based. The two kanons that are assigned for this day, according to Tone One, are attributed to John of Damascus and Kosmas the Melodist. Interspersed with these is an anonymous 'kanon of the Theotokos', which focuses exclusively on the Christological and intercessory importance of the Virgin Mary.[128] The odes of the other two kanons

---

[125] Such liturgical books might be combined in the Byzantine period, as they were in the earlier centuries, according to the needs of individual churches or monasteries. The earliest surviving liturgical book, of Palestinian origin, is called the *Old Tropologion*, Cod. Sinai gr NE/MΓ (ninth century). See Nikiforova 2012; Nikiforova 2013; Smelova 2011, 118–19.

[126] Note, however, that monastic preoccupations and goals could easily transfer themselves to lay devotional contexts. Byzantine lay people regularly attended monastic offices and liturgies in Constantinople and the provinces. They also frequently turned to monastic leaders, instead of the secular clergy, for spiritual direction. See Morris 1995, 90–119.

[127] Ševčenko 1998 (2013), 112–13.

[128] For background on such kanons to the Theotokos, which could be collected in separate manuscripts known as 'theotokaria', see Winkley 1973a.

also end with theotokia, which amplify these themes. Mary's intercessory role is invoked, for example, in the theotokion that follows the fifth ode in the first kanon:

> Do not overlook the prayers of those who pray faithfully, all-praised one, but accept these and present them, O undefiled one, to your Son, the only benevolent God. For we have you as our protector.[129]

Rather surprisingly, the two kanons that are ascribed to John and to Kosmas do not devote praise exclusively to the Virgin Mary in their ninth odes. They focus instead on the crucifixion and resurrection of Christ, probably in accordance with the celebration of the latter on the Sunday of every week. The 'kanon of the Theotokos', however, fills this gap: after alluding to the type of the burning bush (Ex 3:1–8), the hymnographer praises Mary's role in the fulfilment of prophecy and the miracle of her virginal birth-giving.[130] There are no allusions in this ode to Mary's intercessory power.

Turning to the kanons for Wednesday according to the *Parakletike* (Tone One), the themes of the cross and the Theotokos are dominant. It is in this context that we see the penitential – and probably monastic – element becoming more visible. The author of the second kanon (who is named as John of Damascus) dwells constantly on sin and the need for redemption; he blames evil thoughts and passions for distracting him from a pious life, as we see in the third stanza of the first ode:

> As one who is constantly falling down in judgement and being seduced by evil thoughts, having become madly ensnared and wholly available to my enemies – do not despise me, O Lady![131]

The tendency to sin, which brings despair to individual monks and nuns, is balanced by the proximity of a merciful Virgin who is constantly invoked in daily prayer. A polarity is also visible here: the deeper the depths to which the sinner has fallen, the greater is his or her dependence on the Mother of God – and beyond her, Christ her son.

The *Triodion*

The penitential character of this liturgical book reflects its use during the moveable calendar year, extending between the Sunday of the Publican

---

[129] John of Damascus, Kanon in Tone One for *Orthros* on Sunday, Ode Five, Theotokion, 15 (my translation).
[130] Kanon of the Theotokos in Tone One, *Orthros* on Sunday, Ode Nine, *Parakletike*, 20.
[131] John of Damascus, Kanon for *Orthros* on Wednesday, Ode One, *Parakletike*, 52 (my translation).

and the Pharisee (four weeks before the beginning of Lent) and Holy and
Great Saturday, that is, the night before Easter Sunday.[132] The *Triodion*
probably originated at the Monastery of Stoudios, with Theodore and his
brother Joseph (later archbishop of Thessalonike) initiating the project
during the first half of the ninth century.[133] The compilers drew on earlier
hymnographic compositions, including especially the kanons of
Palestinian melodists such as Andrew of Crete, Kosmas the Melodist and
John of Damascus, but also added to this collection. The *Triodion* continued to expand in the course of the ninth century, with
Constantinopolitan poets including Klement, Kassia and the prolific
Joseph the Hymnographer contributing to its content.[134] During its earlier
phases, different versions of the *Triodion* included longer or shorter versions of the Lenten period; according to manuscript evidence, it arrived
approximately at its final form by about the twelfth century.[135]

The *Triodion* offers penitential hymnody for the offices that are celebrated throughout the Lenten period, as well as for Lazarus Saturday, Palm
Sunday and the whole of Holy Week. In comparison with the typological
approach of most festal hymnography, there is more emphasis here on
ethical and allegorical readings of scripture.[136] And, since much of the
Triodion is penitential in character, it is not surprising to find supplication
to the Mother of God, along with holy figures such as St Mary of Egypt, to
intercede on behalf of sinful humanity. As in the case of hymnography of
the *Oktoechos* or *Parakletike*, such pleas for intercession often possess
a more personal quality than do the hymns for the fixed services of the
Menaion. They are usually expressed through the voice of the hymnographer, who speaks for the entire congregation – whether this is monastic
or lay.[137]

Hymnography that honours or addresses Mary, the Theotokos, appears
throughout the *Triodion*, as in other service books, especially in theotokia
and kanons. Andrew of Crete's *Great Kanon* is no exception to this rule.[138]

---

[132] *Triodion katanyktikon*; trans. M. Mary and Ware 1978.   [133] Krueger 2014, 170.
[134] Krueger 2014, 171; on Klement, see Kazhdan 1992; on Kassia, see Tsironis 2002; Simić 2009; on
Joseph the Hymnographer, see Ševčenko 1998 (2013).
[135] Krueger notes, however, that 'later poets continued to write additional selections; copyists made
substitutions' even after this period. See Krueger 2014, 169–72, esp. 172.
[136] Theokritoff 2005, 83–6.
[137] On the construction of a 'liturgical self' with the help of such hymnography, see Krueger 2014, esp.
164–96.
[138] Andrew of Crete, *Great Kanon*. For an important recent study, see Krueger 2014, 130–63. Previous
secondary work on the *Great Kanon* includes Schirò 1961–2; Wellesz 1961, 204–6; Kazhdan 1999,
46–52.

This long hymn, which consists of nine odes that are divided into 250 stanzas or troparia, is sung in sections during the services of Compline in the first week of Lent and in its entirety on Thursday of the fifth week. In the course of identifying himself with many biblical characters, beginning with Adam and Eve, who sinned against God, the hymnographer turns for help to the Mother of God in the theotokia that round off each ode of the kanon as we see in the following example, which follows the first ode:

> O Theotokos, the hope and protection of those who sing your praises, take from me the heavy yoke of sin and, as a pure Lady, accept me in repentance.[139]

At the end of his long composition during which, according to Derek Krueger, the hymnographer 'dramatizes the recognition of the self' in a 'Foucaultian' manner,[140] the focus shifts back to the Virgin Mary as chief defender of Constantinople. In the final theotokion following the ninth ode, Andrew writes:

> Guard your city, O undefiled Progenitor of God; for while ruling faithfully through you, [the city] is made strong by means of your [help]. She is victorious, putting to flight every temptation, despoiling the enemies, and ruling over her subjects.[141]

It is not clear whether verses such as this reflect topical concerns for Andrew of Crete. He certainly lived in Constantinople during parts of his life and experienced Muslim invasions on the island of Crete;[142] however, the theotokion may represent a conventional trope in its appeal to the protective powers of the Theotokos. It does not coincide with the more personal or inward-looking tone of the kanon as a whole, so may represent a scribal addition at a later date.

---

[139] Andrew of Crete, *Great Kanon*, Ode One, Theotokion: Θεοτόκε, ἡ ἐλπίς, καὶ προστασία τῶν σὲ ὑμνούντων· ἆρον τὸν κλοιὸν ἀπ' ἐμοῦ τὸν βαρύν, τὸν τῆς ἁμαρτίας, καὶ ὡς Δέσποινα ἁγνή, μετανοοῦντα δέξαι με, PG 97, 1336C. In the absence of contemporary manuscripts containing the *Great Kanon*, it is impossible to determine whether Andrew himself added these theotokia to each ode of the work. It is likely that once this element had become standard in Byzantine kanons, a later scribe or compiler added appropriate stanzas to the original text. However, a tenth-century manuscript of the *Triodion*, Sinai gr. 735, shows the theotokia firmly in place and written in the same hand – although they are signalled in the margins by the letter Θ. I am grateful to Derek Krueger for alerting me to this manuscript, which is now available online (thanks to the microfilm collection at the Library of Congress) at: www.loc.gov/item/00271075583-ms/.

[140] Krueger 2014, 134.

[141] Andrew of Crete, *Great Kanon*, Ode Nine, Theotokion, PG 97, 1385D.

[142] For discussion of the likely place of the *Great Kanon* in the context of Andrew of Crete's life, see Krueger 2014, 133.

The *Triodion* as a whole, like the *Parakletike*, emerged from a primarily monastic background. This, along with its liturgical setting of Great Lent, may account for its personal and penitential aspect, leading to a greater preponderance of theotokia with an intercessory purpose.[143] However, as liturgical scholars have repeatedly shown, monastic books soon became part of the cathedral and parish liturgical repertoire.[144] The *Great Kanon*, along with other hymns that were originally intended for the monastic office of *Orthros*, began to be chanted – either chorally or as solo performances – in churches that were attended by lay, as well as monastic, Christians. This suggests that the ascetic values that belonged properly to monasticism transferred themselves to lay Christians both in Constantinople and in the Byzantine provinces. Supplication to Mary, the Mother of God, also became more personal and intercessory, thus supplementing the primarily Christological hymnography that we have noted in both daily and festal service books earlier in this chapter.

Theotokia and Stavrotheotokia

The short troparia that are known as theotokia appear in numerous settings throughout the divine offices.[145] As mentioned above, they featured – at least by the beginning of the eighth century – at the end of each ode of most kanons, thus completing that section of the hymn and reminding congregations of the salvation that was inaugurated by Mary's birth-giving. Theotokia could also be sung after stichera (responses) or ainoi ('praises') that were sung after the chanting of Psalm verses in Vespers and the Morning Office, following the final doxology ('Glory ... now and ever ...) in each section – as well as at numerous other points in liturgical celebration.[146] There are different types of theotokia, including those that describe or address the Mother of God, using typology and allegory, poetic imagery and intercessory prayer; the stavrotheotokia, which are devoted to Mary's lament at the crucifixion; and the dogmatika, which elaborate her importance in Christological doctrine.[147] The latter are considered to be

---

[143] For exploration of the penitential and monastic nature of the *Triodion*, see Mellas 2017; Mellas 2020.

[144] Taft 1986, 273–83; Taft 1992, 52–66; Krueger 2014, 132–3.

[145] For useful introductions to this form of hymnography, see Smelova 2011; Hannick 2005; Eustratiades 1930; Baumstark 1920.

[146] Frøyshov 2013, 'Rite of Jerusalem'.

[147] According to Hannick, the dogmatic theotokia belong to the category of hymns known as idiomela; they are thus also preserved in a separate book called the *Sticherarion*, whose earliest witnesses date to the tenth or eleventh century; he also calls them 'works of incomparable exegetical value' on account of their rich use of typology and allegory; see Hannick 2005, 71–6.

the work of John of Damascus,[148] although they were probably revised and expanded by later hymnographers.

To begin with dogmatic theotokia, which are used especially in the office of Vespers before Sunday, we find various methods of exegetical teaching with regard to the Virgin Mary. These include historical or literal, typological and allegorical forms of biblical interpretation. An example of a theotokion which expresses a richly typological account of Mary's role in Christ's incarnation is that which is sung at the end of Vespers for the Sundays of Tone Five:

> The prophecies concerning you have been fulfilled, pure Virgin; for one of the prophets foretold you as the gate in Eden facing towards the East through which none had passed, except your Creator, for the sake of the whole world. Another saw you as a bush aflame with fire, because in you there dwelt the fire of the Godhead and you remained unburned. Another as a holy mountain from which was hewn without human hand a cornerstone and it crushed the image of the spiritual Nebuchanezar. Truly great is the mystery that is in you, Mother of God! Therefore we glorify you, for through you has come the salvation of our souls.[149]

We find a different form of dogmatikon, this time following the stichera for Psalm 140 [141] in the Vespers service preceding Sundays in the sixth tone. Here the hymnographer omits any typological references, preferring to teach Christological doctrine in a more discursive way while addressing himself directly to the Virgin:

> Who will not call you blessed, all-holy Virgin? Who will not hymn your birth-giving without labour? For the only-begotten Son, who shone from the Father beyond time, came forth from you, pure maiden, ineffably incarnate. By nature he is God, by nature he became man for our sakes, not divided in a duality of persons, but known without confusion in a duality of natures. O honoured and all-blessed, implore him to have mercy on our souls.[150]

There is a chiastic structure to this dogmatikon, which helps to emphasise its main dogmatic point.[151] The hymn begins with invocation of the Virgin

---

[148] Hannick supports this thesis by citing the unusual vocabulary that appears in some dogmatika, including αὐθυπάρκτως ('existent in itself') and Φρικτὸν καὶ ἄρρητον ὄντως ('terrible and inexpressible indeed') (both describing the incarnation), found in the *Paraklitike*, 533; see Hannick 2005, 72.

[149] Theotokion following the aposticha in Vespers on Saturday, Tone Five; *Parakletike*, 362; trans. Archimandrite Ephrem (with adjustments) at: https://web.archive.org/web/20160305063629/http:/anastasis.org.uk/

[150] Dogmatikon for Vespers on Saturday, Tone Six, *Paraklitike*, 451; trans. Archimandrite Ephrem (with adjustments) (for internet link to the resource, see above, n. 149).

[151] I am grateful to Elizabeth Theokritoff for making me aware of the chiastic structure of many hymns. See also Breck 2008.

Mary. The following lines lead from her miraculous birth-giving to the two
natures of Christ that are embodied in one Person, with allusion to the
definition of the Council of Chalcedon. Then the hymnographer ends by
calling again on the Theotokos, appealing to her as intercessor before the
God-man, Christ.

Turning now to the intercessory content of many theotokia, we again
find abundant evidence. Supplication to the Mother of God, with appeals
to her role as intercessor before Christ and protector of the faithful, may fill
whole theotokia or else be confined to their closing phrases. A theotokion
that focuses entirely on intercessory prayer reads as follows:

> Look upon the supplication of your servants, O all-unblemished one,
> bringing to an end the dread assaults that beset us and calming all our
> distress; for we have only you as safe and sure anchor, and we have obtained
> your protection. Sovereign Lady, may we who entreat you not be put to
> shame; make haste to hear the supplication of us who cry to you with faith:
> Hail, Sovereign Lady, help, joy, and protection of all, and salvation of our
> souls.[152]

In contrast to this, we find Christological and intercessory themes combined in another theotokion:

> Pure Virgin, you alone were declared the dwelling of the Light which shone
> out from the Father; therefore I cry to you: make bright my soul, darkened
> by the passions, with the light of the virtues, and make her dwell in tents of
> light on the day of judgement, O immaculate one![153]

In addition to showing how the separate strands of invocation may or may
not be combined in one short hymn, these examples (which are chosen
almost at random from the *Parakletike*) reveal the difference between
collective and personal prayer to the Virgin. The first of the two theotokia
appeals to her on behalf of the whole congregation whereas the second
assumes the voice of a solitary supplicant. It is tempting to assume, as in the
case of so much of the hymnographic material in the *Parakletike*, that the
hymnographers are praying on behalf not only of themselves but also of
a largely monastic congregation. The frequent references to passions,
demonic assaults and other forces that impede spiritual growth seem to

---

[152] Theotokion following the resurrection stichera of the aposticha, Great Vespers on Saturday, Tone
Four; *Parakletike*, 274; trans. Archimandrite Ephrem (with adjustments) (for internet link to the
resource, see above, n. 149).
[153] Theotokion for Vespers following 'Lord I have cried', on Monday, Tone One; *Parakletike*, 36–7;
trans. Archimandrite Ephrem (with adjustments) (for internet link to the resource, see above,
n. 149).

reflect the preoccupations of such a background. Although it must be borne in mind that the affect which pervades some hymns in the *Parakletike* is rhetorical, it reflects the penitential spirit that would have been encouraged especially in monasteries not only during Lent but also in the weekday offices throughout the liturgical years. The monastic hymnographers cry out both to Christ and to the Mother of God to save them from 'drowning' in the passions and offences that afflict them in their wretched states.

This tendency appears most vividly in the stavrotheotokia that are sung especially in the offices for Wednesday and Friday each week. These short hymns reflect a strand of hymnography that goes back to Romanos the Melodist and perhaps beyond.[154] Romanos elaborates the story of Mary's lament in his kontakion on this subject, inventing a dramatic dialogue between her and her suffering son as he was being dragged towards the cross.[155] Whereas the Virgin is portrayed as suffering and crying out from 'deep grief and great sorrow' (ἐκ λύπης βαρείας καὶ ἐκ θλίψεως πολλῆς),[156] Christ himself remains stoic in the face of his torments. He tells his mother to stop grieving since she will be the first to witness his resurrection. In the course of this dialogue, much theological teaching is provided, mostly in the voice of Christ, as he goes through the story of God's dispensation for salvation, beginning with his incarnation as the 'second Adam' and being fulfilled in his crucifixion and resurrection. The kontakion ends with the hymnographer's invocation of the Saviour, along with an allusion to Mary's 'freedom of speech' (*parresia*), which allows her to act as intercessor for the rest of humanity.[157]

The stavrotheotokia expand further the theme of Mary's heartfelt grief at the sight of her son dying on the cross. As Niki Tsironis has suggested, a growing theological emphasis on the reality of the incarnation (which could be conveyed in both lyrical and discursive terms) from about the late seventh century onward found expression in various homilies of this period.[158] It is possible that these texts influenced the writers of the stavrotheotokia that were produced in such quantities for the *Parakletike*, the *Triodion* and other service books. I suggest again that the frequency

---

[154] Tsironis 1998. For further discussion of stavrotheotokia, see Constas 2016, esp. 11–14, 17–21.

[155] Romanos the Melodist, *Kontakion on Mary at the Cross*, ed. Maas and Trypanis 1963, 142–9.

[156] Ibid., stanza 4, Maas and Trypanis 1963, 143.

[157] Ibid., stanza 17, Maas and Trypanis 1963, 148–9. For further discussion of Romanos' kontakion on Mary at the cross, see Chapter 1, 63–5.

[158] Tsironis cites John of Damascus, *Homily on Holy Saturday*, (ps-)Germanos of Constantinople, *Homily on the Burial of the Lord's Body*, and Theodore of Studios, *On Holy Easter* as possible sources for the stavrotheotokia; see Tsironis 1998, 220–30. Beck ascribes the *Homily on the Burial of the Lord's Body* to Germanos II, not Germanos I; see Beck 1959, 668.

with which Mary's lament is evoked throughout the liturgical year may be associated with the monastic themes of sin and compunction. By identifying their own pain with that of the Mother of God at the foot of the cross, hymnographers urged their audiences to pray for healing and forgiveness from the suffering Christ.

Among the many stavrotheotokia that are sung in Vespers before Wednesday each week, we find, for example, the following juxtaposition between the situation of the hymnographer (who sings on behalf of a monastic audience) and Mary at the foot of the cross:

> Wretch that I am, since I am bowed down beneath dreadful passions, and I have done wholly profligate deeds of shame, whose base images and fantasies even now batter, confuse, and turn me to sensual enjoyment of them in the sensations of my heart. But do you, O pure one, save me.

> My life has become full of many temptations, O all-pure one, from the many evils with which I have offended; but ransom me from both and give me both a mind and a life that are without offence and a sober reason, that in faith I may call you blessed and glorify your godly name . . .

> . . . The Virgin, when she saw your unjust slaughter, O Christ, cried out to you in bitter grief, 'My sweetest Child, how are you suffering unjustly? How hanging on the tree, you that hung the whole earth on the waters? Do not, compassionate Benefactor, leave me alone, your mother and your servant.'[159]

Such a connection, which is set out here in the ordering of the troparia, is unequivocal. Monastic worshippers (and by extension all Christians) are urged to face and experience the depths of grief that Mary felt at the foot of the cross. This state, which involves a sense of complete abandonment, leads to greater dependence on God. It is also prompted by the selfless love that belongs above all to grieving mothers. In the case of Mary, such pain also represents the fulfilment of Symeon's prophecy that a sword would pierce her soul (Lk 2:35), as we see in the following stavrotheotokion:

> A sword passed through your heart, O all-pure one, when you looked towards your Son on the cross and you cried out, 'Do not leave me childless, my Son and my God, who kept me a virgin after childbirth!'[160]

Fr Maximos Constas has provided a vivid assessment of Mary's position in liturgical texts that deal with her lament at the foot of the cross:

---

[159] Sticheron after 'Lord I have cried', Vespers on Tuesday, Tone One; *Parakletike*, 49; trans. Archimandrite Ephrem (for internet link to the resource, see above, n. 149).

[160] Stavrotheotokion after 'Lord I have cried' in Vespers on Tuesday, Tone Three; *Parakletike*, 50; trans. Archimandrite Ephrem (for internet link to the resource, see above, n. 149).

Mary, both virgin and mother, is a paradoxical figure. In a single moment, in the very form of her being, she embodies all the inviolability of virginity and all the pain of motherhood. In her virginity she is a 'sealed book that no man may open' (cf. Is 29:11-12). Yet in the experience of mourning for her lost son, the seals of her being are torn apart, rent like the veil of the temple, for this is her real childbirth, in which her hair is loose, her eyes leak, and midwives anxiously attend to her. In her pain she is one with the wounded Christ: she is porous, poured out, kenotic . . .[161]

Paradox thus lies at the heart of the incarnation; it manifests itself not only in Christ's birth, death and resurrection, but also in the Virgin Mary's place within these events. Hymnographers deliberately contrasted Mary's virginal conception and birth of Christ, which occurred entirely without rupture or pain, with her vulnerability and 'porousness' at the foot of the cross. The two events revealed her simultaneous closeness to God and human nature: the Theotokos remained inviolate but was vulnerable to pain and suffering. This reflected – and helped to reveal – the two natures, divine and human, of her son, Jesus Christ.

Both homiletic and hymnographic evocations of this doctrine express historical, moral and spiritual layers of meaning. Although the lay and monastic faithful may have assimilated such messages to varying degrees, it is possible that their daily exposure to hymnography allowed them gradually to gain better theological understanding. The typological references may be complex, but rhetorical devices including vivid description (*ekphrasis*), exclamation (*exclamatio*) and character portrayal (*ethopoiia*) would have allowed congregations to enter into the kind of emotional state that engenders real spiritual growth.

Conclusions

I have surveyed in the course of this chapter the hymnography in praise of Mary, the Theotokos, that survives in various Byzantine service books for both the fixed and moveable liturgical years. Although some hymns offered innovative teaching of Marian theology, the majority provided concise and formulaic approaches to their holy subject. Hymnographers, like icon painters, sought to convey well-established exegetical teaching, which could be expressed best by the use of accepted phrases, prophecy and typology. Although these elements might be combined in different ways, they reappeared constantly in both festal and daily hymnography.

---

[161] Constas 2014, 127–9.

Congregations, including both lay and monastic Christians, would have recognised and understood the biblical references to the Theotokos – and would perhaps also have appreciated the variety of ways in which she was described or invoked, according to the different feasts and ordinary days of the year. The emphasis in most hymns, as I have suggested throughout this chapter, was Christological; however, both daily and Lenten services consistently provided suitable occasions for penitential and intercessory prayer to the Virgin Mary.

Like homiletics, hymnography employed a range of rhetorical tools in its teaching of Christological doctrine. In addition to invoking and praising the Mother of God with the help of a huge range of biblical types and metaphors, hymnographers used *ekphrasis* (vivid description), *diegesis* (narrative), *ethopoiia* (the painting of character by means of dramatic monologue or dialogue) and many other persuasive tools that helped to bring alive this biblical, but also legendary, character. Scholars have noted the overlap between homilies and hymns while also pointing out their unique characteristics.[162] The question whether either genre inspired or influenced the other is rendered more difficult because many writers, such as Andrew of Crete, John of Damascus and George of Nikomedia, wrote both homilies and hymns. These preachers and melodists were masters at condensing complex Christological teaching into poetic praise and narrative. Such a message is transmitted more directly in hymnography than in homiletics, owing to the metrical limitations of the former liturgical genre; whereas preaching may have offered a more discursive, and therefore experimental, opportunity for teaching of this kind, the composition of hymns was focused and deliberate. It is likely therefore that hymnographers drew on the theological inspiration of both patristic and contemporary preachers – even when they were themselves involved in both processes.

In addition to listening to well-known hymns on a daily basis, congregations may have participated in singing their refrains.[163] Music, in the form of the well-known tonal melodies that were used in the Byzantine Church, would also have helped the assimilation of theological teaching. The liturgical services, which took place both inside and outside churches and in which every class from emperors to ordinary men and women played a role, taught incarnational theology with the help not only of words, but also of music, incense and images.[164] The Virgin Mary played a central role in this theology since

---

[162] Hannick 2005; Tsironis 2005.   [163] See above, n. 81.

[164] For a recent and evocative treatment of the sensory power of the Byzantine liturgy, see Pentcheva 2010.

she symbolised the receptive creation, or body, which the divine Son of God chose to enter. It is this message above all that the dogmatic theotokia and other Marian hymns emphasised.

That hymnography was valued for its didactic as well as its devotional function is revealed by the glosses and commentaries – especially on the poetic kanons that were attributed to John of Damascus – which began to appear from the end of the ninth century onward.[165] This literary process, which has been receiving increasing scholarly attention, opens up an entirely different context for the reception of Byzantine hymnography.[166] Photios Demetracopoulos and Dimitris Skrekas have shown that some, mainly eighth-century, hymns that were considered to contain the most sophisticated theological teaching and poetry became teaching tools in Byzantine schools especially in the twelfth century. Indeed this phenomenon continued in the later and even post-Byzantine period.[167] It is worth emphasising here that only certain hymns received such treatment.[168] They included the iambic kanons that were attributed to John of Damascus, as well as some by his colleague and possibly adopted brother, Kosmas. The works of writers including Romanos the Melodist, Joseph, Theophanes Graptos and George of Nikomedia were meanwhile considered clear enough in meaning not to need exegetical commentaries.[169] There were two main settings in which the iambic kanons might be explained. First, they appear to have been used in private, or more closed, settings in which the audience might be expected to have a high standard of rhetorical and philosophical learning. This context is suggested by statements by the authors of commentaries, such as Gregory Pardos of Corinth, Theodore Prodoromos or Eustathios, that their work has been requested – or is offered to – scholars and philomatheis ('lovers of learning').[170] Second, however, internal evidence suggests that the same commentaries were delivered to students in the Patriarchal or other theological schools in Constantinople.[171] In addition to exegetical lectures on the kanons, which might subsequently be published by the commentators, teaching in these settings included schedography, or the

---

[165] Skrekas 2008, xx–xxxi.
[166] See, for example, the excellent critical edition of an iambic hymn for Pentecost that is attributed to John of Damascus in Eustathios of Thessalonike, *Exegesis*.
[167] Demetracopoulos 1979; Skrekas 2008, xx–xxxiv.
[168] The corpus included the religious poetry of Gregory Nazianzen, along with some other selected works. See Krumbacher 1897, 679–80; Demetracopoulos 1979, 143–6.
[169] Demetracopoulos 1979, 148.   [170] Demetracopoulos 1979, 140, n. 34.
[171] Demetracopoulos 1979, 150–2. On the Patriarchal School in Constantinople, see Browning 1962.

imitation of short poetic pieces by students.[172] Above all, this evidence suggests that the theological content of religious poetry (which included the more sophisticated hymnography of John of Damascus and Kosmas the Melodist) was taken seriously by such highly educated figures as Theodore Prodromos and Eustathios of Thessalonike. It could be discussed and elucidated in the more sophisticated setting of the Constantinopolitan Patriarchal School while also being sung at the appropriate liturgical moment in churches throughout the empire.

Much work remains to be done not only on Marian but also other forms of Byzantine hymnography. Although this lies beyond the scope of the present study, texts should be considered along with their musical settings: hymnographers were also musicians who composed – or re-used – the melodies to which they set their verses. Their compositions offered congregations a harmonious form of theological teaching that was expressed not only in words, but also in music. It should also be recognised that this vast body of material represents one of the most important surviving sources of official teaching on the theological place of the Virgin Mary in Christian doctrine. Hymnography is not as easy to access as homiletics or theological treatises for the many reasons that I set out at the beginning of this chapter; however, this literary and musical genre probably reached the church-going public in a way that more refined or technical texts did not. The melodists and the singers who performed their works sought to inspire joy, understanding and penitence in the Byzantine faithful, depending on the time or day of the year that was appropriate for each state of mind. Whether they were clerical, lay or monastic worshippers, those who heard these hymns would have understood their didactic message. The Mother of God occupied a central place in the services of the Church that were celebrated throughout the year; after all, 'she who was more spacious than the heavens'[173] '[gave] birth to the Maker of all things'.[174]

---

[172] 'Besides the iambic canons, other religious poems were also used in schedography, as the Ἔπη of Gregory Nazianzus, students and teachers σχεδογράφοι imitated ecclesiastical poems, "ἰαμβίζοντες" in dodecasyllabic verses, and even parodies of canons were written'; Demetracopoulos 1979, 145–6 (see also nn. 15–19).

[173] John the Monk, Sticheron at the Lity, Vespers for Christmas Day, *Menaion*, vol. 2 (Nov.– Dec.), 659.

[174] Germanos of Constantinople, Sticheron at the Lity, Vespers for Christmas Day, *Menaion*, vol. 2 (Nov.–Dec.), 659.

CHAPTER 5

Narratives about the Panagia
Miracle Stories, Hagiography and Apocalypses

It is convenient to include miracle stories and narrative accounts concerning the Virgin Mary's birth, life, death and posthumous activities within an
all-encompassing category which I shall call 'hagiography' in this chapter.
Such material shares certain characteristics: it may (although there are
significant exceptions to this rule) be written in a low-brow or even
colloquial style,[1] display an interest in historical narrative and deviate –
sometimes quite intriguingly – from more 'official' or theological literary
treatment of the Theotokos.[2] After the anomalous second- or third-century
apocryphal text known as the *Protevangelion of James*,[3] mention of the
Virgin Mary in hagiographical texts did not begin to appear until about the
middle of the fourth century.[4] Even after this, with the exception of the
various accounts of Mary's dormition that began to circulate from about
the end of the fifth century onward,[5] miraculous or hagiographical stories
concerning the Virgin were not produced in any great quantity until the
late sixth or early seventh century. From that period onward, such texts
began to proliferate – although, arguably, they never overtook the quantity
of miracle stories and biographies associated with other saints who had
come to be celebrated in the Byzantine liturgical calendar.[6]

The material to be discussed in this chapter includes stories about
posthumous miracles performed by the Virgin Mary or by her relics
(usually a garment) contained in miracle collections, enkomia or *vitae* of
other saints, as well as some other literary genres such as histories and
chronicles. I will also examine four hagiographical texts that are dedicated
to the Theotokos herself. These works form a group that displays common

[1] Browning 1981; I. Ševčenko 1981.　　[2] See the discussions in Baun 2004; Baun 2011.
[3] *Protevangelion of James*; for discussion, see Introduction, 5–7, and nn. 22, 27, 33, 34.
[4] For background, see Maunder 2008, and especially Shoemaker 2008b.
[5] Jugie 1944, 103–67; Mimouni 1995, 75–344; Shoemaker 2002; also see Chapter 3, 116–19.
[6] For background on this subject, see *BHG*; Efthymiades 2011; the Dumbarton Oaks Hagiography
Database at: www.doaks.org/research/byzantine/resources/hagiography-database.

narrative themes, even if each text possesses unique preoccupations and aims.[7] The four hagiographical texts include a *Life of the Virgin* written by Epiphanios, who may have been a monk at the Constantinopolitan Monastery of Kallistratos towards the end of the eighth or beginning of the ninth century,[8] a more sophisticated composition by the late tenth-century writer John of Geometres,[9] a contemporary Georgian version of Geometres' text by Euthymios the Athonite[10] and another Marian *Life* that is attributed to Symeon the Metaphrast.[11] Finally – as a kind of appendix to the chapter – I shall look briefly at the ninth- or tenth-century apocalypses that deal with Mary's tour of hell and paradise in the period just before or after her death; these texts, which Jane Baun has explored so fruitfully in various recent studies, contain a hagiographical element in that they provide narratives about the Virgin's life or afterlife.[12] And, like miracle stories and *Lives of the Virgin*, they reveal much about the Virgin Mary's cult and intercessory role in Byzantium.[13]

A brief comment on the literary genre, or the validity of assigning many of the texts described above to that of hagiography, is necessary here.[14] We should remind ourselves again that the boundaries between separate genres were porous in the hands of Byzantine writers.[15] Thus, John Geometres' *Life of the Virgin*, although described by scholars as 'hagiography', is also a series of rhetorical meditations, or orations, on events in the life of the Theotokos that correspond with their liturgical celebration as feasts.[16] Many of the middle Byzantine festal sermons which we examined in Chapter 3 take the form of (or are described in manuscripts as) enkomia. And the liturgical or monastic locations at which sermons, enkomia or *Lives* of the Theotokos were delivered may not always have differed. Nevertheless, it is convenient to categorise the literary evidence to be examined in this chapter as 'hagiographical'. We will be concerned above

---

[7] Mimouni 1994; Cunningham 2016.   [8] Epiphanios of Kallistratos, *Life of the Virgin*.

[9] John Geometres, *Life of the Virgin*. As will be evident here as well as later in the present chapter, I am fully convinced by Christos Simelidis' argument that this text served as a basis for the Georgian *Life* that Euthymios the Athonite produced during the final decades of the tenth century; see Simelidis 2020. For further discussion, see below, 192–4.

[10] Georgian *Life of the Virgin*.   [11] Symeon the Metaphrast, *Life of the Virgin*.

[12] Baun 2004; Baun 2007; Baun 2011; cf. Arentzen 2018.

[13] Especially the *Apocalypse of the Theotokos* and the *Apocalypse of Anastasia*. For detailed discussion of these texts and much useful analysis, see Baun 2007.

[14] On the function of literary genres in Byzantium, see Patlagean 1979; Mullett 1990; Mullett 1992; *ODB*, vol. 2, 832; Agapitos 2008.

[15] See Introduction, 23–4; Mimouni 1994 (2011), 75–6; Cunningham 2016, 139–42.

[16] Wenger 1955, 186; Kazhdan 2006, 263 (treating only the 'homily' on the Dormition); Antonopoulou 2011, 26, n. 79.

all with narratives – whether written in a low or high literary style – that deal with Mary's personal history, characteristics and activities in this or the next world. There tends to be less emphasis in these texts on her place in Christological doctrine or in the wider scheme of God's dispensation and more on her relationship with individual Christians – although this may not always be the case in more sophisticated theological works such as John Geometres' *Life of the Virgin*. Such teaching, while popular and apparently acceptable to the official Church, could sometimes (but not always) deviate from more rigorous formulations of Christian atonement and salvation.

Jane Baun has recently challenged theologians and historians to include 'low-brow' and 'popular' religious texts in their studies of the formation of Byzantine Christian doctrine. She suggests, following Cyril Mango, that such literature 'brings us into closer contact with reality than the stilted compositions of the educated élite',[17] arguing that it reflects the beliefs and practices of the Byzantine faithful.[18] Hagiographical and apocalyptic texts which, judging from the number of surviving manuscripts, circulated widely and continued to be read in later centuries not only in Greek but also in many other languages, also helped to shape Christian doctrine. This 'sensus fidelium', as it is called in the Roman Catholic tradition, should not be underestimated as a force in the development of Byzantine ideas about the Mother of God, divine intercession and the afterlife.[19] It is my broad agreement with this thesis that has led me to devote a chapter to miracle stories, hagiography and apocalypses that deal with the Virgin Mary. In the discussion that follows, I shall attempt both to highlight the unique characteristics of these various literary forms and to assess their significance in the Marian cult as a whole.

Miracle Stories Involving the Virgin Mary

Stories of the Virgin Mary's appearance to individual Christians, either in person or in dreams, are rare before about the middle of the sixth century. There are exceptions to this rule, such as Gregory of Nyssa's account, in the fourth century, of Gregory Thaumatourgos' (the Wonderworker's) waking vision of a figure who 'had the appearance of a woman, whose noble aspect

---

[17] Baun 2011, 201, quoting Mango 1981, 52–3.
[18] Discussions of the distinction between 'official' and 'popular' expressions of devotion to the Theotokos appear also in Cameron 2004, 20; Cameron 2005, xxviii–xxx; Shoemaker 2008b; Cameron 2011, 3–4.
[19] Baun 2011, 202–3.

far surpassed normal human beauty'. Gregory of Nyssa tells us that
although the night was dark, she appeared to his namesake 'as if
a burning lamp had been kindled there'. After she and her companion,
who is identified as John the Evangelist, had settled the doctrinal matter
that had been worrying the saint, they disappeared from view.[20] This story
neatly juxtaposes Mary's function as a holy intercessor with her own
importance in doctrinal terms. It remains, however, a somewhat isolated
example against a background of growing Christian devotion towards
saints and their relics, as well as belief in their ability to mediate divine
power in the created world.[21]

It was in the sixth century, beginning in the Latin-speaking West, that
miracle stories involving the Theotokos began to appear in greater quantity. Owing to the fact that many of these stories reflected contact with
Eastern Christendom, either because of pilgrimage to the Holy Land or
simply due to oral transmission from one region to another, it is worth
examining them in the context of this study. Gregory of Tours, writing
between approximately the middle of the sixth century and his death in
594, included several miracles involving the Virgin in his *Libri
miraculorum*.[22] These include a story about builders who were constructing
a basilica in honour of the Virgin during the reign of Constantine and who
were granted a vision in which she showed them how to move heavy
columns with the help of a machine and one about a Jewish boy, son of
a glass-blower, who was thrown into the furnace by his father for having
partaken of the Christian eucharist but survived, thanks to the intervention
of the Theotokos. The second of these stories, along with another concerning a pilgrim who was on his way from Palestine to his home in Gaul,
involved the Virgin Mary's relics: in the former, she spread her mantle over
the boy in the furnace and in the latter, the pilgrim discovered the
indestructibility of pieces of her clothing that he was carrying home after
his pilgrimage.[23] Pope Gregory the Great (*c.* 540–604) told the story of
a young girl called Musa, who experienced a vision of the Virgin Mary one
night. The Theotokos informed Musa of her approaching death and told
her that she would be included in a group of holy virgins belonging to her
entourage. After thirty days, during which she had time to reform her way

---

[20] Gregory of Nyssa, *Life of St Gregory Thaumatourgos*, PG 46, 909D–912C; trans. Gambero 1999,
     93–4.
[21] For general studies of this growing trend, see Brown 1981; Markus 1994; Frank 2000; Dal Santo 2012;
     Hahn and Klein 2015.
[22] Gregory of Tours, *Libri miraculorum*, *In gloria martyrum* 8, 9, 18, ed. Krusch 1885, 493–4, 499–50.
[23] These stories are all summarised or translated (as excerpts) in Gambero 1999, 354–8.

of life, the girl duly died.[24] This story was transmitted to the Byzantine world by means of its inclusion in the eleventh-century spiritual anthology known as the *Evergetinos*;[25] it is also likely that Gregory's *Dialogues* were circulating in a Greek translation well before that period.[26]

John Moschos, perhaps writing in Rome but using material that he and his friend Sophronios, future patriarch of Jerusalem, had gathered in the course of their travels through Palestine and Egypt, added to the collection of miraculous stories involving the Virgin Mary.[27] These tales included that of the Jewish glass-blower's son (also narrated by Gregory of Tours, as we saw above),[28] along with several more disturbing examples of Mary's punishment of unrepentant sinners. In one story, the Mother of God threatens an actor named Gaïanas, who has been performing an act in the theatre in Heliopolis (Lebanese Phoenicia) in which he blasphemes her. She appears three times, warning him to stop performing the scene, but Gaïanas refuses to obey. Finally, when he is taking an afternoon nap, she reappears and cuts off his hands and feet with her finger. On waking up, Gaïanas lies there 'just like a tree trunk' and then admits that he has received a just reward for his actions.[29] In another interesting story, John relates how an abbot had a vision of 'a woman of stately appearance clad in purple', accompanied by 'two reverend and honourable men' (whom he identified as John the Baptist and John the Evangelist), who refused to enter his cell unless he destroyed a book containing writings by Nestorios.[30] Another tale describes how Kosmiana, wife of a patrician named Germanos, was approached by the Mother of God, accompanied by some other women, and forbidden entrance to Christ's tomb in Jerusalem unless she renounced her allegiance to the Miaphysite Church. After being admitted to communion by a Chalcedonian deacon, she was thereafter allowed 'to worship unimpeded at the holy and life-giving sepulchre of Jesus Christ'.[31] Mary is invariably described in these stories as a dignified figure, dressed in purple, who is easily

---

[24] Gregory the Great, *Dialogues* 4.18, ed. Vogüé and Antin 1980, 70–3; PL 77, 348–9; trans. Gambero 1999, 369–70.

[25] *Evergetinon* 1.vii.A.6; trans. Archbishop Chrysostomos and Hieromonk Patapios 2008, vol. 1, 58–9; noted by Baun 2011, 212.

[26] Fischer 1950; Dagens 1981. For scepticism concerning the authenticity of this work, see Clark 1987.

[27] John Moschos, *The Spiritual Meadow*.

[28] John Moschos, *The Spiritual Meadow, Supplementary Tales* 12; ed. Mioni 1951, 93–4; trans. Wortley 1992, no. 243, 227–9.

[29] John Moschos, *The Spiritual Meadow* 47; PG 87, 2901D; trans. Wortley 1992, 38.

[30] Ibid. 46; PG 87, 2900D–2901C; trans. Wortley 1992, 37–8.

[31] Ibid. 48; PG 87, 2904A–C; trans. Wortley 1992, 39.

identifiable as the Theotokos. It is likely that such descriptions were based on iconography that was becoming increasingly standard in this period; the confidence with which writers such as Gregory of Tours and John Moschos describe Mary's appearance and garb suggests their familiarity with her portrayal in icons, wall paintings and manuscripts.[32]

Miracle stories were also produced in the middle Byzantine period, although perhaps not in the profusion that one might expect, given the growing importance of the Mother of God both during and after the period of Iconoclasm. Stephen the Deacon's *Life of St Stephen the Younger*, probably composed at the beginning of the ninth century, relates how the saint's mother (named Anna like her forerunner in the Old Testament) prayed for a child during the all-night vigil at the church of Blachernai. On falling asleep as she prayed for the third time, Anna received a vision of the Mother of God who promised that she would conceive a son.[33] The ninth-century *Life of St Irene of Chrysobalanton*, another Constantinopolitan saint, tells how this abbess was granted a vision of the Mother of God in response to her prayers concerning a nun who had become possessed by demons.[34] St Theodora, consort of the iconoclast emperor Theophilos, dreamed that she saw the holy Theotokos, holding the infant Christ in her arms, reproaching her husband and beating him because of his stance against icons.[35] And, dating probably from the tenth century, there is the famous account in the *Life of St Andrew the Fool* in which the Mother of God appeared to all who were present at the all-night vigil in the church of Blachernai, emerging from the sanctuary accompanied by a large retinue of prophets, patriarchs and saints. She prayed on behalf of everyone there, as well as for the whole world, and then spread out her veil over the congregation. According to the hagiographer, 'for a long while the admirable men [Andrew and Epiphanios] saw it stretched out over the people, radiating the glory of the Lord like amber. As long as the most holy Theotokos was there the veil was also visible, but when she had withdrawn they could no longer see it.'[36]

The Virgin Mary makes brief, but significant appearances not only in the *Life of St Andrew the Fool*, but also in the probably contemporary *Life of*

---

[32] Barber 2000; Maguire 2011; Lidova 2019.
[33] *Life of St Stephen the Younger* 4, ed. Auzépy 1997, 92–3; trans. 183–4.
[34] *Life of St Irene of Chrysobalanton* 13, ed. Rosenqvist 1986, 52–64.
[35] *Life of the Empress Theodora* 8; trans. Talbot 1998, 372.
[36] *Life of St Andrew the Fool*, ed. and trans. Rydén 1995, vol. 2, 254–5. See also Rydén 1976.

St Basil the Younger.[37] Both texts provide lengthy accounts, inspired by apocalyptic literature, of the heavenly kingdom with its Ruler, Christ, the Mother of God, and the ranks of attendant angels. In one significant passage, the author of the *Life of St Basil the Younger*, Gregory, describes his vision of Christ crowning and robing his mother in this context:

> The first to come to Him was the Mother of His holy incarnation and His nurturer, the immaculate and supremely holy Virgin Mary, the undefiled tabernacle of His awe-inspiring incarnation. Immediately taking the wondrous crown He wore on His holy and immaculate head, a crown of multicoloured flowers, precious gems, and noetic pearls, fabricated in many colours and in a divine fashion, He placed it on her holy head ... In addition He gave her also the first robe, which was awesomely woven and noetically fabricated from heavenly imperial linen and purple (cf. Lk 16:19, Rev. 18:12, 16), the robe which He Himself wore after His incarnation ... After honouring her as His Mother, He rose up and seated her on the most awe-inspiring divine and fiery throne of His glory (Mt 19:28, 25:31) positioned near Him, having extolled and praised her in the presence of all the saints from the ages, for her spiritual purity and magnanimous and very great divine forbearance amid terrible circumstances ...[38]

The hagiographer ranks the Virgin as second only to Christ; after her comes John the Baptist 'whom [Christ] honoured worthily and extolled above all and deemed worthy of rank and honor second only to the Mistress and Lady of all'.[39] Although Epiphanios, the narrator in the *Life of St Andrew the Fool*, experiences a similar vision, he does not see the Mother of God in glory. An angel (described as 'a dazzling man dressed in a garment that was like a shining cloud') explains her absence as follows:

> Our distinguished Lady, the Queen of the heavenly powers and God-bearer, is not present here, for she is in that vain world to support and help those who invoke God's Only Son and Word and her own all-holy name.[40]

Whether they envision her in heaven or on earth, these tenth-century hagiographers stress the Virgin's glory and power. Her devotees regularly visit her shrines in Constantinople, where they can expect to find forgiveness of sins and healing. A young thief in the *Life of St Andrew the Fool* flees

---

[37] *Life of St Basil the Younger*; on the probable date and provenance of the *Life*, see Sullivan, Talbot and McGrath 2014, 7–11. The editors discuss the relationship between the *Lives of St Andrew the Fool* and *St Basil the Younger* on p. 9.

[38] *Life of St Basil the Younger* 116, ed. and trans. Sullivan, Talbot and McGrath 2014, 645–7.

[39] Ibid. 117, ed. and trans. Sullivan, Talbot and McGrath 2014, 647.

[40] *Life of St Andrew the Fool*, ed. and trans. Rydén 1995, vol. 2, 60–1 (with one adjustment).

to the Virgin's oratory of the Myrelaion after breaking his promise to reform himself. After anointing himself with oil and praying to the Virgin for help, he sees 'a woman standing before the doors of the holy sanctuary dressed in fine linen and purple. Her face [is] shining, more dazzling than the sun'. The vision expels the demon that has seized the boy, after which he addresses her icon, offering 'fervent thanks to the Mother of God, swearing an oath that he [will] never more steal, nor fornicate nor fraternize with fools and sinners'.[41]

The contexts or audiences for which these *Lives* were intended unfortunately remain unclear. Sullivan, Talbot and McGrath suggest (with respect to the *Life of St Basil the Younger*) that the text may have circulated in a monastery or monasteries where it offered ethical teaching to the brethren. They also posit that the text was consumed in sections throughout the year, rather than as a single reading on the feast-day of the saint. Both the length of the *Life* and its organisation into discrete sections or episodes support this hypothesis. However, it is also possible that the text was composed for a lay audience since it concerns itself with people of all classes and genders: the ethical teaching, which stresses charity as a virtue, relates especially to people who have the means to do good works. Above all, the lively narratives that are contained in both *Lives*, including both apocalyptic visions and cautionary tales, would have attracted readers or audiences from diverse social backgrounds.[42]

From about the tenth century onward, miracle stories associated with water also began to be recorded in Constantinople. Three important Marian shrines, namely, the complexes at Blachernai, the Hodegon Monastery and the shrine of the *Pege* ('Source'), contained baths (*lousmata*) or springs (*pegai*). According to the anonymous tenth-century text known as the *Patria*, miracles took place at the spring of the Hodegon Monastery: 'many blind people saw again at the spring there, and many miracles happened'.[43] Another important Constantinopolitan shrine of the Virgin that incorporated water was the Blachernai church and monastery.[44] The empress Verina probably founded this shrine, which was originally located just outside the Theodosian land walls (and later included within

---

[41] Ibid., ed. and trans. Rydén 1995, vol. 2, 110–11.

[42] See the extensive discussion of this question in the *Life of St Basil the Younger*, ed. Sullivan, Talbot and McGrath 2014, 19–24.

[43] *Patria* III.27, ed. and trans. Berger 2013, 150–1; Magdalino 2007, 35.

[44] Other pools associated with Marian shrines in Constantinople included the Theotokos *ta Areobindou* and *ta Armatiou*. See Magdalino 2007, 34; *Patria* III.59, 62, ed. and trans. Berger 2013, 170–3. Such pools were often run by fraternities.

them),[45] shortly before 475.[46] In its earliest phase, the shrine consisted of a round or octagonal sanctuary (known as the 'Soros'), which contained the most important relic of the Virgin, a robe; several centuries later this would be described as a mantle or mandylion.[47] The early sixth-century emperor Justin I added a three-aisled basilica to the complex, which was re-modelled by Justin II and his consort Sophia, later in the same century.[48] There was also a pool or bath at the Blachernai complex, which must have been there even before its foundation.[49] Most accounts of the Virgin Mary's veneration at the sanctuary focus on her robe or, from the eleventh century onward, a holy icon that performed on a weekly basis what came to be known as 'the usual miracle'.[50] However, the pool played a ceremonial role when the emperor and his entourage paid a special visit to the shrine on certain Fridays during the year.[51] According to the tenth-century *Book of Ceremonies*, the royal visitors first entered the holy *Soros* where they said special prayers and then venerated and lit candles before an icon of the Virgin and Child known as the 'episkepsis'. Following these rites, they immersed themselves three times in the sacred bath that adjoined the Soros.[52] This description suggests a more ceremonial than impromptu role for the Blachernai pool. Nevertheless, it reinforces the association between the Virgin Mary and water, which represented an important aspect of her cult in the imperial city throughout the middle Byzantine period.

The shrine of the Virgin of the Source (*Pege*) was based at a sanctuary that was located just outside the walls of Constantinople. Like the shrine at Blachernai, the *Pege* was believed to have been founded in the second half of the fifth century, again during the reign of Leo I. An anonymous writer collected and wrote down the miracle stories that were associated with this shrine, from the time of its foundation to the tenth century.[53] He described

---

[45] The walls were extended by Herakleios, following the siege of the Avars and Persians in 626. See Janin 1964, 163.

[46] Mango 2000, 19.

[47] Much has been written on the relic of the robe or mantle. See, for example, Ebersolt 1921, 44–53; Baynes 1955; Cameron 1979b; Weyl Carr 2001; Wortley 2005.

[48] Mango 2000, 21.   [49] See Janin 1964, 161–71; Mango 1998, 62–3.

[50] Pentcheva 2006, 145–63.   [51] Ebersolt 1921, 48, 51.

[52] Constantine Porphyrogennetos, *Book of Ceremonies* II.12, ed. Leich and Reiske 1935, trans. Moffatt and Tall 2012, 552–6. According to Janin, the ceremony was performed 'from time to time', but always on a Friday. See Janin 1964, 170.

[53] The collection of forty-seven miracles is preserved in a twelfth-century manuscript in the Vatican Library (Vat. gr. 822, fols. 180v–207v) and was first edited in the *Acta Sanctorum Novembris* III (Brussels, 1910). It is now accessible, along with introduction and commentary, in *Miracles of the Pege*, ed. and trans. Talbot and Johnson 2012. See ibid., xv.

the legendary origins of the shrine, asserting that the fifth-century emperor Leo had discovered a spring just outside the walls of Constantinople when he was searching for water for a thirsty blind man. The Virgin Mary appeared to him, directing him to the spring. When the man drank the water, his sight was miraculously restored. The emperor then built a small shrine on the site, which was called a *kataphygion* or 'place of refuge'.[54] In the sixth century, the emperor Justinian constructed a domed church in honour of the Mother of God after being cured of a urinary infection by water from the *Pege*.[55] This church, to which a male monastery was soon attached, became a focus for both imperial and lay pilgrimage.[56] The Byzantine emperors visited the spring on Ascension Day; on this occasion, the patriarch celebrated a Divine Liturgy, which was followed by a meal.[57]

In addition to such imperial patronage, ordinary people visited the spring throughout the year, seeking healing from the water or sometimes from oil lamps that were hanging before an icon of the Virgin. The miraculous healings that took place at the shrine of the *Pege* were facilitated either by the Theotokos herself, who appeared to her supplicants in visions, or by her icon. However, they were always brought about by means of physical substances – water from the spring, mud from its banks or oil from the lamps that were hanging in the sanctuary. For the most part, the pilgrims ingested these liquids; it is also noticeable that the illnesses were often internal ones, consisting of gastric, urinary or intestinal infections or tumours. Dropsy, or bloating due to fluid retention, was also a common ailment. The beneficiaries of Mary's intercession ranged from emperors and their wives or relatives to common people; she appears to have acted without discrimination in her service to Christians of every gender and class. And, interestingly, the author of the miracles tells us that 'Eudokia', sister-in-law of Maurice (582–602 CE), did not recognise the Virgin when she encountered her in a vision; she appeared to be a woman 'of modest means' (*gynaika tina metrian*).[58] In another story, however, a monk perceived her as 'a woman robed in purple, towering as high as the lintel [of the church doorway] in the majesty of her stature'.[59] Such discrepancies probably reflect the diverse nature of these tales, which were compiled over

---

[54] Ibid. 2, ed. and trans. Talbot and Johnson 2012, 208–11.

[55] Ibid. 3, ed. and trans. Talbot and Johnson 2012, 210–13.

[56] Ibid., ed. and trans. Talbot and Johnson 2012, xv.

[57] Constantine Porphyrogennitos, *Book of Ceremonies* 1.18, ed. Leich and Reiske 1935, trans. Moffatt and Tall 2012, 108–14; Ebersolt 1921, 61–2.

[58] *Miracles of the Pege* 7, ed. and trans. Talbot and Johnson 2012, 220–1. On the identity of this individual, see Introduction, n. 158.

[59] *Miracles of the Pege* 13, ed. and trans. Talbot and Johnson 2012, 234–5.

several centuries; however, they may also reveal something about the status of individual devotees and how they expected to encounter the Mother of God.

Jane Baun suggests various ways of classifying the accounts of Marian miracles, which help us to evaluate their significance. She divides apparitions, for example, into categories on the basis of intention or purpose, which range from healings to intercession. After dividing the material up in this way, Baun is able to distinguish chronological developments with regard to some themes, with instances of Mary appointing tasks to her devotees or combating heresy belonging mainly to the earlier or late antique period, while her assistance in military matters appears increasingly frequently in later texts.[60] Baun also creates a useful distinction between the Virgin's physical and visionary appearances.[61] Her ability to appear to Christians in person even after death is described in a literal fashion in some texts: the miracle stories that were collected at the shrine of the *Pege*, for example, describe her appearances (in various guises) to individuals who pray to her there.[62] It is significant that from about the late ninth century onward, Mary appears less often in person, preferring henceforth to intercede or perform miracles by means of her icons.[63] Baun qualifies her conclusions in this study by admitting that they are based only on a representative selection of miracle stories dating from between the sixth and eleventh centuries. It is unfortunate that the very popularity of anthologies of such texts has led to their neglect by scholars. The numbers of manuscripts in which they are transmitted, combined with the focus of Bollandists and other editors on saints whose cults are objects of historical interest,[64] has caused many collections of Marian miracles to remain unedited.[65] My observation above, concerning the limited amount of

---

[60] Baun 2011, 204–6. Some miracle stories involving the Virgin's robe or mantle appear in middle or late Byzantine histories and chronicles. See, for example, the patriarch Photios' account of the role played by Mary's garment (*stolē*) in the siege of Constantinople by the Rus' in 860 (see Chapter 3, n. 167); the presence of her mantle (*maphorion*) at Romanos I Lekapenos' mission for peace with the Bulgarian ruler Symeon in 926 (Skylitzes, *Synopsis historiarum* 10.12, ed. Thurn 1973, 219, trans. Wortley 2010, 212); and Alexios I Komnenos' use of the same relic as a standard when fighting the Patzinaks in 1089 (Anna Komnene, *Alexiad* VII.3.9, ed. Reinsch and Kambylis 2001, vol. 1, 212, trans. Sewter 1969, 225–7).
[61] Baun 2011, 200–1.   [62] See above, nn. 58–9.
[63] Baun 2011, 206. See also Pentcheva 2006, 75–103. It is also worth remembering here the ongoing debate concerning the physical manifestation of saints, or indeed the Virgin Mary, in visions as opposed to these holy figures' impersonation by angelic or divine powers, which had been taking place from approximately the sixth century onward. See Krausmüller 2008; Dal Santo 2011; Dal Santo 2012.
[64] See, for example, the methods that are outlined in Delehaye 1921; Delehaye 1927.
[65] Baun 2011, 204–5.

such material that survives from the middle Byzantine period, should thus remain tentative – pending future editions of a body of literary texts that is potentially of great interest, not only with regard to the cult of the Mother of God, but also for theological and historical reasons.[66]

In summary, miracle stories convey much about the hope that Byzantine Christians placed in their protector and intercessor, the Mother of God. She could appear, either in person or glimpsed through icons or dreams, to those who placed their faith in her; at the same time, however, she could wreak awful vengeance on sinners and heretics. In theological terms, the portrayal of the Virgin Mary in texts such as these resembled that of other major saints. The Theotokos had the power to persuade, cure and some-times punish Christians who were in trouble. She was not seen as co-redeemer in the sense of having unlimited power as intercessor before God.[67] Rather, endowed with the *parresia* or 'freedom of speech' with God that was shared by other saints, Mary interceded with him on behalf of the rest of the human race. Her feminine, and sometimes explicitly maternal, aspect was increasingly emphasised in texts written during or after the iconoclast period.[68] See, for example, the appeal made by St Stephen the Younger's mother Anna for a child:

> 'Theotokos, refuge of those who run towards you, anchor and protector of those who seek you in pain, most safe port for those who are drowning with faint hearts in the great sea of life and most opportune ally for those who in despair summon you to their aid, glory of mothers and adornment of daughters, you who have transformed into happy assurance, by giving birth to the God-man, the most shameful condemnation of the whole female sex, owing to our first mother Eve – have mercy on me, hearken, and break the bond that is in me, just as was done for your progenitor Anna who bore you, and show your maternal mediation in allowing me to bear a male child that I may offer this gift to your Son and God.'[69]

---

[66] It is worth injecting a plea here for the production of less ambitious (as opposed to critical) editions of hagiographical texts. Instead of the lengthy – and not always productive – exercise of collating hundreds of manuscripts, some scholars are increasingly recognising the value of choosing several of the best manuscripts and publishing editions which, even if not representative of the whole tradition, provide the scholarly world with working tools. See D'Avray 2001, 31–3 (with reference to Western medieval sermons).

[67] For discussion of the extent to which that position was taken by some later Roman Catholic theologians, see Graef 1963 (2009), 332, 377. I do not agree, as will be discussed below, that John Geometres supported the concept of Mary's role as co-redemptress, as Graef (1963, 155–6) argues; cf. Galot 1957; Jugie 1944, 561–2.

[68] Kalavrezou 1990; Kalavrezou 2000.

[69] *Life of St Stephen the Younger* 4.15–24; ed. Auzépy 1997, 92 (my translation).

Nevertheless, as we shall see later in relation to some middle Byzantine *Lives* of saints and apocalypses, Mary could sometimes wield considerable power in the heavenly court. She ranked higher than any other saint or even angelic power because of her maternal relationship with Christ and assumption into heaven after death. The boundary between orthodox and more heterodox views on the Virgin's place in the celestial hierarchy was occasionally permeable, as a few of the surviving texts reveal.[70]

Middle Byzantine *Lives* of the Theotokos

The orthodoxy of four surviving middle Byzantine *vitae* of the Virgin Mary is not in question, although these texts provide teaching that is not always strictly in line with that found in biblical or even well-known apocryphal texts. The four *Lives* offer narrative, praise and supplication in honour of the holy Theotokos.[71] Although they are organised in different ways and display separate preoccupations, the texts are all hagiographical in nature. In other words, they attempt to elucidate the full life story, including the birth, life, death and afterlife of the Mother of God. In view of the silence of the canonical Gospels on so many aspects of Mary's life, our four hagiographers also employ both patristic and apocryphal sources in their pursuit of her story. The practice of stringing together separate apocryphal narratives concerning the Virgin's conception, infancy, motherhood of Jesus, and activities during his ministry and passion, as well as her own death and assumption into heaven, is known to have begun – perhaps first in Syriac-speaking milieux – from about the fifth century onward.[72] Charles Naffah is in the process of classifying and editing fifth- and sixth-century Syriac manuscripts that combine the various phases of the Virgin Mary's life into continuous narratives.[73] It is not known whether the Byzantine *Lives* were inspired by an early Greek translation of such a source or whether this genre evolved independently within the

---

[70] See below, 205–7.

[71] An excellent overview of these *Lives* is provided in Mimouni 1994 (2011). Although he lists a fifth *Life* (*CANT* 94; *BHO* 643–5), which he describes as 'Nestorian', I have omitted it from this study since it seems to have circulated within an eastern Syriac (Nestorian) milieu and remains difficult to date. The earliest manuscripts for this *Life*, which was edited by E. A. W. Budge in 1890, are dated to the thirteenth and fourteenth centuries. See Mimouni 1994 (2011), 105–12. For further discussion of the four *Lives*, see Cunningham 2016, 152–8.

[72] Naffah 2009; Norelli 2009.

[73] Earlier editions of these traditions include Wright 1865; *Syriac Life of the Virgin*, ed. Smith-Lewis 1902. For a fascinating account of the lives and Sinai research projects of the Scottish sisters Agnes Smith-Lewis and Margaret Dunlop Gibson, see Soskice 2009.

Greek-speaking Christian world. What is clear is that the literary and theological tendencies of at least three of the *vitae* reflect a period in which Marian
doctrine and devotion were well developed; they express interest in the Virgin
Mary as an exceptionally holy person in her own right who is capable of
interceding on behalf of Christians and assisting their salvation.

It is necessary first to address questions of date and literary context for
the four hagiographical texts. After this, I shall move on to analyse their
narrative content, before exploring what they reveal about the Marian cult
in Constantinople between the early ninth and late tenth centuries. The
problem raised at the beginning of this chapter regarding 'low' and 'high'
(or popular and élite) styles of hagiographical texts should also be addressed
in relation to these *vitae*. Whereas the late eighth- or early ninth-century
Life by Epiphanios of Kallistratos may have appealed to a wide audience,
judging by its simple literary style and message,[74] the three remaining texts
are complex in literary and theological terms. John Geometres' *Life of the
Virgin* contains sophisticated theological reflection on Christological
themes along with its narrative and devotional content.[75] Symeon the
Metaphrast's *Life*, while short on narrative detail, represents an elegant
panegyrical oration in praise of the Theotokos.[76] And the Georgian *Life*,
which is attributed to Maximos the Confessor but inspired by Geometres'
work,[77] provides a somewhat simplified version of the latter with focus
especially on Mary's ascetic and didactic activities as a disciple of Christ.

Scholarly attention has so far focused mainly on the dating and provenance
of the surviving Byzantine *Lives of the Virgin*. Both Michel van Esbroeck and
Stephen Shoemaker have argued that a lost Greek *Life of the Virgin*, which was
attributed to, but not necessarily composed by, the seventh-century theologian
Maximos the Confessor, was the earliest exponent of the Marian hagiographical tradition in the Greek-speaking Byzantine world.[78] This text was then
translated from Greek to Georgian by the monk Euthymios the Athonite (or
Hagiorite), in the late tenth century.[79] Shoemaker's arguments are based

---

[74] Epiphanios of Kallistratos, *Life of the Virgin*, ed. PG 120, 185–216; Dressel 1843, 13–44.
[75] John Geometres, *Life of the Virgin*, critical ed. forthcoming, Constas and Simelidis, DOML; section
on the Dormition, ed. Wenger 1955, 363–415; see also Simelidis 2020. For a detailed study of John
Geometres' literary achievements, see Kazhdan 2006, 249– 2.
[76] Symeon the Metaphrast, *Life of the Virgin*, ed. Latyshev 1912.   [77] Simelidis 2020.
[78] Georgian *Life of the Virgin*, ed. van Esbroeck 1986, vol. 2, v–xiii; ed. and trans. Shoemaker 2012, 14–
22. Van Esbroeck employs four main arguments, which are mainly literary and historical, to support
the attribution of the *Life* to Maximos. For a summary of these, along with criticism, see Mimouni
1994, 81–5.
[79] I refer to this text in the discussion that follows, along with its references, as 'the Georgian *Life of the
Virgin*'. See van Esbroeck 1988b; Georgian *Life of the Virgin*, ed. and trans. Shoemaker 2012, 2–3.
Euthymios the Athonite was born in Georgia between 955 and 960 and died in Constantinople,

mainly on internal evidence: they include the author's dependence on early
apocryphal sources concerning the Virgin's death and assumption into heaven,
his awareness of both Palestinian and Constantinopolitan traditions regarding
her relics, and the influence of the text on later writers including George of
Nikomedia, John Geometres and Symeon the Metaphrast.[80] Phil Booth and
Christos Simelidis have since challenged such an early date for the
Georgian *Life of the Virgin*, arguing for its production no earlier than
the middle or end of the tenth century.[81] Booth accepts the existence of
a lost Greek prototype for Euthymios the Athonite's Georgian translation
of the text, but prefers to place this in the tenth century.[82] He offers
various arguments that disprove either Maximian or even seventh-century
authorship of the text, finally suggesting that the author was more likely
inspired by George of Nikomedia's homilies on the passion and resurrection
of Christ than the reverse.[83] Simelidis proposes an even simpler explanation
for the date and literary context of the Georgian *Life of the Virgin*. Having
compared it closely with the former work, Simelidis argues that the late
tenth-century translator Euthymios the Athonite based his work directly on
Geometres' text. Thus the bilingual abbot produced a revised, and somewhat
simplified, version of the text for his Georgian readers. This means that the
Georgian *Life* represents nothing more than a paraphrase – albeit a highly
sophisticated one – of a complex theological Greek text that was produced
during the final decades of the tenth century.[84]

The textual analysis that Simelidis provides in his recent article provides,
to my mind, a definitive answer to this long-running debate. He offers
detailed and convincing proof that Euthymios the Athonite depended on
John Geometres' *Life of the Virgin* in order to produce a version that would
appeal to less sophisticated but spiritually motivated audiences in Georgia.
Simelidis focuses on sections in the text that have been simplified in the
Georgian version, along with others that expand the number of biblical
references: both of these features are characteristic of Euthymios' methods

---

c. 1028. He served as *hegumenos* of the monastery of Iveron from 1005 to 1019. Euthymios translated
a number of other theological and hagiographical texts from Greek into Georgian, and a few,
including a work that is inspired by the life of Buddha, known as *Barlaam and Ioasaph* and falsely
attributed to John of Damascus, from Georgian to Greek. See *ODB*, vol. 2, 757; Simelidis 2020, 137–
44. It is worth noting, however, that Shoemaker proposes a different translator, based at the
monastery of St Sabas in Palestine, for the *Life of the Virgin* in an article that he wrote in reponse
to Booth 2015; see Shoemaker 2016b, 135–42.

[80] These arguments are elaborated in Shoemaker's Introduction to the Georgian *Life of the Virgin*, 17–
22; cf. Shoemaker 2005; Shoemaker 2006b; Shoemaker 2011c, 53–6.

[81] Booth 2015; Simelidis 2020.   [82] Booth 2015, 149–50.

[83] Booth 2015, 197–9. Shoemaker responded to Booth's various arguments in Shoemaker 2016b.

[84] Simelidis 2020, esp. 128–9, but also passim.

of translation and metaphrasis.[85] John Geometres, when drawing on
biblical, apocryphal and patristic sources for his composition, manages to
combine a number of literary forms, including narrative, homiletic and
panegyrical, into one harmonious composition. Although the success of
this rhetorical exercise reflects John's literary skill and originality, it also
follows centuries of refinement in Marian liturgical expression. The hymnographic and homiletic genres that have been studied so far in this book
all helped to inspire John Geometres' work. It is also likely that new
emphasis on various aspects of the Virgin Mary's character, including her
ascetic labours, involvement in Christ's ministry and apostolic mission,
and emotional demeanour at the foot of the cross reflect a relatively late,
and highly developed, phase in her cult. Rather than accept Shoemaker's
proposal that these aspects of Marian devotion began much earlier than
was previously thought in the Eastern Christian world,[86] I agree with
Simelidis that they only reached full expression, thanks especially to John
Geometres, in the late tenth century.

Now that we have eliminated a hypothetical early seventh-century
prototype, the hagiographical text that is attributed to the
Constantinopolitan monk Epiphanios of Kallistratos emerges as the earliest example of the genre.[87] This *Life* has received some scholarly attention,
but still awaits detailed literary analysis.[88] Most recent studies agree that
Epiphanios, a monk and priest who may have lived at the Kallistratos
monastery in Constantinople at the end of the eighth and beginning of the
ninth century, produced not only this *vita*, but also one on the apostle
Andrew.[89] Alexander Kazhdan places him among the monastic literati of

---

[85] Simelidis 2020, 145–55.
[86] For this argument, especially in relation to Mary's lament, see Shoemaker 2011b; cf. Georgian *Life of the Virgin*, ed. and trans. Shoemaker 2012, 22–35, 174, n. 71. For studies of the development of affective devotion in Western medieval spirituality, see Bynum 1982; Fulton Brown 2002; McNamer 2010.
[87] Epiphanios of Kallistratos, *Life of the Virgin*. The text is accessible in two editions, PG 120 and Dressel 1843. These are based on separate manuscripts, belonging to the Marciana Library in Venice and the Vatican Library, respectively, and differ significantly in some of their readings. A critical edition would be desirable but is not (to my knowledge) forthcoming. For discussion of the two editions of the texts, see Mimouni 1994 (2011), 89. I am currently preparing a translation and commentary of the text for the TTB series at Liverpool University Press.
[88] Dräseke 1895; Jugie 1944, 258–9; Beck 1959, 513; Kazhdan 1999, 307; Shoemaker 2005, 457–8. A more detailed study appears in Cunningham 2019.
[89] Epiphanios of Kallistratos's *Life* of the apostle (*BHG* 102) is edited in Dressel 1843, 45–82 and in PG 120, 216–60. It should be noted, however, that E. Kurtz placed the *Life of the Virgin* in the eleventh century; see Kurtz 1897, 216, cited in Kazhdan 1999, 307, n. 26. The association of Epiphanios with the Monastery of Kallistratos in Constantinople is not well attested but is widely accepted by scholars.

the early ninth century in Constantinople, who included such important figures as Theodore of Stoudios and his brother Joseph, Theophanes the Confessor and the nun Kassia.[90] Epiphanios' *Life of the Virgin* contains a number of interesting characteristics, which set it off from the tenth-century hagiographical texts that followed it. For example, it is clear that Epiphanios approaches his material with a biographical or 'historical' purpose. He states at the beginning of his text that, since none of the apostles or early Fathers who wrote about Mary provided full accounts of her life from beginning to end, such a biography is needed.[91] Epiphanios seeks at the outset to establish the authority of his literary sources. He avoids texts that he calls 'apocryphal' or 'heretical', but does cite earlier authors including 'James the Hebrew' (either the putative author of the *Protevangelion of James* or that of a polemical early seventh-century text known as the *Doctrina Jacobi*),[92] John of Thessalonike, Andrew of Crete and Eusebios of Caesarea as authoritative sources on various aspects of Mary's life.[93]

After a brief prologue in which he sets out his aims and cites his sources, Epiphanios provides a genealogy for the Virgin Mary. This traces the ancestry of both parents, Joachim and Anna, on the basis not only of the Gospels of Matthew and Luke, but also of apocryphal and patristic traditions.[94] The object of the exercise is, as for some other eighth-century writers, both to demonstrate the royal and priestly lineage of the Virgin Mary (with her father Joachim belonging to the tribe of David and her mother Anna to a priestly line) and to underline her links with the rest of the human race.[95] Epiphanios also stresses the familial relationship between various women who featured prominently in Mary's life, including her cousins Elizabeth (mother of John the Baptist) and Salome who

---

[90] Kazhdan 1999, 396 – 97.
[91] Epiphanios of Kallistratos, *Life of the Virgin*, PG 120, esp. 185–9A; Dressel 1843, 13–15.
[92] *Protevangelion of James*; Sargis of Aberga, *Doctrina Jacobi nuper baptizati*, ed. Déroche 1991. Déroche (1991, 49) suggests this as Epiphanios' source.
[93] Epiphanios of Kallistratos, *Life of the Virgin*, PG 120, 188B; Dressel 1843, 14.
[94] Epiphanios of Kallistratos, *Life of the Virgin*, PG 120, 189; Dressel 1843, 15–16. One of the closest sources for this section of Epiphanios's account is John Damascene's *On the Orthodox Faith* IV.14, ed. Kotter 1973, 199–200. For a good summary of patristic (both Syriac and Greek) traditions concerning Mary's royal and priestly genealogy, see Brock 2006.
[95] Other eighth-century writers (in addition to John of Damascus) who mention Mary's royal and priestly lineage include John of Euboea, *Homily on the Conception of the Virgin Mary*, PG 96, 1489B–C, and Kosmas Vestitor, *Oration on Joachim and Anna*, PG 106, 1012A.

was also a midwife.[96] After an account of Anna's conception of the Virgin, Epiphanios moves on to her birth, infancy in the temple and betrothal to Joseph, followed by the part of her life that overlaps with the canonical Gospel accounts. The *Life* concludes with an account of the Virgin's activities after Christ's ascension into heaven (she led a life of asceticism and performed many miracles for the people of Jerusalem), followed by her death and burial. Epiphanios is careful in his epilogue to calculate the exact number of years that the Theotokos lived (he numbers these at seventy-two),[97] but – unlike the other Marian hagiographers – he does not discuss her assumption into heaven or the translation of her relics to Constantinople.[98] In short, this is a 'factual' (at least in the eyes of its author) account of the Virgin Mary's terrestrial life, which attempts to set straight the discrepancies in the canonical Gospels and to fill in the many gaps that persist in both biblical and patristic sources.

The *Life* by Symeon the Metaphrast (+ *c.* 1000) is the shortest text in the group.[99] Like many of the Metaphrast's reworkings of earlier *Lives* of saints, the redactor aims to produce a polished but somewhat impressionistic account of his subject.[100] It is noticeable that Symeon follows the Gospel narratives more closely than do the other three hagiographers; he also omits many details in Mary's story that belong only to the apocryphal and patristic traditions. Those that he does include, however – among which are a brief account of Anna's conception of Mary, the latter's dedication and upbringing in the temple, and her betrothal to Joseph – reveal similarities with the other three Byzantine *Lives* of the Virgin Mary. Nevertheless, certain features in the hagiographical narratives that reflect

---

[96] Epiphanios of Kallistratos, *Life of the Virgin*, PG 120, 189C, Dressel 1843, 16: Κατὰ μητέρα ἡ θεοτόκος ἦν οὕτως· Ματθὰμ ὁ ἱερεὺς ἀπὸ Βηθλεέμ, εἶχεν θυγατέρας τρεῖς· Μαρίαν, Σωβὴν, καὶ Ἄνναν. Ἡ μὲν Μαρία ἔτεκεν Σαλώμην τὴν μαῖαν· ἡ δὲ Σωβὴ ἔτεκεν τὴν μητέρα Ἰωάννου τοῦ Βαπτιστοῦ· ἡ δὲ Ἄννα ἔλαβεν Ἰωακεὶμ τὸν ἀδελφὸν τοῦ πατρὸς Ἰωσήφ· καὶ κατέβη Ἄννα νύμφη εἰς τὴν Γαλιλαίαν εἰς πόλιν Ναζαρὲτ· καὶ συνῴκησεν Ἄννα τῷ Ἰωακεὶμ ἔτη πεντήκοντα, καὶ τέκνον οὐκ ἐποίησαν. 'With regard to her mother, the [lineage of the] Theotokos was as follows. The priest Matham, who was from Bethlehem, had three daughters, Mary, Sobe and Anna. Mary gave birth to the midwife Salome, while Sobe bore the mother of John the Baptist. But Anna took Joachim, the brother of Joseph's father [as her husband]. And Anna went down as a bride into the city of Nazareth in Galilee and lived with Joachim for fifty years, and they did not produce a child.'

[97] Epiphanios of Kallistratos, *Life of the Virgin*, PG 120, 216B; Dressel 1843, 44.

[98] This leads Mimouni to classify this as a 'dormitionist', as opposed to an 'assumptionist', text in the Byzantine dormition tradition. See Mimouni 1994 (2011), 92.

[99] Symeon the Metaphrast, *Life of the Virgin*. According to Latyshev's edition, the text was intended as a liturgical reading for 15 August. Its title announces that it covers the holy birth and upbringing of our all-holy Lady, the Theotokos, that of her son, Jesus Christ, and aspects of her life including her death and the appearance of her relics in Constantinople. See Latyshev 1912, 347.

[100] On Symeon the Metaphrast's literary methods, see Høgel 2002; Høgel 2014.

a monastic background, such as consistent stress on Mary's ascetic practices and apostolic leadership, are lacking in the Metaphrastic *Life of the Virgin*.[101]

John Kyriotes Geometres, who was a contemporary of Symeon the Metaphrast, went further in producing a long and complex panegyrical work in honour of the Mother of God.[102] Like Symeon, Geometres was one of the most important literary figures of the second half of the tenth century.[103] He began his professional life as an imperial officer, but later retired and possibly became a monk and priest in Constantinople. In addition to the *Life of the Virgin*, John composed epigrams, hagiography in verse and prose, and progymnasmata.[104] His hymns on the Mother of God build on the traditional form of the *chairetismos* while also employing rhetorical wordplay in an innovative manner; his homily on the Annunciation represents a significant contribution to the genre.[105] Although John Geometres' *Life* of the Mother of God remained unedited in its entirety until very recently, it has attracted notice from theologians, liturgists and Marian scholars in the course of the last century.[106] Roman Catholic scholars have been intrigued both by the high Mariology of this text[107] and by its teaching concerning the Virgin's assumption into

---

[101] Scholars including Martin Jugie and Antoine Wenger have debated the relationship of Symeon the Metaphrast's *Life* with that of John Geometres but have reached no definitive conclusions. Whereas Jugie argued that the former was based on the latter, with the Metaphrastic version omitting most of the theological and spiritual content of Geometres' work (to the extent that it is only a fifth of its length), Wenger suggested the reverse. It is just as possible, according to Wenger, that John Geometres, who was a contemporary of Symeon, used both his version and the *Life of the Virgin* by Epiphanios of Kallistratos as a basis for his more meditative (but still narrative) approach to the subject. See Jugie 1923a; Jugie 1944, 320–1; Wenger 1955, 193–5. For a summary of the debate and the lack of a convincing solution, see Mimouni 1994 (2011), 103–5.

[102] It is possible that John was named Kyriotes because he was born in the western district of Constantinople known as *ta Kyrou*; his epithet 'geometer' has no known cause, although it has been suggested that it conveys the sense that he was a 'globe-trotter', or in other words, 'a poor and humble fellow, roaming around'. See Sajdak 1931; Mercati 1935; Kazhdan 2006, 249. Whereas some scholars suggest that John Geometres became a monk, Paul Magdalino argues that he became a member of a lay confraternity at the church of the Theotokos *ta Kyrou*; see Magdalino 2018, 118–19.

[103] For an excellent reassessment of John Geometres' literary achievements, see Simelidis 2020, 129–36; cf. Lauxtermann 1998; Demoen 2001.

[104] Scheidweiler 1952; Kazhdan 2006, 251; Simelidis 2020, 130–5.

[105] John Geometres, *Homily on the Annunciation* (*BHG* 1158). Wenger describes this sermon as 'magnifique' and notes that it provides some indication of the content of the first section of John Geometres' unpublished *Life of the Virgin*. See Wenger 1955, 186, 189. Various works by John, including the Marian texts, are analysed in Kazhdan 2006, 262–6.

[106] See, for example, Jugie 1944, 316–22; Wenger 1955, 185–205; Galot 1957; Baun 2007, 282–5.

[107] J. Galot argues, for example, that John Geometres (alone of Byzantine writers) elevates Mary to the role of 'Co-Redemptrix' with her son, Christ; see Galot 1957. For further discussion, see below, n. 130.

heaven.[108] Geometres promotes an exalted view of the Mother of God, picturing her as 'Queen of all created nature' and as 'standing at the right hand of her Son and King'.[109] Considering the theological importance of this text, it is strange that it has waited so long to receive a critical edition.

As Fr Maximos Constas recently discovered, Michel van Esbroeck and Antoine Wenger planned such an edition from about the middle of the twentieth century. Although a manuscript which van Esbroeck had prepared was thought to have disappeared, it was recently discovered in the archives of Wenger that are held at the Assumptionist House in Paris.[110] Fr Maximos Constas and Christos Simelidis are using this draft as a basis for a new critical edition of the text. Pending the appearance of this long-awaited publication, I have consulted the best surviving manuscript witness, Cod. Vatic. Gr. 504, which was copied in 1105 and contains the entire text, along with Wenger's edition of the final section on the Virgin's dormition and assumption.[111] It has not been possible in the present circumstances to gain a detailed understanding of the text; however,

---

[108] Jugie suggests that Geometres teaches a doctrine of 'double assumption', that is, he suggests that the Virgin's body and soul were raised separately to heaven but, as in the case of all other human beings, await reunification at the final day of judgement; see Jugie 1944, 316–20. Wenger, who describes this section of the *Life* as 'un pur chef d'oeuvre', follows C. Balić and M. Gordillo in contesting Jugie's interpretation, offering a different interpretation of Geometres' somewhat ambiguous wording. He concludes that Geometres follows the mainstream Byzantine view that the Virgin Mary was granted an early resurrection, but avoided stating this explicitly – in other words, he preferred to hint at this event as a 'mystery'. See Balić 1948; Gordillo 1947; Wenger 1955, 196–200.

[109] John Geometres, *Life of the Virgin* 1, ed. and trans. Wenger 1955, 364–5: Βασίλισσάν τε πάσης ἀναρρηθῆναι τῆς γεννητῆς φύσεως … καὶ ἐκ δεξιῶν παραστῆναι τοῦ ταύτης υἱοῦ τε καὶ βασιλέως … This passage is also cited in Graef 1963 (2009), 154.

[110] Constas 2019, 326–31; cf. Shoemaker 2005, 449, n. 27. While scholars waited for this work to be completed, they have at least had access to the final section of the text (about one-fifth), which deals with Mary's death and assumption into heaven. This is published, along with a French translation, in Wenger 1955, 364–415.

[111] I greatly regret the fact that I am unable to wait for the publication of Constas and Simelidis' critical edition of the text. Nevertheless, I would like to acknowledge here their assistance with regard to its content, as well as Simelidis' generosity in sharing his article in *DOP* (Simelidis 2020) with me before it was published. There are four surviving manuscripts that contain the text in its entirety or in fragments. Vatic. Gr. 504 (written in 1105) is undoubtedly the best witness since it transmits the whole text in fols. 173v–194v. The minuscule script is clear and contains few orthographical errors. Paris gr. 215 (thirteenth century) is badly damaged, although Wenger does not indicate exactly which sections of the text are missing. Genoa 32 (fourteenth century) contains the entire text, but was not employed by Wenger for his edition of the section of the *Life* on the dormition. A fourth manuscript, held at the Bodleian library in Oxford, contains a text that is copied from the Genoa witness, according to its Latin translator, Balthasare Corderio. See Wenger 1955, 186–88. It is also important to mention that a separate critical edition of John Geometres' *Life of the Virgin* has been prepared by A. Benia, 'Ἰωάννη Γεωμέτρη, Εξόδιος ἡ προπεμπτήριος εἰς τὴν Κοίμησιν τῆς ὑπερενδόξου Δεσποίνης ἡμῶν Θεοτόκου: Πρώτη ἔκδοση και μελέτη του κειμένου' (unpubl. PhD thesis, University of Athens, 2019). I have not had access to this text either.

I hope at least to comment on aspects of the text that are relevant to this discussion.

John Geometres divides his panegyrical work into distinct sections that correspond to major episodes, or festal celebrations, in the life of the Theotokos.[112] It is possible that these sections were intended as separate readings, either in a private or a liturgical context, for separate days in the liturgical year. They are usually introduced by short titles and are made up of narrative sections accompanied by theological discussion. Nevertheless, the whole text presents the Virgin Mary's life in chronological order, finishing with an extended account of her dormition, assumption into heaven and the translation of the robe to Constantinople. This narrative material is framed throughout the work by prayerful meditation on its theological and spiritual significance. While clearly based (like the other hagiographical texts that we have so far examined) on apocryphal and patristic sources that treat this subject, John Geometres also employs both scripture and his own imagination in developing Marian themes. As part of the hagiographical and exegetical tradition that had been evolving since the early ninth century, this text represents one of the most sophisticated treatments of the Virgin Mary's role in the divine dispensation.

The Georgian *Life of the Virgin* represents, as we saw above, a translation that was completed, either at the Monastery of Iveron on Mt Athos or in Constantinople, by the monk and later abbot Euthymios the Athonite (*c.* 955/60–1028).[113] Eleven manuscripts survive, bearing witness to the popularity of the text in monasteries from Georgia to Mt Sinai.[114] Even if we accept, as I do, Simelidis' conclusion that Euthymios adapted John Geometres' set of orations on the Virgin (known as the *Life*) as he produced a version that would be understandable to a mainly monastic, Georgian audience, the text is significant in its own right. The Athonite translator not only simplified but also enhanced his version of Mary's story in various ways. Since Shoemaker's excellent translation and commentary appeared in English, it has begun to attract notice from scholars who are interested not only in the cult of the Virgin, but also in the role of women in early and medieval Christianity.[115]

---

[112] Wenger characterises the text as 'un traité, sous forme de sermon, destiné à être lu plutôt qu'à être prononcé'. He bases this statement not only on the unusual structure of the text, but also on its literary complexity and even obscurity in some sections. See Wenger 1955, 192.

[113] Georgian *Life of the Virgin*, ed. and trans. Shoemaker 2012, 2–3. If Simelidis is correct in his dating of John Geometres' *Life of the Virgin*, on which this translation was based, then Euthymios' work would have been completed either after 979 or 989 CE; see Simelidis 2020, 155–7.

[114] Van Esbroeck 1986, vol. 2, xxx–xxxii ; Georgian *Life of the Virgin*, ed. and trans. Shoemaker 2012, 3.

[115] See, for example, Kateusz 2019, 131–49.

Following its model, the *Life of the Virgin* by John Geometres, the Georgian version relates the whole story of Mary's life, beginning with her conception, birth and dedication to the temple and ending not only with her death and assumption into heaven, but also with a short excursus on the translation of the relics, a robe and a belt, to Constantinople. Unlike the surviving apocryphal narratives, the *Life* also focuses on Christ's life, passion and resurrection, providing the Virgin Mary with an important role throughout this narrative. Following her son at each stage of his public ministry, Mary attracts female disciples whom she personally guides and teaches. She is present at Christ's interrogation and torture, standing outside the door of the courtroom and transmitting the news to his disciples.[116] She stands at the foot of the cross and is entrusted to the care of the beloved disciple, as the Evangelist himself relates (John 19:26–7), but the hagiographer also describes her suffering in detail: 'And the abundance of the sufferings and the wounds pierced your heart: streams of blood came down from his wounds, but fountains of tears came down from your eyes. How could you bear to behold such a dreadful sight, unless the grace and power of your son and Lord strengthened you and confirmed for you the glory of his mercy?'[117] After the crucifixion, Mary is made responsible for finding a tomb and arranging for the burial of Christ's body.[118] She remains by the tomb and is the first person to see the resurrection; she then informs both the disciples and the myrrh-bearing women of this event.[119] Following Christ's ascension, the Theotokos becomes the apostles' leader and guide: she instructs them in asceticism and directs their missions. The *Life* continues with an account of the Virgin's dormition and assumption, which follows the conventional Greek treatment of this theme in liturgical texts. The author stresses the incorruptibility of Mary's body while asserting the reality of her death; he states that the apostles were afraid, when placing her body in the tomb at Gethsemane, to 'lay their hands upon the holy and utterly blessed body, for they saw the light that enveloped it and the grace of God that was upon it'.[120] This is followed by an account of the translation of Mary's robe to Constantinople (using the traditional narrative involving two fifth-century patricians, Galbius and Kandidus), along with brief mention of the holy belt; the two relics were housed at the shrines in the churches of the Blachernai and the

---

[116] Georgian *Life of the Virgin* 76, ed. and trans. Shoemaker 2012, 103–4.
[117] Ibid. 78, ed. and trans. Shoemaker 2012, 105–6.
[118] Ibid. 86–90, ed. and trans. Shoemaker 2012, 112–17.
[119] Ibid. 92–3, ed. and trans. Shoemaker 2012, 119–21.
[120] Ibid. 115, ed. and trans. Shoemaker 2012, 140.

Chalkoprateia, respectively.[121] The hagiographer concludes with a hymnic section that celebrates Mary with the help of metaphorical, typological and intercessory language,[122] along with reflections on her miraculous assumption into heaven.[123]

All four of the middle Byzantine *Lives of the Virgin* emphasise Mary's importance within the larger story of Christ's incarnation, crucifixion and resurrection. To a greater or lesser extent, their authors are prepared to adapt both New Testament and apocryphal accounts in order to demonstrate this point. Three of the *Lives* (excluding the Metaphrastic one) also share narrative peculiarities, some of which may reflect the monastic (or pious lay) backgrounds of their authors, as I have demonstrated in earlier studies.[124] For example, the Virgin described as receiving a vision in the temple at the age of twelve (while carrying out nightly vigils), attracting female disciples, pursuing an ascetic life especially after the death, resurrection and ascension of Christ, and (in the case of the Georgian *Life of the Virgin*) even directing the missions of the apostles during the years that followed. The prominence of the Mother of God especially within texts such as the Georgian *Life* has led scholars to ask whether this reflects a 'feminist' outlook on the part of the author; as Shoemaker notes in one study, this message 'presents a stark contrast with the exclusion of women from church leadership at the time when the text was composed'.[125]

One explanation for this anomaly might be that the Georgian *Life of the Virgin* (or certain elements within it) preserves earlier traditions concerning the position of women in the Church that were later suppressed.[126] However, the question why Euthymios the Athonite would have included

---

[121] Ibid. 124, ed. and trans. Shoemaker 2012, 147–8. On the main Marian relics in Constantinople, the robe and the belt, see Wenger 1955, 111–39; Cameron 1979b; Weyl Carr 2001; Wortley 2005; Shoemaker 2008a; Krausmüller 2011.

[122] Georgian *Life of the Virgin* 125, ed. and trans. Shoemaker 2012, 149–51.

[123] Ibid. 128, ed. and trans. Shoemaker 2012, 154.

[124] See Cunningham 2016, 152– 6; Cunningham 2019, 313–18. It is noteworthy that Symeon the Metaphrast omits many of these variations, preferring to follow more faithfully the narratives found in the *Protevangelion of James* and other accepted apocryphal sources.

[125] Shoemaker 2005, 455.

[126] Ally Kateusz, for example, argues that the Georgian *Life* preserves much earlier apocryphal teachings, some of which recalled a period when women, including the Virgin Mary, served alongside men as priests. One passage in particular, which survives in the Georgian manuscript Tbilisi A-40, states that 'the holy Theotokos … sacrificed herself as the priest and she was sacrificed'; see Kateusz 2019, 131–49. Van Esbroeck also upheld the authenticity of this passage in his edition and analysis of the Georgian *Life*; see Georgian *Life of the Virgin* 74, ed. and trans. van Esbroeck 1986, vol. 2, 64. Shoemaker argues, however, that the meaning of the passage is ambiguous since it gives no clear indication of the subject's gender; see Shoemaker 2005, 448; *Georgian Life of the Virgin*, ed. and trans. Shoemaker 2012, 190, n. 1.

such radical ideas when rewriting the story of the Virgin remains. Shoemaker suggests that it would have been easier for a monastic (as opposed to a lay or secular) writer to portray Mary, as well as her female followers, as important figures in the early Christian community: 'the absence of actual women may have made this representation considerably less threatening than it would have been in a mixed, urban setting'.[127] Although this explanation helps to explain the freedom with which Euthymios approached his subject, it still does not fully explain his agenda in elevating Mary to such a powerful position throughout the text.

The answer may lie in the high Mariology that characterises both the Georgian *Life of the Virgin* and its source by John Geometres. John elaborates this doctrine especially in the closing chapters of his *Life*, which deal with the dormition and assumption of the Virgin. These events served to reveal – not only to the apostles who witnessed them but also to the wider Christian community in subsequent centuries – the exceptional holiness of Christ's mother Mary. Geometres writes that the apostles carried 'that supercelestial body, which had borne that unlimited nature and contained the uncircumscribable' and placed it in the tomb. This is followed by a return to more earthly imagery when he states that 'she went into the earth, ceding to the common law of nature while also withdrawing towards her Son and Bridegroom, towards the heavenly bridal chamber . . .'[128] The paradoxical juxtaposition of earthly and heavenly natures is thus applied to Mary as well as to Christ in this text; she takes on the glory of heavenly existence while remaining subject to death (but not corruption), like other human beings. The Georgian *Life of the Virgin* employs similar language in its description of Mary's death and assumption. Euthymios, like John Geometres, reminds his audience that this event assured the presence of human nature in heaven – thus guaranteeing the final resurrection of all Christians.[129] In her position of queenly power, as the bride of Christ in heaven, Mary also has the power to intercede on behalf of those who pray to her; she is infinitely generous and merciful towards her devotees. The high-flown quality of passages such as these has led some scholars, including Jean Galot and Hilda Graef, to suggest that John Geometres, alone among Byzantine theologians, accorded the role of 'co-redemptrix' to the Virgin Mary.[130] Since this

---

[127] Shoemaker 2005, 466.
[128] John Geometres, *Life of the Virgin* 30–1, ed. and trans. Wenger 1955, 386–7.
[129] Georgian *Life of the Virgin* 128, ed. and trans. Shoemaker 2012, 154.
[130] This hypothesis rests on a technical definition of Christian redemption, which has been worked out especially in the context of the Roman Catholic theological tradition. It is based on a few key

teaching was not commonly accepted in the Eastern Christian tradition, which preferred to stress Mary's solidarity with the rest of the human race even though she was exalted by her role in the incarnation, it is likely that rhetorical hyperbole rather than dogmatic experimentation lies behind such remarkable passages.

In any case, if we read the late tenth-century *Lives of the Virgin* as carefully constructed theological statements about Mary, then their depiction of her as a powerful mother, disciple and leader of the apostles begins to fall into place. From a rhetorical point of view, we need first to understand that she, as the holy subject of these panegyrical works, is bound to take centre stage. Next we may note that John Geometres and Euthymios the Athonite, building on at least five centuries of liturgical and theological reflection concerning the Mother of God, recognised that Mary represented an essential link in God's saving dispensation for humanity. God entered creation as a human being while remaining fully divine. The Virgin Mary was chosen as the receptacle for the incarnation; however, her feminine qualities also enabled her to maintain a particularly close and emotional relationship with her Son. It is remarkable that meditation on the latter aspect of Mary's position led monastic writers such as Euthymios to picture her at the centre of Christ's mission, passion, resurrection and legacy; we can only speculate that Athonite veneration of the Mother of God encouraged such reflection.[131] It is unlikely that this author intended a radical restructuring of church leadership on the basis of his hagiographical composition. Nevertheless, it offered an idealistic vision of the earliest Christian community in which male and female followers of Jesus served together on equal terms.

It only remains to discuss briefly the circumstances and possible reception of the four middle Byzantine *Lives of the Virgin*. The late eighth- or early ninth-century *Life* by Epiphanios, which was composed by a monk-priest in a Constantinopolitan monastery, was probably intended for a monastic audience. The text might have been read out in an all-night vigil before one of the great Marian feasts in order to educate the audience concerning the Virgin's life story.[132] The literary context and purpose of the

---

passages in John Geometres' text that concern Christ's passion, which suggest that Mary suffered along with him on behalf of humankind. See Galot 1957; Graef 1963 (2009), 154–5.

[131] On the Virgin Mary's role as patroness of the monasteries on Mt Athos, see Speake 2002, 17–18.

[132] According to a sample of manuscripts that are available online, it appears that Epiphanios of Kallistratos's *Life of the Virgin* is usually assigned as a reading either for the feast of her Nativity (8 September) or Dormition (15 August); see the Pinakes database, Institut de Recherches et d'Histoire des Textes in Paris, at https://pinakes.irht.cnrs.fr. For descriptions of the various

longer *Life of the Virgin* by John Geometres was more exclusive. According
to Simelidis, John may have composed this work for performance within
a lay confraternity at the church of the Theotokos *ta Kyrou* in
Constantinople.[133] The text survives in only four manuscripts, which
suggests limited circulation not only at the time of its composition but
also in subsequent centuries.[134] Although this confraternity, which was
made up of devout lay Christians, sought spiritual inspiration at its weekly
'readings', it also expected high-style rhetorical expression that would do
justice to its holy patroness, the Mother of God. According to marks or
titles in the surviving manuscripts, it is likely that the text was divided into
sections for delivery on separate Marian feasts throughout the
liturgical year.[135] John Geometres' *Life of the Virgin* thus follows that of
Epiphanios in including an ascetic focus; however, it also offers fresh
theological and metaphorical reflection on the Theotokos to an audience
that was well versed in this rich liturgical tradition.

The Georgian *Life*, following its erudite model, is also divided into
sections that reflect the festal cycle of the Virgin Mary's life, beginning
with her Nativity in early September and finishing after her death and
assumption in the middle of August. Shoemaker has demonstrated how
these sections were used as readings in Georgian monasteries throughout
the Caucasus and Near East, helping monks and nuns to reflect on the
historical and theological meaning of Mary's life.[136] This work, as Simelidis
has demonstrated, is somewhat simplified in relation to the Life by John
Geometres; however, it also contains long sections of theological reflection
and panegyrical praise of the Mother of God. The *Life* by Symeon the
Metaphrast, like other redactions of this kind, offers an elegant, although
shorter, version of the narrative. This text is included in Metaphrastic
liturgical collections as a reading for the feast of the Dormition (15 August).
It might have been read out in monastic or cathedral vigil services on an
annual basis.

The manuscript evidence for all four middle Byzantine *Lives of the
Virgin* thus suggests that they were written and subsequently disseminated

---

manuscripts, see Ehrhard 1936–52, vols. 1–3, passim. A useful aid for locating Ehrhard's descriptions
of individual manuscripts exists in Perria 1979.
[133] Simelidis 2020, 133. Cf. Magdalino 2018 on this confraternity and its literary as well as devotional
practices.
[134] See above, n. 111.
[135] For example, Vat. gr. 504, fol. 176v, col. 2 (Annunciation); fol. 178r, col. 2 (Nativity of Christ); fol.
184v (the Passion), etc. The scribe also includes marginal notes (in red) that indicate subject matter,
such as Christ's temptation (Mt 4:1–11, etc.) at fol. 183r, col. 2. See also Simelidis 2020, 133–4.
[136] Georgian *Life of the Virgin*, ed. and trans. Shoemaker 2012, 161–4.

for liturgical use – whether this occurred in public or, in the case of John Geometres' *Life*, more restricted settings. The divergence of some of these texts from traditional narratives (whether canonical or apocryphal) concerning the Virgin Mary, along with their surprising emphasis on her personal power and influence among Jesus's followers, must reflect her growing importance during the middle Byzantine centuries. Although Epiphanios of Kallistratos, writing at the beginning of the ninth century (and perhaps aware of iconoclast opposition to her cult), avoided offering excessive praise to the Theotokos and never invoked her intercessory power, Symeon the Metaphrast, John Geometres and Euthymios composed their works a century and a half later for audiences or readers who expected such devotional content. The freedom with which the tenth-century hagiographers approached their subject thus reflects the Virgin's dominant position within the doctrinal and devotional life of the Church in this period.

Apocalyptic Views of the Panagia

My final category of texts is that of the apocalypse, although it should be noted here, as in the case of other genres discussed in this chapter, that the boundaries of this literary form are flexible. Passages conveying apocalyptic visions, or the fate of human beings in heaven and hell, may occur, for example, in hagiographical texts such as the *Life of St Andrew the Fool*, as well as in treatises and homilies.[137] I shall confine my attention here to a few ninth- and tenth-century texts that are exclusively concerned with such narratives, including especially the two that are known as the *Apocalypse of the Holy Theotokos* and the *Apocalypse of Anastasia*. These two accounts of visionary tours of paradise and hell feature in Jane Baun's ground-breaking study of medieval apocalypses as windows into the beliefs and practices of Byzantine Christian communities.[138] They are significant for our purposes both because they deal with the Virgin Mary's role as intercessor and, as Baun argues, because they stretch the theology of Christian redemption to its limits, placing Mary in a position that in fact challenges Christ's role as merciful Saviour of humankind.

---

[137] *Life of St Andrew the Fool*, ed. Rydén 1995, vol. 2, 46–63. See Alexander 1985 for background on this tradition.
[138] Baun 2007.

The *Apocalypse of the Theotokos*, which Baun dates to the ninth or tenth century although it is based on a much earlier literary tradition,[139] opens by describing a vision that is granted to the Virgin Mary as she prays on the Mount of Olives. She is taken first to see Hades, where sinners are punished in many different ways and locations on the basis of their particular transgressions. The 'Panagia Theotokos' is moved by their suffering, although she is less sympathetic to those who denied correct belief in the Trinity or herself, along with Jews and practitioners of incest or other crimes. She seeks an audience with God the Father and prays to him for mercy towards all of the other sinners, calling on the assistance of all the saints when he refuses to listen to her entreaties. God eventually relents and grants a brief period of respite to the sinners, between Easter and Pentecost, when their punishments in Hades will pause. The *Apocalypse of Anastasia*, which Baun dates slightly later, around the turn of the tenth century,[140] is more complex, involving the journey of a nun named Anastasia through six levels of the next world, beginning with the heavenly throne of God and ending with a zone reserved for the punishment of well-to-do sinners. Like the *Apocalypse of the Theotokos*, that of Anastasia not only provides a vivid description of the fate of human beings after death but also acts as a cautionary tale with regard to Christian doctrine and morality. The *Apocalypse of Anastasia*, although less concerned with the intercessory role of the Theotokos than that which focuses solely on that holy figure, does allude to her at various points in the text, describing her in one instance as someone who 'entreats and beseeches God, saying, "Master, have mercy on the creation of your hands, and on your world, and do not destroy them."'[141]

In her exploration of the dynamics of intercession and mercy that are described in these, as well as earlier, apocalyptic texts, Baun highlights their authors' subversion of orthodox or 'official' Christian understanding of salvation. Whereas, according to scripture and mainstream patristic tradition, Jesus Christ should represent the preeminent mediator and saviour for ordinary Christians, he has shifted, according to this literary tradition, into the role of Righteous Judge. Baun argues that, as universal monarchs, God the Father and Christ his Son work on the basis of an 'amnesty' model of relations between rulers and their people. In these circumstances, Christian sinners must seek powerful advocates in order to secure

---

[139] For a discussion of the problems associated with dating such complicated traditions as these apocalypses, both of which were transmitted in numerous manuscripts and versions besides being translated into numerous languages, see Baun 2007, 16–18.
[140] Baun 2007, 60.   [141] *Apocalypse of Anastasia* 14, trans. Baun 2007, 403.

forgiveness and salvation; only the saints or, pre-eminently, the Mother of God, are able to fulfil this function. Thus, from being a figure who aligns herself with the merciful intentions of a benevolent God, Mary is frequently portrayed in apocalyptic texts as being at odds with her divine Father and Son. Baun describes this configuration as 'a dysfunctional family'; Mary, in the *Apocalypse of the Theotokos*, is a 'majestic, militant grandmother' who manipulates her heavenly family in order to achieve the results that she seeks.[142]

The main difference between middle Byzantine apocalypses and the other literary genres that we have examined in the course of this book, including sermons, hymns and hagiography, thus lies in their configuration of the celestial hierarchy. Baun argues that whereas mainstream, or liturgical, texts present Mary as a fully integrated member of the heavenly power structure, enjoying a fond and synergic relationship with her son – who is also merciful and a lover of humanity (*philanthropos*) – the medieval apocalypses depict her as an outsider. According to the *Apocalypse of the Theotokos*, Mary demands to be taken on a tour of the underworld and, on being shocked by what she sees there, storms 'the gates of heaven to badger an unwilling God and Christ into acting in a way contrary to their normal inclinations'.[143] These different perceptions of the dynamics of Christian salvation, which Baun labels 'orthodox' and 'popular', must have co-existed in Byzantine spirituality. Judging by the numbers of apocalyptic manuscripts that survive, not only in Greek but also in other languages, the latter outlook exerted considerable influence even if it was not expressed in mainstream theological or liturgical settings.

Conclusions

The material that I have surveyed in this chapter, which can be described in general terms as 'hagiographical', presents an aspect of the Virgin Mary which at times seems far removed from the more theological, or Christological, view that predominates in liturgical poetry and homiletics. Mary, as a dignified but powerful woman – usually dressed in purple – intercedes, according to hagiographical texts, on behalf of all Christians who appeal to her. Whereas many *Lives* of saints, including those that celebrate the Mother of God herself, emphasise Mary's loving relationship and cooperation with her divine Son, some Byzantine apocalypses picture

---

[142] See the discussion in Baun 2007, 267–318.   [143] Baun 2007, 278.

her as a determined advocate who is forced at times to oppose God's righteous will.

Two main issues require discussion in my conclusion to this brief overview of the Marian hagiographical tradition between approximately 600 and 1000 CE. First, it is worth asking whether significant developments occurred in the portrayal of Mary, the Theotokos, in hagiographical or apocalyptic texts throughout these centuries. Second, we should return to the question that Jane Baun has posed concerning the relationship between 'official' and 'popular' strands of the Marian tradition.

With regard to developments in the hagiographical, or panegyrical, treatment of the Virgin Mary in this period, it is necessary to allude once again to the significant 'spanner in the works' that van Esbroeck and Shoemaker introduced by their early dating of the Georgian *Life of the Virgin Mary* that is attributed to Maximos the Confessor.[144] The widely accepted scholarly view that the Virgin Mary came to be viewed as a tender and maternal figure in response to Iconoclasm, achieving full-blown literary and iconographical treatment especially after the middle of the ninth century, needed to be reassessed in the light of this evidence.[145] However, if the Georgian *Life* was indeed based on that of the late tenth-century writer, John Geometres, then it fits well with parallel literary developments of this period. George of Nikomedia would remain an early proponent of this movement, with his affective treatment of Mary's lament at the cross and the tomb of Christ influencing not only hagiographers, but also hymnographers and hagiographers of the tenth century.[146] The growing emphasis on emotion and the senses, which Tsironis traces in liturgical and hagiographical writing of the eighth and ninth centuries, thus follows a trajectory that begins in festal homilies and spreads into hymnography and devotional works such as the tenth-century *Lives* by (ps-)Maximos, John Geometres and Symeon the Metaphrast.[147] Although I thus adhere to the view that affective literary treatment of the Mother of God flourished especially after the end of Iconoclasm, it is worth remembering that such rhetorical emphasis is present (although not dominant) in earlier liturgical texts. As we have seen in earlier chapters, hymns and homilies of the

[144] For discussion of the dating of this text, see above, 192–4.
[145] Shoemaker 2011c, in response to Kalavrezou 1990; Kalavrezou 2000; Tsironis 2000; Tsironis 2005.
[146] See especially George of Nikomedeia, *Homilies on Great Friday* and *On the Virgin Mary at the Tomb*. Studies on the influence of these homilies on post-Iconoclast art include Maguire 1981, 96–108; Barber 1994, 204–5; Ševčenko 2011.
[147] Tsironis 2011, esp. 195–6.

sixth to early eighth centuries could also focus on Mary's motherly qualities, in relation to both the infancy and the suffering of Christ. Romanos the Melodist provided dramatic dialogues in order to portray the Virgin's emotional relationship with her son. Eighth-century preachers including Germanos of Constantinople and Andrew of Crete developed these themes in their sermons on Marian feasts, emphasising the reality of Christ's incarnation by means of his mother's humanity.[148] Even as such texts prefigure later developments in the tradition, it is possible to perceive trends in hagiographical writing between the early seventh and late tenth centuries. The later witnesses in this tradition, including the *Lives* by John Geometres, Euthymios the Athonite (the Georgian *Life*) and Symeon the Metaphrast, epitomise a movement towards a higher and more mystical style of panegyrical celebration of the Mother of God. As in the case of late ninth- and early tenth-century preachers, these hagiographers avoid precise statements about the Virgin's physical nature – whether these concern her conception or death and assumption into heaven. Unlike some early eighth-century counterparts, the middle Byzantine writers stress the theological rather than the literal meaning of Mary's life. They are conscious not only of the misconceptions that might arise from detailed scrutiny but are also influenced by the increasingly exalted style of Marian praise that by this time permeated all liturgical worship. Such awareness does not prevent a theologian such as John Geometres from exploring his subject with expansive enthusiasm; however, he is more inclined to digress into theological and poetic meditation than to investigate the historical basis for his narrative.

How then do we assess the influence of high-style texts such as the *Lives* of Symeon the Metaphrast and John Geometres, as opposed to those that display a more 'popular' aspect? One way of approaching this question is to look at the reception of the various genres by Byzantine Christians. Judging by the numbers of surviving manuscripts, along with the translation of individual texts into other languages, it appears that lower-style, more narrative, hagiographical and apocalyptic texts enjoyed a wider audience than did more literary works such as John Geometres' orations on the Virgin Mary. It is surprising, considering their frequently heterodox content, that the official Church apparently condoned the writing and dissemination of apocalypses and miracle stories about the Virgin Mary. Orthodox Christians from a variety of

---

[148] Cunningham 2008a, 252.

backgrounds and ranks – even within the ecclesiastical hierarchy – probably read and enjoyed this literature, perhaps regarding it as morally and spiritually improving.

We may conclude that modern concerns with regard to the 'subversive' nature of such material may be misplaced. Like many believers of the twenty-first century, Byzantine Christians were capable of assimilating conflicting messages as long as they understood their literary or theological contexts. Miracle stories and apocalypses, which were known to have a mythical or legendary aspect, could be appreciated as moral tales or simply enjoyed for their entertainment value. The liturgical life of the Church, which was packed with more orthodox teaching with regard to the Mother of God, would have guided the faithful successfully in their understanding both of her importance in Christological terms and of her submission to the Trinitarian God. Most importantly, the tradition as a whole maintained a consistent emphasis on the Virgin's physical link with the rest of humanity. This rule applies as much to high-style panegyrical texts such as John Geometres' *Life of the Virgin Mary* as it does to collections of miracle stories or apocalypses throughout the Byzantine period.

Conclusion

Mary, the holy Virgin and Mother of God, remained a paradoxical presence in Byzantine religious culture. As we have seen in the course of this book, she assumed different aspects according to the settings in which she appeared. To some extent, such variations reflected the aims and intended audiences that writers or artisans had in mind: the Virgin's roles as symbol of the incarnation according to Christological doctrine that began to be elaborated from the early fifth century onward or as protector and intercessor for Christians throughout the Eastern Roman empire received emphasis in different literary or liturgical contexts. By focusing on three main literary genres, namely, homiletics, hymnography and hagiography during the period of roughly the fifth to the tenth centuries, I have demonstrated only some of the myriad of ways in which the Virgin could be presented. According to this analysis, preachers and hymnographers focused especially on Mary's Christological importance – although they also invoked her intercessory power – while hagiographers were more interested in her physical (albeit legendary) presence as human mother, protector and intercessor. All of these aspects of the Theotokos were significant for the Byzantines, whether or not some (such as her female gender, power and intercessory role) fascinate modern researchers into her cult to a greater degree. For this reason, I have devoted as much attention to elaborating and explaining the theological meaning of Marian liturgical praise as to manifestations of her miraculous power. Above all, however, it is important to recognise that the two strands of this tradition are inextricably linked: most Byzantine writers saw Mary's power as emanating from her status as the virginal Mother of God. She thus assumed a place in the celestial hierarchy that went far beyond the holiness, or deification, of patriarchs, martyrs and saints. At the same time, however, Byzantine theologians were keen to emphasise Mary's humanity. Her human and physical nature guaranteed the reality of Christ's incarnation and the extent of his self-emptying (kenosis) when he chose to enter creation while remaining the Son and Word of God.

The decision to divide the book into chapters that are based on the three literary genres, hymnography, homiletics and hagiography (with the first two categories being divided chronologically into two sections simply because they are so large), has yielded some interesting results. Although the categories overlap in significant ways, they each offer distinct readings of the Virgin Mary. Hymnography, especially after the development of hymn forms (such as kontakia, kanons, stichera and others) for specific liturgical slots and according to the usage of the Ecclesiastic and Hagiopolitan rites in Constantinople from about the seventh century onward,[1] provided concise theological teaching that could take discursive, typological or other forms. Invocation of the protective and merciful Virgin took place in this context, but usually only in specific sections of longer hymns or in shorter hymns (such as theotokia and stavrotheotokia) that were devoted to this purpose. Homiletics also offered an opportunity for theological teaching; however, this genre also allowed more opportunity for narrative or dramatic development of biblical and apocryphal stories about the Virgin Mary. Middle Byzantine preachers also increasingly invoked the Theotokos as intercessor, although as in hymnography, this preoccupation was confined to certain sections (especially the epilogues) of festal homilies. The category that I called 'occasional', however, could focus more – or even entirely – on Mary's role as defender and intercessor for Byzantine Christians. Finally, hagiography offered various generic opportunities for elaboration of the Virgin's intercessory (or occasionally punitive) interaction with Christian supplicants. These included short miracle stories, such as those associated with the shrine of the Source (*Pege*) in Constantinople, and longer *Lives* of the Virgin in which her legendary (or apocryphal) dealings with Christ and his disciples as well as with later followers received narrative treatment. Although the overlap between all three genres (in the form of hymnic sections, Christological teaching and other elements) remains significant, I have thus been able to distinguish significant differences in their treatment of the holy subject.

Another preoccupation of this book, which received detailed treatment in the Introduction and attention throughout the following chapters, has been to test the relevance of gendered approaches to the Byzantine cult of the Virgin Mary. I suggested at the beginning that gender is indeed a crucial issue in this field: Mary was pre-eminently a symbol of feminine

---

[1] I follow the terminology for the two rites that is adopted in Frøyshov 2020, esp. 351–2.

virtue and activity for the Byzantines. As the 'Second Eve', who undid the sin of the first human woman according to the Jewish and Christian creation narrative, Mary became the archetypal wielder of human free will according to God's original intention. This theological narrative, which is shared by Eastern and Western Christians, places females at the heart of the divine dispensation. One woman opened up the possibility of sin; another initiated the way back to redemption. Mary's other theological roles, including especially her virginal birth-giving of Christ, are also dependent on her female nature. It was only from about the late fifth century onward, however, that Byzantine liturgical writers began to emphasise Mary's human, or maternal, involvement in this process. This innovation may have occurred for didactic reasons: preachers and hymnographers realised that the reality of Christ's incarnation could be understood better in the context of his mother's humanity. However, it may also reflect an increasing interest in Mary as a figure of dignity in her own right; this is the period in which other manifestations of Marian devotion were becoming more visible. Further aspects of Mary's female gender received attention in the course of our period, but especially after about the middle of the ninth century (or the end of Iconoclasm); these included her devotion to asceticism and prayer, leadership of both female and male disciples of Christ, and lament at the cross. By about the tenth century, we are presented with the Mother of God as a fully developed human figure on the basis of homilies, hymns and hagiography. As such, however, Mary embodies the best characteristics of both genders. She is a model for all Christians to emulate and with whom to identify. Mary thus represents by the end of our period the quintessential example of the faithful Christian, or 'bride of Christ'; although this symbolism is female, it is open to Christians of both genders.

Although women did seek cures or help – sometimes of a specifically gynaecological nature – from Mary, it is not clear that they outstripped men in their supplications. The Byzantines used gender-based symbolism that transcended the literal division of people into distinct categories. Feminine imagery carried a host of meanings, which often had more to do with ethical behaviour than with biological identity. To behave like a woman involved the demonstration of particular virtues that were associated with the feminine gender, such as modesty, obedience and receptivity. Masculine virtues included bravery, endurance, strength and self-restraint. Both women and men could display the whole range of characteristics, although women had to surmount their innate weaknesses in order to acquire 'manliness'. By the tenth century, Mary had begun to embody the ideal virtues of both genders; emphasis on her determination and even leadership in hagiographical texts such as the Georgian *Life of the Virgin* demonstrated her 'male' credentials in addition to her 'female' ones. But long before this, as we have seen, she featured as the successful 'male' warrior, fighting on the walls of Constantinople during the siege of 626.[2]

That preachers and hymnographers viewed the Theotokos as a model for female Christians in particular is undeniable: it became a *topos*, or convention, to encourage virgins, mothers and widows (as identifiable female categories) to venerate and imitate Mary, as we see in the following example:

> Mothers and virgins, praise the one who alone was both mother and always virgin. Brides, go before her who remained an unmarried maiden, the incorrupt one who, uniquely free from the pangs of childbirth, brought forth the incomprehensible one. Childless people and widows, applaud her who 'did not know man' (Lk 1:34), but who changed the laws of infertility. Maidens, dance joyfully before the incorruptibility that gave birth to a child.[3]

Such passages, when read in context, however, invoke the symbolic (gendered) categories of the human race more than they do the actual categories of Christians who were assembled in church on any given day. Andrew of Crete also calls on patriarchs, prophets, apostles, martyrs, saints, kings and those who are ruled; other preachers, in similar tropes, invoke significant Old Testament women, beginning with Eve, who have been saved by Mary.[4] Gender is thus primarily a symbolic way of thought and expression: although contemporary women were encouraged to identify with female biblical models, including Mary, men could also participate in this activity.[5]

---

[2] Pentcheva 2006, 61–103.
[3] Andrew of Crete, *Homily III on the Dormition*, PG 97, 1104C; trans. Daley 1998, 147 (12).
[4] See, for example, Proklos of Constantinople's *Homily V.3, On the Holy Virgin Theotokos*: 'On account of Mary all women are blessed. No longer does the female stand accused, for it has produced an offspring which surpasses even the angels in glory. Eve is fully healed (cf. Gen 3:17); the Egyptian woman has fallen silent (cf. Gen 39:7–18); Delilah is wrapped tightly in a shroud (cf. Judg 16:4–22); Jezebel has fallen into oblivion (cf. 3 Kgs 16:31; 18:4 [1 Kgs 16:31; 18:4]); and Herodias has been stricken from memory (Mk 6:14–29). And now the assembly of women is admired: Sarah is praised as the fertile seedbed of nations (cf. Gen 17:15–20); Rebeccah is honoured as shrewd purveyor of blessings (cf. Gen 27:6–17); Leah also is admired as the mother of the ancestor (of Christ) according to the flesh (Gen 29:35; cf. Lk 3:30); Deborah is praised because she overcame nature and fought as a leader in combat (cf. Judg 4:4–14); Elizabeth is also called blessed because she conceived in her womb the leapings of the Forerunner of grace ... (Lk 1:44)'; ed. and trans. Constas 2003, 260–3.
[5] See Krueger's interesting analysis of such practices in the formation of the Christian 'self': Krueger 2014, 8–24.

The richness of imagery, which includes narrative, description, meta-phor and typology, in the portrayal of the Mother of God remains one of the most striking, but also inexplicable, aspects of the Byzantine liturgical tradition. Why, we may ask, does this human figure – who does not feature prominently in the canonical New Testament – attract such a wealth of narratives and epithets?[6] Why did her cult develop in the way that it did, especially following the endorsement of the title 'Theotokos' at the Council of Ephesus in 431?[7] Krastu Banev's suggestion that Mary took over the symbolic role of the Church, along with a well-developed tradition of typology associated with that concept, from about this date onward goes some way towards explaining her growing importance.[8] However, it is also likely that her basis in history, at least for believing Christians, and humanity played a part in this process. Eastern and Western Christians began to feel the need for a female figure in the celestial hierarchy; they also sought, in the face of increasingly hierarchical and bureaucratic social systems, an intercessor before Christ, as Righteous Judge, as he sat on his imperial throne in heaven. Mary's transition from theological symbol to merciful intercessor appears to have been sanctioned and managed by church leaders in this period: bishops preached about the Christological importance of the Theotokos, feasts were added to the official liturgical calendars, and shrines that housed her relics were founded and maintained by emperors and empresses from the second half of the fifth century onward. The texts that were produced in order to support the burgeoning Marian cult, which took many forms in addition to homiletics, hymnog-raphy and hagiography, continued to be read in liturgical and other public settings throughout the Byzantine period.

The reception of such literature by populations that were largely illiter-ate has become a stimulating field of scholarly study.[9] Recent contributions to this subject explore the performative aspect of many literary genres, the differences between oral and written delivery, and the extent to which various genres were understood. In the course of the present study, I have emphasised the ways in which texts went through different phases of delivery and transmission. The surviving Marian homilies, whether festal or occasional, were probably delivered extempore or from memory at the first occasion; after this, they would be edited, either by the preacher

---

[6] On the place of the Virgin Mary in the New Testament, see Brown, Donfried, Fitzmyer and Reumann 1978; Pelikan 1996, 7–21; Maunder 2007; Maunder 2008, 23–39; Maunder 2019, 21–39.
[7] Price 2007; Price 2008; Price 2019.   [8] Banev 2014, esp. 93–9.
[9] Mullett 1992; Antonopoulou 2010; Pizzone 2014; White 2015; Shawcross 2018; Jeffreys and Jeffreys 2018.

himself or by scribes, and compiled into liturgical collections that were then read out at future liturgical offices, sometimes on an annual basis.[10] This does not exclude, however, the possibility that literate monks or lay Christians read such books for personal devotional reasons.

In the case of hymns, which represent even more refined literary compositions, a process of selection took place. Those that were considered the best or most apposite for a given feast or day of the year were included in service books that began to be compiled from about the eighth century onward.[11] From that time onward, they would be sung during highly codified liturgical services that took place throughout the fixed and moveable church years, according to the typika that were appropriate to any given cathedral, monastery or parish church. Owing to the simpler and more formulaic language of hymns, as opposed to homilies, it is likely that this genre above all others taught basic doctrine to Byzantine Christians, which included the central role that the Virgin Mary played in the incarnation of Christ. Hymns also allowed congregations, especially through participation in the singing of refrains, to pray directly to the Mother of God for help and healing. The Byzantines' own recognition of the theological and devotional importance of hymnography is borne out in the use of this genre for educational purposes in Constantinopolitan schools and *theatra* from about the twelfth century onward.[12]

Some forms of hagiography, including collections of miracle stories and *Lives* of the Virgin Mary, seem to have circulated less widely than homilies and hymns, judging by the numbers of manuscripts that survive.[13] Such texts often retained an association with a local shrine, such as the Source (*Pege*) in Constantinople, where they were probably read at annual festivals or other celebrations. Some of the higher style *Lives* of the Virgin, such as those by John Geometres or Symeon the Metaphrast, may have served smaller, more educated clienteles; it is possible that they were read aloud in sections in particular monasteries or pious gatherings, such as lay fraternities.[14] Euthymios the Athonite's Georgian *Life of the Virgin*

---

[10] Ehrhard 1936–52; Cunningham 2011b.   [11] Velkovska 1997.

[12] Demetracopoulos 1979; Skrekas 2008, xx–xxxiv; Skrekas 2018.

[13] This varies of course, depending on the text. *Lives* of saints that were chosen as readings on an annual basis in churches and monasteries throughout the Byzantine empire survive in numerous manuscripts. However, the miracle stories associated with the *Pege* shrine in Constantinople are transmitted in just one witness; see Talbot and Johnson 2012, xv; the *Life of the Virgin* by John Geometres in four; see Wenger 1955, 186–9. This can be contrasted with the transmission of many festal homilies in upwards of 100 manuscripts. On the transmission of homilies and *vitae* in Byzantine manuscripts, see Ehrhard 1936–52, passim.

[14] Antonopoulou 2010; Magdalino 2018.

circulated in monasteries of Georgia, Palestine and Mount Sinai: some of the surviving manuscripts contain markings that indicate the feasts on which the separate sections of the *Life* should be read aloud.[15] One other genre that I included in my discussion of 'hagiography', namely, the middle Byzantine apocalypses, attracted much wider readership.[16] It is possible that the entertaining nature of such texts, with their vivid descriptions of heaven and hell, along with their dynamic portrayal of Mary's intercessory power, helped them to gain such popularity.

I have offered as a hypothesis throughout this book that Byzantine readers and auditors were sophisticated in their understanding of the various roles that the Virgin Mary could play. Their judgement must have been helped by the separate contexts (liturgical, devotional or didactic) in which texts were delivered and by what they expected to hear. The solemn setting of liturgical worship in the great church of Hagia Sophia, over which the mosaic image of the Virgin and child presided from the apse,[17] evoked her importance as one who is 'greater in honour than the cherubim and beyond compare more glorious than the seraphim'.[18] Monks or lay people who gathered to hear a homily or sections of a *Life* of the Virgin being delivered for the first time, or read out on an annual basis in later centuries, also expected Christological teaching – although this might be embroidered with apocryphal or legendary narrative, dramatic dialogue or other rhetorical embellishments. The reading out of miracle stories or apocalypses, on the other hand, evoked a somewhat different picture of the Mother of God. It was in such literary contexts that she came to life as an active female personage who intervened on behalf of the faithful at times of war or appeared to individuals who needed personal help. Such diverse – even paradoxical – portrayals of the Virgin Mary were possible because of the variety of settings and requirements that she filled. However, there is also a theological reason for this phenomenon: the Theotokos symbolised the paradox that lies at the heart of Christian doctrine. She, after all, was the human virgin who contained the uncontainable God. Her humanity encompassed a range of attributes, as we have seen, while her purity revealed her ability to give birth to Christ, the Son and Word of God.

---

[15] Georgian *Life of the Virgin*, ed. Shoemaker 2012, 3, 161–4.

[16] The *Apocalypse of Anastasia* and the *Apocalypse of the Theotokos* survive in numerous manuscripts and were translated into a variety of medieval languages; see Baun 2007, 16–20.

[17] For illustrations and discussion of this famous mosaic, see Cormack 1985, 146–58; Barber 2002, 135–6; James 2017, 317–19.

[18] Τὴν τιμιωτέραν τῶν Χερουβεὶμ καὶ ἐνδοξοτέραν ἀσυγκρίτως τῶν Σεραφεὶμ . . ., *Divine Liturgy of John Chrysostom*, trans. Lash 2011, 47.

Finally, it is worth adding a few words concerning the ways forward that this study suggests. The project as a whole was originally conceived along much more ambitious lines. Leslie Brubaker and I hoped, following initial funding for the work by the British funding body the Academic and Humanities Research Council, to provide a comprehensive introduction to the literary and material evidence concerning the Virgin Mary between about 400 and 1200 CE.[19] Owing to the huge amount of evidence, we decided in the end, with regret, to narrow the project down. Instead of including numerous other literary genres that bear witness to the cult of the Theotokos in the Eastern Roman world, I have chosen to focus only on hymnography, homiletics and hagiography, also limiting my timescale somewhat, in the present book. I hope nevertheless that other researchers will turn their attention to other rich sources for study along the lines that I have suggested: these might include poetry and epigrams, letters, histories and chronicles, and polemical texts. On the basis of work that I have carried out so far, it is likely that each of these genres will yield diverse results: even more aspects of the 'multifaceted' Virgin Mary may appear. Leslie Brubaker meanwhile plans to publish her work on the material evidence, which includes monumental art, manuscripts, icons and other media, as an accompanying volume to this one. We hope that this second instalment will appear soon; much of the research has been completed and it simply remains for the work to be written up. Brubaker and I will no doubt display differences in our approaches to the subject on which we have worked together for so long; however, we remain unified in our understanding that the Byzantine Virgin Mary was a multifaceted and paradoxical figure whose many aspects depended, to a large extent, on the various contexts in which Byzantine Christians encountered her.

---

[19] The AHRC provided a grant, covering the costs of a full-time research assistant, at the University of Birmingham between 2003 and 2006 (see Acknowledgements, viii–ix). Two other products of this grant have so far appeared: Cunningham 2008b; Brubaker and Cunningham 2011.

Bibliographies

Abbreviations

AASS	*Acta Sanctorum* (Antwerp, 1643–1770; Brussels, 1780–6, 1845–83, and 1894, etc.; Tongerloo, 1794; Paris, 1875–87)
AB	*Analecta Bollandiana*
ACCS	*Ancient Christian Commentary on Scripture*, 29 vols., ed. T. C. Oden et al. (Downers Grove, IL, 2000–10)
ACO	*Acta Conciliorum Oecumenicorum*, ser. I, ed. E. Schwartz (and later J. Straub and R. Schieffer), 19 vols. in 4 (Berlin and Leipzig, 1927–74); ser. 2, ed. R. Riedinger, 4 vols. in 2 (Berlin, 1984–95)
BBGG	*Bolletino della Badia Greca di Grottaferrata*
BBOM	Birmingham Byzantine and Ottoman Monographs
BBTT	Belfast Byzantine Texts and Translations
BF	*Byzantinische Forschungen*
BHG	*Bibliotheca hagiographica graeca*, ed. F. Halkin (Brussels, 1957), 3 vols.
BHO	*Bibliotheca hagiographica orientalis*, ed. Society of Bollandists (Brussels, 1910)
BMCR	*Bryn Mawr Classical Review*
BMGS	*Byzantine and Modern Greek Studies*
BZ	*Byzantinische Zeitschrift*
CANT	*Clavis apocryphorum Novi Testamenti*, ed. M. Geerard (Turnhout, 1992)
CCT	Corpus Christianorum in Translation (Turnhout, ongoing)
CCCM	Corpus Christianorum. Continuatio Mediaevalis (Turnhout, ongoing)
CCL	Corpus Christianorum. Series Latina (Turnhout, ongoing)
CCSA	Corpus Christianorum. Series Apocryphorum (Turnhout, ongoing)
CCSG	Corpus Christianorum. Series Graeca (Turnhout, ongoing)
CPG	*Clavis patrum graecorum*, ed. M. Geerard, 4 vols. (Turnhout, 1983, 1974, 1979, 1980); ed. M. Geerard and F. Glorie, vol. 5 (Turnhout, 1987)

CPG, Suppl.	*Clavis patrum graecorum. Supplementum* (Turnhout, 1998)
CSCO	Corpus scriptorum christianorum orientalium (Paris and Louvain, 1903–)
CSHB	Corpus scriptorum historiae byzantinae (Bonn, 1828–97)
DACL	*Dictionnaire d'archéologie chrétienne et de liturgie*, ed. C. Cabrol and H. Leclercq, 15 vols. (Paris, 1924 – 53)
DOML	Dumbarton Oaks Medieval Library (Cambridge, MA, and London)
DOP	*Dumbarton Oaks Papers*
DS	*Dictionnaire de Spiritualité*, ed. M. Viller et al., 16 vols. with index (Paris, 1937–95)
ECR	*Eastern Churches Review*
EEBS	*Epeteris Hetaireias Byzantinon Spoudon*
EO	*Échos d'Orient*
FOTC	The Fathers of the Church (Washington, DC)
GCS	Die griechischen christlichen Schriftsteller der ersten drei Jahrhunderte
GRBS	*Greek, Roman and Byzantine Studies*
JECS	*Journal of Early Christian Studies*
JÖB	*Jahrbuch der Österreichischen Byzantinistik*
JRS	*Journal of Roman Studies*
JTS n.s.	*Journal of Theological Studies*, new series
KretChron	*Kretika Chronika*
LXX	*The Septuagint*, ed. J. W. Wevers, *Septuaginta: Vetus Testamentum Graecum auctoritate Academiae Scientiarum Gottingensis* (Göttingen, 1974); trans. A. Pietersma and B. G. Wright, *A New English Translation of the Septuagint* (Oxford and New York, 2007). [References to the LXX and Hebrew Bible (which sometimes differ in their names and numberings of books such as 1–2 Samuel, 1–2 Kings and the Psalms) are indicated first according to the LXX, followed by Hebrew names or numbers in square brackets.]
Mansi	J. D. Mansi, *Sacrorum conciliorum nova et amplissima collectio*, 31 vols. (Florence, 1759–88)
Mus	*Le Muséon: Revue d'études orientales*
NHS	Nag Hammadi Studies
NRSV	*Holy Bible. New Revised Standard Version. Anglicized Edition* (Oxford, 1995)
OCA	Orientalia Cristiana Analecta
OCP	*Orientalia christiana periodica*
ODB	*Oxford Dictionary of Byzantium*, ed. A. Kazhdan et al. (Oxford, 1991), 3 vols.
ParOr	*Paroles de l'Orient*
PG	Patrologia Graeca cursus completus, series Graeco-Latina, ed. J.-P. Migne (Paris, 1857–66, 1880–1903)

PGM	K. Preisendanz, E. Heitsch and A. Henrichs, eds., *Papyri Graecae Magicae:Die griechischen Zauberpapyri*, 2nd ed., 2 vols. (Stuttgart, 1974)
PL	Patrologia Latina cursus completus, series Latina, ed. J.-P. Migne (Paris, 1844–1974)
PO	Patrologia orientalis, eds. R. Graffin and F. Nau (Paris, 1930–)
PTS	Patristische Texte und Studien, im Auftrag der Patristischen Kommission der Akademien der Wissenschaften zu Göttingen, Heidelberg, München und der Akademie der Wissenschaften und der Literatur zu Mains, ed. K. Aland and W. Schneemelcher (Berlin and New York, 1964–)
REB	*Revue des études byzantines*
REG	*Revue des études grecques*
SBN	*Studi bizantini e neoellenici*
SC	Sources chrétiennes (Paris, 1942–)
SL	*Studia Liturgica*
SP	*Studia Patristica*
ST	Studi e Testi (Vatican City)
StMed	*Studi medievali*
SubsHag	Subsidia Hagiographica
SVTQ	*St Vladimir's Theological Quarterly*
Synax. CP	*Synaxarium Constantinopolitanum*, ed. H. Delehaye, *Propylaeum ad AS Novembris* (Brussels, 1902)
TTB	Translated Texts for Byzantinists (Liverpool, ongoing)
TTH	Translated Texts for Historians (Liverpool, ongoing)
TM	Travaux et mémoires (Paris, ongoing)
TU	Texte und Untersuchungen zur Geschichte der altchristlichen Literatur. Archiv für die griechisch-christlichen Schriftsteller der ersten drei Jahrhunderte (Leipzig and Berlin, 1882, ongoing)
VC	*Vigiliae Christianae*

Primary Sources

Abraham of Ephesus, *Homily on the Annunciation* (*CPG* 7380, *BHG* 1136h). Ed. M. Jugie, *Homélies mariales byzantines*, vol. 1, PO 16, fasc. 3, no. 79 (Paris, 1922; repr. Turnhout, 2003), 442–7 (hereafter Jugie 1922 [2003])

Abraham of Ephesus, *Homily on the Hypapante* (*CPG* 7381, *BHG* 1954). Ed. Jugie 1922 (2003), 448–54

Acts of Seventh Ecumenical Council of Nicaea (787). Ed. E. Lamberz, *Concilium universale Nicaenum secundum: Concilii actiones* (Berlin, 2008–12); trans. R. Price, *The Acts of the Second Council of Nicaea (787)*, TTH 68 (Liverpool, 2018)

Afentoulidou, *Die Hymnen*. Ed. E. Afentoulidou, *Die Hymnen des Theoktistos Studites auf Athanasios I. von Konstantinopel. Einleitung, Edition, Kommentar*, Wiener byzantinistische Studien 28 (Vienna, 2008)

Akathistos Hymn. Ed. C. A. Trypanis, *Fourteen Early Byzantine Cantica*, Wiener byzantinische Studien 5 (Vienna, 1968), 29–39; E. Wellesz, *The Akathistos Hymn*, Monumenta musicae Byzantinae Transcripta 9 (Copenhagen, 1957); trans. Peltomaa 2001, 3–19 (see Secondary Sources)

Ambrosius Autpertus, *Homily on the Assumption of Mary*. Ed. R. Weber, CCCM 27B (Turnhout, 1979), 1027–36

Analecta hymnica graeca. Ed. D. Gonzato, A. Schirò et al., *Analecta hymnica graeca e codicibus eruta Italiae inferioris*, 12 vols. (Rome, 1966–80)

Ancient Iadgari. Ed. E. Metreveli, C. Čankievi and L. Hevsuriani, *Udzveliesi Iadgari* (Tbilisi, 1980); trans. H.-M. Schneider, *Lobpreis im rechten Glauben: Die Theologie der Hymnen an den Festen der Menschwerdung der alten Jerusalemer Liturgie im Georgischen Uszvelesi Iadgari* (Bonn, 2004) (feasts of the Incarnation); ed. and trans. C. Renoux, *Hymnes de la Résurrection*, vol. 1: *Hymnographie liturgique géorgienne. Textes du Sinaï 18* (Paris, 2000); ed. and trans. C. Renoux, *Hymnes de la Résurrection*, vols. 2–3: *Hymnographie liturgique géorgienne. Textes des manuscrits Sinaï 40, 41 et 34*, PO 52, fasc. 1, no. 231; *Textes des manuscrits Sinaï 26 et 20 et Index analytique des trois volumes*, PO 52, fasc. 2, no. 232 (Turnhout, 2010) (resurrection hymns)

Andrew of Crete, *Great Kanon* (*CPG* 8219). PG 97, 1329– 85; *Triodikon katanyktikon*, 463–91; ed. W. Christ and M. K. Paranikas, *Anthologia graeca carminum christianorum* (Leipzig, 1871), 147–61 (abridged version); trans. Mother Mary and Archimandrite Kallistos Ware, *The Lenten Triodion* (London, 1978), 378–415.

Andrew of Crete, *Homily on the Annunciation* (*CPG* 8174, *BHG* 1093g). PG 97, 881–913; trans. M. B. Cunningham, *Wider Than Heaven: Eighth-Century Homilies on the Mother of God* (Crestwood, NY, 2008) (hereafter Cunningham 2008b), 197–219

Andrew of Crete, *Homilies I– III on the Dormition* (*CPG* 8181–3, *BHG* 1122, 1115, 1109, *BHG*n 1115a). PG 97, 1045–1109; trans. B. E. Daley, *On the Dormition of Mary: Early Patristic Homilies* (Crestwood, NY, 1998) (hereafter Daley 1998), 103–52

Andrew of Crete, *Homilies I–IV on the Nativity of the Virgin Mary* (*CPG* 8170–3, *BHG*a 1082, *BHG*n 1082a, *BHG* 1080, *BHG*a 1127, *BHG*a 1092, 1092b). PG 97, 805–81; trans. Cunningham 2008b, 71–138

Andrew of Crete, *Kanon on the Conception of St Anna* (*CPG* 8219). PG 97, 1306–15

Anna Komnene, *Alexiad*. Ed. D. R. Reinsch and A. Kambylis, *The Alexiad*, 2 vols. (Berlin, 2001); trans. E. R. A. Sewter, *The Alexiad of Anna Comnena* (Harmondsworth, 1969)

Anonymous, *Homily on the Translation of the Belt of the Theotokos* (*CPG* 8026, *BHG* 1147). Ed. F. Combefis, *Graecolat: Patrum bibliothecae novum auctarium*, vol. 2 (Paris, 1648), 790–802(from a damaged manuscript); for a slightly different version, which the editor attributes to the early tenth-century monk and synkellos, Michael, see D. Krausmüller, 'Praising Mary's Girdle: The

Encomium BHG 1146M Attributed to Michael the Monk and *Synkellos'*, *Journal for Late Antique Religion and Culture* 15 (2021), 1–18

Anonymous, *Hymns on Mary*. Ed. T. J. Lamy, *Sancti Ephraem Syri Hymni et Sermones*, vol. 2 (Malines, 1886), 519–90; trans. Brock 1994 (2010), 32–66 (see below, *Bride of Light*)

Anonymous, *Inventio vestis* (PVO). Ed. and trans. A. Wenger, *L'Assomption de la très sainte Vierge dans la tradition Byzantine du VIe au Xe siècle* (Paris, 1955), 294–303 on the basis of Codd. Paris. gr. 1447 (10th c.), fols. 255–8, Palat. gr. 317 (11th c.), fols. 36v–39, Ottob. gr. 402 (11th–12th c.)

Anonymous, *Inventio vestis* (S). Ed. and trans. Wenger 1955, 306–11, on the basis of Cod. Sinait. 491, fols. 252–8 (9th c.)

Anonymous, *Kontakia*. Ed. C. A. Trypanis, *Fourteen Early Byzantine Cantica*, Wiener Byzantinische Studien 5 (Vienna, 1968) (hereafter Trypanis 1968)

Anonymous, *Kontakion on the Holy Fathers*. Ed. Trypanis 1968, 93–100

Anonymous, *Soghyatha*. Various editions, see Brock 1994 (2010), 17; trans. Brock 1994, 125–50 (see below, *Bride of Light*)

Anthologia graeca carminum. Ed. W. Christ and M. Paranikas, *Anthologia graeca carminum christianorum* (Leipzig, 1871)

Antony of Choziba, *The Miracles of the Holy Mother of God at Choziba* (*CPG* 7842, *BHG* 1215). Ed. C. Houze, *AB* 7 (1888), 360–70; trans. T. Vivian and A. N. Athanassakis, *The Life of St George of Choziba and the Miracles of the Most Holy Mother of God at Choziba* (San Francisco, 1994)

Apocalypse of Anastasia. Ed. R. Homburg, *Apocalypsis Anastasiae, ad trium codicum auctoritatem Panormitani Ambrosiani Parisini* (Leipzig, 1903); trans. Baun 2007 (see Secondary Sources), 401–24

Apocalypse of the Theotokos. Ed. I. I. Sreznevskii and G. S. Destunis, *Drvniie Pamiatniki Russkago Pis'ma I Iazyk (X–XIV viekov): obshchee porvremennoie obozrenie* (St Petersburg, 1863), 204–17; ed. K. Tischendorf, *Apocalypses apocryphae* (Leipzig, 1866; repr. Hildesheim, 1966), xxvii–xxx; ed. M. R. James, *Apocrypha anecdota*, Texts and Studies 2.3 (Cambridge, 1893), 109–26; trans. Baun 2007, 391–400

Armenian Lectionary. Ed. and trans. A. Renoux, *Le Codex Arménien Jérusalem 121*, 2 vols., PO 35, fasc. 1, PO 36, fasc. 2 (Turnhout, 1971)

Athanasios of Alexandria, *First Letter to Virgins*. Ed. and trans. L. Th. Lefort, *S. Athanase: Lettres festales et pastorales en copte*, CSCO 151, Scriptores Coptici 20 (Louvain, 1955), 73–99; trans. Brakke 1995, 274–91 (see Secondary Sources)

Athanasios of Alexandria, *Second Letter to Virgins*. Ed. J. Lebon, 'Athanasiana Syriaca II: une letter attribuée à saint Athanase d'Alexandrie', *Mus* 41 (1928), 169–216; trans. Brakke 1995, 292–302

(ps-)Athanasios of Alexandria, *Sermon on the Annunciation* (*CPG* 2268, *BHGa* 1147t). PG 28, 917–40

(ps-)Athanasios of Alexandria, *Sermon on the Presentation* (*CPG* 2271, *BHGa* 1968). PG 28, 973–1000

(ps-)Basil of Seleukeia, *Homily XXXIX, On the Annunciation* (*CPG* 6656. 39, *BHG* 1112p). PG 85, 425–52

Bride of Light. Trans. S. P. Brock, *Bride of Light: Hymns on Mary from the Syriac Churches, Mōrān 'Eth'ō 6* (Kerala, 1994; repr. Piscataway, NJ, 2010)

Christos Paschon. Ed. and trans. A. Tuilier, *Grégoire de Nazianze, La Passion du Christ. Tragédie,* SC 149 (Paris, 1969)

Chronicon pascale. Ed. L. Dindorf, 2 vols., CSHB 16–17 (Bonn, 1832); trans. M. and M. Whitby, *Chronicon Paschale, 284–628 A.D.,* TTH 7 (Liverpool, 1989)

Chrysippos of Jerusalem, *Homily on the Holy Theotokos Mary* (*CPG* 6705, *BHG* 1144n). Ed. M. Jugie, *Homélies mariales,* vol. 2, PO 19, fasc. 3, no. 93 (Paris, 1926; repr. Turnhout, 1990), 336–43(hereafter Jugie 1926 [1990])

Clement of Alexandria, *Stromata* (*CPG* 1377). Ed. O. Stählin and L. Früchtel, *Clemens Alexandrinus,* vol. 2: *Stromata 1–6,* GCS 52 [15] (Berlin, 1960); vol. 3: *Stromata 7–8,* GCS 17² (Berlin, 1970)

Constantine Porphyrogennetos, *Book of Ceremonies.* Ed. J. H. Leich and J. J. Reiske, *Constantinus Porphyrogenitus, De Cerimoniis Aulae Byzantinae,* CSHB, 2 vols. (Bonn, 1935 and 1939); ed. and trans. A. Vogt, *Le livre des ceremonies,* 4 vols. (Paris, 1935–40); trans. A. Moffatt and M. Tall, *Constantine Porphyrogennetos: The Book of Ceremonies,* Byzantina Australiensia (Leiden, 2012); ed. G. Dagron, B. Flusin, and D. Feissel, *Constantin VII Porphyrogénète: Le livre des cérémonies.* Corpus fontium historiae byzantinae 52. 1-5 (Paris, 2020), 5 vols.

Corippus, *In laudem Iustini Augusti minoris.* Ed. and trans. Averil Cameron, *Flavius Cresconius Corippus, In laudem Iustini Augusti minoris, Libri VI* (London, 1976)

Cyril of Alexandria, *Homily XII, On the Presentation* (*CPG* 5256, *BHG* 1963). PG 77, 1039–49

Cyril of Alexandria, *Homily IV, On the Virgin Mary* (*CPG* 5248, *BHG* 1151). Ed. E. Schwartz, *ACO* 1. 1. 2, 102–4; PG 77, 992–6

Cyril of Alexandria, *Homily XI, On the Virgin Mary* (*CPG* 5255, *BHG* 1154). PG 77, 1029–40

Cyril of Alexandria, *Second Letter to Nestorios* (*CPG* 5302). Ed. E. Schwartz, *ACO* 1. 1. 1, 23–5; PG 77, 40–1; trans. L. R. Wickham, *Cyril of Alexandria. Select Letters* (Oxford, 1983), 2–11

Cyril of Alexandria, *Third Letter to Nestorios* (*CPG* 5303). Ed. E. Schwartz, *ACO* 1. 1. 1, 25; PG 77, 44; trans. Wickham 1983, 12–33

Cyril of Skythopolis, *Vita s. Theodosii.* Ed. E. Schwartz, *Kyrillos von Skythopolis,* TU 49.2 (Leipzig, 1939)

Dialogue Poems on Mary. Trans. S. P. Brock, *Mary and Joseph, and Other Dialogue Poems on Mary,* Texts from Christian Late Antiquity 8 (Piscataway, NJ, 2011)

(ps-)Dionysios the Areopagite, *The Celestial Hierarchy* (*CPG* 6600). PG 3, 120–369; Ed. G. Heil and A.M. Ritter, *Corpus Dionysiacum,* vol. 2: *Pseudo-Dionysius Areopagita, De coelesti hierarchia, de ecclesiastica hierarchia, de mystica theologia, epistulae* (Berlin and New York, 1991), 5–59; trans. C. Luibheid, *Pseudo-Dionysius. The Complete Works* (London, 1987), 145–91 (hereafter Luibheid 1987) (ps-)Dionysios the Areopagite, *The Divine Names* (*CPG* 6602). PG 3, 585–984; ed. B. R. Suchla, *Corpus Dionysiacum*, vol. 1: *Pseudo-Dionysius Areopagita. De divinis nominibus*, PTS 33 (Berlin, 1990); trans. Luibheid 1987, 49–131

Divine Liturgy of John Chrysostom. Trans. Archimandrite Ephrem Lash, *The Divine Liturgy of our Father among the Saints, John Chrysostom: The Greek Text together with a Translation into English* (London, 2011)

Dostoyevsky, *The Brothers Karamazov*. Trans. D. McDuff, F. Dostoyevsky, *The Brothers Karamazov: A Novel in Four Parts and an Epilogue* (London, 1993; rev. ed. 2003)

Egeria, *Journal*. Ed. and trans. H. Pétré, *Éthérie, Journal de Voyage*, SC 21 (Paris, 1971); trans. J. Wilkinson, *Egeria's Travels* (Warminster, 1999)

Ephrem the Syrian, *Hymns on Faith*. Ed. E. Beck, *Des heiligen Ephraem des Syrers Hymnen de fide*, CSCO 154–5 (Louvain, 1955); trans. J. T. Wickes, *St Ephrem the Syrian, The Hymns on Faith*, FOTC 130 (Washington, DC, 2015)

Ephrem the Syrian, *Hymns on Mary*. Ed. T. J. Lamy, *Sancti Ephraem Syri Hymni et Sermones*, vol. 2 (Malines, 1886), 519–90; trans. Brock 1994 (2010), 36–73 (see above, *Bride of Light*)

Ephrem the Syrian, *Hymns on the Nativity*. Ed. E. Beck, *Des heiligen Ephraem des Syrers Hymnen de Nativitate*, CSCO 186–87 (Louvain, 1959); trans. K. McVey, *Ephrem the Syrian. Hymns* (New York and Mahwah, NJ, 1989), 61–217; trans. Brock 1994 (2010), 18–27 (see above, *Bride of Light*)

Epiphanios of Kallistratos, *Life of the Virgin* (*CANT* 91, *BHG* 1049). PG 120, 185–216; ed. A. Dressel, *Epiphanii monachi edita et inedita* (Leipzig, 1843), 13–44

Epiphanios of Salamis, *Panarion* (*CPG* 3745). Ed. K. Holl, *Epiphanius*, vol. 1: *Ancoratus und Panarion (haer. 1–33)*, GCS 25 (Leipzig, 1915), 153–464; vol. 2: *Panarion (haer. 34–64)*, GCS 31 (Leipzig, 1922); vol. 3: *Panarion (haer. 65–8)*, GCS 37 (Leipzig, 1933)

Eusebios of Caesarea, *Proof of the Gospel* (*CPG* 3487). Ed. I. A. Heikel, *Eusebius Werke*, vol. 6: *Die Demonstratio evangelica*, GCS 23 (Leipzig, 1913)

Eustathios of Thessalonike, *Exegesis*. Ed. P. Cesaretti and S. Ronchey, *Eustathii Thessalonicensis exegesis in canonem iambicum pentecostalem. Recensuerunt indicibusque instruxerunt*, *Supplementa Byzantina* 10 (Berlin, Munich and Boston, 2014)

Eustratiades *Theotokarion*. S. Eustratiades, *Theotokarion*, vol. 1: Ἁγιορειτικὴ Βιβλιοθήκη 7–8 (Chennevières-sur-Marne, 1931)

Euthymiac Legend (*CPG* 8062 = *Homily on the Dormition II*, chap. 18). Ed. B. Kotter, *Die Schriften des Johannes von Damaskos*, vol. 5, PTS 29 (Berlin and New York, 1988), 536.18.5 – 539.18.68; trans. Daley 1998, 224–6

Euthymios the Athonite, Georgian *Life of the Virgin* (*CANT* 90). Ed. and trans. M. van Esbroeck, *Maxime le Confesseur: Vie de la Vierge*, 2 vols., CSCO 478–9, Scriptores Iberici 21–2 (Louvain, 1986); ed. and trans. S. J. Shoemaker, *Maximus the Confessor, The Life of the Virgin* (New Haven and London, 2012)

Euthymios of Constantinople, *Homily Ia on the Conception of the Virgin Mary* (*BHG* 134c). Ed. M. Jugie 1922 (2003), 499–514

Euthymios of Constantinople, *Enkomion on the Holy Belt* (*BHG* 1138). Ed. Jugie 1922 (2003), 505–14

Euthymios of Constantinople, *Homilies I–II on the Conception of the Virgin Mary* (*BHG* 134a–134b). Ed. Jugie 1926 (1990), 441–7; 448–55

Evagrios, *Ecclesiastical History*. Ed. J. Bidez and L. Parmentier, *The Ecclesiastical History of Evagrius with the Scholia* (London, 1898); trans. M. Whitby, *The Ecclesiastical History of Evagrius Scholasticus*, TTH 33 (Liverpool, 2000)

Evergetinon. Ed. V. Matthaios, *Evergetinos etoi Synagoge*, 4 vols. (Athens, 1957); trans. Archbishop Chrystomos and Hieromonk Patapios, *The Evergetinos: A Complete Text*, 4 vols. (Etna, CA, 2008).

Garitte 1958. G. Garitte, *Le calendrier palestino-géorgien du Sinaiticus 34 (Xe siècle)* (Brussels)

Gelasian Decree. Ed. E. von Dobschütz, *Das Decretum Galasianum de libris recipiendis et non recipiendis im Kritischen Text herausgegeben und untersucht*, TU 38 (Leipzig, 1912); trans. W. Schneemelcher, *New Testament Apocrypha*, vol. 1: *Gospels and Related Writings*, Eng. trans. R. M. Wilson (Cambridge and Louisville, KT, 1991)

George of Nikomedia, *Homily on the Conception of Anna* (*BHG* 131). PG 100, 1353–76

George of Nikomedia, *Homily on Good Friday* (*BHG* 1139) = *Oratio de Deipara iuxta crucem*. PG 100, 1457–89

George of Nikomedia, *Homily on the Virgin Mary at the Tomb* (*BHG* 1156) = *Oratio in immaculatae Virginis in sepulchro assistentiam, et gratiarum action pro gloriosa resurrection*. PG 100, 1489–1504

George of Pisidia, *Bellum Avaricum*. Ed. A. Pertusi, *Giorgio di Pisidia poemi. I. Panegirici epici. Edizione critica traduzione e commento* (Freising, 1959), 179–200

George of Pisidia, *Carmi*. Ed. L. Tartaglia, *Carmi di Giorgio di Pisidia* (Turin, 1998)

Georgian Lectionary. Ed. M. Tarchnishvili, *Le grand lectionnaire de l'Eglise de Jérusalem (Ve–VIIIe siècle)*, CSCO 188–9, 204–5 (Leuven, 1959–60)

Georgian *Life of the Virgin*. See Euthymios the Athonite, Georgian *Life of the Virgin*

Germanos I of Constantinople, *Homily on the Annunciation* (*CPG* 8009). PG 98, 320–40 (incomplete); ed. D. Fecioru, *Biserica ortodoxă română* 64 (1946), 65–91, 180–92, 386–96; trans. Cunningham 2008b, 221–46

Germanos I of Constantinople, *Homilies I–III on the Dormition* (*CPG* 8010–12, *BHG* 1119). PG 98, 340–72; trans. Daley 1998, 153–81

Germanos I of Constantinople, *Homilies I–II on the Entrance* (*CPG* 8007–8, *BHG* 1103, *BHGa* 1104). PG 98, 292–320; trans. Cunningham 2008b, 145–72

Germanos I of Constantinople, *Homily on the Holy Belt* (*CPG* 8013, *BHG* 1086). PG 98, 372–84; trans. Cunningham 2008b, 247–55

Germanos I of Constantinople, *Homily on the Deliverance of Constantinople* (*CPG* 8014). Ed. V. Grumel, 'Homélie de Saint Germain sur la délivrance de Constantinople', *REB* 16 (1958), 183–205

(ps-)Germanos I of Constantinople, *Homily on the Burial of the Lord's Body* (*CPG* 8031). PG 98, 244–90 (ps-)Germanos I of Constantinople, *Homily on the Dormition* (*CPG* 8025, *BHG*a 1146q). Ed. A. Wenger, 'Un nouveau témoin de l'assomption, une homélie attribuée à Saint Germain de Constantinople', *REB* 16 (1958), 43–58

Geyer, *Itineraria*. P. Geyer, *Itineraria et alia geographica* (Turnhout, 1965)

Gigante 1964. Ed. M. Gigante, *Versus Iambici*, Testi e Monumenti 10 (Palermo, 1964)

Gospel of Mary. Ed. R. McL. Wilson and G. W. MacRae, in D. M. Parrott, ed., *Nag Hammadi Codices V, 2–5 and VI with Papyrus Berolinensis 8502, 1 and 4*, NHS 11 (Leiden, 1979)

Gospel of Ps-Matthew (*CANT* 51). Ed. C. Tischendorf, *Evangelia apocrypha* (Leipzig, 1853), 50–105 (Hildesheim, 1987), 51–111; ed. E. Amann, *Le protévangile de Jacques et ses remaiements latins* (Paris, 1910), 272–339; ed. J. Gijsel, *Libri de Nativitate Mariae. Pseudo-Matthaei Evangelium, Textus et Commentarius*, CCSA 10 (Turnhout, 1997)

Gospel of Nikodemos (Byzantine recensions). Ed. and trans. R. Gounelle, *Les recensions byzantines de l'Évangile de Nicodème* (Turnhout, 2007)

Greek Transitus (*CANT* 102, *BHG* 1056d). Ed. and trans. Wenger 1955, 210–41; ed. F. Manns, *Le récit de la dormition de Marie (Vat. gr. 1982), Contribution à l'étude des origines de l'exégèse chrétienne*, Studium Biblicum Franciscanum, Collectio Maior 33 (Jerusalem, 1989)

Gregory the Great, *Dialogues*. Ed. and trans. A. de Vogüé and P. Antin, *Grégoire le Grand. Dialogues*, 3 vols., SC 251, 260 and 265 (Paris, 1978–80); O. J. Zimmermann, trans., *St Gregory the Great, Dialogues* (Washington, DC, 1959)

Gregory Nazianzen, *Festal Orations* (*CPG* 3010). *Oration 1*, ed. and trans. J. Bernardi, *Grégoire de Nazianze, Dicourse 1–3*, SC 247 (Paris, 1978); *Orations 38–41*, ed. and trans. C. Moreschini, *Grégoire de Nazianze: Discours 38–41*, SC 358 (Paris, 1990); trans. M. Vinson, *St Gregory of Nazianzus. Select Orations*, FOTC 107 (Washington, DC, 2003); trans. B. E. Daley, SJ, *Gregory of Nazianzus* (London and New York, 2006), 62–161; trans. N. V. Harrison, *St Gregory of Nazianzus. Festal Orations* (Crestwood, NY, 2008)

Gregory of Nyssa, *Homily on the Nativity of Christ* (*CPG* 3194, *BHG* 1915). Ed. F. Mann, 'Die Weihnachtspredigt Gregors von Nyssa: Überlieferungsgeschichte und Text' (unpubl. thesis, Münster, 1975); PG 46, 1128–49

Gregory of Nyssa, *Life of Moses* (*CPG* 3159). Ed. E. Mülenberg and G. Maspero, *Gregorii Nysseni opera* (Leiden, 2010–13) online at: https://referenceworks.brillonline.com/browse/gregorii-nysseni-opera ; ed. and trans. J. Daniélou, *La vie de Moïse, ou, Traité de la perfection en matière de vertu* (Paris, 1955); trans. A. J. Malherbe and E. Ferguson, *Gregory of Nyssa, The Life of Moses* (New York, Ramsey and Toronto, 1978)

Gregory of Nyssa, *Life of St Gregory Thaumatourgos* (*CPG* 3184, *BHG*a 715–715b). PG 46, 493–957

(ps-)Gregory Thaumatourgos (ps-John Chrysostom), *Homily on the Annunciation* (*CPG* 4677, *BHG*a 1144h). PG 62, 763–70 (ps-)Gregory Thaumatourgos, *Homily I, On the Annunciation* (*CPG* 1175, *BHG* 1139n). PG 10, 1145–56

(ps-)Gregory Thaumatourgos, *Homily II, On the Annunciation* (*CPG* 1776, *BHG* 1092w). PG 10, 1156–69

(ps-)Gregory Thaumatourgos ([ps-] John Chrysostom), *Homily III, On the Annunciation* (*CPG* 4519, *BHG* 1128f). PG 10, 1172–7 = PG 50, 791–6

Gregory of Tours, *Libri miraculorum*. Ed. B. Krusch, *Miracula et opera minora, In gloria martyrum, Monumenta Germaniae Historica, Scriptores rerum Merovingicarum* (Hanover, 1885), 484–561

Hesychios of Jerusalem, *Homilies V and VI, On the Theotokos Mary* (*CPG* 6568–9, *BHG* 1132–3). Ed. and trans. M. Aubineau, *Les homélies festales d'Hésychius de Jérusalem*, vol. 1: *Les homélies I–XV*, SubsHag 59 (Brussels, 1978) (hereafter Aubineau 1978), 158–68, 194–204

Hesychios of Jerusalem, *Homilies I and II, On Hypapante* (*CPG* 6565–6, *BHG* 1956–7). Ed. and trans. Aubineau 1978, 24–43, 61–75

Hippolytus of Thebes, *Chronicle*. Ed. F. Diekamp, *Hippolytos von Theben* (Münster, 1898); PG 117, 1025–56

Horologion, Sinai. Ed. and trans. M. L. Ajjoub with J. Paramelle, SJ, *Livre d'heures du Sinaï (Sinaiticus graecus 864): Introduction, texte critique, notes et index*, SC 486 (Paris, 2004)

Horologion, Syriac. Ed. M. Black, *A Christian Palestinian Syriac Horologion* (Berlin Ms. Or. Oct. 1019) (Cambridge, 1954)

Hymnal of St Sabas. Ed. and trans. C. Renoux, *L'Hymnaire de Saint-Sabas (Ve–VIIIe siècle): Le manuscrit géorgien H 2123*, vol. 1: *Du samedi de Lazare à la Pentecôte*, PO 50:3 (Turnhout, 2008)

Irenaeus of Lyons, *Against Heresies, Bk III*. Ed. and trans. F. Sagnard, *Irénée de Lyon, Contre les hérésies III*, SC 34 (Paris, 1952)

Jacob of Serugh, *Homilies I, II, III, V on the Mother of God*. Ed. P. Bedjan, *S. Martyrii, qui et Sahdona quae supersunt omnia* (Paris and Leipzig, 1902), 614–85, 709–19; trans. M. Hansbury, *Jacob of Serug, On the Mother of God* (Crestwood, NY, 1998)

James Kokkinobaphos, *Homilies*. Ed. A. Ballerini, *Sylloge monumentorum ad mysterium conceptionis immaculatae Virginis deiparae illustrandum* (Rome, 1854–8); PG 127, 543–700. A critical edition is currently being prepared by Elizabeth Jeffreys.

Jerome, *On Illustrious Men*. Trans. T. P. Halton, *St Jerome, On Illustrious Men*, FOTC 100 (Washington, DC, 1999)

John of Bolnisi, *Homilies*. Ed. S. Verhelst, *Jean de Bolnisi, Homélies*, SC 580 (Paris, 2015)

John of Damascus, *On the Divine Images* (*CPG* 8045, *BHG* 1391e–g). Ed. B. Kotter, *Die Schriften des Johannes von Damaskos*, vol. 3, PTS 17 (Berlin and New York, 1975), 65–200; trans. A. Louth, *St John of Damascus, Three Treatises on the Divine Images* (Crestwood, NY, 2003)

John of Damascus, *Homilies I–III on the Dormition* (*CPG* 8061–3, *BHG*a 1114, 1097, *BHG* 1126n, *BHG*a 1089). Ed. B. Kotter, *Die Schriften des Johannes von*

Damaskos, vol. 5, PTS 29 (Berlin and New York, 1988), 483–500, 516–40, 548
55; trans. Daley 1998, 183–239

John of Damascus, *Homily on Holy Saturday* (*CPG* 8059). Ed. Kotter 1998, 121–56;
PG 96, 601–44

John of Damascus, *On Orthodox Faith* (*CPG* 8043). Ed. B. Kotter, *Die Schriften
des Johannes von Damaskos*, vol. 2, PTS 12 (Berlin, 1973); trans. F. H. Chase,
Jr, *St John of Damascus, Writings*, FOTC 37 (Washington, DC, 1958)

(ps-)John of Damascus, *Sermon on the Presentation of Christ into the Temple* (*CPG*
8066, *BHG* 1953). Ed. Kotter 1988, 371–95

(ps-)John of Damascus, *Homily on the Nativity of the Virgin Mary* (*CPG* 8060,
BHGa 1114). Ed. Kotter 1988, 169–82; trans. Cunningham 2008b, 53–70

John of Euboea, *Homily on the Conception of the Virgin Mary* (*CPG* 8135, *BHG*
1117). PG 96, 1460–1500; trans. Cunningham 2008b, 173–95

John Geometres, *Homily on the Annunciation* (*BHG* 1158). PG 106, 811–48

John Geometres, *Life of the Virgin* (*CANT* 92, *BHG* 1102g–1102h, 1123m, 1143c). A
critical edition by Fr Maximos Constas and Christos Similides is forthcoming; section on the Dormition (based on Vatic. Gr. 504, fols. 190–194v):
(*BHG* 1143c); ed. and trans. Wenger 1955, 363–415; another critical edition has
recently appeared in A. Benia, Ἰωάννη Γεωμέτρη, Ἐξόδιος ἡ προπεμπτήριος
εἰς τὴν Κοίμησιν τῆς ὑπερενδόξου Δεσποίνης ἡμῶν Θεοτόκου: Πρώτη
ἔκδοση καὶ μελέτη τοῦ κειμένου (unpublished PhD thesis, University of
Athens, 2019)

John Moschos, *The Spiritual Meadow* (*CPG* 7376, *BHG* 1441–2). PG 87,
2852–3112; trans. J. Wortley, *The Spiritual Meadow of John Moschos*,
Cistercian Studies Series 139 (Kalamazoo, MI, 1992)

John Moschos, *The Spiritual Meadow, Supplementary Tales*. Ed. E. Mioni, 'Il
Pratum Spirituale di Giovanni Mosco: gli episodi inediti del Cod. Marciano
greco II.21', *OCP* 17 (1951), 61–94

John of Thessalonike, *Homily on the Dormition* (*CPG* 7924, *BHG* 1144–1144c). Ed.
Jugie 1925 (1990), 375–405; trans. Daley 1998, 47–70

Joseph the Hymnographer, *Kanon on the Nativity of the Virgin Mary, Mariale*. PG
105, 983–92

Joseph the Hymnographer, *Kanon on the Honourable Belt of the Supremely Holy
Theotokos, Mariale*. PG 105, 1011–17

Justin Martyr, *Dialogue with Trypho* (*CPG* 1076). Ed. M. Marcovich, *Dialogus
cum Tryphone* (Berlin, 1997); PG 6, 472 800; trans. T. B. Falls, *St Justin
Martyr, Dialogue with Trypho* (Washington, DC, 2003)

Justinian, *Novels*. Ed. Z. von Lingenthal, *Imperatoris Iustiniani novellae*, 2 vols.
(Leipzig, 1881)

Kedrenos, *Historiarum compendium*. Ed. I. Bekker, 2 vols., CSHB (Bonn, 1838–9)

Kosmas Vestitor, *Oration on Joachim and Anna* (*CPG* 8151, *BHG* 828). PG 106,
1005–12; trans. Cunningham 2008b, 139–44

Kosmas Vestitor, *Homilies I–IV on the Dormition* (*CPG* 8155–8, in Latin). Ed. and
trans. Wenger 1955, 315–33; ed. A. P. Orbán, *Sermones in Dormitiones Mariae.
Sermones patrum graecorum praesertim in Dormitionem Assumptionemque*

beatae Mariae Virginis in Latinum translati, ex codice Augiensi LXXX (saec. IX), CCCM 54 (Turnhout, 2000), 99–126

Leontios of Constantinople, *Homilies* (*CPG* 7888–98). Ed. C. Datema and P. Allen, *Leontii Prebyteri Constantinopolitani Homiliae*, CCSG 17 (Turnhout and Leuven, 1987); trans. P. Allen with C. Datema, *Leontius, Presbyter of Constantinople, Fourteen Homilies*, Byzantina Australiensia 9 (Brisbane, 1991)

Leontios of Neapolis, *Homily on Symeon* (*CPG* 7880, *BHG* 1955). PG 93, 1565–81

Leo VI ('the Wise'), *Homilies I, XII, XV, and XX, On the Annunciation, Dormition, Nativity and Entrance of the Virgin Mary*. Ed. T. Antonopoulou, *Leonis VI Sapientis imperatoris byzantini*, CCSG 63 (Turnhout, 2008), 5–11, 167–79, 221–41, 267–76

Leo Grammatikos, *Chronographia*. Ed. I. Bekker, *Leonis Grammatici Chronographia*, CSHB (Bonn, 1842), 1–331

Liber pontificalis. Ed. L. Duchesne, *Le Liber pontificalis: texte, introduction et commentaire* (Paris, 1886–1957), 3 vols.

Life of St Andrew the Fool. Ed. and trans. J. Rydén, *The Life of St Andrew the Fool*, vol. 2: *Text, Translation and Notes*, Acta Universitatis Upsaliensis, Studia Byzantina Upsaliensia 4:2 (Uppsala, 1995)

Life of St Basil the Younger (*BHG* 264–264f). Three separate versions appear in Veselovskii 1889–92; Vilinskii 1911 and *AASS*, 26 March, 20–32; ed. and trans. D. F. Sullivan, A.-M. Talbot, and S. McGrath, *The Life of Saint Basil the Younger*, Dumbarton Oaks Studies 45 (Washington, DC, 2014)

Life of St Euthymios, Patriarch of Constantinople. Ed. P. Karlin-Hayter, *Bibliothèque de Byzantion* (Brussels, 1970)

Life of St Irene of Chrysobalanton. Ed. and trans. J. O. Rosenquist, *The Life of St Irene, Abbess of Chrysobalanton* (Uppsala, 1986)

Life of St Stephen the Younger (*BHG* 1666). Ed. and trans. M.-F. Auzépy, *La Vie d'Étienne le Jeune par Étienne le diacre*, BBOM 3 (Aldershot, 1997)

Life of the Empress Theodora. Ed. A. Markopoulos, *Symmeikta* 5 (1983), 249–85, text 257–71 (*BHG* 1732–5 and *Synax. CP*, 456, 458–60); trans. M. Vinson, in A.-M. Talbot, ed., *Byzantine Defenders of Images. Eight Saints' Lives in English Translation* (Washington, DC, 1998), 353–82

Mansi J. D., ed., *Sacrorum conciliorum nova et amplissima collectio* (Florence, 1759-)

(ps-)Maximos the Confessor, *Life of the Virgin*. See Euthymios the Athonite

Maximos the Confessor and Anastasios, *Dispute at Bizya*. Ed. P. Allen and B. Neil, *Scripta saeculi VII vitam Maximi Confessoris illustrantia*, CCSG 39 (Turnhout, 1999), 73–151

Menaion Menaia tou olou eniautou, 6 vols. (Rome, 1888–1902). For a modern translation of the hymnography for nine great feasts, see Mother Mary and Archimandrite Kallistos Ware, trans., *The Festal Menaion* (London, 1969; repr. South Canaan, PA, 1990)

Metaphrast, Simeon the, *Life of the Virgin* (*CANT* 93, *BHG* 1047–8a). Ed. V. Latyshev, *Menologii anonymi byzantini saeculi X quae supersunt II* (St Petersburg, 1912), 127–32

Miracles of the Pege. Ed. and trans. A.-M. Talbot and S. F. Johnson, *Miracle Tales from Byzantium*, DOML 12 (Cambridge, MA, and London, 2012), 203–97

Miracles of St Artemios. Ed. A. Papadopoulos-Kerameus, *Varia graeca sacra* (St Petersburg, 1909), 1–75; trans. J. Nesbitt and V. Crisafulli, *The Miracles of St Artemios: A Collection of Miracle Stories by an Anonymous Author of Seventh-Century Byzantium* (Leiden, New York and Cologne, 1997)

(ps-)Modestos of Jerusalem, *Enkomion on the Dormition* (*CPG* 7876, *BHG* 1085). PG 86, 3277–312; trans. Daley 1998, 83–102

Morcelli Calendar. Ed. S. A. Morcelli, *Kalendarium Ecclesiae Constantinopolitanae e Biblitheca Romana Albanorum in lucem editum et veterum monumentorum comparatione diurnisque commentaries illustratrum,* 2 vols. (Rome, 1788)

Neophytos the Recluse, *Homilies on the Nativity and the Entrance into the Temple of the Virgin Mary.* Ed. Jugie 1922 (2003), 528–38

Nikephoros, *Antirrhetikoi i–iii adversus Constantinum Copronymum.* PG 100, 205–522; trans. M.-J. Mondzain-Baudinet, *De notre bienheureux père et archévêque de Constantinople Nicéphore discussion et refutation des bavardages ignares, athées et tout à fait creux de l'irreligieux Mamon contre l'incarnation de Dieu et le Verbe notre sauveur. Discours contre les iconoclasts* (Paris, 1989), 57–296

Nikephoros Basilakes, *Rhetorical Exercises.* Ed. and trans. J. Beneker and C. A. Gibson, *The Rhetorical Exercises of Nikephoros Basilakes. Progymnasmata from Twelfth-Century Byzantium,* DOML 43 (Cambridge, MA, and London, 2016)

Nikephoros Kallistos Xanthopoulos, *Ecclesiastical History.* PG 145, 559 – PG 147, 448

Obsequies of the Holy Virgin (*CANT* 120). Ed. W. Wright, *Contributions to the Apocryphal Literature of the New Testament* (London, 1865), 55–65

Odes of Solomon. Ed. and trans. J. H. Charlesworth, *The Odes of Solomon* (Oxford, 1973); ed. M. Lattke, *Oden Salomos: Text, Übersetzung, Kommentar,* 4 vols. (Freiburg, 1999–2005)

Oktoechos. Ed. I. K. Papachrone, *Oktoechos tou en hagiois patros hemon Ioannou tou Damaskenou* (Katerine, 1988)

Origen, *Comm. in Mt* (*CPG* 1450). Ed. E. Klostermann and E. Benz, *Origenes Matthäusklärung des Origenes,* TU 47.2, (Leipzig, 1931)

Origen, *Contra Celsum* (*CPG* 1476). Ed. and trans. H. Borret, *Origène. Contre Celse,* vol. 1: Bks. 1–11, SC 132 (Paris, 1967, rev. ed. 2005)

Origen, *Homilies on Luke* (*CPG* 1451). Ed. and trans. H. Crouzel, F. Fournier and P. Périchon, *Origène. Homélies sur Luc,* SC 87 (Paris, 1962)

Origen, *On First Principles* (*CPG* 1482). Ed. P. Koetschau, *Origenes Werke V. De principiis,* GCS 22 (Leipzig, 1913); ed. and trans. H. Crouzel and M. Simonetti, *Origène. Traité des principes,* vols. 1–4, SC 252, 253, 268, 269 (Paris, 1978–80); trans. G. W. Butterworth, *Origen, On First Principles* (Gloucester, MA, 1973); trans. J. Behr, *Origen. On First Principles: A Reader's Edition* (Oxford, 2019)

Palestinian Syriac Horologion. Ed. M. Black, *A Christian Palestinian Syriac Horologion* (Berlin MS. Or. Oct. 1019) (Cambridge, 1954)

Parakletike etoi Oktoechos e Megale (Rome, 1885); trans. D. Guillaume, *Paraclitique ou grand Octoèque* (Rome, 1977)

Parastaseis. Ed. and trans. A. Cameron and J. Herrin, *Constantinople in the Early Eighth Century: The Parastaseis Syntomoi Chronikai* (Leiden, 1984)

Patria. Ed. T. Preger, *Scriptores originum Constantinopolitanarum,* 2 vols. (Leipzig, 1901–7; repr. New York, 1975); ed. and trans. A. Berger, *Accounts of Medieval Constantinople. The Patria,* DOML 24 (Cambridge, MA and London, 2013)

Paul the Deacon, *Homilies I–II on the Assumption.* PL 95, 156–74; ed. L. Buono, 'Le omelie per l'Assunzione di Paolo Diacono. Introduzione e edizione', *StMed* ser.3, 58:2 (2017), 697–756

Peter of Argos, *Homily on the Conception of St Anna* (*BHG* 132). PG 104, 1352–65

Photios, *Bibliotheca.* Ed. and trans. R. Henry, *Photius, Bibliothèque* (Paris, 1959–91), 8 vols.; PG 104, 9–430

Photios, *Homilies.* Ed. B. Laourdas, *Photiou Omiliai* (Thessaloniki, 1959); trans. C. Mango, *The Homilies of Photius, Patriarch of Constantinople* (Cambridge, MA, 1958)

Pilgrim Accounts, Russian. Ed. B. de Khitrowo, *Itinéraires russes en Orient* (Osnabrück, 1966)

Pliny the Younger, *Letters.* Trans. B. Radice, *Pliny. Letters and Panegyricus,* vol. 2: *Letters, Books VIII–X and Panegyricus* (Cambridge, MA, 1975)

Proklos of Constantinople, *Homilies I–V* (*CPG* 5800–4, *BHGa* 1129, *BHG* 1899k, 1914d, 1900, *BHGa* 1134). Ed. and trans. N. Constas, *Proclus of Constantinople and the Cult of the Virgin in Late Antiquity. Homilies 1–5, Texts and Translations* (Leiden and Boston, 2003), 125–272; trans. J. Barkhuizen, *Proclus Bishop of Constantinople, Homilies on the Life of Christ,* Early Christian Studies 1 (Brisbane, 2001), 63–96

(ps-)Proklos, *Homily VI, On the Theotokos* (*CPG* 5805, *BHGa* 1110, *BHGn* 1126e). Ed. F. J. Leroy, *L'homilétique de Proclus de Constantinople. Tradition manuscrite, inédits, études connexes,* ST 247 (Rome, 1967), 298–324

Proklos of Constantinople, *Tomus ad Armenios* (*CPG* 5897). Ed. E. Schwartz, *ACO* IV, vol. 2, 187–95

Prokopios, *Buildings.* Trans. H. B. Dewing, *Procopius, On Buildings,* Loeb Classical Library 343 (Cambridge, MA, 1940)

Protevangelion of James (*CANT* 50). Ed. C. Tischendorf, *Evangelia apocrypha* (Leipzig, 1876; repr. Hildesheim, 1966 and 1987), 1–50; ed. E. de Strycker, *La forme la plus ancienne du Protévangile de Jacques,* SubsHag 33 (Brussels, 1961), 64–191; trans. Elliott 1993 (2004), 57–67; trans. G. Postel, *Protevangelion sive de natalibus Iesu Christi ... sermo historicus divi Iacobi minoris* (Basel, 1552; Strasbourg, 1570)

Psellos, Michael, *Sermon on the Annunciation.* Ed. Jugie 1922 (1990), 517–25; ed. E. A. Fisher, *Orationes hagiographicae* (Stuttgart and Leipzig, 1994), 96–113 (hereafter Fisher 1994)

Psellos, Michael, *Sermon on the Entrance into the Temple.* Ed. Fisher 1994, 258–66

Psellos, Michael, *Oration on the 'Usual Miracle' at Blachernai*. Ed. Fisher 1994, 200–29

Romanos the Melodist, *Kontakia*. Ed. P. Maas and C. A. Trypanis, *Sancti Romani Melodi Cantica. Cantica Genuina* (Oxford, 1963; repr. 1997); ed. and trans. J. Grosdidier de Matons, *Romanos le Mélode, Hymnes*, 5 vols., SC 99, 110, 114, 128, 283 (Paris, 1964–81); trans. Archimandrite Ephrem Lash, *St Romanos the Melodist. Kontakia on the Life of Christ* (San Francisco, London and Pymble, 1995); ed. and trans. R. Maisano, *Cantici di Romano il Melodo*, 2 vols. (Turin, 2002); ed. and trans. J. Koder, *Romanos Melodos: Die Hymnen*, 2 vols. (Stuttgart, 2005); trans. J. H. Barkhuizen, *Romanos the Melodist: Poet and Preacher* (Durbanville, SA, 2012)

Sargis of Aberga, *Doctrina Jacobi nuper baptizati*. Ed. and trans. V. Déroche, TM 11 (Paris, 1991), 47–229

The Septuagint. Ed. J. W. Wevers, *Septuaginta: Vetus Testamentum Graecum Auctoritate Academiae Scientiarum Gottingensis* (Göttingen, 1974); trans. A. Pietersma and B. G. Wright, *A New English Translation of the Septuagint* (Oxford and New York, 2007)

Severos of Antioch, *Homily II, On the Annunciation* (*CPG* 7035). Ed. M. Brière and F. Graffin (with C. J. A. Lash and J.-M. Sauget), *Les homiliae cathédrales de Sévère d'Antioche, traduction syriaque de Jacob d'Édesse*, PO 38, fasc. 2, no. 175 (Turnhout, 1976), 272–91

Severos of Antioch, *Homily XIV, On the Memory of the* Theotokos (*CPG* 7035). Ed. Brière and Graffin 1976, 400–15; trans. Allen and Hayward 2004, 111–18

Severos of Antioch, *Homily XXXVI, On the Nativity of Christ* (*CPG* 7035). Ed. M. Brière, F. Graffin and C. J. A. Lash, *Les homélies cathédrales de Sévère d'Antioche, traduction syriaque de Jacob d'Édesse*, PO 36, fasc. 3, no. 169 (Turnhout, 1972), 458–73

Severos of Antioch, *Homily LXVII, On Holy Mother of God and Ever-Virgin* (*CPG* 7035). Ed. M. Brière, PO 8. 2 (Paris, 1912; repr. Turnhout, 1971), 349–67

(ps-)Sextus Julius Africanus, *De rebus persicis post Christum natum*. Ed. E. Bratke, *Das sogennante Religionsgespräch am Hof der Sasaniden*, TU 19.3 (Leipzig, 1899); PG 10, 97–108

Six Books on the Dormition of the Virgin (*CANT* 123, *BHO* 620–5). Ed. W. Wright, 'The Departure of My Lady Mary from the World', *Journal of Sacred Literature and Biblical Record* 6 (1865), 417–48 and 7 (1865), 108–60

Skylitzes, *Synopsis historiarum*. Ed. J. Thurn, *Ioannis Scylitzes Synopsis Historiarum*, CFHB 5 (Berlin and New York, 1973); trans. B. Flusin, J.-C. Cheynet, comm., *Jean Skylitzès. Empereurs de Constantinople, Réalités byzantines* 8 (Paris, 2003); trans. J. Wortley, *John Skylitzes, A Synopsis of Byzantine History, 811–1057* (Cambridge, 2010)

Socrates, *Ecclesiastical History* (*CPG* 6028). Ed. G. C. Hansen, *Socrates Scholasticus, Historia ecclesiastica*, GCS, n.s., I (Berlin, 1995)

Sophronios of Jerusalem, *Homily IV on the Presentation* (*CPG* 7641; *BHG* 808). Ed. H. Usener, *Sophronii de Praesentatione Domini sermo* (Bonn, 1889), 8–18; ed.

and trans. J. M. Duffy, *Sophronios of Jerusalem. Homilies*, DOML 64 (Cambridge, MA, and London, 2020), 102–47

Sophronios of Jerusalem, *Homily V on the Annunciation* (*CPG* 7638; *BHG* 1098). PG 87, 3217–88; ed. Duffy 2020, 148–245

Sub tuum praesidium. Ed. A. S. Hunt, J. de M. Johnson, and C. H. Roberts, *Catalogue of the Greek Papyri in the John Rylands Library, Manchester*, 4 vols. (Manchester, 1911–52), vol. 3, 46–7

Symeon the Metaphrast, *Life of the Virgin* (*CANT* 93, *BHG* 1047–8a). Ed. V. Latyshev, *Menologii anonymi byzantini saeculi X quae supersunt*, vol. 2 (St Petersburg, 1912), 345–83

(ps-)Symeon the Metaphrast, *Lament of the Virgin = Oratio in lugubrem lamentationem sanctissimae Deiparae pretiosum corpus Domini nostri Jesu Christi amplexantis*. PG 114, 209–18. (This work is now ascribed to the twelfth-century rhetorician, Nikephoros Basilakes. See his *Rhetorical Exercises*, above).

Symeon the New Theologian, *Hymns*. Ed. A. Kambylis, *Symeon Neos Theologos, Hymnen*, Supplementa Byzantina 3 (Berlin and New York, 1976)

Synax. CP. Ed. H. Delehaye, *Synaxarium Constantinopolitanum, Propylaeum ad AS Novembris* (Brussels, 1902)

Syriac Life of the Virgin (*CANT* 124, *BHO* 626–30). Ed. A. Smith-Lewis, *The Protevangelion Jacobi and Transitus Mariae, with Texts from the Septuagint, the Corân, the Peshitta, and from a Syriac Hymn in a Syro-Arabic Palimpsest of the Fifth and Other Centuries*, Studia Sinaitica 11, Apocrypha Syriaca (London, 1902)

Tarasios of Constantinople, *Homily on the Entrance* (*BHG* 1149). PG 98, 1482–1500

Theodore II Dukas Laskaris, *Homily* ἀκαθίστῳ. Ed. P. Themelis, *Nea Sion* 6 (1907), 826–33; crit. ed. Giannouli 2001, 272–83

Theodore Anagnostes, *Ecclesiastical History* (*CPG* 7503). PG 86, 165–228; ed. G. C. Hansen, *Theodoros Anagnostes, Kirchengeschichte*, GCS (Berlin, 1971), 1–95

Theodore of Petra, *Vita s. Theodosii* (*BHG* 1776). Ed. H. Usener, *Vita Theodosii, Der heilige Theodosius, Schriften des Theodoros und Kyrillos* (Leipzig, 1890), 4–42

Theodore of Stoudios, *Antirrhetici tres adversus iconomachus*. PG 99, 327–436; trans. C. P. Roth, *St Theodore the Studite, On the Holy Icons* (Crestwood, NY, 1981)

Theodore of Studios, *Letters*. Ed. G. Fatouros, *Theodori Studitae epistulae* (Berlin, 1992)

Theodore of Studios, *On Holy Easter*. PG 99, 709–20

Theodore Synkellos, *Inventio* (*CPG* 7935, *BHG* 1058). Ed. F. Combefis, *Theodore Synkellos, Inventio et deposito vestis in Blachernis, Novum auctarium* (Paris, 1648), vol. 2, 751–86; ed. C. Loparev, *VizVrem* 2 (1895), 592–612; emend. E. Kurtz, *BZ* 5 (1896), 369–70

Theodore Synkellos, *De obsidione* (*CPG* 7936, *BHG* 1061). Ed. L. Sternbach, *Theodore Syncellus, De obsidione Constantinopolitana sub Heraclio imperatore, Analecta Avarica* (Krakow, 1900), 2–24; var. lect. 24–37; trans. F. Makk, *Traduction et commentaire de l'homélie écrite probablement par Théodore le*

Syncelle sur le siège de Constantinople en 626, Opuscula Byzantina III (Szeged, 1975), 9–71

Theodosios, *De situ terrae sanctae*. Ed. P. Geyer, *Itineraria et alia Geographica*, CCL 175 (Turnhout, 1965)

Theodotos of Ankyra, *Homily I, On the Nativity of the Lord* (*CPG* 6125, *BHG* 1901). Ed. E. Schwartz, ACO I. I. 2, 80–90; PG 77, 1349–69

Theodotos of Ankyra, *Homily III, Against Nestorios* (*CPG* 6127, *BHG* 932p). Ed. E. Schwartz, ACO I. I. 2, 71–3

Theodotos of Ankyra, *Homily on the Holy Virgin and on Symeon* (*CPG* 6128, *BHG* 1966). PG 77 1389–1412

(ps-)Theodotos of Ankyra, *On the Virgin Mary and on the Nativity of the Lord* (*CPG* 6136, *BHG* 1143 g). Ed. Jugie 1926 (1990), 318–35

Theophanes Confessor, *Chronicle*. Ed. C. de Boor, *Chronographia* (Leipzig, 1883; repr. Hildesheim, 1963); trans. C. Mango and R. Scott, *The Chronicle of Theophanes Confessor. Byzantine and Near Eastern History, A.D. 284–813* (Oxford, 1997)

Theophylact Simocatta, *History*. Ed. C. de Boor, *Theophylacti Simocattae Historia* (Leipzig, 1887); emend. P. Wirth (Stuttgart, 1972); trans. M. and M. Whitby, *The History of Theophylact Simocatta* (Oxford, 1986)

Theoteknos of Livias, *Homily on the Dormition* (*CPG* 7418, *BHG* 1083 n). Ed. Wenger 1955, 272–91; trans. Daley 1998, 71–81

Transitus of (ps-)John the Evangelist (*CANT* 101, *BHG* 1055–6). Ed. C. Tischendorf, *Apocalypses apocryphae* (Leipzig, 1866; repr. Hildesheim, 1966), 95–112; trans. James 1989, 201–9; Elliott 1993 (2004), 701–8

Triodion katanyktikon = Triodion katanyktikon, periechon apasan tēn anēkousan autō akolouthina tēs hagias kai megalēs tessarakostēs (Τριώδιον κατανυκτικόν, περιέχον ἄπασαν τὴν ἀνήκουσαν αὐτῷ ἀκολουθίαν τῆς ἁγίας καὶ μεγάλης Τεσσαρακοστῆς) (Rome, 1879); trans. Mother Mary and Archimandrite Kallistos Ware, *The Lenten Triodion* (London and Boston, 1978)

Typikon of the Great Church. Ed. and trans. J. Mateos, *Le Typikon de la Grande Église: Ms. Sainte-Croix no. 40, Xe siècle*, 2 vols. (Rome, 1962–3)

Secondary Sources

Agapitos, Panagiotis A. (2003). 'Ancient Models and Novel Mixtures: The Concept of Genre in Byzantine Funerary Literature from Patriarch Photios to Eustathios of Thessalonike', in G. Nagy and A. Stavrakopoulou, eds., *Modern Greek Literature: Critical Essays* (New York and London), 5–23

(2008). 'Literary Criticism', in Jeffreys, Haldon and Cormack 2008, 77–85

Alexander, Paul J. (1985). *The Byzantine Apocalyptic Tradition* (Berkeley, Los Angeles and London)

Alexiou, Margaret (1974). *The Ritual Lament in Greek Tradition* (Cambridge); rev. ed. with D. Yatromanolakis and P. Roilos (Lanham, MD, Boulder, CO, New York and Oxford, 2002)

(1975). 'The Lament of the Virgin in Byzantine Literature and Modern Greek Folk Song', *BMGS* 1, 111–40

(2002). *After Antiquity: Greek Language, Myth and Metaphor* (Ithaca, NY)

Allen, Pauline (1996). 'Severus of Antioch and the Homily: The End of the Beginning?', in P. Allen and E. Jeffreys, eds., *The Sixth Century: End or Beginning?*, Byzantina Australiensia 10 (Brisbane), 163–75

(1998). 'The Sixth-Century Greek Homily: A Reassessment', in Allen and Cunningham 1998, 201–25

(2007). 'The Greek Homiletic Tradition of the Feast of the Hypapante: The Place of Sophronios of Jerusalem', in Belke, Kislinger, Külzer and Stassinopoulou 2007, 1–12

(2011). 'Portrayals of Mary in Greek Homiletic Literature (6th–7th Centuries)', in Brubaker and Cunningham 2011, 69–88

Allen, Pauline and Cunningham, Mary B., eds. (1998). *Preacher and Audience: Studies in Early Christian and Byzantine Homiletics* (Leiden, Boston and Cologne)

Allen, Pauline and Hayward, C.T.R. (2004). *Severus of Antioch* (London and New York)

Allen, Pauline, Külzer, Andreas, and Peltomaa, Leena Mari, eds. (2015). *Presbeia Theotokou: The Intercessory Role of Mary across Times and Places in Byzantium (4th–9th Century)* (Vienna)

Alwan, K. (1986). 'Bibliographie générale raisonnée de Jacques de Saroug', *ParOr* 13, 313–84

Andreopoulos. Andreas (2016). 'The Dormition of the Theotokos', *Analogia: The Pemptousia Journal for Theologial Studies* 1, 77–86

Antonopoulou, Theodora (1997). *The Homilies of the Emperor Leo VI* (Leiden, New York and Cologne)

(1998). 'The Homiletic Activity in Constantinople around 900', in M. Cunningham and P. Allen, eds., *Preacher and Audience: Studies in Early Christian and Byzantine Homiletics* (Leiden), 317–48

(2004). 'A Kanon on Saint Nicholas by Manuel Philes', *REB* 62, 197–213

(2010). 'On the Reception of Homilies and Hagiography in Byzantium: the Recited Metrical Prefaces', in A. Rhoby and E. Schiffer, eds., *Imitatio – Aemulatio – Variatio. Akten des Internationalen Wissenschaftlichen Symposions zur byzantinischen Sprache und Literatur (Wien, 22.–25. Oktober 2008)* (Vienna), 57–79

(2011). 'A Survey of Tenth-Century Homiletic Literature', *Parekbolai* 1, 7–36

(2013). 'Byzantine Homiletics: An Introduction to the Field and Its Study', in K. Spronk, G. Rouwhorst and S. Royé, eds., *Challenges and Perspectives: A Catalogue of Byzantine Manuscripts in Their Liturgical Context, Subsidia* 1 (Turnhout), 183–98

Arentzen, Thomas (2013). '"Your Virginity Shines": The Attraction of the Virgin in the Annunciation Hymn by Romanos the Melodist', in M. Vinzent, ed., *SP* 68 (Leuven, Paris and Walpole, MA), 125–32

(2014). *Virginity Recast. Romanos and the Mother of God* (publ. PhD thesis, Lund University)

(2016). 'Voices Interwoven: Refrains and Vocal Participation in the Kontakia', *JÖB* 66, 1–10

(2017). *The Virgin in Song: Mary and the Poetry of Romanos the Melodist* (Philadelphia, PA)

(2018). 'The Virgin in Hades', in G. Ekroth and I. Nilsson, eds., *Round Trip to Hades in the Eastern Mediterranean Tradition. Visits to the Underworld from Antiquity to Byzantium* (Leiden and Boston), 287–303

(2019). 'The Dialogue of Annunciation: Germanos of Constantinople versus Romanos the Melode', in Arentzen and Cunningham 2019, 151–69

(2021). 'The *Chora* of God: Approaching the Outskirts of Mariology in the Akathistos', *Journal of Orthodox Christian Studies* 4 (Autumn, 2021)

Arentzen, Thomas and Cunningham, Mary B., eds. (2019). *The Reception of the Virgin in Byzantium. Marian Narratives in Texts and Images* (Cambridge)

Arentzen, Thomas and Krueger, Derek (2016). 'Romanos in Manuscript: Some Observations on the Patmos Kontakarion', delivered orally at the 23rd International Congress of Byzantine Studies, Belgrade, 23 Aug. 2016

Atanassova, Antonia (2015). 'The Theme of Marian Mediation in Cyril of Alexandria's Ephesian Writings', in Allen, Külzer and Peltomaa 2015, 109–13

Aubineau, Michel (1969). 'Une homélie grecque inédite attribuée à Théodote d'Ancyre sur le baptême du Seigneur', *ΔΙΑΚΟΝΙΑ ΠΙΣΤΕΩΣ (Mélanges J. A. de Aldama)* (Granada), 5–30

(1972). 'Bilan d'une enquête sur les homélies de Proclus de Constantinople', *REG* 85, 572–96 = Aubineau 1988, ch. 26

(1978). *Les homélies festales d'Hésychius de Jérusalem*, vol. 1: *Les homélies I–XV*, SubsHag 59 (Brussels)

(1988). *Chrysostome, Sévérien, Proclus, Hésychius, et alii: patristique et hagiographie grecques: inventaires de manuscrits, textes inédits, traductions, études* (London)

Auzépy, Marie-France (1990). 'La destruction de l'icône du Christ de la Chalcé par Léon III: propagande ou réalité?', *Byzantion* 60, 445–92

(1995a). 'L'évolution de l'attitude face au miracle à Byzance (VIIe–IXe siècles)', *Miracles, prodiges et merveilles au Moyen Age, XXVe Congrès de la S.H.M.E.S. (Orléans, juin 1994)* (Paris), 31–46

(1995b). 'La carrière d'André de Crète', *BZ* 88, 1–12

(2001). 'Les Isauriens et l'espace sacré: l'église et les réliques', in Kaplan 2001, 13–24

Avdokhin, Arkadiy (2016). 'The Quest for Orthopraxy. Narrating and Negotiating Christian Prayers and Hymns in Late Antiquity' (unpubl. PhD thesis, King's College London)

Avner, Rina (1999). 'Birth Pangs on the Bethlehem Road' (in Hebrew), *Judea and Samaria Research Studies: Proceedings of the Eighth Annual Meeting 1998 (Kedumim-Ariel)*, 155–60; English summary, xviii–xix

238   *Bibliographies*

(2011). 'The Initial Tradition of the Theotokos at the Kathisma: Earliest Celebrations and the Calendar', in Brubaker and Cunningham 2011, 9–29

Bagatti, B. , Piccirillo, M. and Prodomo, A. , OFM (1975). *New Discoveries at the Tomb of Virgin Mary at Gethsemane*, Studium Biblicum Franciscanum, Collectio Minor 17 (Jerusalem)

Bagnoli, Martina, ed. (2010). *Treasures of Heaven: Saints, Relics and Devotion in Medieval Europe* (New Haven, CT)

Baldovin, John F. (1987). *The Urban Character of Christian Worship: The Origins, Development, and Meaning of Stational Liturgy*, OCA 228 (Rome)

Balić, C. (1948). *Testimonia de Assumptione Beatae Virginis Mariae ex omnibus saeculis. Pars prior: ex aetate ante concilium tridentine*, vol. 1 (Rome)

Baltoyanni, Chryssanthi (2000). 'The Mother of God in Portable Icons', in Vassilaki 2000, 139–53

Banev, Krastu (2014). '"Myriad of Names to Represent Her Nobleness": the Church and the Virgin Mary in the Psalms and Hymns of Byzantium', in J. A. Mihoc and L. Aldea, eds., *A Celebration of Living Theology: A Festscrift in Honour of Andrew Louth* (London, New Delhi, New York and Sydney), 75–103

Barber, Charles (1994). 'The Monastic Typikon for Art Historians', in M. E. Mullett and A. Kirby, eds., *The Theotokos Evergetis and Eleventh-Century Monasticism*, BBTT 6.1 (Belfast), 198–214

(2000). 'Early Representations of the Mother of God', in Vassilaki 2000, 253–61

(2002). *Figure and Likeness: On the Limits of Representation in Byzantine Iconoclasm* (Princeton)

Barker, Margaret (1991). *The Gate of Heaven: The History and Symbolism of the Temple in Jerusalem* (London)

(2004). *Temple Theology: An Introduction* (London)

(2011). 'Wisdom Imagery and the Mother of God', in Brubaker and Cunningham 2011, 91–108

Barkhuizen, Jan H. (1998). 'Proclus of Constantinople: A Popular Preacher in Fifth-Century Constantinople', in Allen and Cunningham 1998, 179–200

(2001). *Proclus, Bishop of Constantinople, Homilies on the Life of Christ*, Early Christian Studies 1 (Brisbane)

(2012). *Romanos the Melodist: Poet and Preacher* (Durbanville, S. Africa)

Barré, H. (1939). 'La royauté de Marie pendant les neufs premiers siècles', *Recherches de science religieuse* 29, 303–34

Baumstark, Anton (1920). 'Ein frühchristliches Theotokion in mehrsprachiger Überlieferung und verwandte Texte des ambrosianischen Ritus', *Oriens Christianus* 9, 36–61

Baun, Jane (2004). 'Discussing Mary's Humanity in Medieval Byzantium', in Swanson 2004, 63–72

(2007). *Tales from Another Byzantium: Celestial Journey and Local Community in the Medieval Greek Apocrypha* (Cambridge)

(2011). 'Apocalyptic Panagia: Some Byways of Marian Revelation', in Brubaker and Cunningham 2011, 199–219

Baynes, Norman (1949). 'The Supernatural Defenders of Constantinople', *AB* 67, 165–77

(1955). 'The Finding of the Virgin's Robe', in N. Baynes, *Byzantine Studies and Other Essays* (London), 240–7

Beattie, Tina (2002). *God's Mother, Eve's Advocate* (London and New York)

Beck, Hans-Georg (1959). *Kirche und theologische Literatur im byzantinischen Reich* (Munich)

Beeley, Christopher A. (2008). *Gregory of Nazianzus on the Trinity and the Knowledge of God: In Your Light Shall We See Light* (Oxford)

Belke, K., Kislinger, E., Külzer, A. and Stassinopoulou, M. A., eds. (2007). *Byzantina Mediterranea: Festschrift für Johannes Koder zum 65. Geburtstag* (Vienna, Cologne and Weimar)

Betancourt, Roland (2020). *Byzantine Intersectionality: Sexuality, Gender and Race in the Middle Ages* (Princeton, NJ, and Oxford)

Beyers, Rita (2011). 'La règle de Marie: caractère littéraire et inspiration monastique', *Apocrypha* 22, 49–86

(2012). 'The Transmission of Marian Apocrypha in the Latin Middle Ages', *Apocrypha* 23, 117–40

Blowers, Paul M. and Martens, Peter W., eds. (2019). *The Oxford Handbook of Early Christian Biblical Interpretation* (Oxford)

Bodin, Helena (2020). '"Paradise in a Cave": The Garden of the Theotokos in Byzantine Hymnography', in H. Bodin and R. Hedlund, eds., *Byzantine Gardens and Beyond*, Studia Byzantina Upsaliensia 13 (Uppsala), 129–47

Bolman, Elizabeth (2005). 'The Enigmatic Coptic Galaktotrophousa and the Cult of the Virgin Mary in Egypt', in Vassilaki 2005, 13–22

Booth, Phil (2015). 'On the *Life of the Virgin* Attributed to Maximus Confessor', *JTS*, n.s. 66, 149–203

Booth, Phil, Dal Santo, Matthew and Sarris, Peter, eds. (2011). *An Age of Saints? Power, Conflict, and Dissent in Early Medieval Christianity* (Leiden and Boston)

Boss, Sarah Jane, ed. (2007). *Mary: The Complete Resource* (London and New York)

Botte, B. (1932). *Les origines de la Noël et de l'Épiphanie*, Textes et études liturgiques (Louvain)

(1949). 'Le lectionnaire arménien et la fête de la Théotokos à Jérusalem au 5e siècle', *Sacris Erudiri* 2, 111–22

Bouby, E. (1902). 'Les origines de la fête de la Présentation', *Revue Augustinienne* (December), 581–94

Bradshaw, Paul F. (2002). *The Search for the Origins of Christian Worship. Sources and Methods for the Study of Early Liturgy* (London)

Brakke, David (1995). *Athanasius and Asceticism* (Baltimore and London)

Breck, John (2008). *The Shape of Biblical Language: Chiasmus in the Scriptures and Beyond* (Crestwood, NY)

Briere, Elizabeth A. (1983). 'Scripture in Hymnography: A Study in Some Feasts of the Orthodox Church' (unpubl. DPhil thesis, Oxford University)

Brock, Sebastian P. (1983). 'Dialogue Hymns of the Syriac Churches', *Sobornost incorporating Eastern Churches Review* 5:2,35–45

(1985). *The Luminous Eye* (Rome)

(1987). 'Dramatic Dialogue Poems', in H. J. W. Drijvers, R. Lavenant, C. Molenberg and G. J. Reinink, eds., *IV Symposium Syriacum. Literary Genres in Syriac Literature*, OCA 229 (Rome), 135–47

(1989). 'From Ephrem to Romanos', in E. A. Livingstone, ed., *SP* 20 (Leuven), 139–51 = Brock 1999, ch. 4

(1991). 'Syriac Dispute Poems: The Various Types', *Dispute Poems and Dialogues, Orientalia Lovaniensia Analecta* 42 (Leuven), 109–19 = Brock 1999, ch. 7

(1994). *Bride of Light: Hymns on Mary from the Syriac Churches, Mōrān 'Eth'ō* 6 (Kottayam, India, 1994; rev. ed. Piscataway, NJ, 2010) [Although the two editions do not differ except for the addition of a preface in the 2010 publication, page numbers vary. I have used the 2010 edition in my references throughout the present book.]

(1999). *From Ephrem to Romanos: Interactions between Syriac and Greek in Late Antiquity* (Aldershot and Brookfield, VT)

(2006). 'The Genealogy of the Virgin Mary in Sinai Syr. 16', *Scrinium* 2, 58–71

(2011). *Mary and Joseph, and Other Dialogue Poems on Mary*, Texts from Christian Late Antiquity 8 (Piscataway, NJ)

Brown, Peter (1971). 'The Rise and Function of the Holy Man in Late Antiquity', *JRS* 61, 80–101

(1981). *The Cult of the Saints: Its Rise and Function in Latin Christianity* (London)

Brown, R. E., Donfried, K. P., Fitzmyer, J. A. and Reumann, J., eds. (1978). *Mary in the New Testament* (New York and Mahwah, NJ)

Browning, Robert (1962). 'The Patriarchal School at Constantinople in the Twelfth Century', *Byzantion* 32:1, 167–202

(1981). 'The "Low Level" Saint's Life in the Early Byzantine World', in S. Hackel, ed., *The Byzantine Saint* (London, 1981), 117–27

Brubaker, Leslie (1998). 'Icons before Iconoclasm?', *Settimane di studio del Centro italiano di studi sull' alto medioevo* 45, 1215–54

(2001). 'Topography and the Creation of Public Space in Early Medieval Constantinople', in M. De Jong and F. Theuws, with C. van Rhijn, eds., *Topographies of Power in the Early Middle Ages* (Leiden, Boston and Cologne), 31–43

(2019). 'The Virgin at Daphni', in Arentzen and Cunningham 2019, 120–48

Brubaker, Leslie and Cunningham, Mary B. (2007). 'Byzantine Veneration of the Theotokos: Icons, Relics, and Eighth-Century Homilies', in H. Amirav and B. ter Haar Romeny, eds., *From Rome to Constantinople. Studies in Honour of Averil Cameron*, Late Antique History and Religion 1 (Leuven, Paris and Dudley, MA), 235–50

eds. (2011). *The Cult of the Mother of God in Byzantium: Texts and Images* (Farnham and Burlington, VT)

Brubaker, Leslie and Haldon, John (2001). *Byzantium in the Iconoclast Era (ca. 680–850): The Sources*, Birmingham Byzantine and Ottoman Monographs 7 (Aldershot and Burlington, VT)

(2011). *Byzantium in the Iconoclast Era, c. 680–850: A History* (Cambridge)

Brubaker, Leslie and Smith, Julia M. H., eds. (2004). *Gender in the Early Medieval World: East and West, 300–900* (Cambridge)

Bruyn, Theodore de (2015). 'Appeals to Intercessions of Mary in Greek Liturgical and Paraliturgical Texts from Egypt', in Allen, Külzer and Peltomaa 2015, 115–29

Bryer, A. A. M. and Herrin, Judith, eds. (1977). *Iconoclasm: Papers Given at the Ninth Spring Symposium of Byzantine Studies, University of Birmingham, March 1975* (Birmingham)

Bucur, B. G. (2007). 'Exegesis of Biblical Theophanies in Byzantine Hymnography: Rewritten Bible?', *Theological Studies* 68, 92–112

Bynum, Caroline Walker (1982). *Jesus as Mother: Studies in the Spirituality of the High Middle Ages* (Berkeley, CA)

Calabuig, I. M., OSM (2000). 'The Liturgical Cult of Mary in East and West', in Chupungco 2000, vol. 5, 219–97

Cameron, Averil (1975). 'The Byzantine Sources of Gregory of Tours', *JTS*, n.s. 26, 421–26

(1978). 'The Theotokos in Sixth-Century Constantinople: A City Finds Its Symbol', *JTS*, n.s. 29, 79–108

(1979a). 'Images of Authority: Elites and Icons in Late Sixth-Century Byzantium', *Past and Present* 84 (1979), 2–35

(1979b). 'The Virgin's Robe: An Episode in the History of Early Seventh-Century Constantinople', *Byzantion* 49, 42–56

(1980). 'The Artistic Patronage of Justin II', *Byzantion* 50, 62–84

(1983). 'The History of the Image of Edessa: The Telling of a Story', in C. Mango and O. Pritsak, eds., *Okeanos: Essays Presented to Ihor Ševčenko on his Sixtieth Birthday by his Colleagues and Students*, Harvard Ukrainian Studies 7 (Cambridge, MA), 80–94

(1991a). *Christianity and the Rhetoric of Empire: The Development of Christian Discourse* (Berkeley, Los Angeles and Oxford)

(1991b). 'Disputations, Polemical Literature and the Formation of Opinion', in A. Cameron, 'Byzantines and Jews: Some Recent Work on Early Byzantium', in G. J. Reinink and H. L. J. Vanstiphout, eds., *Dispute Poems and Dialogues in the Ancient and Medieval Near East*, Orientalia Lovaniensia Analecta 42 (Leuven) 91–108 = A. Cameron, *Changing Cultures in Early Byzantium* (Aldershot, 1996), ch. 3

(1992). 'The Language of Images: The Rise of Icons and Christian Representation', in D. Wood, ed., *The Church and the Arts*, Studies in Church History 28 (Oxford), 1–42

(2004). 'The Virgin in Late Antiquity', in Swanson 2004, 1–21

(2005). 'Introduction', in Vassilaki 2005, xxvii–xxxii

(2011). 'Introduction: The Mother of God in Byzantium: Relics, Icons, Texts', in Brubaker and Cunningham 2011, 1–5

(2014). *Dialoguing in Late Antiquity* (Washington, DC)

Cameron, Averil and Hoyland, Robert G., eds. (2011). *Doctrine and Debate in the East Christian World, 300–1500* (Farnham and Burlington, VT)

Capelle, Dom B. (1943). 'La fête de la Vierge à Jérusalem au ve siècle', *Mus* 56, 1–33

(1954). 'Typologie mariale chez les Pères et dans la liturgie', *Les questions liturgiques et paroissiales* 35 (Louvain), 109–21

Carlton, C. Clark (2006). '"The Temple that Held God": Byzantine Marian Hymnography and the Christ of Nestorius', *SVTQ* 50:1–2, 99–125

Caro, Roberto, SJ (1971–3). *La homilética Mariana griega en el siglo V*, 3 vols. (Dayton, OH)

Carpenter, Marjorie (1932). 'The Paper that Romanos Swallowed', *Speculum* 7:1, 3–22

Carruthers, Mary J. (1990) *The Book of Memory: A Study of Memory in Medieval Culture* (Cambridge, 2nd ed., 2008)

Chestnut, Roberta C. (1976). *Three Monophysite Christologies: Severus of Antioch, Philoxenus of Mabbug and Jacob of Sarug* (Oxford)

Chevalier, C. (1937). 'Les trilogies homilétiques dans l'élaboration des fêtes mariales, 650–850', *Gregorianum* 18,361–78

Chirat, Henri (1945). 'Les origines de la fête du 21 novembre: St Jean Chrysostom et S. André de Crète', *Psomia Diaphora, Mélanges E. Podechard* (Lyons), 121–33

Cholij, Roman (2002). *Theodore the Stoudite: The Ordering of Holiness* (Oxford)

Chupungco, A. J., OSB, ed. (2000). *Handbook for Liturgical Studies,* vol. 5: *Liturgical Time and Space* (Collegeville, MN)

Clark, Francis (1987). *The Pseudo-Gregorian Dialogues*, 2 vols. (Leiden)

Clayton, Mary (1990). *The Cult of the Virgin Mary in Anglo-Saxon England*, Cambridge Studies in Anglo-Saxon England 2 (Cambridge)

(1998). *The Apocryphal Gospels of Mary in Anglo-Saxon England*, Cambridge Studies in Anglo-Saxon England 6 (Cambridge)

Clivaz, C., Dettwiler, A., Devillers, L. and Norelli, E., with Bertho, B., eds. (2011). *Infancy Gospels: Stories and Identities* (Tübingen)

Conomos, Dimitri (1984). *Byzantine Hymnography and Byzantine Chant* (Brookline, MA)

Constantinou, Stavroula and Meyer, Mati, eds. (2019). *Emotions and Gender in Byzantine Culture* (Cham, Switzerland)

Constas, Nicholas (1995). 'Weaving the Body of God: Proclus of Constantinople, the Theotokos, and the Loom of the Flesh', *JECS* 3.2, 169–94

(2003). *Proclus of Constantinople and the Cult of the Virgin in Late Antiquity: Homilies 1–5, Texts and Translations* (Leiden)

(2005). Review of Peltomaa 2001, *SVTQ* 49, no. 3,355–8

Constas, Fr. Maximos (formerly Nicholas) (2014). *The Art of Seeing. Paradox and Perception in Orthodox Hymnography* (Alhambra, CA)

(2016). 'Poetry and Painting in the Middle Byzantine Period. A Bilateral Icon from Kastoria and the *Stavrotheotokia* of Joseph the Hymnographer', in S.E. J. Gerstel, ed., *Cultural and Political Agency in the Medieval and Early Modern Mediterranean* (Turnhout), 2–22

(2019). 'The Story of an Edition: Antoine Wenger and John Geometres' *Life of the Virgin Mary*', in Arentzen and Cunningham 2019, 324–40

Cooper, Kate (1998). 'Contesting the Nativity: Wives, Virgins, and Pulcheria's *Imitatio Mariae*', *Scottish Journal of Religious Studies* 19, 31–43

Cormack, Robin (1985). *Writing in Gold. Byzantine Society and Its Icons* (London)

Cothenet, E. (1961). 'Marie dans les Apocryphes', in H. Du Manoir, SJ, ed., *Maria: Études sur la Sainte Vierge* 6 (Paris), 71–156

Cullmann, Oscar (1991). Protevangelion of James', in W. Schneemelcher, ed., *New Testament Apocrypha*, vol. 1: *Gospels and Related Writings* (Cambridge and Louisville, KY), 421–39

Cunningham, Mary B. (1990). 'Preaching and the Community', in R. Morris, ed., *Church and People in Byzantium* (Birmingham), 29–47

(1996). 'The Sixth Century: A Turning-Point for Byzantine Homiletics?', in P. Allen and E. Jeffreys, eds., *The Sixth Century: End or Beginning?*, Byzantina Australiensia 10 (Brisbane, 1996), 176–86

(1999). 'Polemic and Exegesis: Anti-Judaic Invective in Byzantine Homiletics', *Sobornost incorporating Eastern Churches Review* 21:2, 46–68

(2003). 'Dramatic Device or Didactic Tool? The Function of Dialogue in Byzantine Preaching', in E. Jeffreys, ed., *Rhetoric in Byzantium* (Aldershot), 101–13.

(2004). 'The Meeting of the Old and the New: The Typology of Mary the Theotokos in Byzantine Homilies and Hymns', in R. N. Swanson, ed., *The Church and Mary*, Studies in Church History 39 (Woodbridge, Suffolk), 52–62

(2006). '"All-Holy Infant": Byzantine and Western Views on the Conception of the Virgin Mary', *SVTQ* 50:1–2, 127–48

(2008a). 'The Reception of Romanos in Middle Byzantine Homiletics and Hymnography', *DOP* 62, 251–60

(2008b). *Wider Than Heaven: Eighth-Century Homilies on the Mother of God* (Crestwood, NY)

(2008c). 'Homilies', in Jeffreys, Haldon and Cormack 2008, 872–81

(2010). 'Byzantine Views of God and the Universe' in James 2010, 149–60

(2011a). 'The Use of the *Protevangelion of James* in Eighth-Century Homilies on the Mother of God', in Brubaker and Cunningham 2011, 163–78

(2011b). 'Messages in Context: The Reading of Sermons in Byzantine Churches and Monasteries', in A. Lymberopoulou, ed., *Images of the Byzantine World: Visions, Messages and Meanings: Studies Presented to Leslie Brubaker* (Aldershot), 83–98

(2012). 'The Kanon and the Theotokos: The Development of a Middle Byzantine Hermeneutic', communication delivered at the Byzantine Studies Conference, Boston 2012 (unpubl.)

(2015). 'Mary as Intercessor in Constantinople During the Iconoclast Period', in Allen, Külzer and Peltomaa 2015, 139–52

(2016). 'The *Life* of the Virgin Mary according to Middle Byzantine Preachers and Hagiographers: Changing Contexts and Perspectives', *Apocrypha* 27, 137–59

(2019). 'The *Life of the Theotokos* by Epiphanios of Kallistratos: A Monastic Approach to an Apocryphal Story', in Arentzen and Cunningham 2019, 309–23

Dagens, C. (1981). 'Grégoire le Grand et le monde oriental', *Rivista di storia e letteratura religiosa* 17, 243–52

Dagron, Gilbert (1992). 'L'hagiographie en question, VIe–XIe siècle', *DOP* 46, 59–68.

Daley, Brian E., SJ (1998). *On the Dormition of Mary: Early Patristic Homilies* (Crestwood, NY)

(2006). *Gregory of Nazianzus* (London and New York)

(2015). 'Antioch and Alexandria: Christology as Reflection on God's Presence in History', in F. A. Murphy, ed., *The Oxford Handbook of Christology* (Oxford and New York), 121–38

(2018). *God Visible: Patristic Christology Reconsidered* (Oxford)

Dal Santo, Matthew (2011). 'Text, Image and the "Visionary Body" in Early Byzantine Hagiography: Incubation and the Rise of the Christian Image Cult', *Journal of Late Antiquity* 4, 31–54

(2012). *Debating the Saints' Cults in the Age of Gregory the Great* (Oxford)

Daniélou, Jean (1950). *Sacramentum futuri: Études sur les origines de la typologie biblique* (Paris)

(1956). *The Bible and the Liturgy* (Notre Dame, IN)

(1960). *From Shadows to Reality: Studies in the Biblical Typology of the Fathers* (London)

Darrouzès, Jean (1987). 'Deux traités inédits du patriarche Germain', *REB* 45, 5–13

D'Avray, David (2001). *Medieval Marriage Sermons: Mass Communication in a Culture without Print* (Oxford)

Delehaye, Hippolyte (1921). *Les passions des martyrs et les genres littéraires* (Brussels)

(1927). *Les légendes hagiographiques* (Brussels)

Dell'Acqua, Francesca (2019). 'Mary as "Scala Caelestis" in Eighth-Century Italy', in Arentzen and Cunningham 2019, 235–56

(2020). *Iconophilia: Politics, Religion, Preaching, and the Use of Images in Rome, c. 680–880* (London and New York)

Della Dora, Veronica (2016). *Landscape, Nature and the Sacred in Byzantium* (Cambridge)

Demetracopoulos, Photios A. (1979). 'The Exegeses of the Canons in the Twelfth Century as School Texts', *Diptycha* 1, 143–57

Demoen, Kristoffel (2001). 'Classicizing Elements in John Geometres' Letters about His Garden', in *Πρακτικὰ ΙΑ Διεθνοῦς Συνεδρίου Κλασσικῶν Σπουδῶν, Καβάλα 24–30 Αὐγούστου 1999*, 3 vols. (Athens, 2001), vol. I, 215–30

Demus, Otto (1948). *Byzantine Mosaic Decoration: Aspects of Monumental Art in Byzantium* (London and Henley)

Déroche, Vincent (1991). 'La polémique anti-judaique aux VIe et VIIe siècles. Un momento inédit, les Kephalaia', TM 11 (Paris), 275–311

    (1994). *L'apologie contre les Juifs de Léontios de Néapolis*, TM 12 (Paris), 45–104

Detorakis, T. (1987–9),'Ἀνέκδοτα μεγαλυνάρια τοῦ Μεγάλου Σαββάτου', *EEBS* 47, 221–46

Dobschütz, E. von (1899). *Christusbilder: Untersuchungen zur christlichen Legende*, TU 18 (Leipzig)

    (1912). *Das Decretum Galasianum de libris recipiendis et non recipiendis*, TU 38.4 (Leipzig)

Dölger, Franz (1950). 'Iohannes von Euboia', *AB* 68 = *Mélanges P. Peeters II* (1950), 5–26

Downey, Glanville (1961). *A History of Antioch in Syria: from Seleucus to the Arab Conquest* (Princeton)

Dräseke, J. (1895). 'Der Mönch und Presbyter Epiphanios', *BZ* 6,346–62

Duff, David, ed. (2000). *Modern Genre Theories* (Harlow)

Ebersolt, Jean (1921). *Sanctuaires de Byzances: Recherches sur les anciens trésors des églises de Constantinople* (Paris)

Edelman, D. V. (2014). *The Origins of the 'Second' Temple: Persian Imperial Policy and the Rebuilding of Jerusalem* (rev. ed. Oxford and New York)

Efthymiades, Stephanos, ed. (2011). *The Ashgate Research Companion to Byzantine Hagiography*, vol. 1: *Periods and Places* (Farnham and Burlington, VT)

    (2014). *The Ashgate Research Companion to Byzantine Hagiography*, vol. 2: *Genres and Contexts* (Farnham and Burlington, VT)

Ehrhard, Albert (1936–52). *Überlieferung und Bestand der hagiographischen und homiletischen Literatur der griechischen Kirche von den Anfängen bis zum Ende des 16. Jahrhunderts, I: Die Überlieferung, Texte und Untersuchungen zur Geschichte der altchristlichen Literatur*, 3 vols. (Leipzig and Berlin)

Elliott, J. K., ed. (1993). *The Apocryphal New Testament: A Collection of Apocryphal Christian Literature in an English Translation based on M. R. James* (Oxford; repr. 2004)

Elm, Susanna (2012). *Sons of Hellenism, Fathers of the Church: Emperor Julian, Gregory of Nazianzus, and the Vision of Rome* (Berkeley, Los Angeles, CA, and London)

Eriksen, Uffe Holmsgaard (2013). *Drama in the Kontakia of Romanos the Melodist: A Narratological Analysis of Four Kontakia* (publ. PhD thesis, Aarhus University)

Esbroeck, Michel van (1968–9). 'La lettre de l'empereur Justinien sur l'Annonciation et la Noël en 561', *AB* 86 (1968), 351 = 71; correction in M. van Esbroeck, 'Encore la lettre de Justinien. Sa date: 560 et non 561', *AB* 87 (1969), 442–4

    (1981). 'Les textes littéraires sur l'assomption avant le Xe siècle', in F. Bovon, ed., *Les Actes apocryphes des apôtres* (Geneva), 265–85 = van Esbroeck 1995, ch. 1

    (1988a). 'Le culte de la vierge de Jérusalem à Constantinople aux 6e–7e siècles', *REB* 46 (1988), 181–90 = van Esbroeck 1995, ch. 10

(1988b). 'Euthyme l'Hagiorite: le traducteur et ses traductions', *Revue des Études Géorgiens et Caucasiennes* 4, 73–107

(1995). *Aux origines de la Dormition de la Vierge* (Aldershot and Brookfield, VT)

Eustratiades, Sophronios (1930). *Ή Θεοτόκος ἐν τῇ ὑμνογραφίᾳ* (Paris)

(1931–33) "Ὁ ἅγιος Ἰωάννης ὁ Δαμασκήνος καὶ τὰ ποιητικὰ αὐτοῦ ἔργα', *Nea Sion* 26 (1931): 385–401, 497–512, 530–8, 610–17, 666–81, 721–36; 27 (1932), 28–44, 111–23, 165–77, 216–24, 329–53, 415–22, 450–72, 514–34, 570–85, 644–64, 698–719; 28 (1933), 11–25, 28

(1937–38). "Ή ἀκολουθία τοῦ Μεγάλου Σαββάτου καὶ τὰ μεγαληνάρια τοῦ Ἐπιταφίου', *Nea Sion* 32 (1937), 16–23, 145–52, 209–26, 273–88, 337–53, 465–80, 529–45, 593–608, 657–73; 33 (1938), 19–28, 370–7, 433–52

Evangelatou, Maria (2014). 'Threads of Power: Clothing Symbolism, Human Salvation and Female Identity in the Illustrated Homilies by Iakobos of Kokkinobaphos', *DOP* 69, 59–116

(2019). 'Krater of Nectar and Altar of the Bread of Life: The Theotokos as Provider of the Eucharist in Byzantine Culture', in Arentzen and Cunningham 2019, 77–119

Evans, Helen C. and Wixom, William D., eds. (1997). *The Glory of Byzantium. Art and Culture of the Middle Byzantine Era, A.D. 843–1261* (New York)

Finnegan, Ruth H. (1988). *Literacy and Orality: Studies in the Technology of Communication* (Oxford and New York)

Fischer, E. H. (1950). 'Gregor der Grosse und Byzanz', *Zeitschrift der Savigny-Stiftung für Rechtsgeschichte. Kanonistische Abteilung* 67, 15–144

Fisher, Elizabeth A. (2011). 'Michael Psellos on the "Usual Miracle" at Blachernai, the Law, and Neoplatonism', in D. Sullivan, E. A. Fisher and S. Papaioannou, eds., *Byzantine Religious Culture: Studies in Honor of Alice-Mary Talbot* (Leiden), 187–204

Fletcher, R. A. (1958). 'Three Early Byzantine Hymns and Their Place in the Liturgy of the Church of Constantinople', *BZ* 51, 53–65

(1962). 'Celebrations at Jerusalem on March 25th in the Sixth Century AD', F. L. Cross, ed., *SP* 5 (Berlin), 30–4

Follieri, Henrica (1960–6). *Initia hymnorum ecclesiae graecae*, ST 211–5, 5 vols. (Vatican City)

Förster, H. (1995). 'Zur ältesten Überlieferung der marianischen Antiphon "Sub tuum praesidium"', *Biblos* 44, 183–92

(2005). 'Die ältesten marianische Antiphon ein Fehldatierung? Überlegungen zum "ältesten Beleg" des Sub tuum praesidium', *Journal of Coptic Studies* 7, 99–109

Foucault, Michel (1989). *The Order of Things: An Archaeology of the Human Sciences* (London and New York)

Frank, Georgia (2000). *The Memory of the Eyes: Pilgrims to Living Saints in Christian Late Antiquity* (Berkeley and London)

(2005). 'Dialogue and Deliberation: The Sensory Self in the Hymns of Romanos the Melodist', in D. Brakke, M. L. Satlow and S. Weitzman, eds., *Religion and the Self in Antiquity* (Bloomington-Indianapolis), 163–79

(2006). 'Romanos and the Night Vigil in the Sixth Century', in D. Krueger, ed., *A Peoples' History of Christianity*, vol. 3: *Byzantine Christianity* (Minneapolis, MN), 59–78

(2019). 'Singing Mary: The Annunciation and Nativity in Romanos the Melode', in Arentzen and Cunningham 2019, 170–79

Frost, Carrie Frederick (2019). *Maternal Body. A Theology of Incarnation from the Christian East* (New York and Mahwah, NJ)

Frøyshov, Stig S. R. (2000). 'La réticence à l'hymnographie chez des anachorètes de l'Égypte et du Sinaï du 6e au 8e siècles', in A. M. Triacca and A. Pistoia, eds., *L'Hymnographie: Conférences Saint-Serge* (Rome), 229–45

(2007a). 'The Cathedral – Monastic Distinction Revisited. Part 1: Was Egyptian Desert Liturgy a Pure Monastic Office?', *SL* 37, 198–216

(2007b). 'The Early Development of the Liturgical Eight-Mode System in Jerusalem', *SVTQ* 51:2–3, 139–78

(2012). 'The Georgian Witness to the Jerusalem Liturgy: New Sources and Studies', in B. Groen, S. Hawkes-Teeples and S. Alexopoulos, eds., *Inquiries into Eastern Christian Worship. Selected Papers of the Second Intl. Congress of the Society of Oriental Liturgy, Rome, 17–21 Sept. 2009, Eastern Christian Studies* 12 (Leuven, Paris and Walpole, MA), 227–67

(2013). 'Byzantine Rite', 'Rite of Constantinople' and 'Rite of Jerusalem', in *The Canterbury Dictionary of Hymnology* at:https://hymnology.hymnsam.co.uk/b/byzantine-rite [by subscription]

(2020). 'The Early History of the Hagiopolitan Daily Office in Constantinople: New Perspectives on the Formative Period of the Byzantine Rite', *DOP* 74, 351–82

Frye, Northrop (1981). *The Great Code: The Bible and Literature* (New York and London)

Fulton Brown, Rachel (2002). *From Judgment to Passion: Devotion to Christ and the Virgin Mary, 800–1200* (New York)

Gador-Whyte, Sarah (2013). 'Changing Conceptions of Mary in Sixth-Century Byzantium: The Kontakia of Romanos the Melodist', in Neil and Garland 2013, 77–92

(2017). *Theology and Poetry in Early Byzantium: The Kontakia of Romanos the Melodist* (Cambridge)

Galadza, Daniel (2018). *Liturgy and Byzantinization in Jerusalem* (Oxford)

Galot, Jean (1957). 'La plus ancienne affirmation de la corédemption mariale: le témoignage de Jean le Géometre', *Recherches de Science Religieuse* 45, 187–208.

Gambero, Luigi (1999). *Mary and the Fathers of the Church: The Blessed Virgin Mary in Patristic Thought* (San Francisco, CA)

(2009). 'Biographies of Mary in Byzantine Literature', *Marian Studies* 60, 31–50

Gaul, Niels (2018). 'Performative Reading in the Late Byzantine *Theatron*', in Shawcross and Toth 2018, 215–33

Gaventa, Beverly R. (1999). *Mary: Glimpses of the Mother of Jesus* (Edinburgh)

Gero, Stephen (1973). *Byzantine Iconoclasm during the Reign of Leo III with particular attention to the Oriental sources*, CSCO 346, Subsidia 41 (Louvain)

(1977). *Byzantine Iconoclasm during the Reign of Constantine V with particular attention to the Oriental sources*, CSCO 384, Subsidia 52 (Louvain)

Gerstel, Sharon E. J. (1998). 'Painted Sources for Female Piety in Medieval Byzantium', *DOP* 52, 89–111

(1999). *Beholding the Sacred Mysteries: Programs of the Byzantine Sanctuary* (Seattle and London, 1999)

Geschwandtner, C. M. (2013). '"All Creation Rejoices in You": Creation in the Liturgies for the Feasts of the Theotokos', in J. Chryssavgis and B. V. Foltz, eds., *Toward an Ecology of Transfiguration: Orthodox Christian Perspectives on Environment, Nature, and Creation* (New York), 307–23

Getcha, Job (2012). *The Typikon Decoded: An Explanation of Byzantine Liturgical Practice* (Yonkers, NY)

Giamberardini, G. (1969). 'Il "sub tuum praesidium" e il titolo "Theotokos" nella tradizione egiziana', *Marianum* 31, 324–62

(1975). *Il culto mariano in Egitto* (Jerusalem), vol. 1

Giannelli, Ciro (1953), 'Témoignages patristiques en faveur d'une apparition du Christ ressuscité à la Vierge Marie', *REB* 11, 106–19

Giannouli, Antonia (2001). 'Eine Rede auf das Akathistos-Fest und Theodoros II. Dukas Laskaris (*BHG* 1140, *CPG* 8197)', *JÖB* 51, 259–83

(2013). 'Catanyctic Religious Poetry: A Survey', in A. Rigo, P. Ermilov and M. Trizio, eds., *Theologica Minora: The Minor Genres of Byzantine Theological Literature*, Byzantios: Studies in Byzantine History and Civilisation (Turnhout), 86–109

Golitzen, Alexander (2007). 'The Image and Glory of God in Jacob of Serug's Homily, "On That Chariot that Ezekiel the Prophet Saw"', *Scrinium* 3:1, 180–212

Goody, Jack (1987). *The Interface between the Written and the Oral* (Cambridge)

Goppelt, Leonhard (1982). *Typos: The Typological Interpretation of the Old Testament in the New*, trans. D. H. Madvig (Grand Rapids, MI)

Gordillo, M. (1947). 'L'Assunzione corporale della SS. Vergine madre di Dio nei teologi bizantini (sec. x–xv)', *Marianum* 9, 44–89

Gordley, Matthew E. (2011). *Teaching through Song in Antiquity: Didactic Hymnody among Greeks, Romans, Jews, and Christians* (Tübingen)

Graef, Hilda (1963). *Mary: A History of Doctrine and Devotion* (London; repr. Notre Dame, IN, 2009)

Gray, Patrick T. (1979). *The Defense of Chalcedon in the East (451–533)* (Leiden)

Grillmeier, Aloys, SJ (1975). *Christ in the Christian Tradition*, vol. 1: *From the Apostolic Age to Chalcedon*, trans. J. Bowden, rev. ed. (Louisville, KY)

with T. Hainthaler (1995). *Christ in Christian Tradition*, vol. 2: *From the Council of Chalcedon (451) to Gregory the Great (590–604)*, pt 2: *The Church of Constantinople in the Sixth Century*, trans. J. Cawte and P. Allen (London and Louisville, KY)

Grosdidier de Matons, J. (1977). *Romanos le Mélode et les origins de la poésie religieuse à Byzance* (Paris)

(1980–1). 'Liturgie et hymnographie: kontakion et canon', *DOP* 34–5, 31–43

Grumel, V. (1931). 'Le "miracle habituel" de Notre-Dame des Blachernes', *EO* 30, 129–46
  (1933). 'Le jeûne de l'Assomption dans l'église grecque. Étude historique', *EO* 32, 163–94
Haarer, Fiona (2006). *Anastasius I: Politics and Empire in the Late Roman World* (Leeds)
Hahn, Cynthia and Klein, Holger A., eds. (2015), *Saints and Sacred Matter: The Cult of Relics in Byzantium and Beyond*, Dumbarton Oaks Symposia and Colloquia 6 (Washington, DC)
Hamblin, W. J. and Seely, D. R. (2007). *Solomon's Temple: Myth and History* (London)
Hamington, Maurice (1995). *Hail Mary? The Struggle for Ultimate Womanhood in Catholicism* (New York)
Hannick, Christian (2002). *Dogmatika in den acht Tönen aus einer Handschrift aus dem Ende des 16. Jahrhunderts, Anthologie zur ukrainischen sakralen Monodie* 1 (Lvov)
  (2005). 'The Theotokos in Byzantine Hymnography', in Vassilaki 2005, 69–76
Harrison, Nonna Verna (1996). 'Gender, Generation, and Virginity in Cappadocian Theology', *JTS*, n.s. 47, p t1, 38–68
  (2006). 'The Entry of the Mother of God into the Temple', *SVTQ* 50:1–2, 149–60
Harrison, Carol (2013). *The Art of Listening in the Early Church* (Oxford)
Harvey, Susan Ashbrook (1994). 'The Odes of Solomon', in E. Schüssler Fiorenza, ed., *Searching for the Scriptures*, vol. 2: *A Feminist Commentary* (New York), 86–98
  (2005). 'Revisiting the Daughters of the Covenants: Women's Choirs and Sacred Song in Ancient Syriac Christianity', *Hogoye* 8:2, at http://syrcom.cua.edu/Hogoye/Vol-8No2/HV8N2Harvey.html
  (2006). *Scenting Salvation: Ancient Christianity and the Olfactory Imagination* (Berkeley, Los Angeles and London)
  (2010). *Song and Memory: Biblical Women in Syriac Tradition* (Milwaukee, WI)
  (2019). 'Afterword', in Arentzen and Cunningham 2019, 341–7
Harvey, Susan Ashbrook and Hunter, David G., eds. (2008). *The Oxford Handbook of Early Christian Studies* (Oxford)
Harvey, Susan Ashbrook and Mullett, Margaret, eds. (2017), *Knowing Bodies, Passionate Souls. Sense Perceptions in Byzantium* (Washington, DC)
Hayward, C. T. R. (1996). *The Jewish Temple. A Non-Biblical Sourcebook* (London and New York)
Hennephof, H. (1969). *Textus Byzantinos ad iconomachiam pertinentes in usum academicum*, Byzantina Neerlandica, ser. A. Textus, fasc. 1 (Leiden)
Hennessy, Cecily (2012). 'The Chapel of Saint Jacob at the Church of the Theotokos Chalkoprateia in Istanbul', in R. Matthews and J. Curtis, eds., *Proceedings of the 7th International Congress on the Archaeology of the Ancient Near East: 12 April – 16 April 2010, The British Museum and UCL* (London), 351–66
Herrin, Judith (2000). 'The Imperial Feminine in Byzantium', *Past and Present* 169 (2000), 3–35
  (2001). *Women in Purple: Rulers of Medieval Byzantium* (Princeton, N.J.)

(2013). *Unrivalled Influence: Women and Empire in Byzantium* (Princeton, N.J.)

Hinterberger, Martin (2014). 'Byzantine Hagiography and Its Literary Genres. Some Critical Observations', in Efthymiades 2014, 25–60

Hofer, Andrew, OP (2019). 'Scripture in the Christological Controversies', in Blowers and Martens 2019, 455–72

Høgel, Christian (2002). *Symeon Metaphrastes: Rewriting and Canonization* (Copenhagen)

(2014). 'Symeon Metaphrastes and the Metaphrastic Movement', in Efthymiades 2014, 181–96

Holum, Kenneth G. (1982). *Theodosian Empresses: Women and Imperial Dominion in Late Antiquity* (Berkeley and London)

Horn, Cornelia (2015). 'Ancient Syriac Sources on Mary's Role as Intercessor', in Allen, Külzer and Peltomaa 2015, 153–75

Hovorun, Cyril (2008). *Will, Action and Freedom: Christological Controversies in the Seventh Century* (Leiden and Boston, MA)

Huglo, M. (1951). 'L'ancienne version latine de l'Hymne Acathiste', *Mus* 64, 27–61

Humphries, M. T. G. (2014). *Law, Power, and Imperial Ideology in the Iconoclast Era, c. 680–850* (Oxford)

Hunger, Herbert (1978). *Die hochsprachliche profane Literatur der Byzantiner*, 2 vols. (Munich)

Hurbanič, Martin (2019). *The Avar Siege of Constantinople in 626. History and Legend* (Cham, Switzerland)

Hutter, Irmgard and Canard, P. (1991). *Das Marienhomilar des Monchs Jakobos von Kokkinobaphos: Codex Vaticanus Graecus 1162* (Zürich)

Iverites, Fr Evgenios (2019). 'Christological and Ecclesiological Narratives in Early Eighth-Century Greek Homilies on the Theotokos', in Arentzen and Cunningham 2019, 257–80

James, Liz, ed. (1997). *Women, Men and Eunuchs: Gender in Byzantium* (London and New York)

(2001). 'Bearing Gifts from the East: Imperial Relic Hunters from Abroad', in A. Eastmond, ed., *Eastern Approaches to Byzantium* (Aldershot and Brookfield, VT), 119–31

(2005). 'Female Piety in Context: Understanding Developments in Private Devotional Practice', in Vassilaki 2005, 145–52

(2007). 'Senses and Sensibility in Byzantium', *Art History* 27:4, 522–37

ed. (2010). *A Companion to Byzantium* (Oxford)

(2017). *Mosaics in the Medieval World: From Late Antiquity to the Fifteenth Century* (Cambridge)

Janin, Raymond (1953). *La géographie ecclésiastique de l'empire byzantin*, pt I: *Le siège de Constantinople et le patriarcat oecuménique*, vol. 3: *Les églises et les monastères* (Paris)

(1964). *Constantinople Byzantine: développement urbain et repertoire topographique* (Paris, 2nd ed.)

(1966). 'Les processions religieuses à Byzance', *REB* 24, 69–88

Jansma, T. (1965). 'Die Christologie Jacobs von Serugh und ihre Abhängkeit von der alexandrinsichen Theologie und der Frömmigkeit Ephraems des Syrers', *Mus* 78, 5–65

Jeffery, Peter (1991). 'The Sunday Office of Seventh-Century Jerusalem in the Georgian Chantbook (Iadgari): A Preliminary Report', *SL* 21, 52–75

Jeffreys, Elizabeth (2014). 'The Sevastokratorissa Eirine as Patron', in M. Grünbart, M. Mullett and L. Theis (with G. Fingarova and M. Savage), eds., *Female Founders in Byzantium and Beyond* (Vienna) = *Wiener Jahrbuch der Kunstgeschichte* 60/61, 2011/12 (publ. 2014), 177–94

(2019). 'The Homilies of James of Kokkinobaphos in Their Twelfth-Century Context', in Arentzen and Cunningham 2019, 281–306

Jeffreys, Elizabeth, Haldon, John and Cormack, Robin, eds. (2008). *The Oxford Handbook of Byzantine Studies* (Oxford)

Jeffreys, Elizabeth and Jeffreys, Michael (2018), 'Afterword: Reading and Hearing in Byzantium', in Shawcross and Toth 2018, 626–37

Johnson, M. E. (2008). '"Sub tuum praesidium": The Theotokos in Christian Life and Worship before Ephesus', *Pro Ecclesia* 17:1,52–75

Jugie, Martin, AA (1913). 'L'église de Chalcopratia et le culte de la ceinture de la Sainte Vierge à Constantinople', *EO* 16, 308–12

(1922). *Homélies mariales Byzantines: textes grecs édités et traduits en Latin*, vol. 1, PO 16, fasc. 3, no. 79 (Paris; repr. Turnhout, 2003)

(1923a). 'Sur la vie et les procédés littéraires de Syméon le Métaphraste. Son récit de la vie de la Sainte Vierge', *EO* 22, 5–10

(1923b). 'La première fête Mariale et l'Avent primitif en Orient', *EO* 22, 129–52; repr. in Jugie 1925 (1990), 297–309

(1925). *Homélies mariales byzantines. Textes grecs édités et traduits en Latin*, vol. 2, PO 19, fasc. 3, no. 93 (Paris; repr. Turnhout, 1990)

(1926). 'Le récit de l'Histoire Euthymiaque sur la mort et l'assomption de la Sainte Vierge', *EO* 25, 385–92

(1943). 'La fête de la Dormition et de l'Assomption de la sainte Vierge en Orient et en Occident', *L'Année théologique* 4, 11–42

(1944). *La mort et l'assomption de la très sainte Vierge: Étude historico-doctrinale*, ST 114 (Vatican City)

(1952). *L'Immaculée Conception dans l'Écriture Sainte et dans la tradition orientale* (Rome)

Kaestli, Jean-Daniel (2011). 'Mapping an Unexplored Second-Century Apocryphal Gospel: *The Liber de Nativitate Salvatoris* (*CANT* 53)', Clivaz, Dettwiler, Devillers and Norelli 2011, 506–59

Kalavrezou, Ioli (1990). 'When the Virgin Mary Became *Meter Theou*', *DOP* 44, 165–72

(2000). 'The Maternal Side of the Virgin', in Vassilaki 2000, 41–5

Kallistos of Diokleia (1990). 'The Meaning of the Divine Liturgy for the Byzantine Worshipper', in R. Morris, ed., *Church and People in Byzantium* (Birmingham), 7–28

Kaplan, Michel, ed. (2001). *Le sacré et son inscription dans l'espace à Byzance et en occident*, Byzantina Sorbonensia 18 (Paris)

Kateusz, Ally (2019). *Mary and Early Christian Women. Hidden Leadership* (London)

Kazhdan, Alexander (1992). 'An Oxymoron: Individual Features of a Byzantine Hymnographer', *Rivista di studi bizantini e neoellenici* 29, 19–58

Kazhdan, Alexander, with Franklin, Simon, eds. (1984). *Studies on Byzantine Literature of the Eleventh and Twelfth Centuries* (Cambridge)

Kazhdan, Alexander, with Sherry, Lee F. and Angelidi, Christine, eds. (1999). *A History of Byzantine Literature (650–850)* (Athens)

Kazhdan, Alexander, with Angelidi, Christine, eds. (2006). *A History of Byzantine Literature (850–1000)* (Athens)

Kecskeméti, J. (1993). 'Doctrine et drame dans la predication grecque', *Euphrosyne* 21, 29–68

Kekelidze, G. (1912). *Données sur S. Maxime le Confesseur fournies par les sources géorgiennes* (in Russian), *Trudi*, Ecclesiastical Academy of Kiev, 1–41, 451–86

Kennedy, George A. (1994). *A New History of Classical Rhetoric* (Princeton)

Kishpaugh, Mary Jerome, OP (1941), 'The Feast of the Presentation of the Virgin Mary in the Temple: An Historical and Literary Study' (unpubl. PhD thesis, Catholic University of America, Washington, DC)

Klein, Holger A. (2004). 'Eastern Objects and Western Desires: Relics and Reliquaries Between Byzantium and the West', *DOP* 58, 283–314

Koder, Johannes (2010). 'Imperial Propaganda in the Kontakia of Romanos the Melodist', *DOP* 62, 275–91

Koutrakou, Nike (2005). 'Use and Abuse of the "Image" of the Theotokos in the Political Life of Byzantium (with Special Reference to the Iconoclast Period', in Vassilaki 2005, 77–89

Krausmüller, Dirk (1998–9). 'God or Angels as Impersonators of Saints: A Belief in the Refutation of Eustratius of Constantinople and in the Writings of Anastasius of Sinai', *Gouden Hoorn* 6:2 = https://goudenhoorn.com/2014/05/13/god-or-angels-as-impersonators-of-saints-a-belief-and-its-contexts-in-the-refutation-of-eustratius-of-constantinople-and-in-the-writings-of-anastasius-of-sinai/

(2008). 'Denying Mary's Real Presence in Apparitions and Icons: Divine Impersonation in the Tenth-Century Life of Constantine the Ex-Jew', *Byzantion* 78, 288–303

(2011). 'Making the Most of Mary: The Cult of the Virgin in the Chalkoprateia from Late Antiquity to the Tenth Century', in Brubaker and Cunningham 2011, 219–45

(2013). 'The Flesh Cannot See the Word: "Nestorianizing" Chalcedonians in the Seventh to Ninth Centuries AD', *VC* 67, 1–24

Krueger, Derek (2004). *Writing and Holiness: The Practice of Authorship in the Early Christian East* (Philadelphia, PA)

(2005). 'Christian Piety and Practice in the Sixth Century', in M. Maas, ed., *The Cambridge Companion to the Age of Justinian* (Cambridge), 291–315

(2006). 'Romanos the Melodist and the Christian Self in Early Byzantium', in E. Jeffreys, ed., *Proceedings of the 21st International Congress of Byzantine Studies. London, 21–26 August 2006* (Aldershot and Burlington, VT), vol. 1: Plenary Papers, 255–74

ed. (2010). *Byzantine Christianity: A People's History of Christianity*, vol. 3 (Minneapolis, MN)

(2014). *Liturgical Subjects: Christian Ritual, Biblical Narrative, and the Formation of Self in Byzantium* (Philadelphia, PA)

(2019). 'Adam and Eve on the Threshold of Lent: Counterpoint and Intercession in a Kanon for Cheesefare Sunday', in Arentzen and Cunningham 2019, 180–91

Krumbacher, Karl (1897). *Geschichte der byzantinischen Literatur von Justinian bis zum Ende des oströmischen Reiches (527–1453)* (Munich)

Kurtz, E. (1897). 'Ein bibliographisches Monitum für den Verfasser des Aufsatzes "Der Mönch und Presbyter Epiphanios"', *BZ* 4, 214–17

Ladouceur, Paul (2006). 'Old Testament Prefigurations of the Mother of God', *SVTQ* 50:1–2, 5–57

Lafontaine-Dosogne, Jacqueline (1964). *Iconographie de l'enfance de la Vierge dans l'Empire byzantin et en Occident*, vol. 1 (Brussels; repr. 1992)

(1975). 'Iconography of the Cycle of the Life of the Virgin', in P. Underwood, ed., *The Kariye Djami: Studies in the Art of the Kariye Djami and Its Intellectual Background* (London), vol. 4, 161–94

Lambot, D. (1934). L'homélie du Pseudo-Jérôme sur l'Assomption et l'Évangile de la Nativité de Marie, d'après une lettre inédite d'Hincmar', *Revue Bénédictine* 44, 265–82

Lampe, G. W. H. and Woollcombe, K. J. (1957). *Essays in Typology, Studies in Biblical Theology* 22 (London)

La Piana, George (1912). *Le rappresentazioni sacre nella letteratura bizantina dale origini al sec. IX* (Grottaferrata; repr. London, 1971)

(1936). 'The Byzantine Theatre', *Speculum* 11, 171–211.

Lash, Archim. Ephrem (1990). 'Mary in Eastern Church Literature', in A. Stacpoole, OSB, ed., *Mary in Doctrine and Devotion* (Dublin), 58–80

(2008). 'Biblical Interpretation in Worship', in M. B. Cunningham and E. Theokritoff (eds), *The Cambridge Companion to Orthodox Christian Theology* (Cambridge), 35–48

Laurentin, René (1954). 'Table rectificative des pièces mariales inauthentiques ou discutées contenues dans les deux Patrologies de Migne', in R. Laurentin, *Court traité de théologie mariale* (Paris), 119–73

Lauxtermann, Marc D. (1998). 'John Geometres: Poet and Soldier', *Byzantion* 68 (1998), 356–80

(2003). *Byzantine Poetry from Pisides to Geometres: Texts and Contexts*, vol. 1 (Vienna)

(2015). Review of *Eustathios of Thessalonike, Exegesis*, in *BMCR*, 09.48

Leclercq, H. (1948). 'Présentation de Jésus au Temple (Fête de la)', *DACL* 14, cols. 1722–9

Ledit, Joseph (1976). *Marie dans la liturgie de Byzance* (Paris)

Lemerle, Paul (1986). *Byzantine Humanism. The First Phase: Notes and Remarks on Education and Culture in Byzantium from Its Origins to the 10th Century*, trans. H. Lindsay and A. Moffatt, Byzantina Australiensia 3 (Canberra)

Lenain de Tillemont, L.- S. (1637–98). *Mémoires pour servir à l'histoire écclésiastique des six premiers siècles*, 16 vols. (Paris)

Leroy, F. J., SJ (1967). *L'homilétique de Proclus*, ST 247 (Vatican City)

Lidova, Maria (2019). 'Embodied Word: Telling the Story of Mary in Early Christian Art', in Arentzen and Cunningham 2019, 17–43

Limberis, Vassiliki (1994). *Divine Heiress: The Virgin Mary and the Creation of Christian Constantinople* (London and New York)

Linardou, Kallirroe (2004). 'Reading Two Byzantine Illustrated Books: The Kokkinobaphos Manuscripts (Vat.gr. 1162 and Paris gr. 1208) and their Illustration' (unpubl. PhD thesis, University of Birmingham)

    (2007). 'The Kokkinobaphos Manuscripts Revisited: The Internal Evidence of the Books', *Scriptorium* 56, 384–407

Lingas, Alexander (1995). 'The Liturgical Place of the Kontakion in Constantinople', in C. C. Akentiev, ed., *Liturgy, Architecture, and Art in the Byzantine World: Papers of the XVIII International Byzantine Congress (Moscow, 8–15 August 1991)*, Byzantinorossica 1 (St Petersburg), 50–7

    (2008). 'Music', in Jeffreys, Haldon and Cormack 2008, 915–35

Louth, Andrew (2002). *St John Damascene: Tradition and Originality in Byzantine Theology* (Oxford)

    (2005). 'Christian Hymnography from Romanos the Melodist to John Damascene', *JECS* 57:3, 195–206

    (2011). 'John of Damascus on the Mother of God as a Link Between Humanity and God', in Brubaker and Cunningham 2011, 153–61

    (2013). *Introducing Eastern Orthodox Theology* (Downers Grove, IL)

Luijendijk, A. (2014). *Forbidden Oracles: The Gospel of the Lots of Mary*, Studien und Texte zu Antike und Christentum 89 (Tübingen)

Maas, Paul (1906). 'Die Chronologie der Hymnen des Romanos', *BZ* 15:1, 1–44

    (1910). 'Das Kontakion', *BZ* 19, 285–306

MacMullen, Ramsay (1989). 'The Preacher's Audience (AD 350–400)', *JTS* n.s. 40, 503–11

Magdalino, Paul (2003). 'The Year 1000 in Byzantium', in P. Magdalino, ed., *Byzantium in the Year 1000* (Leiden),233–70

    (2004). 'L'Église du Phare et les reliques de la passion à Constantinople (VIIe/ VIIIe–XIIIe siècles)', in J. Durand and B. Flusin, eds., *Byzance et les reliques du Christ*, Centre de Recherche d'Histoire et Civilisation de Byzance, Monographies 17 (Paris), 15–30

    (2007). 'Medieval Constantinople', in P. Magdalino, *Studies on the History and Topography of Byzantine Constantinople* (Aldershot), ch. 1

    (2018). 'The Liturgical Poetics of an Elite Religious Confraternity', in Shawcross and Toth 2018, 116–32

Magdalino, Paul and Nelson, Robert, eds. (2010). *The Old Testament in Byzantium* (Washington, DC)

Maguire, Henry (1981). *Art and Eloquence in Byzantium* (Princeton)

(1996). *The Icons of Their Bodies: Saints and Their Images in Byzantium* (Princeton)

(2010). 'Metaphors of the Virgin in Byzantine Literature and Art', in A. Rhoby and E. Schiffer, eds., *Imitatio – Aemulatio – Variatio: Akten des internationalen wissenschaftlichen Symposions zur byzantinischen Sprache und Literatur. Wien, 22.–25. Oktober 2008* (Vienna),189–94

(2011). 'Body, Clothing, Metaphor: The Virgin in Early Christian Art', in Brubaker and Cunningham 2011, 39–51

(2012a). *Nectar and Illusion. Nature in Byzantine Art and Literature* (Oxford)

(2012b). 'Pangs of Labour without Pain': Observations on the Iconography of the Nativity in Byzantium', in D. Sullivan, E. Fisher and S. Papaioannou, eds., *Byzantine Religious Culture: Studies in Honor of Alice-Mary Talbot* (Leiden), 205–16

Mango, Cyril (1969–70). 'Notes on Byzantine Monuments', *DOP* 23, 369–72

(1981). 'Discontinuity with the Classical Past in Byzantium', in M. Mullett and R. Scott, eds., *Byzantium and the Classical Tradition*, University of Birmingham Thirteenth Spring Symposium of Byzantine Studies 1979 (Birmingham), 48–57

(1990). 'Constantine's Mausoleum and the Translation of Relics', *BZ* 83, 51–62 = C. Mango, *Studies on Constantinople* (Aldershot and Brookfield, VT, 1993), ch. 5

(1993–4). 'The Chalkoprateia Annunciation and the Pre-Eternal Logos', *Deltion tes christianikes archaiologikes etaireias* 4:17, 165–70

(1998). 'The Origins of the Blachernai Shrine at Constantinople', *Actes du XIIIe Congrès International d'Archéologie Chrétienne*, vol. 2 (Vatican City and Split), 61–76

(2000). 'Constantinople as Theotokoupolis', in Vassilaki 2000, 17–25

Markopoulos, Athanasios (2008). 'Education', in Jeffreys, Haldon and Cormack 2008, 785–95

(2014). 'Teachers and Textbooks in Byzantium, Ninth to Eleventh Centuries', in S. Steckel, N. Gaul and M. Grünbart, eds., *Networks of Learning. Perspectives on Scholars in Byzantine East and Latin West, c. 1000–1200* (Zürich),2–15

Markus, Robert A. (1994). 'How on Earth Could Places Become Holy?' Origins of the Christian Idea of Holy Places', *JECS* 2, 257–71

Marx, Benedikt (1940). *Procliana: Untersuchungen über den homiletischen Nachlass des Patriarchen Proklos von Konstantinople* (Münster in Westfalen)

Mathews, Thomas F. (1971). *The Early Churches of Constantinople, Architecture and Liturgy* (University Park, PA)

Maunder, Chris (2007). 'Mary in the New Testament and Apocrypha', in Boss 2007, 11–46

ed. (2008). *The Origins of the Cult of the Virgin Mary* (London and New York)

ed. (2019). *The Oxford Handbook of Mary* (Oxford)

Mayer, Wendy (1998). 'John Chrysostom: Extraordinary Preacher, Ordinary Audience', in Allen and Cunningham 1998, 105–37

(2008). 'Homiletics', in Harvey and Hunter 2008, 565–83

McCracken, David (1994). *The Scandal of the Gospels: Jesus, Story, and Offense* (New York)

McFague, Sally (1982). *Metaphorical Theology: Models of God in Religious Language* (Philadelphia, PA)

McGuckin, John A. (1994). *St Cyril of Alexandria and the Christological Controversy* (Leiden; repr. Crestwood, NY, 2004)

(2001a). *St Gregory of Nazianzus: An Intellectual Biography* (Crestwood, NY)

(2001b). 'The Paradox of the Virgin-Theotokos: Evangelism and Imperial Politics in the Fifth-Century Byzantine World', *Maria* 2, 8–25

(2008). 'The Early Cult of Mary and Inter-Religious Contexts in the Fifth-Century Church', in Maunder 2008, 1–22

McKinnon, James W. (1986). 'On the Question of Psalmody in the Ancient Synagogue', *Early Music History* 6, 159–81 = J. W. McKinnon, *The Temple, The Church Fathers, and Early Western Chant* (Aldershot, 1998), ch. 8

McNamer, Sarah (2010). *Affective Meditation and the Invention of Medieval Compassion* (Philadelphia, PA)

Mellas, Andrew (2017). 'Tears of Compunction in Byzantine Hymnody. The Hymnography of Romanos the Melodist, Andrew of Crete, and Kassia' (unpubl. PhD thesis, University of Sydney)

(2020). *Liturgy and the Emotions in Byzantium* (Cambridge)

Mercati, S. G. (1935). 'Que significa Γεωμέτρης?', *SBN* 4, 302–4

Meyendorff, John (1974). *Byzantine Theology: Historical Trends and Doctrinal Themes* (New York)

Mimouni, Simon Claude (1993a). 'La lecture liturgique et les apocryphes du Nouveau Testament. Le cas de la Dormitio grecque du Pseudo-Jean', *OCP* 59,403–25

(1993b). 'Les Transitus Mariae sont-ils vraiment des apocryphes?', E. A. Livingstone, ed., *SP* 25 (Leuven), 122–28

(1994). 'Les Vies de la Vierge: état de la question', *Apocrypha* 5, 211–48 = repr. Mimouni 2011a, 75–115 [page numbers of the more recent publication of this article are used]

(1995). *Dormition et assomption de Marie: Histoire des traditions anciennes*, Théologie Historique 98 (Paris)

(2011a). *Les traditions anciennes sur la Dormition et l'Assomption de Marie. Études littéraires, historiques et doctrinales* (Leiden and Boston)

(2011b). 'La virginité de Marie: entres textes et contextes (1ᵉʳ–11ᵉ siècles)', in Clivaz, Dettwiler, Devillers and Norelli 2011, 33–46

Mitsakis, Kariophiles (1971). *Βυζαντινή Υμνογραφία* (Thessalonike)

Momigliano, Arnaldo (1972). 'Popular Religious Beliefs and the Late Roman Historians', in G. J. Cuming and D. Baker, eds., *Popular Belief and Practice*, Studies in Church History 8 (Cambridge), 1–18

Morris, Rosemary (1995). *Monks and Laymen in Byzantium, 843–1118* (Cambridge)

Mulard, C. (2016). *La pensée symbolique de Romanos le Mélode* (Turnhout)

Mullett, Margaret (1990). 'Dancing with Deconstructionists in the Gardens of the Muses: New Literary History vs ?', *BMGS* 14, 258–75

(1992). 'The Madness of Genre', *DOP* 46: *Homo Byzantinus: Papers in Honour of Alexander Kazhdan*, 233–43

(2011). 'Conclusion – Not the Theotokos Again?', in Brubaker and Cunningham 2011, 279–88

Munitiz, Joseph,SJ (1997). Chrysostomides and C. Dendrinos, eds., *The Letter of the Three Patriarchs to Emperor Theophilos and Related Texts* (Camberley)

Murray, Robert, SJ (1971). 'Mary, the Second Eve in the Early Syriac Fathers', *ECR* 3:4, 372–84

(1975). *Symbols of Church and Kingdom: A Study in Early Syriac Tradition* (Cambridge; republ. London and New York, 2004)

Naffah, Charles (2009). 'Les "histoires" syriaques de la Vierge: traditions apocryphes anciennes et récentes', *Apocrypha* 20, 137–88

Nau, F. (1919). 'Documents pour servir à l'histoire de l'église nestorienne', *PO* 13 (Paris; repr. Turnhout 1974)

Neil, Bronwen (2019). 'Mary as Intercessor in Byzantine Theology', in Maunder 2019, 140–53

Neil, Bronwen and Garland, Linda, eds. (2013). *Questions of Gender in Byzantine Society* (Aldershot and Burlington, VT)

Neville, Leonora (2019), *Byzantine Gender* (Leeds)

Nikiforova, Alexandra (2012). *Iz istorii Minei v Vizantii: gimnograficheskie pamiatniki VIII–XII vv. Iz sobraniia monastyria sviatoi Ekateriny na Sinae* (Moscow) (in Russian)

(2013). 'The Tropologion Sin. Gr. NE/MΓ 56–5 of the Ninth Century: A New Source for Byzantine Hymnography', *Scripta* 12, 157–85

Norelli, Enrico (2009). *Marie des apocryphes: enquête sur la mère de Jésus dans le christanisme antique* (Geneva)

Nutzman, Megan (2013). 'Mary in the Protevangelium of James: A Jewish Woman in the Temple?', *GRBS* 52, 551–78

Olivar, Alexandre (1991). *La predicación cristiana antigua*, Sección de teología y filosofia 189 (Barcelona)

Olkinuora, Jaakko (2015). *Byzantine Hymnography for the Feast of the Entrance of the Theotokos*, Studia Patristica Fennica 4 (Helsinki)

Omont, Henri (1928). *Miniatures des Homélies sur la Vierge du moine Jacques* (ms. gr. 1208 de Paris) (Paris)

Ong, Walter (1982). *Orality and Literacy: The Technologizing of the Word* (London)

Ouspensky, Leonid and Lossky, Vladimir (1983). *The Meaning of Icons* (Crestwood, NY)

Panou, Eirini (2011). 'Aspects of St Anna's Cult in Byzantium' (unpubl. PhD thesis, University of Birmingham)

(2018). *The Cult of St Anna in Byzantium* (London and New York)

(2019). 'The Theological Substance of St Anna's Motherhood in Byzantine Homilies and Art', in Arentzen and Cunningham 2019, 62–76

Papaioannou, Stratis (2001). 'The "Usual Miracle" and an Unusual Image: Psellos and the Icons of Blachernai', *JÖB* 51, 177–88

(2013). *Michael Psellos: Rhetoric and Authorship in Byzantium* (Cambridge)

Papaconstantinou, Arietta (2000). 'Les sanctuaires de la Vierge dans l'Égypte byzantine et omeyyade. L'apport des textes documentaires', *Journal of Juristic Papyrology* 30, 81–94

Papoutsakis, Emmanuel (2007). 'The Making of a Syriac Fable: From Ephrem to Romanos', *Mus* 120, 29–75

Parpulov, Georgi R. (2010). 'Psalters and Personal Piety in Byzantium', in P. Magdalino and R. Nelson, eds., *The Old Testament in Byzantium* (Washington, DC), 77–105

Parry, Kenneth (1996). *Depicting the Word. Byzantine Iconophile Thought of the Eighth and Ninth Centuries* (Leiden, New York and Cologne)

Parys, M. J. van (1971). 'L'évolution de la doctrine christologique de Basile de Séleucie', *Irénikon* 44, 493–514

Patlagean, Evelyne (1979). 'Discours écrit, discours parlé: Niveaux de culture à Byzance aux VIIIe–XIe siècles', *Annales ESC* 34, 264–78

Pelikan, Jaroslav (1996). *Mary Through the Centuries: Her Place in the History of Culture* (New Haven, CT, and London)

Peltomaa, Leena Mari (1997). 'The *Tomus ad Armenios de Fide* of Proclus of Constantinople and the Christological Emphasis of the *Akathistos Hymn*', *JÖB* 47, 25–35

(2001). *The Image of the Virgin Mary in the Akathistos Hymn* (Leiden, Boston and Cologne)

(2007). 'Romanos the Melodist and the Intercessory Role of Mary', in Belke, Kislinger, Külzer and Stassinopoulou 2007, 1–12

(2010). 'Roles and Functions of Mary in the Hymnography of Romanos Melodist', in J. Baun, A. Cameron, M. Edwards and M. Vinzent, eds., *SP* 44 (Leuven, Paris and Walpole, MA), 487–98

(2015). '"Cease your Lamentations, I shall Become an Advocate for You": Mary as Intercessor in Romanos' Hymnography', in Allen, Külzer and Peltomaa 2015, 131–7

Pentcheva, Bissera V. (2002). 'The Supernatural Protector of Constantinople: the Virgin and Her Icons in the Tradition of the Avar Siege', *BMGS* 26, 2–41

(2006). *Icons and Power: The Mother of God in Byzantium* (University Park, PA)

(2010). *The Sensual Icon: Space, Ritual, and the Senses in Byzantium* (University Park, PA)

Perria, Lidia (1979). *I manoscritti citati da Albert Ehrhard*, Testi e Studi Bizantino-Neoellenici 4 (Rome)

Petersen, W. L. (1985). *The Diatesseron and Ephrem Syrus as Sources of Romanos the Melodist*, CSCO 475, Sub. 74 (Louvain)

Pitra, J. B. (1867). *Hymnographie de l'église grecque* (Rome)

Pizzone, Aglae M. V., ed. (2014). *The Author in Middle Byzantine Literature: Modes, Functions, and Identities* (Berlin and Boston)

Price, Richard M. (2004). 'Marian Piety and the Nestorian Controversy', in Swanson 2004, 31–8

(2007). 'Theotokos: The Title and Its Significance in Doctrine and Devotion' in Boss 2007, 56–73

(2008). 'The Theotokos and the council of Ephesus', in Maunder 2008, 89–103

(2019). 'The Virgin as Theotokos at Ephesus (AD 431) and Earlier', in Maunder 2019, 67–77

Quasten, J. (1986–94). *Patrology*, 4 vols. (Westminster, MD)

Reynolds, Brian K. (2012). *Gateway to Heaven. Marian Doctrine and Devotion: Image and Typology in the Patristic and Medieval Periods*, vol. 1: *Doctrine and Devotion* (Hyde Park, NY)

(2019). 'Marian Typological and Symbolic Imagery in Patristic Christianity', in Maunder 2019, 78–92

Riant, P. E. D. (1877–1904). *Exuviae sacrae Constantinopolitanae. Fasciculus documentorum minorum, ad byzantina lipsana in occidentem saeculo XIIIe translate, spectantium et historiam quarti belli sacri imperii; gallo-graeci illustrantium*, 3 vols. (Geneva)

Ricoeur, Paul (1978). *The Rule of Metaphor. The Creation of Meaning in Language*, trans. R. Czerny with K. McLaughlin and J. Costello, SJ (London and New York; repr. 2008)

Riehle, Alexander (2014). 'Authorship and Gender (and) Identity. Women's Writing in the Middle Byzantine Period', in Pizzone 2014, 245–62

Ringrose, Kathryn M. (2003). *The Perfect Servant: Eunuchs and the Social Construction of Gender in Byzantium* (Chicago)

Römer, C. (1998). 'Christliche Texte 11', *Archiv für Papyrusforschung* 44, 129–39

Rouillard, P., OSB (2000), 'The Cult of Saints in the East and the West', in Chupungco 2000, vol. 5, 299–316

Rowe, G. O. (1997). 'Style', in S. E. Porter, ed., *Handbook of Classical Rhetoric in the Hellenistic Period, 330 BC – AD 400* (Leiden, New York and Cologne), ch. 5, 121–57

Rubin, Miri (2009). *Mother of God: A History of the Virgin Mary* (London and New York)

Ruether, Rosemary Radford (1969). *Gregory of Nazianzus, Rhetor and Philosopher* (Oxford)

(1977). *Mary – The Feminine Face of the Church* (Philadelphia, PA)

Russell, Norman (2000). *Cyril of Alexandria* (London and New York)

(2004). *The Doctrine of Deification in the Greek Patristic Tradition* (Oxford)

Rydén, Lennart (1976). 'The Vision of the Virgin at Blachernae and the Feast of Pokrov', *AB* 94, 63–82

Saenger, Paul Henry (1982). 'Silent Reading: Its Impact on Late Medieval Script and Society', *Viator* 13, 367–414

Sajdak, J. (1931). 'Que signifie Κυριώτης Γεωμέτρης?', *Byzantion* 6, 343–53

Santer, M. (1975). 'The Authorship and Occasion of Cyril of Alexandria's Sermon on the Virgin (Hom. Diu. IV)', in E. A. Livingstone, ed., *SP* 12 (Berlin), 144–50

Savas, Savas J. (1983). *Hymnology of the Eastern Orthodox Church* (n.p.)

Scheer, A. H. M. (1977). 'Aux origines de la fête de l'Annociation', *Les questions liturgiques et paroissiales* 58, 97–169

Schirò, Guiseppe (1961–2). 'Caratteristiche dei canoni di Andrea Cretese, *KretChron* 15–16, 113–39

Schork, R. J. (1995). *Sacred Song from the Byzantine Pulpit: Romanos the Melodist* (Gainesville, FL)

Sheidweiler, F. (1952). 'Studien zu Johannes Geometres', *BZ* 45, 277–319

Seibt, W. (1987). 'Die Darstellungen der Theotokos auf byzantinische Bleisiegeln besonders im 11. Jahrhundert', in N. Oikonomides, ed., *Studies in Byzantine Sigillography* (Washington, DC),3–56

Seppälä, Serafim (2011). 'Reminiscences of Icons in the Qur'an?', *Islam and Christian–Muslim Relations* 22:1, 3–21

Ševčenko, Ihor (1977). 'Hagiography of the Iconoclast Period', in Bryer and Herrin 1977, 113–31

(1981). 'Levels of Style in Byzantine Prose', *JÖB* 31, I.1, 289–312

Ševčenko, Nancy P. (1991). 'Icons in the Liturgy', *DOP* 45, 45–57 = Ševčenko, N. P. 2013, ch. 11, 1–41

(1994). 'The Limburg Staurothek and Its Relics', in Θυμίαμα στη μνήμη της Λασκαρίνας Μπούρα (Athens), 289–95 = Ševčenko, N. P. 2013, ch. 16, 1–13

(1998). 'Canon and Calendar: The Role of a Ninth-Century Hymnographer in Shaping the Celebration of Saints', in L. Brubaker, ed., *Byzantium in the Ninth Century: Dead or Alive?* (Aldershot), 101–14 = Ševčenko 2013, ch. 1

(2011). 'The Service of the Virgin's Lament Revisited', in Brubaker and Cunningham 2011, 247–62

(2013). *The Celebration of the Saints in Byzantine Art and Liturgy* (Farnham and Burlington, VT)

Shawcross, Teresa and Toth, Ida, eds. (2018). *Reading in the Byzantine Empire and Beyond* (Cambridge)

Shawcross, Teresa (2018). 'Byzantium: A Bookish World', in Shawcross and Toth 2018, 3–36

Shoemaker, Stephen J. (1999). '"Let Us Go and Burn Her Body": The Image of the Jews in the Early Dormition Traditions', *Church History* 68:4, 775–823

(2001a). 'Gender at the Virgin's Funeral: Men and Women as Witnesses to the Dormition', in M. F. Wiles and E. J. Yarnold, eds., *SP* 34 (Leuven), 552–8

(2001b). 'The (Re?) Discovery of the Kathisma Church and the Cult of the Virgin in Late Ancient Palestine', *Maria: A Journal of Marian Studies* 2, 21–72

(2002). *Ancient Traditions of the Virgin Mary's Dormition and Assumption* (Oxford)

(2005). 'The Virgin Mary in the Ministry of Jesus and the Early Church According to the Earliest *Life of the Virgin*', *The Harvard Theological Review* 98, 441–67

(2006a). 'Death and the Maiden: The Early History of the Dormition and Assumption Apocrypha', *SVTQ* 50, 59–97

(2006b). 'The Georgian *Life of the Virgin* Attributed to Maximus the Confessor: Its Authenticy (?) and Importance', in A. Muraviev and B. Lourié, eds., *Mémorial R. P. Michel van Esbroeck, S.J., Scrinium 2* (St Petersburg), 307–28

(2007). 'Marian Liturgies and Devotion in Early Christianity', in Boss 2007, 130–45

(2008a). 'The Cult of Fashion: The Earliest *Life of the Virgin* and Constantinople's Marian Relics', *DOP* 62 (2008), 53–74

(2008b). 'The Cult of the Virgin in the Fourth Century: A Fresh Look at Some Old and New Sources', in Maunder 2008, 71–87

(2008c). 'Epiphanius of Salamis, the Kollyridians, and the Early Dormition Narratives: The Cult of the Virgin in the Later Fourth Century', *JECS* 16, 369–99

(2010). 'Asceticism in the Early Dormition Narratives', in J. Baun, A. Cameron, M. Edwards and M. Vinzent, eds., *SP* 44 (Leuven, Paris and Walpole, MA),509–13

(2011a). 'From Mother of Mysteries to Mother of the Church: The Institutionalization of the Dormition Apocrypha', *Apocrypha* 22, 11–47

(2011b). 'Mary at the Cross, East and West: Maternal Compassion and Affective Piety in the Earliest *Life of the Virgin* and the High Middle Ages', *JTS*, n.s. 62,570–606

(2011c). 'A Mother's Passion: Mary at the Crucifixion and Resurrection in the Earliest *Life of the Virgin* and Its Influence on George of Nikomedeia's Passion Homilies', in Brubaker and Cunningham 2011, 53–67

(2015). 'The Ancient Dormition Apocrypha and the Origins of Marian Piety: Early Evidence of Marian Intercession in Late Ancient Palestine', in Allen, Külzer and Peltomaa 2015, 23–39

(2016a). *Mary in Early Christian Faith and Devotion* (New Haven and London)

(2016b). 'The (Pseudo?-)Maximus *Life of the Virgin* and the Byzantine Marian Tradition, *JTS*, n.s., 67, pt 1, 115–42

Simelidis, Christos (2020). 'Two *Lives of the Virgin*: John Geometres, Euthymios the Athonite, and Maximos the Confessor', *DOP* 74, 125–59

Simić, Kosta (2009). 'Life According to Nature: Ascetic Ideals in a Sticheron by Kassia', *Church Studies. Annual Journal of the Centre of Church Studies* (Niš) 6, 111–21

(2017). 'Liturgical Poetry in the Middle Byzantine Period: Hymn attributed to Germanos I, Patriarch of Constantinople (715–730)' (unpubl. PhD thesis, Australian Catholic University)

Skrekas, Dimitrios (2008). 'Studies in the Iambic Canons attributed to John of Damascus: A Critical Edition with Introduction and Commentary' (unpubl. DPhil thesis, University of Oxford)

(2018). 'Late Byzantine School Teaching through the Iambic Canons and Their Paraphrase', in Shawcross and Toth 2018, 377–91

Smelova, Natalia (2011). 'Melkite Syriac Hymns to the Mother of God (9th–11th Centuries): Manuscripts, Language and Imagery', in Brubaker and Cunningham 2011, 117–31

Soskice, Janet M. (1985). *Metaphor and Religious Language* (Oxford)

(2009). *Sisters of Sinai: How Two Lady Adventurers Found the Hidden Gospels* (London)

Speake, Graham (2002). *Mount Athos: Renewal in Paradise* (New Haven and London)

Speck, Paul (2003). 'Classicism in the Eighth Century? The Homily of Patriarch Germanos on the Deliverance of Constantinople', in P. Speck, *Understanding Byzantium* (Aldershot and Burlington, VT), 123–42

Szövérffy, Joseph (1978–9). *A Guide to Byzantine Hymnography: A Classified Bibliography of Texts and Studies*, 2 vols. (Brookline, MA, and Leiden)

Starowieyski, M. (1989). 'Le titre Θεοτόκος avant le concile d'Ephèse', in E. A. Livingstone, ed., *SP* 19 (Leuven), 236–42

Stegmüller, O. (1952). '*Sub tuum praesidium*: Bemerkungen zur ältesten Überlieferung', *Zeitschrift für katholische Theologie* 74, 76–82

Stevenson, J., trans. (1987). *A New Eusebius. Documents Illustrating the History of the Church to AD 337* (London, rev. ed.)

Stewart-Sykes, Alistair (2001). *From Prophecy to Preaching: A Search for the Origins of the Christian Homily* (Leiden and Boston)

Swanson, R. N., ed. (2004). *The Church and Mary: Papers Read at the 2001 Summer Meeting and the 2002 Winter Meeting of the Ecclesiastical History Society*, Studies in Church History 39 (Woodbridge)

Taft, Robert F., SJ (1980–1). 'The Liturgy of the Great Church: An Initial Synthesis of Structure and Interpretation on the Eve of Iconoclasm', *DOP* 34–5 (Washington, DC), 45–75 = R. F. Taft, SJ, *Liturgy in Byzantium and Beyond* (Aldershot, 1995), ch. 1.

(1986). *The Liturgy of the Hours in East and West: The Origins of the Divine Office and Its Meaning for Today* (Collegeville, MN)

(1990). 'In the Bridegroom's Absence. The *Paschal Triduum* in the Byzantine Church', in *Analecta Liturgica* 14 = *Studia Anselmiana* 102 (Rome), 71–97; repr. in Taft 1995, ch. 5.

(1992). *The Byzantine Rite: A Short History* (Collegeville, MN)

(1998). 'Women at Church in Byzantium: Where, When – and Why?', *DOP* 52, 27–87; repr. Taft 2001, ch. 1

(2000a). 'The Liturgy of the Hours in the East', in Chupungco 2000, vol. 5, 29–57

(2000b). 'The Theology of the Liturgy of the Hours', in Chupungco 2000, vol. 5, 119–32

(2001). *Divine Liturgies – Human Problems in Byzantium, Armenia, Syria and Palestine* (Aldershot and Burlington, VT)

(2005). 'Cathedral vs. Monastic Liturgy in the Christian East: Vindicating a Disctinction', *BBGG*, 2nd ser. 3, 173–219

(2006). *Through Their Own Eyes: Liturgy as the Byzantines Saw It* (Berkeley, CA)

Talbot, Alice-Mary (1994). 'Epigrams of Manuel Philes on the Theotokos tes Peges and its art', *DOP* 48, 137–65

(1996). 'Women and Mt Athos', in A. A. M. Bryer and M. B. Cunningham, eds., *Mt Athos and Byzantine Monasticism* (Aldershot and Brookfield, VT), 67–79

(2001). *Women and Religious Life in Byzantium* (Aldershot and Burlington, VT)

(2010). 'The Devotional Life of Laywomen', in Krueger 2010, 201–20

(2019). *Varieties of Monastic Experience in Byzantium, 800–1453* (Notre Dame, IN)

Talbot, Alice-Mary and Kazhdan, Alexander (1991–2). 'Women and Iconoclasm', *BZ* 84/85, 391–408

Talley, Thomas J. (1986). *The Origins of the Liturgical Year* (Collegeville, MN)

Theokritoff, Elizabeth (2005). 'Praying the Scriptures in Orthodox Worship', in S. T. Kimbrough, Jr (ed.), *Orthodox and Wesleyan Scriptural Understanding and Practice* (Crestwood, NY), 73–87

(2008). 'Creator and Creation', in M.B. Cunningham and E. Theokritoff, eds, *The Cambridge Companion to Orthodox Christian Theology* (Cambridge),63–77

Thomas, Gabrielle (2019). *The Image of God in the Theology of Gregory of Nazianzus* (Cambridge)

Tomadakis, N. V. (1965–9). *Eisagoge eis ten Byzantinen philologian*, 2 vols. (Athens)

Toniolo, E. M. (1991). 'L'Akathistos nella Vita di Maria di Massimo il Confessore', in I. M. Calabuig, ed., *Virgo Liber Dei. Miscellanea di studi in onore di P. Giuseppe M. Besutti, O.S.M.* (Rome), 209–28

Tóth, Peter (2011). 'Way out of the Tunnel? Three Hundred Years of Research on the Apocrypha: A Preliminary Approach', in L. Delezalova and T. Visy, eds., *Retelling the Bible: Literary, Historical and Social Contexts* (Bern), 45–84

Tougher, Shaun (2008). *The Eunuch in Byzantine History and Society* (London and New York)

Touliatos-Banker, D. H. (1984). *The Byzantine Anomos Chant of the Fourteenth and Fifteenth Centuries* (Thessalonike)

Treadgold, Warren (1988). *The Byzantine Revival, 780–842* (Stanford, CA)

Trypanis, C. A. (1968). *Fourteen Early Byzantine Cantica*, Wiener Byzantinische Studien 5 (Vienna)

(1972). 'Three New Early Byzantine Hymns', *BZ* 65, 334–8

Tsironis, Niki (1997). 'George of Nicomedia: Convention and Originality in the Homily on Good Friday', in E. A. Livingstone, ed., *SP* 33 (Leuven), 573–7

(1998). 'The Lament of the Virgin Mary from Romanos the Melode to George of Nicomedia: An Aspect of the Development of the Marian Cult' (unpubl. PhD thesis, King's College London)

(2000). 'The Mother of God in the Iconoclastic Controversy', in Vassilaki 2000, 27–39

(2002). 'Κασσιανὴ ἡ ὑμνωδός', *Athena*, 7–20

(2005). 'From Poetry to Liturgy: The Cult of the Virgin in the Middle Byzantine Era', in Vassilaki 2005, 91–102

(2010). 'Desire, Longing and Fear in the Narrative of Middle-Byzantine Homiletics', in J. Baun, A. Cameron, M. Edwards and M. Vinzent, eds., *SP* 44 (Leuven, Paris and Walpole, MA), 515–20

(2011). 'Emotion and the Senses in Marian Homilies of the Middle Byzantine Period', in Brubaker and Cunningham 2011, 179–96

Uthemann, Karl-Heinz (1998). 'Forms of Communication in the Homilies of Severian of Gabala: A Contribution to the Reception of the Diatribe as a Method of Exposition', in Allen and Cunningham 1998, 139–77

Vailhé, S. (1901). 'La fête de la Présentation', *EO* 5, 221–4

(1906). 'Origines de la fête de l'Annonciation', *EO* 9, 138–45

Valiavitcharska, Vessela (2013). *Rhetoric and Rhythm in Byzantium: The Sound of Persuasion* (Cambridge)

Vasiliev, A. A. (1946). *The Russian Attack on Constantinople* (Cambridge, MA)

Vassilaki, Maria, ed. (2000). *Mother of God: Representations of the Virgin in Byzantine Art* (Athens and Milan)

ed. (2005). *Images of the Mother of God: Perceptions of the Theotokos in Byzantium* (Aldershot and Burlington, VT)

Velkovska, E. V. (1997). 'Byzantine Liturgical Books', in A. J. Chupungco, OSB, ed., *Handbook*

(2000). 'The Liturgical Year in the East', in Chupungco 2000, vol. 5, 157–76

Voicu, Sever J. (2011). 'Ways to Survival for the Infancy Apocrypha', in Clivaz, Dettwiler, Devillers and Norelli 2011, 401–17

Vuong, Lily C. (2011). '"Let Us Bring Her up to the Temple of the Lord": Exploring the Boundaries of Jewish and Christian Relations Through the Presentation of Mary in the *Protevangelion of James*', in Clivaz, Dettwiler, Devillers and Norelli 2011, 418–32

(2013). *Gender and Purity in the Protevangelion of James* (Tübingen)

Wade, A. (1984). 'The Oldest Iadgari: The Jerusalem Tropologion, v–viiie c.', *OCP* 50, 451–6

Warner, Marina (1976). *Alone of All Her Sex: The Myth and Cult of the Virgin Mary* (London)

Weissenrieder, A. and Coote, R. B., eds. (2010). *The Interface of Orality and Writing: Speaking, Seeing, Writing in the Shaping of New Genres* (Tübingen)

Wellesz, Egon (1961). *A History of Byzantine Music and Hymnography* (Oxford; rev. ed., first publ. 1949)

(1956). 'The "Akathistos": A Study in Byzantine Hymnography', *DOP* 9–10, 141–74

Wenger, Antoine (1953). 'Les homélies inédites de Cosmas Vestitor sur la Dormition', *REB* 11 (Mélanges M. Jugie), 284–300

(1955). *L'Assomption de la très sainte Vierge dans la tradition Byzantine du VIe au Xe siècle*, Archives de l'Orient Chrétien 5 (Paris)

(1959). 'Foi et piété mariale à Byzance', in D. Du Manoir, ed., *Maria: Études sur la Sainte Vierge*, vol. 5 (Paris), 923–81

Wessel, Susan (2004). *Cyril of Alexandria and the Nestorian Controversy: The Making of a Saint and a Heretic* (Oxford)

Weyl Carr, Annemarie (2001). 'Threads of Authority: The Virgin Mary's Veil in the Middle Ages', S. Gordon, ed., *Robes and Honor: The Medieval World of Investiture* (New York), 59–94

(forthcoming), 'Epithet and Emotion: Reflections on the Quality of *Eleos* in the Mother of God *Eleousa*', in S. Ashbrook Harvey and M. E. Mullett, eds., *Managing Emotion: Passions, Emotions, Affects, and Imaginings in Byzantium* (Abingdon)

Whitby, Mary (2020). 'The Patriarch Sergius and the Theotokos', *JÖB* 70, 403–25

White, Andrew Walker (2015). *Performing Orthodox Ritual in Byzantium* (Cambridge)

Wickes, Jeffrey (2019). *Bible and Poetry in Late Antique Mesopotamia: Ephrem's Hymns on Faith* (Oakland, CA)

Wilkinson, John (1977). *Jerusalem Pilgrims before the Crusades* (Warminster)

Williams, Rowan (1987). *Arius: Heresy and Tradition* (London)

Winkley, Stephen (1973a). 'A Bodleian Theotokarion', *REB* 31, 267–73

(1973b). 'The Canons of John of Damascus to the Theotokos' (unpubl. DPhil thesis, Oxford)

Woodfin, Warren T. (2012). *The Embodied Icon: Liturgical Vestments and Sacramental Power in Byzantium* (Oxford)

Wortley, John (1977). 'The Oration of Theodore Syncellus (*BHG* 1058) and the Siege of 860', *Byzantine Studies / Études Byzantines* 4, 111–26

(1982). 'Iconoclasm and Leipsanoclasm: Leo III, Constantine V and the Relics', *BF* 8, 253–79

(2005). 'The Marian Relics at Constantinople', *GRBS* 45: 2, 171–87

(2009). *Studies on the Cult of Relics in Byzantium up to 1204* (Farnham and Burlington, VT)

Wright, William (1865). *Contributions to the Apocryphal Literature of the New Testament, collected and edited from Syriac Manuscripts in the British Museum* (London)

Xevsuriani, L. (1978). 'The Problem of the Composition of Sin. 34', *Mravaltavi* 6, 88–123 (in Georgian)

Young, Frances M. (1983). *From Nicaea to Chalcedon: A Guide to the Literature and Its Background* (London)

(1997). *Biblical Exegesis and the Formation of Christian Culture* (Cambridge)

Index

CPSIA information can be obtained
at www.ICGtesting.com
Printed in the USA
LVHW011419140922
728333LV00009B/558